lonely planet

Paris

Montmartre & Northern Paris p126

Belleville & Ménilmontant p168

Champs Élysées & Grands Boulevards p80

Louvre & Les Halles p96

Eiffel Tower & Western Paris p60

Le Marais p150

St-Germain & Les Invalides p240

The Islands p204

Bastille & Eastern Paris p184

Latin Quarter p222

Montparnasse & Southern Paris p268

Mary Winston Nicklin, Alexis Averbuck, Jean-Bernard Carillet, Fabienne Fong Yan, Rooksana Hossenally, Nicola Leigh Stewart, Rowan Twine, Peter Yeung

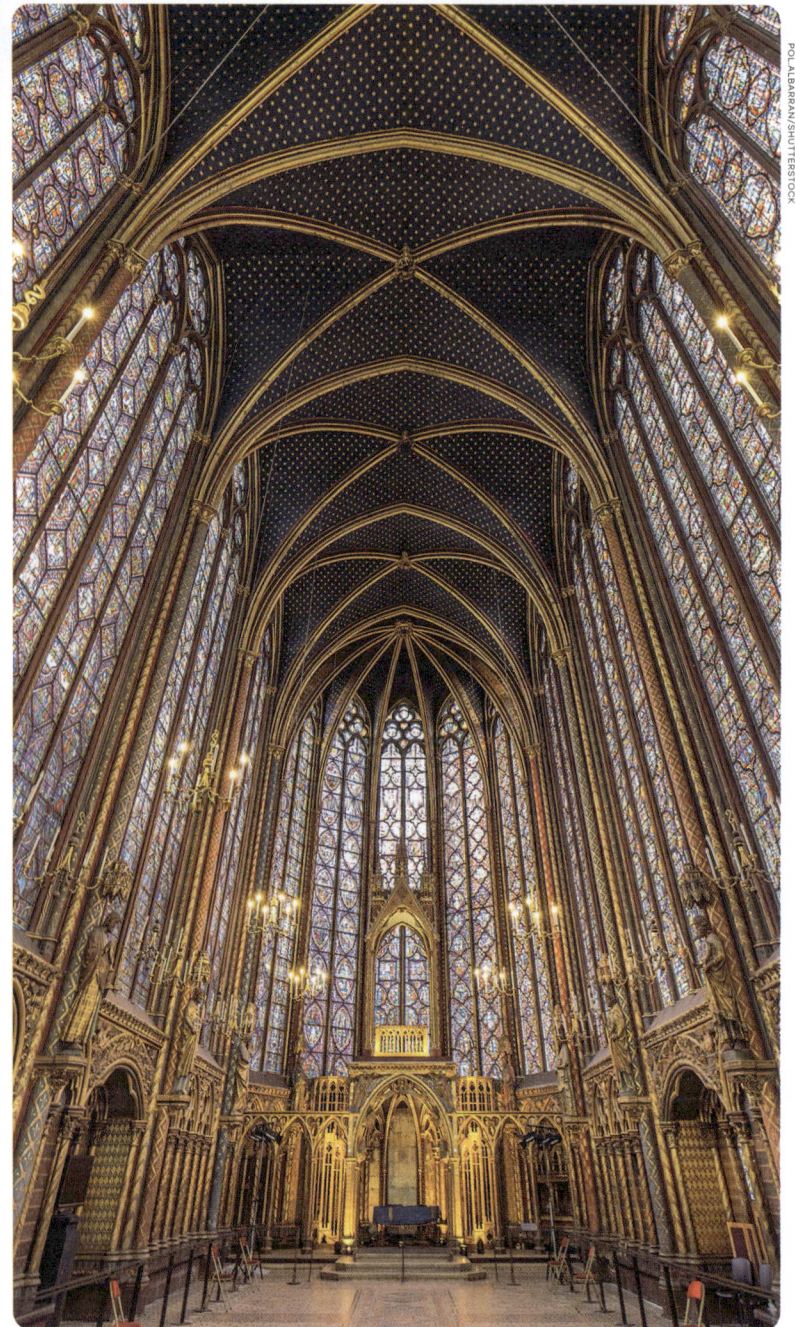

Sainte-Chapelle (p214)

CONTENTS

Plan Your Trip

The Journey Begins Here 4
Our Picks 8
Perfect Days 24
When to Go 26
Get Prepared for Paris 28
Getting There 30
Getting Around 32
Dining Out 36
Explore Paris' Bread & Cheese Purveyors 40
Bar Open 42
Showtime 46
Shop 48
Outdoor Thrills 50
Family Fun 53

The Guide

Neighbourhoods at a Glance 58
Eiffel Tower & Western Paris 60
Champs-Elysées & Grands Boulevards 80
Louvre & Les Halles 96
Montmartre & Northern Paris 126
Le Marais 150
Belleville & Ménilmontant 168
Bastille & Eastern Paris 184
The Islands 204
Latin Quarter 222
St Germain & Les Invalides 240
Montparnasse & Southern Paris 268
Day Trips from Paris 288
Where to Stay 306

Toolkit

Money 316
Family Travel 317
Food, Drink & Nightlife 318
LGBTIQ+ Travellers 320
Health & Safe Travel 321
Responsible Travel 322
Accessible Travel 324
Nuts & Bolts 325
Language 326

Storybook

A History of Paris in 15 Places 330
Meet the Parisians 334
Paris' Marvellous Metro 336
Paris on Location 340
Paris' Alternative Arts Scene 344
Les Années Folles & the Cocktail Craze in Paris 348

Bistro, Montmartre (p126)

Strolling beside the Seine

PARIS
THE JOURNEY BEGINS HERE

Where else can you play *pétanque* in a Roman amphitheatre, drool over the bounty of an open-air market, people-watch for hours at a sidewalk cafe, gawk at Impressionist masterpieces, drink a cocktail with Hemingway's ghost and dance the tango by the Seine? Such an embarrassment of riches could only be Paris. The city is a multi-layered millefeuille of culture and history just waiting for you to sink your teeth into. For me, falling for Paris wasn't a coup de foudre (love at first sight) when I saw the Eiffel Tower as a kid. But as a long-time resident, I find that 'lightning strike' happening on a daily basis. I'll be at an exhibit opening, or digging into a divinely delicious bistro meal or listening to a band during the Fête de la Musique, and suddenly be bowled over by the beauty of Paris, smitten by its irrepressible joie de vivre.

Mary Winston Nicklin

marywinstonnicklin.com

Mary Winston Nicklin is a Franco-American writer and editor based on the Left Bank of Paris. She wrote the Plan Your Trip, Eiffel Tower & Western Paris, Day Trips and Toolkit chapters, and the history essay.

My favourite experience is to go for an urban hike across the city, looking for street art and stories. Paris is peppered with surprising, serendipitous delights at every turn. A close second is a Seine-side summer *apéro* (predinner drink) when the sunset casts a golden glow on the limestone monuments.

WHO GOES WHERE

Our writers and experts choose the places which, for them, define Paris.

I always anchor my time in Paris with a first walk along the Seine...following the quays and crossing the **bridges** (p217) to the Île de la Cité and Île St-Louis. By day, for fresh air and changing clouds scudding across the sky over the monuments...also, of course, for fascinating people-watching. By night, for shimmering lights and ambience, the best in the world.

Alexis Averbuck

alexisaverbuck.com

Alexis paints and writes about her adventures for Lonely Planet, National Geographic UK and other outlets. Alexis wrote the Islands chapter.

The **13e** *arrondissement* (p268) is one of Paris' most underrated. It has a smattering of village-like neighbourhoods, parks, cafes, bistros, bars and restaurants. It's a fast-changing area – this is where the future of Paris lies!

Jean-Bernard Carillet

@jb.carillet_photography

Jean-Bernard is a writer, photographer and videographer focused on travel, nature and culture. He wrote the Montparnasse & Southern Paris chapter.

The **Belvédère de Belleville** (p179) brings a unique perspective of Paris, not only because of its lesser-known beautiful panoramic view. It could have stayed a characterless functional building, but the way the neighbourhood's children and artists have completely taken it over through street art makes it a powerful place of life, creation, and a visible sign of togetherness – a place which really belongs to the people.

Fabienne Fong Yan

@a.fab.journey

Fabienne is a writer and content creator about food, travel and culture. She wrote Louvre & Les Halles and Belleville & Ménilmontant.

The longer I live in Paris, the more convinced I am that the real Paris isn't in what you do but how you do it. It's about taking as much time as possible to wander the streets, to look at every detail in the architecture, to sit at a cafe and watch life go by. It's not queuing outside a trending restaurant or taking as many snaps as possible. Personally, what I love the most about Paris is walking around **Montmartre** (p126) especially, and also sometimes the Marais and central islands, by night, because the city is beautiful lit up, highlighting details that go unnoticed in the daytime.

Rooksana Hossenally

@roxy.inparis

Rooksana is a travel and culture writer and she is the author of What's Up, Paris? She wrote the Montmartre & Northern Suburbs and the Latin Quarter chapters.

The best thing to do in Paris is simply to look. In a city filled with so much beauty, there is always more to discover and admire. Walking through the winding streets, sitting in the sun at **Café La Perle** (pictured; 167), or sipping a coffee at **Causeries** (p166). Taking time to watch the people walking past, the flowers, the façades. A moment to daydream about the layers of history built up on this former marsh.

Rowan Twine

@rowan.rt

Rowan is a writer and photographer who's always hungry for a story or a meal. She wrote the Le Marais chapter.

St-Germain des Prés (p240) for me is perhaps the most quintessentially Parisian part of Paris; it's as close as you can get to stepping back in time here, *Midnight in Paris*–style. Streets are lined with traditional Haussmannian architecture, bistros retain their old world decor, and there's typically Parisian terraces for lingering over glasses of wine. It really is a place where you can just *flânerie*, popping in and out of bookshops and bakeries, and really take your time to absorb this classic side of Paris.

Nicola Leigh Stewart

@nicolaleighstewart

Nicola is a travel, food and drinks writer based in Paris. She wrote the Champs-Élysées & Grands Boulevards and the St-Germain & Les Invalides chapters.

I grew to fall in love with **Le Sedaine Bar** (p192) during my research for this guidebook. It's a charming, refreshingly uncool locals' cafe run by an adorable old couple for nearly 40 years. I wrote good chunks of my chapter while sipping on their cloudlike cappuccinos. I've had all-the-trimmings, wine-filled lunches there. I've had a restorative croque monsieur while hungover. I've chatted with friends at the bar counter with an espresso. This is the Paris I love.

Peter Yeung

@ptr_yeung

Peter is a Paris-based journalist and photographer who writes human-centred stories about culture, food and the arts. He wrote the Bastille & Eastern Paris chapter.

THE ICONS

Packed with architectural stunners that are instantly recognisable, Paris has a timeless familiarity for visitors. Famous monuments have become synonymous with the city itself – some even spawning international copycats. From the wrought-iron spire soaring over the skyline to the glittering glass pyramid gracing the world's most popular museum, the masterpieces are myriad and marvellous.

Gustave's Folly

No one could imagine Paris without its most famous symbol, the Eiffel Tower, though Gustave Eiffel only constructed the tower as a temporary exhibit for the 1889 Exposition Universelle (World Fair).

The Beloved Cathedral

The city's geographic and spiritual heart, Notre Dame was meticulously restored by 1000 artisans after the devastating 2019 fire.

Sweeping Views

Take in some of Paris' best vistas atop the magnificent Arc de Triomphe on the Champs-Élysées.

FROM LEFT: FOKKE BAARSSEN/SHUTTERSTOCK, ANDY SOLOMAN/SHUTTERSTOCK, SALVADOR MANIQUIZ/SHUTTERSTOCK

Palais Garnier (p90)

BEST MONUMENTAL EXPERIENCES

Climb to the top of the 130m-high Butte de Montmartre to admire the white-domed ❶ **Basilique du Sacré-Cœur** (p129).

Go ghost hunting for the *Phantom of the Opera* at the opulent 19th-century opera house ❷ **Palais Garnier** (p90) that inspired the hit book and musical.

Visit the ❸ **Louvre** (p100) at night for the marvellous ambience of this immense palace-turned-museum.

Gape at Napoléon's tomb beneath the gold dome inside the 17th-century ❹ **Hôtel des Invalides** (p263), built as a residence for disabled war veterans.

Imagine the grisly guillotine executions that took place during the French Revolution in ❺ **place de la Concorde** (p87), the city's largest square.

CULINARY CORNUCOPIA

As a world food capital, Paris is a bastion of French culinary tradition, drawing chefs from across the globe to sharpen their knives in Michelin-starred kitchens. This is where baguettes are judged in an annual contest and *pâtissiers* compete with artful pastries almost too pretty to eat. It's also a multicultural hub incorporating the full spectrum of global flavours. Believe the hype – Paris is a fabulous feast.

Bistros & Bouillons

Creative chefs and clever restaurateurs are reviving traditional restaurant concepts – the small neighbourhood joint known as the bistro, and the *bouillon*, a big hall serving classics on the cheap.

Pastry Paradise

Forget macarons. There's never been a better time to find pastry nirvana in Paris. Culinary maestros such as Claire Damon and Cédric Grolet draw lines to their jewellery-box shops.

Cafe Life

Cafes are a cornerstone of local life. In every neighbourhood, table-packed terraces draw Parisians for drinks and leisurely people-watching – at every hour of the day.

Cafe, rue de Montorgueil

BEST CULINARY EXPERIENCES

Get your picnic from your market of the day (paris.fr), like ❶ **Marché des Enfants Rouges** (p159) with fresh produce stalls and counter-service eateries.

Experience ❷ **Le Procope** (p256), one of the oldest restaurants in Paris, with a spectacular dining room in which traditional French fare is elegantly served.

Shop for foodie delights on ❸ **rue Montorgueil** (p97), a bustling market street that's a vestige of the historic Les Halles marketplace.

Splurge on a Michelin-starred lunch at legendary ❹ **La Tour d'Argent** (p234) or try Substance, Prunier, Le George or Pavyllon.

Explore the 15e's culinary temptations on a ❺ **gourmet bike tour** (p285), a curated epicurean jaunt across southern Paris.

Jardin des Plantes (p236)

GREEN ESCAPES

While Paris is Europe's most densely populated capital, it's easy to find outdoor havens. The city's beautiful parks serve as its apartment-dwelling residents' communal backyards, and sprawling lawns such as the Champ de Mars beckon for picnics. Leafy squares and carefully landscaped gardens complement the nature-filled expanses of the Bois de Boulogne and Bois de Vincennes, appreciated as the city's *poumons* (lungs).

Urban Oasis

With formal terraces, fruit orchards and lawns, the Jardin du Luxembourg has a special place in Parisians' hearts – a playground for young and old.

Symmetry & Grandeur

Part of the *axe historique* (historic axis), adjacent to the Louvre, the Jardin des Tuileries were designed by André Le Nôtre in the 17th century.

BEST FRESH-AIR EXPERIENCES

Explore ❶ **Bois de Boulogne** (p70), the former royal hunting ground brimming with rose gardens, tropical greenhouses and more.

Search for famous tombs amidst the greenery in the city's biggest cemetery, ❷ **Cimetière du Père Lachaise** (p172), a bastion of biodiversity.

Discover the natural treasures of ❸ **Jardin des Plantes** (p236), the historic botanical garden.

Embrace summer in Paris, paddling lazily around the central isles of Lac Daumesnil in the ❹ **Bois de Vincennes** (p196).

Join the locals sunbathing, dancing and picnicking in quirky ❺ **Parc des Buttes-Chaumont** (p183), complete with a craggy butte rising from a lake.

SECRET UNDERGROUND

Beneath the cobblestone streets and elegant boulevards of Paris, there's a sprawling underground realm. The buildings admired on the surface were constructed from limestone excavated from a maze of subterranean quarries, some of which house the catacombs today. Layers of metro tunnels, sewers and hidden hideouts punctuate this alluring underground domain.

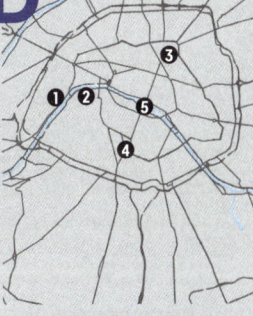

BEST UNDERGROUND EXPERIENCES

Wander through the vaulted 15th-century cellars of ❶ **M Musée du Vin** (p68), where monks once stored their barrels in former quarries beneath Passy.

Explore the bowels of Paris in the quirky sewer museum, ❷ **Musée des Égouts de Paris** (p260), following in the footsteps of 19th-century tourists.

Sail through the tunnels beneath the 11e and look up to see the Bastille, on a Canauxrama cruise on ❸ **Canal St-Martin** (p140).

Wind through the labyrinthine, skull-and-bone-lined tunnels of ❹ **Les Catacombes** (p272), one of the world's largest ossuaries.

Marvel at the ancient Gallo-Roman ruins of ❺ **Crypte Archéologique** (p211) hidden under the Notre Dame forecourt.

Metro Ghost Stations

While riding metro lines 8 and 9, keep a lookout for the abandoned St-Martin station, now sometimes used for illuminated advertising campaigns.

WWII Bunker

Inside the Musée de la Libération de Paris, discover the air raid shelter where brave Resistance fighters created an underground command post during WWII.

Phantom of the Opera

The Palais Garnier, famed home to the fictional phantom, really does have a subterranean 'lake' – originally built as a reservoir.

WHAT'S NEW

The gargoyled churches, lamplit bridges spanning the Seine and art nouveau cafes spilling onto wicker-chair-lined terraces are indelibly etched in the minds of anyone who's visited the city. But despite initial appearances, Paris isn't static. Constant renovations and new construction add to the sparkle of the cityscape, while revolutions in urban planning have added abundant greenery, pedestrian spaces and new transport links. No matter how many times you've made the trip, there are always new thrills to discover.

Grand Paris Express

This giant public transport project is extending existing metro lines and also adding new ones that bypass the centre of Paris.

Olympic Legacy

Paris invested in a big way for the 2024 Summer Olympics, refurbishing existing venues, such as the Grand Palais, to lower the carbon footprint, and cleaning up the Seine.

Greenery Galore

As part of its environmental initiatives, Paris is landscaping historically traffic-clogged squares, such as the Place de la Concorde, and planting 'urban forests' – check out the trees around the Hôtel de Ville.

Paris 2024 Cauldron (p108), created by Mathieu Lehanneur

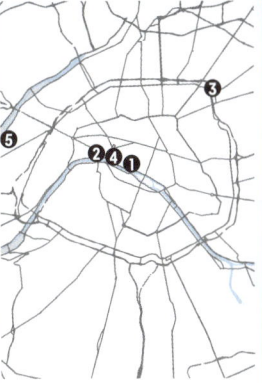

BEST NEW EXPERIENCES

Admire contemporary art at ❶ **Fondation Cartier's** (p114) dazzling new home designed by Jean Nouvel.

Gape at the results of the restoration of the ❷ **Grand Palais** (p89), the glass-capped monument first built for the 1900 Exposition Universelle (World's Fair).

Dance the night away at ❸ **Mia Mao** (p138) in a former industrial hall of La Villette – an electro scene giving Berlin a run for its money.

Watch the magical summertime spectacle as the hot-air-balloon-inspired ❹ **Paris 2024 Cauldron** (p108) rises over the Tuileries (until the 2028 Games in Los Angeles).

Step inside the petite palace of ❺ **Château de Bagatelle** (p71), linked to Marie Antoinette, after a years-long restoration.

THE LIFE AQUATIC

Flanked by famous monuments, the River Seine is Paris' lifeblood. The Left and Right Banks are connected by 37 bridges, and the quays – perfect for promenades – are a UNESCO World Heritage site. It's central to Parisian life: browse for books, picnic at the water's edge, party on houseboats and even go for a swim.

Les Bouquinistes

Likened to an open-air bookshop, the riverbanks are lined with hundreds of traditional green stalls where booksellers showcase antiquarian books and other treasures.

Île aux Cygnes

Ideal for strolls, this untouristed artificial island was created in western Paris in 1827. A Statue of Liberty replica stands tall near the Port de Grenelle.

Colossal Clean-Up

The city invested €1.4 million to make the river swimmable again in time for the 2024 Olympics. Three supervised swimming spots are open in the summer.

Batobus (p221) & Pont Neuf (p217)

BEST WATER EXPERIENCES

Go sightseeing on the Batobus, indulge in a gourmet meal or hire your own captained boat on a ❶ **Seine cruise** (p67).

Dive into the ❷ **Piscine Joséphine Baker** (p279), then watch the river boats sail by.

Sip an *apéro* (predinner drink) or catch a concert on one of the ❸ **converted houseboats** (p261) moored near the Bibliothèque Nationale de France.

Fall under the spell of island life on ❹ **Île St-Louis** (p217), settling in at a cafe or dancing to buskers on the Pont St-Louis.

Hire a boat from ❺ **Akwa Experience** (p142) to explore the Bassin de la Villette and the Canal de l'Ourcq, a Seine tributary.

View from the Eiffel Tower (p64)

VIBRANT VISTAS

The magnificent cityscape of Paris is best admired from above. As the capital's tallest structure, the Eiffel Tower offers pinch-me panoramas, but other vantage points abound: rooftop restaurants, hotel terraces and a bevy of bars where you can drink in the views along with a killer cocktail. The highest bar hangout is at the TOO Hotel, located inside the Jean Nouvel–designed Tours Duo.

Montparnasse Monster

When the Tour Montparnasse opened in 1973, it was considered an eyesore. But as the city's second-tallest building, its 56th-floor observation deck overlooks all the sights, including the Eiffel Tower.

Prime Perches

Rooftop bars are blossoming across the city, from Le Perchoir atop an industrial building in Ménilmontant to the trendy Maggie Rooftop at the Hôtel Rochechouart.

BEST SKY-HIGH EXPERIENCES

Summit the centuries-old ❶ **Tour St-Jacques** (p121) that is the starting point for the St-Jacques de Compostelle pilgrimage.

Toast the sunset from the hilltop Belvédère in ❷ **Parc de Belleville** (p179), offering panoramic views and a multitude of murals made by street artists.

Get dizzying, bird's-eye views of Paris from the top of the ❸ **Eiffel Tower** (p64), Paris' most famous landmark, with a flute of Champagne in hand.

Enjoy a veggie-vibrant lunch on the 8th-floor terrace of the historic department store ❹ **Galeries Lafayette Haussmann** (p93).

Take a lift to the 27th floor of the Philippe Starck–designed hotel for views with serious wow factor at ❺ **TOO Tac Tac Sky Bar** (p278).

LIVE IT UP, PARIS STYLE

The reputation of the demure Parisian goes out the window when you click into nightlife mode. Neighbourhoods light up when cafes morph into bars and concert halls, and edgy alt-scene venues fill for live music and DJ sets. All you need is a spirit of adventure and a commitment to join in.

FROM LEFT: AMIR HAMJA FOR LONELY PLANET, JEREMY ALLEN/LONELY PLANET

Cocktail Renaissance

Paris' cocktail scene spans glitzy hotel bars like the Hôtel de Crillon, backstreet speakeasies and former hostess bars in hip SoPi ('south Pigalle').

Vinyl Revival

Listening bars are having a moment in Paris – a concept first popularised in Japan, now booming as records come back in style.

North Paris Music Scene

North Paris has a wealth of music venues: Boule Noire, Cigale, Elysée-Montmartre, Trabendo, Zénith Paris, Grande Halle de la Villette, Cabaret Sauvage, New Morning and Philharmonie.

BEST NIGHTLIFE EXPERIENCES

Hang out near happening Ménilmontant at ❶ **rue Oberkampf and rue St-Maur** (p176), where bars stay open late and are popular for all ages.

Mingle with moviegoers at the iconic, art deco cinema ❷ **Grand Rex** (p124) for karaoke movie nights.

Join a Belleville institution at one of the city's oldest cabaret bars, ❸ **Aux Folies** (p177), dating to the late 18th century.

Catch a jazz concert at a storied club like **Caveau de la Huchette** (p234) or the ❹ **Duc des Lombards** (p120).

Dance the night away at ❺ **Café de la Danse** (p192), conveniently near restaurants and bars at the beating heart of Bastille nightlife.

OUR PICKS | PLAN YOUR TRIP

ARTISTIC TREASURES

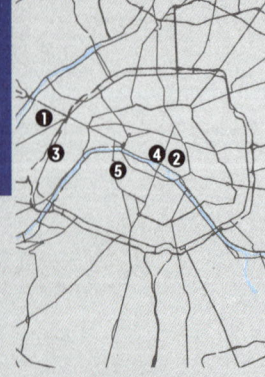

With an illustrious artistic pedigree – Renoir, Picasso and Van Gogh are but a few of the masters who have worked here – Paris is one of the world's great art repositories. In addition to famous museums such as the Louvre and the Orsay, scores of smaller establishments feature every imaginable genre. Not to mention the glorious street art.

BEST ART EXPERIENCES

Make the trip to the Frank Gehry–designed contemporary art centre, ❶ **Fondation Louis Vuitton** (p71), which resembles a glass-panelled ship sailing over the Bois de Boulogne.

Get inspired on a ❷ **gallery-hopping walk** (p166) through the historic Marais district.

Admire the world's largest collection of Claude Monet works in ❸ **Musée Marmottan Monet** (p69), a former hunting lodge that's sumptuously decorated.

Step off one of Paris' most prominent streets to discover ❹ **59 Rivoli** (p120), a former squat filled with artist studios.

Marvel at Auguste Rodin's former workshop, showroom and garden at ❺ **Musée Rodin** (p264), filled with sculptural masterpieces such as *The Kiss*.

The Star Museum

Once a fortress and now the world's most visited museum, the Louvre is embarking on a vast restoration project to better welcome its nearly nine million annual visitors.

FROM LEFT: NIKOLPETR/SHUTTERSTOCK, STEVE ESTVANIK/SHUTTERSTOCK

Medieval Magic

Inside a 15th-century mansion built on Roman thermal baths, Musée de Cluny shows off gorgeous stained glass, objets d'art and tapestries such as the famed *Lady and the Unicorn*.

Art Incubators

POUSH is the largest of Paris' art incubators, with hundreds of artists on its books and a huge venue of studios and exhibition spaces in Aubervilliers.

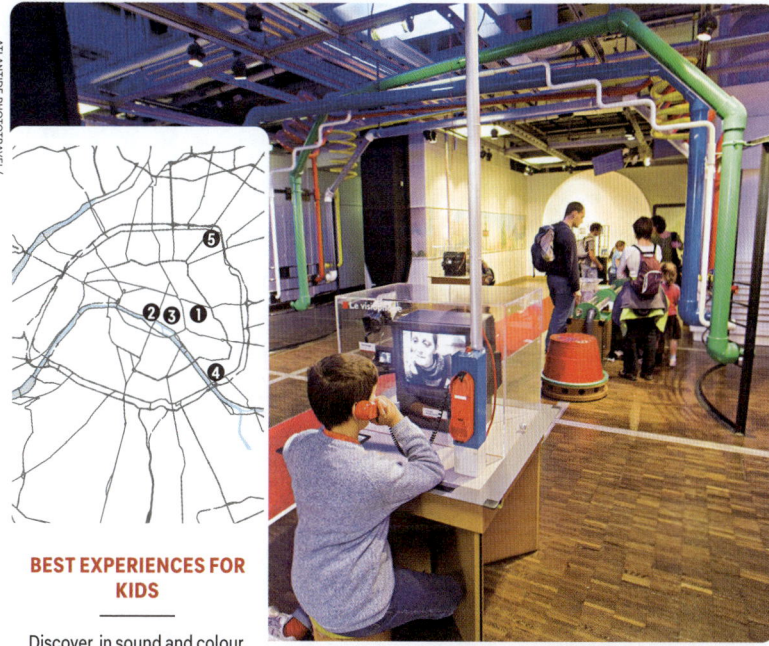

Cité des Sciences et de l'Industrie (p143)

PARIS WITH KIDS

Paris is an endlessly entertaining destination for kids. Crammed with cultural riches that can be explored with audioguides, smartphone apps and high-quality tours, the city is also rich in outdoor escapes, from its rambling gardens, urban playgrounds and river-based activities, to its climbable monuments and street-front cafe terraces.

BEST EXPERIENCES FOR KIDS

Discover, in sound and colour, animated works of the world's greatest painters like Klimt and Chagall at ❶ **Atelier des Lumières** (p178).

Introduce your tots to art and culture at ❷ **Musée en Herbe** (p122), a museum designed for children three and up.

Go on a treasure hunt looking for the ❸ **pixelated mosaics** (p159) created by French street artist Invader, racking up points on the app.

Gape at vintage merry-go-rounds at the whimsical ❹ **Musée des Arts Forains** (p202) inside the old Bercy wine warehouses.

Delve into science at the huge industrial-style children's exploratorium, ❺ **Cité des Sciences et de l'Industrie** (p143), complete with La Géode immersive cinema.

Garden Play

Craft outdoor adventures in the Jardin du Luxembourg with its merry-go-round and toy sailboats, the giant Bois de Boulogne or Tuileries and Seine river parks.

Museum Multitude

You're spoilt for choice when it comes to Paris museums, many of which are free for kids. Dedicated children's workshops are engaging and entertaining.

UNDER THE RADAR

Paris does not limit itself to iconic monuments and sights. The city is full of unexpected treasures that reflect its cosmopolitan spirit and new-wave creativity. For those in search of something quirkier or lesser known, there are plenty of options. Go off the beaten path and see the city through a new lens.

BEST UNDER-THE-RADAR EXPERIENCES

Get lost in the village-like atmosphere of the tiny district of **❶ La Butte aux Cailles** (p273) near Place d'Italie.

Soak up the old-school Passy vibes at Honoré de Balzac's dreamy writing studio and garden with Eiffel Tower views at **❷ Maison de Balzac** (p72).

Sit on the deck of **❸ Paname Brewing Company** (p144) overlooking the Bassin de la Villette and sip a beer brewed on-site.

Go for a hike through biodiverse habitats along the former railway known as the **❹ Petite Ceinture** (p286; 'Little Belt').

Grab a drink at the cafe and catch an art show inside the vaulted limestone gallery of the medieval Cistercian **❺ Collège des Bernardins** (p228).

Alternative Arts & Music Hubs

Explore Paris' independent creative spirit at music and alt-art hubs like La Bellevilloise, La Gare/Le Gore, Hasard Ludique, La REcyclerie, Le 104 (pictured) or La Flèche d'Or.

Bastille Industrial Passages

Secret courtyards, private alleys and picturesque passages, once occupied by workshops, now give an impression of a small village around Bastille.

Beyond the Périph

Outside Paris' ring road, suburbs like Pantin and St-Ouen are flourishing with lively hybrid spaces like the Magasins Généraux, La Cité Fertile and Mains d'Œuvres.

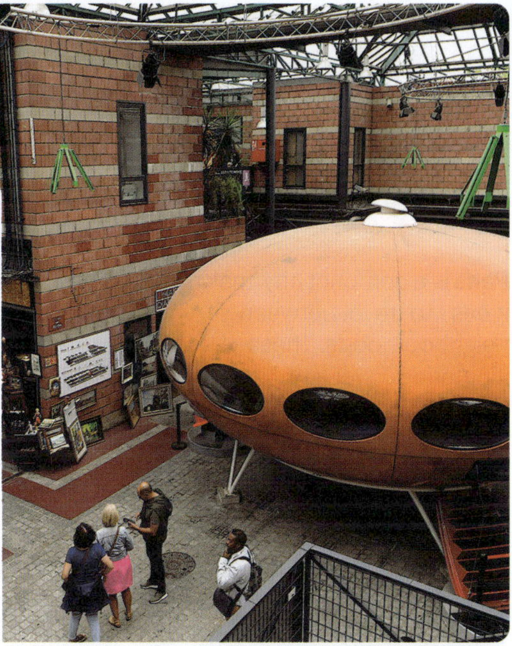

OLIVEROUGE 3/ SHUTTERSTOCK

Marché aux Puces de St-Ouen (p148)

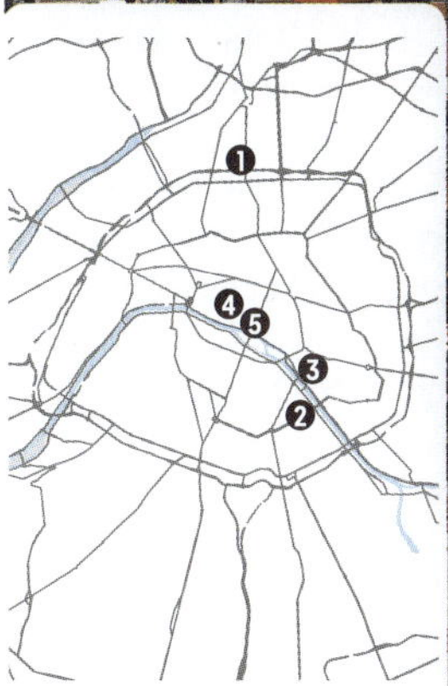

BEST FREE EXPERIENCES

Enjoy many free hours of entertainment at ❶ **Marché aux Puces de St-Ouen** (p148), a sprawling complex of 11 interconnected markets.

Follow our walking tour of the giant, open-air museum in the 13e filled with works by international artists on a ❷ **street art tour** (p277).

Amble the world's first elevated park, ❸ **Promenade Plantée** (p286), atop a 19th-century railway viaduct.

Join the crowd ❹ **dancing at Pl Colette** (p111) to live musical performances on weekends outside the Palais Royal.

Take a free walking tour (donation encouraged) with ❺ **Parisien d'un Jour – Paris Greeters** (p54) by booking in advance for a personalised excursion.

FREE

FOR FREE

Paris might be home to *haute couture, haute cuisine* and historic luxury hotels, but if you're still waiting for your lottery numbers to come up, don't despair. There are a wealth of ways to soak up the French capital without spending a *centime* (or scarcely any, at least).

Magnificent Churches

Some of Paris' most magnificent buildings are free-to-enter places of worship. Not only exceptional architecturally and historically, they contain exquisite art and treasures.

Free Museums

Municipal museums (parismusees.paris.fr) are free! Many others have a free day per month, generally the first Sunday.

Perfect Days

Paris is a compact city, making it easy to travel between neighbourhoods. These itineraries cover key sights and offbeat wonders. But always leave time for wandering and noticing – this is a city for the *flâneur*.

Sacré-Cœur basilica (p129)

DAY 1

The Islands/Latin Quarter

Start your day on the Île de la Cité, the site of **Notre Dame** (p208), painstakingly restored after the 2019 fire. For wow-worthy stained glass, don't miss **Sainte-Chapelle** (p214). Cross the Pont St-Louis to browse the boutiques and galleries on charming Île St-Louis. Then continue into the Latin Quarter to see the open-air sculpture garden on the Seine, Gallo-Roman ruins at **Arènes de Lutèce** (p227) and the market delights of rue Mouffetard.

Lunch Delicious bistro fare at **Café de la Nouvelle Mairie** (p227).

St-Germain & Les Invalides

Laze in the lovely **Jardin du Luxembourg** (p256), the city's most popular park, or pop by a storied cafe like **La Palette** (p254) for coffee on the sidewalk terrace. Swoon over Impressionist masterpieces in the magnificent **Musée d'Orsay** (p250), admire Delacroix murals in the **Église St-Sulpice** (p262) and scout out the backstreet boutiques of St-Germain.

Dinner French classics on the quay at **Le Voltaire** (p264).

Louvre & Les Halles

Catch a concert at one of the jazz clubs along the rue des Lombards such as **Sunset/Sunside**, **Duc des Lombards** or **Le Baiser Salé** (p120).

DAY 2

Louvre & Les Halles

☀ IM Pei's glass pyramid is your compass point to enter the labyrinthine **Louvre** (p100). Once you've had your fill, stroll through the elegant **Jardin des Tuileries** (p108), wander the **Jardin du Palais Royal** (p98) and visit the beautiful church **Église St-Eustache** (p120). Tap into the soul of the former Les Halles wholesale markets along backstreet legacies like rue Montorgueil.

Lunch Slurp ramen at **Kodawari Ramen Tsukiji** (p115).

Le Marais

☀ Scope out Victor Hugo's house in **Place des Vosges** (p155), then wander through the Marais' narrow streets to uncover hidden gardens, treasure-filled museums and trendy boutiques. Linger for a drink at **La Belle Hortense** (p160), where you can also browse books. Or if you'd rather have an *apéro* at one of the district's speakeasy-style bars, opt for **Candelaria** or **Sotto** (p157).

Dinner Insanely good sourdough pizza at **Oobatz** (p176).

Bastille & Eastern Paris

🌙 The Bastille neighbourhood calls for a cafe crawl: classics include **L'Atelier Saisonnier** (p192). Grab a beer at **Les Cuves de Fauve** (p192), or catch live music at **Les Disquaires** (p192) or funk and hip-hop at **Badaboum** (p193).

DAY 3

Montmartre & Northern Paris

☀ Montmartre's slinking streets and steep staircases lined with crooked ivy-clad buildings are enchanting places to meander, especially in the early morning. Head to the hilltop **Sacré-Cœur basilica** (p129). Then head to the **Canal St-Martin** (p140), spanned by wrought-iron bridges, to stroll the shaded towpaths.

Lunch Refined French fare in retro style at **Les Enfants Perdus** (p140).

Eiffel Tower & Western Paris

☀ This cultural neighbourhood is home to the world's largest Monet collection at the **Musée Marmottan Monet** (p69), contemporary art at the **Palais de Tokyo** (p73), a fashion feast at **Musée Yves Saint Laurent** (p75) and Asian masterpieces at the **Musée Guimet** (p79). Sunset is the best time to ascend the **Eiffel Tower** (p64), to experience both dizzying views during daylight hours and the glittering City of Light by night.

Dinner Art deco splendour at **Le Dôme** (p279) or **La Coupole** (p279).

Montparnasse & Southern Paris

🌙 Nothing beats a sultry, Seine-side party at night. Check out the floating bars and nightclubs moored near the **Bibliothèque Nationale de France** (p279).

WHEN TO GO

Paris is timeless. A city of life and light, you can ebb and flow like the Seine and adapt to the changing conditions.

A highlight of virtually all traveller's lifetime itineraries, Paris is a magnet for all. Spring (especially April and May) and autumn (particularly September and October) are ideal with gentle weather and less-crowded central streets. Summer (June to August) is the main tourist season, but many establishments close during August when Parisians generally leave. Sights are quieter and prices are lower during winter (November to February).

When planning a visit, it's also worth checking out Paris' extensive festival and events calendar. One of the world's best cultural cities, you can arrange a trip that includes anything from special operas and hip-hop dance premieres to French Open tennis.

Accommodation Lowdown

Paris' plentiful accommodation spans all budgets, but it is often fully booked well in advance, particularly during peak times (April to October, as well as public and school holidays). Reservations are essential at these times, but are also recommended year-round.

⊛ I LIVE HERE

SUMMER BLOOM

Janine Eberle is a local writer. @janinemaree

Sometime in May, a run of warm days unofficially heralds the beginning of summer and the city transforms. Winter gloom lifts; we're suddenly a city of giddy optimists, determined to profit from every sunny moment, rushing en masse to find a *terrasse* and order a glass of rosé. Picnickers swarm the banks of the Seine and canals, armed with baguettes, *fromage*, charcuterie, and COVID-era temporary outdoor seating (allowed during the warm months) reclaims parking places.

Final stage, Tour de France

MAY HOLIDAYS

The temperate month of May, which is a top time to visit Paris, also has more public holidays than any other month in France. Watch out for widespread closures, particularly on May Day (1 May).

Weather Through the Year

JANUARY	FEBRUARY	MARCH	APRIL	MAY	JUNE
Avg. daytime max: **8°C**	Avg. daytime max: **9°C**	Avg. daytime max: **13°C**	Avg. daytime max: **17°C**	Avg. daytime max: **20°C**	Avg. daytime max: **24°C**
Days of rainfall: 9	Days of rainfall: 8	Days of rainfall: 9	Days of rainfall: 8	Days of rainfall: 9	Days of rainfall: 8

SUMMER SUN

During the Parisian summer, when daylight can last around 16 hours, 'beaches' – complete with sunbeds, lounge chairs and palm trees – line the banks of the Seine, Paris Pride rocks the June streets and shoppers hit the summer *soldes* (sales).

Rocking Out

Fête de la Musique (p193) This national music festival welcomes in summer on the solstice with fabulous staged and impromptu live performances of jazz, reggae, classical and more. Held at venues all over the city. **June**

We Love Green (p197) This music festival lights up the Bois de Vincennes with international bands and top-tier DJ sets. **June**

Bastille Day The capital celebrates France's national day with a morning military parade along av des Champs-Élysées, accompanied by a fly-past of fighter aircraft and helicopters. *Feux d'artifice* (fireworks) light up the sky above the Champ de Mars by night. **July**

Rock en Seine Headlining acts perform at the Domaine National de St-Cloud, on the city's southwestern edge, at this popular three-day music festival. **August**

Culture & Cycling

Chinese New Year (p276) During Chinese New Year, get thrilled by parades thronging through the 13e *arrondissement* and firecrackers lighting up the night. **February**

Tour de France The last of 21 stages of this prestigious, 3500km-long cycling event finishes with a race up the av des Champs-Élysées on the third or fourth Sunday of July. **July**

Quartier du Livre (p233) The Latin Quarter comes even more alive than usual during this festival when independent booksellers and writers set up stands or take over cafes throughout the neighbourhood. **June**

Nuit Blanche From sundown to sunrise, this artistic and cultural extravaganza brings contemporary art installations to the city streets, plus museums stay open for one 'White Night' ('All Nighter'). **June**

I LIVE HERE

AUTUMN ENCOUNTER

Rafael Sinclair Mahdavi is co-author of *The Dishwasher Dialogues*. rafaelmahdavi.com

It was a fall afternoon...By the Louvre, I jumped off the bus and joined the queue at the glass pyramid. I struck up a conversation with an elderly woman. She hailed from Wichita, Kansas, and I told her my mother was from there. 'You see,' I said. 'That's Paris for you. You queue up to meet Caravaggio and you get to know a lady from Wichita.'

Autumn in Paris

WINTER ICE SKATING

Come winter, ice-skating rinks pop up across the city, including in some truly picturesque spots, such as Galeries Lafayette's panoramic rooftop. Skating is usually free, with a charge for skate hire. The Grand Palais offers the world's biggest indoor rink – complete with a DJ and disco ball at night.

JULY	**AUGUST**	**SEPTEMBER**	**OCTOBER**	**NOVEMBER**	**DECEMBER**
Avg. daytime max: **26°C**	Avg. daytime max: **25°C**	Avg. daytime max: **22°C**	Avg. daytime max: **17°C**	Avg. daytime max: **11°C**	Avg. daytime max: **8°C**
Days of rainfall: **7**	Days of rainfall: **6**	Days of rainfall: **7**	Days of rainfall: **8**	Days of rainfall: **9**	Days of rainfall: **9**

GET PREPARED FOR PARIS

Useful things to load in your bag, your ears and your brain.

Clothes

Stylish Threads As the cradle of *haute couture*, Paris is chic: don your smarter threads and accessories. Though keep in mind, Parisians have a finely tuned sense of aesthetics. They take meticulous care in their presentation and every component fits perfectly. They favour style and simplicity – classic items – over bling, mixing basics from chain stores like H&M with designer pieces, vintage and flea-market finds, and statement-making accessories. You'll also stand out less as a tourist and therefore be less of a target for pickpockets.

Cruising Shoes Bring sturdy shoes whatever the season, whether trainers, which are ubiquitous, or walking shoes – cobbled streets aren't kind on high heels.

Scarf A scarf can double as a style accessory and covering for bare shoulders in cathedrals and other religious sites where you should dress respectfully.

Manners

Always greet and say goodbye to anyone you interact with, such as shopkeepers, using *Bonjour* (*bonsoir* at night) and *Au revoir*. It's not viewed as a formality but as basic respect.

Take your time at meals or in cafes – eating is relaxation in Paris.

Talking about money (salaries or spending outlays) in public is taboo. Food and drink aside, conversations often revolve around philosophy, art and sports.

READ

A Moveable Feast (Ernest Hemingway; 1964) Hemingway's posthumously published memoir about his tumultuous life in 1920s Paris.

Notre Dame de Paris (Victor Hugo; 1831) The classic tale of the hunchback of Notre Dame, which saved the cathedral of the same name.

Exteriors (Annie Ernaux; 1993) Novel about living on the Paris periphery by the author who won the Nobel Prize for Literature in 2022.

Parisians: An Adventure History of Paris (Graham Robb; 2010) The British historian recounts the city's history through fascinating characters.

Words

'**Bonjour**' (bon-zhoor) is how you say 'hello' in Paris.
'**Au revoir**' (o-rer-vwa) translates to something close to 'til next time', and is used for 'goodbye'.
'**Excusez-moi**' (ek-skew-zay-mwa) is how you interrupt someone or get attention ('excuse me').
If you bump into someone, say '**pardon**' (par-don).
To say 'yes', use '**oui**' (wee), or make it more informal, almost like *yeah*, by drawing out the pronunciation (weah).
'No' is easy: '**non**' (noh).
'**S'il vous plaît**' (seel-voo-play) is the way to say 'please', and you can also use it to get the waiter's attention.
'Thank you' is a must. Just say '**merci**' (mair-see). And if someone thanks you, reply with '**de rien**' (der ree-en) for 'you're welcome'.

If someone hits you with a stream of French, you can let them know 'I don't understand' by saying '**je ne comprends pas**' (zher ner kom-pron pa).
Then you can ask them 'Do you speak English?' with '**Parlez-vous anglais?**' (par-lay-voo ong-glay).
To enquire of a hotelier or a shopkeeper the price of something, say '**Quel est le prix?**' (kel ay ler pree).
To ask someone how they are doing, '**Comment allez-vous?**' (ko-moh ta-lay-voo) is the more formal way to go. Or more casually, ask '**Ça va?**' (sa va), which is similar to 'How's it going?'
If they ask how you are, and you're doing well, you can respond 'Fine, thank you, and you?' with '**Bien, merci. Et vous?**' (byun mair-see ay voo).

WATCH

Call My Agent! (various directors; 2015–2020) Light-hearted look at life in a Parisian talent agency, chock-a-block with celeb cameos.

Amélie (Jean-Pierre Jeunet; 2001) Endearing story of a winsome young Parisian in a whimsical Montmartre.

Le Ballon Rouge (Albert Lamorisse; 1956) A 34-minute classic following a young boy's adventures with a red balloon in the streets of Ménilmontant.

Intouchables (Olivier Nakache and Éric Toledano; 2011) One of the highest-grossing French films, starring Omar Sy and François Cluzet.

L'Histoire de Souleymane (Boris Lojkine; 2024; pictured above) Drama about an undocumented migrant working as a delivery biker rocked the Cannes Film Festival.

LISTEN

The New Paris Podcast (2017–present) Author Lindsey Tramuta's podcast deep dives into the evolving French capital with local experts.

La Vie en Rose (Édith Piaf; 1946) One of many stirring classic chansons by Belleville-born La Môme Piaf (the Little Sparrow), covered by Grace Jones and others.

NI (Ninho; 2023) The rapper from the Parisian suburb of Yerres is behind a string of number-one albums like this one.

Famille (Ben Mazué; 2025) Latest album from the award-winning singer/songwriter who's based in Paris.

Above: Gare du Lyon; right: RER B line from Charles de Gaulle

GETTING THERE

Paris is the main point of entry for visitors to France. Most international airlines fly to Aéroport Charles de Gaulle, 28km northeast of central Paris, or Orly, 19km south of central Paris. Five major train stations offer international services.

RER Train

Trains are the best way to get to and from Paris' airports. The RER B line from Charles de Gaulle crosses under the middle of Paris, with stops including Gare du Nord, Châtelet–Les Halles, St-Michel–Notre Dame and Luxembourg. Some trains run express through the suburbs, saving about 10 minutes. An even faster express route is slated for 2027. From Orly, you can connect to the city via line 14 of the metro, or on the RER B after taking the OrlyVal shuttle.

Taxis

Allow 40 to 80 minutes to central Paris, depending on traffic. Take an official taxi from the clearly marked ranks at each terminal's Arrivals level. The government mandates fixed prices for taxis to the Right and Left Banks. Note that rideshare services do not have access to Paris' fast taxi lanes, so they're more susceptible to traffic jams.

Visas

EU citizens have no entry restrictions. From 2026, citizens of countries that can visit the Schengen area visa-free (eg, Australia, Canada, UK, USA) will need prior authorisation under the online ETIAS scheme.

SIM Cards

You'll get a better deal buying a SIM in the city. It's also hard to find advice on the best packages and set-up at the airport. To buy one immediately, get a local SIM (such as the prepaid Mobicarte Orange) at a Relay shop in the terminal.

Money

ATMs dispensing euros are easily found in airports, train stations and across central Paris. Avoid currency-exchange services *(bureaux de change)* because of the high fees.

FROM AIRPORTS TO THE CITY CENTRE

From Charles de Gaulle Airport

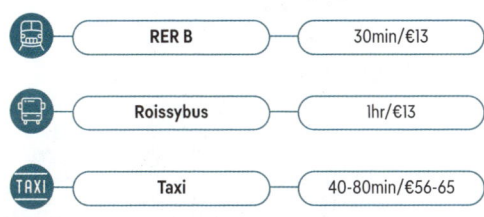

🚆	RER B	30min/€13
🚌	Roissybus	1hr/€13
🚕	Taxi	40-80min/€56-65

From Orly Airport

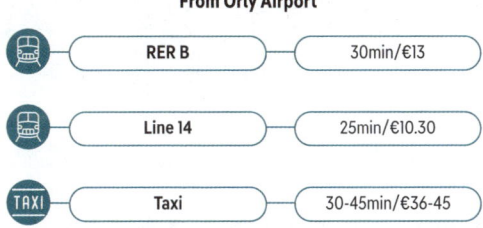

🚆	RER B	30min/€13
🚇	Line 14	25min/€10.30
🚕	Taxi	30-45min/€36-45

TIP

Download **Bonjour RATP** *(bonjour-ratp.fr/en)*, the app from the Paris metro authority, to get real-time traffic updates and itinerary options. You can also buy tickets on your phone. **Citymapper** *(citymapper.com)* is invaluable for trip planning. Easily book a taxi with the app offered by **G7 taxis** *(g7.fr/en)*.

Bonjour RATP

Citymapper

ELENA CHEVALIER/SHUTTERSTOCK

OTHER POINTS OF ENTRY

Eurostar

The high-speed London–Paris line runs from St Pancras International to Gare du Nord in northern Paris. Voyages take 2¼ hours. Fees vary greatly, starting from €44 each way. The popular **'Snap' tickets** *(snap.eurostar.com/rw-en)* offer reduced fares on last-minute journeys. Eurostar now also operates the routes to Brussels, Antwerp and Amsterdam previously handled by Thalys.

TGV

France's national railway company, the SNCF, operates high-speed TGV trains to international destinations. In partnership with the Renfe railway company in Spain, a train connects Barcelona and the Gare du Lyon (starting from €85 each way). The Gare du Lyon is also the station for Lyria trains serving Swiss destinations, and the Trenitalia to Milan.

Bus

Various companies, such as FlixBus and BlaBlaCar, operate long-distance coach routes connecting Paris with other destinations across Europe. Arguably the cheapest way to arrive in Paris (fares starting at €19 from Amsterdam with BlaBlaCar bus, €21.50 from London), the comfy buses are equipped with a toilet, snacks, plug sockets to keep devices charged and free wi-fi; some services are overnight. Book as far ahead as possible to bag the cheapest ticket.

Tramway

GETTING AROUND

The Paris metro is fast and convenient, while the comprehensive bus system allows you to sightsee while travelling. A surge in new bike lanes and infrastructure has prompted a cycling revolution. For many, however, walking the beautiful streets is the way to go.

Metro & RER

The fastest way to get around, the metro runs from about 5.30am to around 1.15am (about 2.15am on Friday and Saturday evenings). Serving the suburbs, RER trains save time crossing the city because they have fewer stops in the centre. As part of the enormous Grand Paris Express infrastructure project, four new metro lines are being added in the Paris region, and other lines have been extended, like the driverless line 14 which now serves Orly airport. Currently the metro lines are numbered 1 to 14. The RER has five main lines, though visitors usually only need to use lines A, B and C.

TIP
Beware of pickpockets who occasionally target busy tourist areas, such as metro lines 1 and 9, and also the RER train to Disneyland Paris. Keep bags zipped and close to your body. Do not leave phones in your back pocket.

Bus

With no stairs, buses are widely accessible and are good for parents with prams/strollers and people with limited mobility. Bus lines complement the metro: for some journeys a bus is the more direct – and

---

Metro Etiquette | Keep your voice down and use headphones to avoid disrupting the peace. | Don't sit on a *strapotin* (folding seat) during rush hour. Stand to make room for other passengers. | Give up your seat for elderly, pregnant and/or people with a disability. | Always let passengers off the trains before you board.

scenic – way to go. Stops show schedules, routes and often the waiting time until the next bus.

Tramway

A network of tram lines on the outskirts of Paris complements the other modes of public transport. These are popular with Parisians in outlying neighbourhoods.

Boat

Combining scenery and convenience, the **Batobus** *(batobus.com)* is a handy hop-on, hop-off service stopping at nine key destinations along the Seine. In warmer months the service runs regularly through the day and offers the chance for a river cruise at a fraction of the price of a tour boat.

Walking

Easily navigable, Paris is a walker's paradise. The city is so compact you can actually traverse it in about two hours. Serious urban hikers can explore several Grandes Randonnées (long-distance trails) in Paris, including the GR75, a 50km loop around the city that was launched in 2017 in support of Paris' bid for the 2024 Olympic and Paralympic Games.

> **TIP**
> Validate your Navigo pass or ticket for each journey, and have it handy to show to ticket inspectors, who periodically board trains or stop commuters in stations to check.

 PUBLIC TRANSPORT ESSENTIALS

Navigo Easy Card

The cheapest, easiest way to use Paris' public transport is via the Navigo Easy card. Sold for €2 at metro and RER ticket windows and RATP-affiliated outlets (eg, tobacconists and markets), this credit-card-sized fare card is used for all your ticketing needs; or charge up a virtual one on the RATP app. Navigo, like London's Oyster card or Hong Kong's Octopus card, is a system that provides a full range of fare options. As Paris phases out paper tickets, Navigo Easy cards are the future. You can load the reusable, contactless card with tickets, which are then deducted for each ride.

Understanding the Fares

As of January 2025, a new fare system was put into place, which eliminates the confusing zone system. Previously ticket prices were higher for trips to the suburbs, including Versailles. Now you can travel all over the Île-de-France region by train for the price of a single, one-way fare at €2.50. The ticket is valid for a duration of two hours. Note that buses and trams have a different price, which is set at €2. You can load a variety of ticket types onto a Navigo Easy card: metro-train-RER, bus-tram, RoissyBus, Paris airports, Navigo Day Pass. Use one of the multilingual machines found at metro and train stations, get assistance from an RATP agent at the service window or load tickets via the RATP app on your phone.

Navigo Day Pass

If you anticipate using public transport a lot on a single day, the Navigo Day Pass is better value at €12 for unlimited rides on all transportation modes in the Île-de-France (excluding airport access).

DESIGN DREAM

The Paris metro isn't just a fast and convenient way to get around. It's also a showcase for beautiful design – from the splendid art nouveau station entrances to the signature ceramic tiles. Resist the urge to rush out of the trains and stop and admire the details: the Louvre Rivoli station displays sculptures along the quay, Bastille offers murals depicting the French Revolution, Pont Neuf/La Monnaie has ceramic coins on the ceiling in a nod to the nearby Paris Mint. Parmentier is a potato-filled homage to the station namesake, while St-Germain des Prés celebrates the bohemian writers who made this Left Bank quarter their stomping grounds. Perhaps the most marvellous of all is the Arts et Métiers station, clad in copper in a steampunk tribute to Jules Verne.

If you need to recharge your phone while you're out exploring the city, outlets can be found in the public bus kiosks.

Cycling

The Vélib' bike-share scheme has over 20,000 bikes, both classic (green) and electric (blue), at nearly 1480 docking stations in the city and surrounding region. In Paris proper, stations are found every 300m. Buy a subscription online (velib-metropole.fr/en) or at docking stations. There are single-trip, day and multi-way options. Other bike-sharing service operators include Lime and Dott. Before choosing your bike, be sure to check the tyres, brakes and gears. Be aware of the rules of the road, and note that some cycling lanes share traffic with buses. Do not ride on the footpath.

Taxi & Rideshare

Find taxis at official stands or via companies such as **Taxis G7** (g7.fr). There are queues of cabs at major train stations. You can flag one on the street if the sign on the roof is green. Taxis are expensive but are a blessing if you have luggage, or can't face the metro. Taxis must accept payment by credit card. The *prise en charge* (flagfall) is €3 (if using the app, it's €4 to order immediately, €7 in advance). The minimum journey cost is €8. Aside from airport trips, which are a fixed flat-rate fare, the cost of the taxi journey is determined by the taximeter located inside the vehicle – strictly regulated by law. Beware of the taxi driver, particularly queuing around the Eiffel Tower or other tourist zones, who claims an outrageous flat fare for a ride. Take note of the official taxi permit number fixed to the front right-hand side of the windshield, which you can report in an online complaint to the Préfecture de Police. Rideshare apps like Uber are active in Paris. Note that rideshare vehicles do not have access to the city's fast taxi lanes.

Driving

As part of its sustainability and environmental initiatives, the city of Paris has closed many streets to cars. In fact, the centre (1er, 2e, 3e and 4e *arrondissements*) is a car-free zone, only allowing access to residents, officials and emergency vehicles. (Through traffic is completely banned.) Other measures have included eliminating parking spots and tripling the parking fees for SUVs. Though car traffic has been dramatically reduced, traffic jams can be a real problem – the metro is much faster. All this is to say, driving is not recommended in Paris. And with such an excellent public transport system, there's really no need to hire a car.

Cycling, Le Marais

PREPARING FOR THE METRO

Rush Hour
The Paris region public transport system is the busiest in the world after Tokyo with 9.4 million trips every day. If your plans are flexible, consider travelling outside the peak hours of 8am to 10am and 5pm to 7pm. Commuting Parisians pack the trains and they can become uncomfortably crowded.

Stairs
The Paris metro is notorious for the flights of stairs. If you have a physical impairment or a lot of luggage, consider taking a bus or taxi, particularly if a metro route would require changing lines.

Heat
In the warmer months, the metro can become uncomfortably stuffy and hot. Some lines have refrigerated ventilation systems (1, 2, 5, 9, 11, 14 and part of line 4), which cool the air inside the trains with less energy than traditional air-conditioning. Other lines rely on ventilation to get the air moving.

Repairs
Parisians sometimes take for granted a system that seems to run so seamlessly. But the infrastructure requires constant maintenance and improvement. Generally the RATP will schedule work on stations or portions of the metro lines for nights or weekends. The schedule for this work is posted on signs in individual trains and also on the Bonjour RATP app. If there's a line closure, alternative routes are suggested.

Delays
Signs in the metro indicate the wait times for trains – usually between two to four minutes during the day. If there are delays or stoppages, this information is indicated on the signs, and also via station agents over the loudspeakers. The Bonjour RATP app gives traffic information for each line in real time.

TRAVEL COSTS

Metro/RER
Single fares are €2.50 with a Navigo Easy card

Bus
Single fares are €2 with a Navigo Easy card

Bicycle
A single Vélib' ride is €3

NEED TO KNOW

Children under four travel for free on the Paris public transport system. Under 10s use reduced fare tickets (half price).

ACCESSIBILITY

First opened in 1900, the vintage metro system is not fully accessible. The vast number of stairs and lack of elevators at older stations put it out of reach for those who have a physical disability or are in a wheelchair. Improvements are being made, and the new stations inaugurated as part of the Grand Paris Express project are all wheelchair accessible. Note that metro line 14 – equipped with station elevators – is fully accessible. Paris buses are all accessible, equipped with dedicated ramps, low floors and wide doors. Likewise, all tramway lines are accessible.

Bouillon Julien (p38)

DINING OUT

Home to one of the world's greatest culinary traditions, Paris wows – whether with multicourse meals, crusty baguettes or gooey Camembert.

The inhabitants of some cities rally around local sports teams, but in Paris they rally around *la table* – and everything on it. Pistachio macarons, shots of tomato consommé, decadent bœuf bourguignon, a gooey wedge of Camembert running onto the cheese plate...food isn't fuel here – it's the reason you get up in the morning.

Blessed with access to a rich and varied French landscape and farmers with a strong sense of regional identity, plus a culture that celebrates life's daily pleasures, it's no surprise that Parisian chefs have long been synonymous with gastronomic genius. In recent decades, a new generation of chefs has emerged, displaying a willingness to push the boundaries of traditional tastes. They are open to culinary traditions originating outside France, while at the same time downplaying the

---

Best Parisian Specialities

BAGUETTES Born in Paris, the wand-shaped loaf is on UNESCO's list of intangible heritage.

PARISIAN BRIE Stand-out cows-milk bries include Provins, Melun, Montereau and Meaux.

ONION SOUP Delicious beef broth and onions with crispy croutons and melted Gruyère.

MACARONS Soft pillows of almond flour with delectable fillings, from chocolate to rose or matcha.

importance of Michelin stars and instead embracing street-front bistro and style-forward settings. Decadent work-of-art pastries aren't going anywhere. Instead, Parisian cuisine is continuing to innovate and shine. For more on Food, Drink & Nightlife, see p318.

Vegetarians & Vegans

In a meat-centric country like France, where *viande* (meat) once also meant 'food', vegetarians and vegans have been hard-pressed for dining options. Yet a slew of new addresses in Paris are shaking things up, from casual *cantines* and vegan burger, pizza and hot-dog joints to gourmet vegetarian and vegan restaurants, such as the fine-dining hotspot **Faubourg Daimant** and trendy Maslow (p116) overlooking the Seine. There's even vegan sushi at BrEAThe (p116). Check out the food tours and vegan tourist map offered by Franck Adandé, the vegan influencer behind @vegantouristparis.

In general, there's been a shift towards a greener way of eating with plant-forward dishes taking pride of place on restaurant menus. It's not uncommon to see vegetarian choices – or ask your waiter about options. Another good bet for vegetarians is non-French cuisine, like Middle Eastern food. Chef Alan Geaam even spun off a vegetarian version of his popular Lebanese spot, called **Qasti Green**. See happycow.net for more vegan and vegetarian options in Paris.

Bistro Boom

Legend has it that the bistro was born at La Mère Catherine in Montmartre. After Napoleon's fall in 1814, occupying Cossack soldiers – sneaking away from their posts without their officers' permission – shouted '*Bistro! Bistro!*' (Hurry! Hurry!) when ordering drinks. The bistro's origins remain murky, but the tradition is firmly established.

These small neighbourhood restaurants, offering chalkboard menus, are often decorated with a zinc-topped bar and mosaic floors. In recent years, concern for the

Fête des Vendanges de Montmartre

FOOD, WINE & BEER FESTIVALS

Salon International de l'Agriculture Appetising nine-day agricultural fair with France-wide fare (February–March).

Paris Café Festival Coffee roasters from France and beyond gather – it's great for speciality-coffee amateurs to sample brews (April/May).

Paris Beer Festival Craft beer's popularity in Paris peaks over 10 days across the city (May).

Rice le marché Treiz'Asiatique A new(ish) Asian street food festival in the 13e. (September).

Fête des Vendanges de Montmartre Five days celebrating Montmartre's grape harvest with costumes, concerts, food and a parade (October).

Salon du Chocolat Chocoholics shouldn't miss this five-day festival of tastings, workshops, demonstrations and kids' activities (October–November).

OEUF MAYO	**JAMBON-BEURRE**	**STEAK TARTARE**	**PARIS-BREST**
Classic bistro dish made of hard-boiled eggs and mayonnaise.	Quintessential Parisian sandwich of sliced baguette with butter and ham.	Raw ground beef paired with everything from capers to raw egg.	Hoop of choux pastry filled with hazelnut and/or almond praline cream.

Pastries from Stohrer (p116)

PARIS FOOD WEBSITES

Le Fooding (lefooding.com) The French movement that's giving Michelin a run for its money, with a mission to shake up the establishment. A good balance of quirky, under-the-radar reviews and truly fine dining.

Paris by Mouth (parisbymouth.com) Capital dining and drinking with articles and recommendations searchable by *arrondissement*.

David Lebovitz (davidlebovitz.com) Expat US pastry chef and cookbook author with insights and recommendations.

La Fourchette (thefork.com) Offers user reviews and great deals of up to 50% off in Paris restaurants.

bistro as a dying breed has led to protective measures, government stimulus and restaurateur investment. Top chefs such as Jean-François Piège have revived classics like **À L'Épi d'Or**, and the popularity of new haunts like the **Bistrot des Tournelles** and the Bistrot des Fables (p68) show the bistro's staying power. In fact, there's been a veritable bistro boom – an alluring melange of traditional spots and stylish neobistros offering affordable feasts crafted with carefully sourced ingredients.

The Rise of the Bouillon

The *bouillon* was born back in 1855, when the butcher Baptiste-Adolphe Duval set up shop near Les Halles. His vast hall could accommodate 500 people at a time, and served *bouillon*, or broth-based recipes. Nowadays the *bouillons* are undergoing a renaissance with places like Bouillon Pigalle (p134) complementing historic spots like the **Bouillon Julien**, Bouillon Chartier (p84) and Le Petit Bouillon Pharamond (p120). Expect to see queues snaking down the street. The winning formula: simple, hearty cuisine for a cheap price, served in a lively, spacious setting.

Street Food

Like many cosmopolitan cities, Paris has seen its fair share of food fads. From the food truck to the *crookie* (a croissant-chocolate-chip-cookie hybrid), there are trends that come and go. Some have real staying power. The gourmet hamburgers that arrived on the scene more than a decade ago are now ubiquitous, and outlets serving *bành mì* (the Vietnamese sandwich) are on the rise.

Street food is not new to Paris. After all, this is the city that pioneered the *frite*, with vendors selling fried sliced potatoes on the Pont Neuf at the end of the 18th century. Options nowadays for street food run the gamut from kebabs and falafel sandwiches to crêpes.

Gourmet Pizza

The French are firm fans of pizza, consuming on average a pizza a week. Pizza joints can be found all over Paris, and there are some that are real foodie destinations. Chief among them is Oobatz (p176) in the 11e *arrondissement,* which serves sourdough pizza (the dough is naturally fermented) and an interesting selection of natural wines. Also in the 11e is hot spot **Rori**, where you can order small plates along with your slice.

Food Shopping Parisian Style

One of the excellent privileges of life in Paris is to buy food from small neighbourhood shops, each with its own speciality. Prepare for a cultural moment, standing in little queues to fill the fridge (or assemble a picnic), chatting with the purveyor at each stop.

Patisseries are similar to *boulangeries* (bakeries) but are generally a notch up on sophistication. *Fromageries* specialise in cheese: whether hard goat's cheese or creamy Époisses. The *boucherie* (butcher's shop) sells a huge array of animal products, but short-term visitors usually focus on charcuterie (prepared meats) such as pâtés, *saucissons* (salami) and *rillettes* (meat spreads). Similar to a deli, the *traiteur* specialises in prepared dishes. *Marchés alimentaires* (open-air and covered markets) are also a staple of Parisian life. And don't forget the *caviste* (wine shop), with wines usually much more affordable than overseas.

Urban Agriculture

Seasonality has long been a hallmark of French cuisine, and Parisian chefs are mindful in their sourcing of ingredients. An example is **Les Résistants**, a farm-to-table group by restaurateur Florent Piard, a champion of the Slow Food movement. His restaurants showcase fine fish, meat and vegetables sourced from a network of 150 independent farms and fishers. Some chefs use ingredients from their own kitchen gardens, or highlight products cultivated in Paris itself.

Urban agriculture is having a moment, with unused spaces such as rooftops and car parks blooming with greenery. **La Caverne**, situated in a former garage in the 18e, is the largest underground farm in the Île-de-France region. Organic mushroom production follows in the tradition of the historic Paris mushroom farmers who used to grow the *champignons de Paris* in underground quarries. You may also spot restaurant ingredients from rooftop farms such as BienÉlevées (saffron grown on top of the Opera Bastille), Beaugrenelle shopping mall (aromatic herbs and edible flowers) and Nature Urbaine (fruits and vegetables from a vast farm atop the Paris Expo Porte de Versailles convention centre).

Crêpe

Baguettes for sale

TRIP PLANNER

EXPLORE PARIS' BREAD & CHEESE PURVEYORS

Few things in France are as tantalising as the smell of just-baked buttery croissants wafting out of an open bakery door, and few can resist the temptation of the hundreds of cheese varieties available in the capital. Here, we give you a quick primer on how to dive right in to two of Paris' signature foods.

Sample the Daily Bread

With roughly 1200 *boulangeries* (bakeries) in Paris – or 11.5 per sq km – you should absolutely find your way to one (or more!) at some point during your stay.

As you'll notice in the extravagant display windows, bakeries bake much more than baguettes: they also sell croissants, chocolate éclairs, quiches, pizzas and an astounding array of pastries and cakes. If you're eating lunch on the cheap, a trip to the closest bakery will do you right.

Specialist patisseries, often headed by big-name pastry chefs, create astonishing works of art. Their delicacies fall into several categories: bavarois (gelatine-set, cream-based desserts), gateaux (literally 'cakes', but spanning everything from a sponge-based chocolate-and-coffee *opéra* to layered-pastry mille-feuille), cookie-style treats like shell-shaped madeleine cakes and macarons, choux (puff pastry, such as éclairs and profiteroles), *entremets* (eg flans) and *viennoiseries* (yeast-based baked goods including croissants and *pains au chocolat*).

When buying bread from a *boulangerie*, try to familiarise yourself with the varieties

🥐 TOP BOULANGERIES & PATISSERIES

Le Bricheton Breads made using ancient grains like Khorasan wheat, ground in the bakery's own mill.

Boulangerie MieMie Turns out distinctive croissants, some of the best in Paris.

Stohrer Rue Montorgueil landmark in business since 1730.

Boulangerie Basil Organic bakery brimming with delights in the 16e.

Sacha Finkelsztajn – La Boutique Jaune Traditional Jewish bakery in the Marais.

Laurent Duchêne Prize-winning croissants vie with macarons for attention.

VG Pâtisserie Indulge in plant-based vegan treats in the 11e.

Jacques Genin Assembled-to-order millefeuilles.

Fou de Pâtisserie One-stop shop for treats by some of France's top pastry chefs.

---

on sale while you're standing in the queue – not all baguettes are created equal. Most Parisians today will ask for a *baguette tradition* (traditional-style baguette), distinguished by its pointy tips and coarse, handcrafted surface. Other breads you'll see include *boules* (round loaves), *pavés* (flattened rectangular loaves) and *ficelles* (skinny loaves that are half the weight of a baguette).

The shape of a baguette (literally 'stick' or 'wand') evolved when Napoléon Bonaparte ordered army bakers to create loaves for soldiers to stuff down their trouser legs on the march.

Every spring *boulangers* (bakers) battle it out in the official Grand Prix de la Meilleure Baguette de Paris (Best Baguette in Paris). The winner is not only awarded a cash prize but also provides the French president with baguettes for a year.

Choose Cheese

Charles de Gaulle once famously asked how it was possible to govern a country with 246 types of cheese (now countless more). So how on earth to choose what to buy at the *fromagerie* (cheese shop)?

The variety on offer can be overwhelming, but vendors will always allow you to sample before you buy, and they are usually very generous with their guidance and pairing advice. For more insights, pop by the new Musée Vivant du Fromage (p221; Living Cheese Museum) on the Île St-Louis.

SEEK THE FIVE BASIC CHEESE TYPES

Fromage à pâte demi-dure
- 'Semi-hard cheese' means uncooked, pressed cheese. Try Tomme de Savoie, made from either raw or pasteurised cow's milk; Cantal, a cow's-milk cheese from Auvergne that tastes something like cheddar; St-Nectaire, a pressed cheese that has a strong, complex taste; and Ossau-Iraty, a ewe's-milk cheese made in the Basque Country.

Fromage à pâte dure
- 'Hard cheese' is always cooked and then pressed. Try Beaufort, a grainy cow's-milk cheese with a slightly fruity taste from Rhône-Alpes; Comté, a cheese made with raw cow's milk in Franche-Comté; and Mimolette, an Edam-like dark-orange cheese from Lille aged for up to 36 months.

Fromage à pâte molle
- 'Soft cheese' is moulded or rind-washed. Camembert, a classic moulded cheese from Normandy, and Brie de Meaux are both made from raw cow's milk. Munster from Alsace, mild Chaource and strong-smelling Langres from Champagne are rind-washed, fine-textured cheeses.

Fromage à pâte persillée
- 'Marbled' or 'blue cheese' is so called because the veins often resemble *persil* (parsley). Roquefort is a ewe's-milk veined cheese that is to many the king of French cheeses. Fourme d'Ambert is a mild cow's-milk cheese from Rhône-Alpes.

Fromage de chèvre
- 'Goat's-milk cheese' is usually creamy and both sweet and slightly salty when fresh, but it hardens and gets much saltier as it matures. Try Ste-Maure de Touraine, a creamy, mild cheese from the Loire region, or Crottin de Chavignol, a classic though saltier variety from Burgundy.

Aux Folies (p177)

BAR OPEN

You'll find all species of thirst-quenching or caffeine-quaffing venues in Paris, from chic wine bars and neighbourhood dives to speciality taprooms.

For the French, drinking and eating go together like wine and cheese, and the boundary between a cafe, bistro, brasserie and bar is blurred. The line between drinking and clubbing is often nonexistent – a cafe that's quiet mid-afternoon might have DJ sets in the evening and dancing later on.

For most Parisians living in tiny apartments, cafes and bars have traditionally served as the salon they don't have – a place where they can meet with friends over *un verre* (glass of wine), read for hours over a *café au lait*, debate politics while downing an espresso at a zinc counter, swill cocktails during *apéro* (apéritif; predinner drink) or get the party started aboard a floating club on the Seine.

The clubbing scene has never been so good, with a variety of venues offering music and ambience for all types. What used to be underground and mobile – the best DJs would move on following short stints, and the hippest *soirées clubbing* (clubbing events) would float between venues – has been transformed by the arrival of new dance-all-night destinations. Case in point: the Berlin-style electro Mia Mao (p138), housed in a cavernous industrial hall in La Villette, which is changing Paris into a clubbing destination *par excellence*.

Rooftop Bars

Innovative drinking and dining spaces are carving out their place on the city's rooftops, with panoramic views over the skyline

---

Lonely Planet's Top Bars

BAR DES FERRAILLEURS	**SEPTIME LA CAVE**	**CRAVAN**	**ST JAMES**
Creative cocktails and a fun vibe on festive rue de Lappe. **p192**	Hip spot for natural wine in the IIe. **p192**	Excellent cocktails and cool design in chic St-Germain. **p73**	Just one of many high-end hotel bars (eg Le Bristol, Hôtel de Crillon). **p73**

strung with Parisian landmarks. La Bellevilloise (p177), a top music and cultural venue in Belleville, has a sprawling, two-level rooftop decorated with potted plants and stylish flea-market finds. Seasonal rooftop bar-restaurants sprout on department stores Galeries Lafayette (p94) and Le Printemps (p94). Cultural centre Point Éphémère (p143) opens a rooftop in warm weather on the banks of Canal St-Martin. The Institut Français de la Mode is crowned with the Café Oz Rooftop (p278), overlooking the Seine, while La Tour d'Argent (p234) – the celebrated dining destination – features a lovely landscaped rooftop with Notre Dame views.

Some of the most spectacular spaces are at hotels. On the Left Bank, a cool crowd queues at the Hôtel Dame des Arts (p257) in the 6e. Rooftop watering holes on the Right Bank include Grands Boulevards Experimental (p94), **Hôtel Madame Rêve**, **SO/ Paris** and **Hôtel Rochechouart**. There's also Mama Shelter (p311) and **Terrass" Hôtel**. TOO Tac Tac Sky Bar (p278) is the highest of them all.

One of the originals is still one of the best: Le Perchoir (p178) is situated atop a former industrial building in Ménilmontant. The same team also runs the bar and restaurant atop the Pavillon 6 of Paris Expo Porte de Versailles, using produce grown at its 14,000-sq-m urban rooftop farm (the world's largest).

Wine & Wine Bars

Paris has been a wine-drinking town since the days when its outskirts were blanketed in vineyards. There's a tremendous selection of wine bars and *caves à vin* (bottle-stocked cellars where you can also get a glass). Favourites include Le Bar-av (p155), **Magnum**, **Chez Nous**, L'Etiquette (p220) on the Île Saint-Louis and Septime La Cave (p192) – a popular alternative to the always-booked restaurant. Hot spot **Folderol** offers ice cream, too.

Though Bordeaux bashing is no longer *au courant*, the current trend is all about natural wine, *pétillant naturel* (a young sparkling natural wine, *pet' nat* for short) and orange wine. Of course fine-dining restaurants are impervious to such trends, boasting some of the world's most glorious wine cellars – La Tour d'Argent has more than 300,000 bottles, a historic collection that was successfully hidden from the Nazis during WWII.

Happy hour drinks board

NEED TO KNOW

Tiered Pricing Drinking in Paris means paying for the space you take up. So it costs more to sit at a table than to stand at the counter, more for coveted terrace seats, more on a fancy square than a backstreet, more in the 8e than the 18e.

Average Costs Glass of wine from €4. Cocktail €12 to €30. *Demi* (half-pint) of beer €4 to €7. In clubs and chic bars, prices can double. Club admission is from free to €30, often cheaper before 1am.

Happy Hour Parisian 'happy hour' – called just that (no French translation) – ushers in reduced-price drinks for two or three hours, usually between 5pm and 8pm.

Closing Time Cafes and bars close around 2am, though some have licences until dawn. Club hours vary depending on venue and event but start late.

LITTLE RED DOOR
Famous speakeasy with award-winning mixologists. **p157**

FREEDJ
Le Marais staple gay bar, better for mingling and dancing than drinks. **p165**

BATEAU EL ALAMEIN
Floating venue in the 13e with live music and a Seine-side terrace. **p279**

AUX FOLIES
Iconic 1870s cabaret turned bar with a large, lively terrace. **p177**

Beer & Breweries

Beer hasn't traditionally had a high profile in France and mass-produced varieties such as Kronenbourg 1664 (5.5%), brewed in Strasbourg, used to dominate. However French beer consumption is on the rise, gaining popularity and in some cases displacing wine as the elixir of choice. Paris' growing *bière artisanale* (craft beer) scene is booming, with cafes offering limited-production brews on tap, specialised shops like **Biérocratie** organising tasting workshops and dedicated beer bars like **A la Bière Comme à la Bière** and **La Fine Mousse** delighting hopheads.

What's more, a number of city breweries have cropped up, led by frontrunner **Brasserie la Goutte d'Or**, which opened in the Barbès district in 2012. At the Paname Brewing Company (p144) in the 19e, you can sip one of the freshly brewed beers on tap on the waterfront deck overlooking the Bassin de la Villette. (It also has a taphouse at the Cité Fertile in Pantin, Gare Montparnasse and CDG airport.) Microbrewery Balthazar (p178) in Ménilmontant offers eight beers and kombucha on tap and a large, sun-dappled terrace to enjoy them. Brewpub Les Cuves de Fauve (p192) in Bastille is another top pick. As part of the city's urban agriculture movement, hops are grown on the sides of buildings across town.

In the surrounding Paris region, favourite breweries include **La Parisienne** and **Deck & Donohue**, a certified B-Corp business that sources local malt and other ingredients from Seine et Marne farmers. The city's artisan-beer fest, the **Paris Beer Festival**, takes place in brasseries, bars and specialist beer shops throughout the city.

GUINGUETTES A GOGO

Riverside revelry is part of the fabric of Paris. Along the banks of the Seine and tributaries like the Marne and Oise, open-air dance halls and cabarets known as *guinguettes* have been going strong for centuries. The name is believed to be derived from *guinguet*, a sparkling wine once made from Paris region grapes. Historically the establishments were set up outside the city limits, to avoid taxes on wine, and – in the 19th century when train travel put the suburbs in easy reach – to provide a relaxing, pastoral setting for urban workers to unwind on the weekends. In recent years, there's been a *guinguette* revival, with sultry seasonal spots popping up on houseboats and the quays.

ICONIC PARIS COCKTAILS

SERENDIPITY
(Bar Hemingway) A *calvados* and champagne creation invented by legendary barman Colin Field.

SIDECAR
(Harry's New York Bar) Brandy and Cointreau blend born at Harry's (though the Ritz Paris also claims the honour).

BOULEVARDIER
(Little Red Door) The 1920s brainchild of American writer Erskine Gwynne, who also founded a Paris magazine with the same name.

FRENCH 75
(Cravan) Forget the classic kir. Gin takes this champagne-based cocktail to the next level.

Cocktail Cravings

In Paris, you aren't limited to beer or wine libations. Mixology is an art form, with *couture*-style craft and attention to detail (and often *couture*-style prices to match). Watering holes range from hidden speakeasies, **Moonshiner** and Candelaria (p157), to glamorous hotels dripping with finery – Les Ambassadeurs at Hôtel de Crillon (p85), Bar Hemingway at the Ritz Paris (p111). The Experimental Cocktail Group was a taste-making pioneer of the Paris cocktail craze. Also try Little Red Door (p157), CopperBay (p85), Cravan (p73), **Danico** and **Combat**.

Coffee Decoded

Coffee has always been Parisians' drink of choice to kick-start the day. So it's surprising that Parisian coffee long lagged behind world standards, with poor-quality beans and unrefined preparation. The bitter brew – often taken as a *petit noir* at a cafe or bar counter – is more of a caffeine pick-me-up than a drink that's meant to be savoured. But the urban palate has changed. A veritable coffee revolution is now underway, initiated by pioneers **La Caféothèque** and Coutume (p88) more than a decade ago.

A new wave of local roasteries and speciality coffee shops serving Anglo-inspired flat whites and pour-overs has diversified options for coffee lovers. The city still keeps a list of places where you can drink an espresso for a euro (check the paris.fr website and map), but you can also find seriously good coffee crafted by a trained barista courtesy of roasteries like L'Arbre à Café, Artesano, Ten Belles, Belleville Brûlerie, Terres de Café and Noir. Craving a matcha latte? Speciality drinks abound at new independent joints.

Some helpful orders:

Un café Single shot of espresso.
Un café allongé Espresso lengthened with hot water (sometimes served separately).
Un café au lait Coffee with milk.
Un café crème Shot of espresso lengthened with steamed milk.
Un double Double shot of espresso.
Une noisette Shot of espresso with a spot of milk.

Paname Brewing Company (p144)

Crazy Horse

SHOWTIME

Catching a performance in Paris is a treat. Whether you're into indie rock or ballet, you're spoilt for choice.

Paris has long been a destination par excellence for entertainment. From Molière's hilarious plays in the 17th century to the rip-roaring cabarets of the Belle Époque, the city has a history of putting on a good show. The reputation continues today. French and international opera, ballet, theatre companies and cabaret dancers take to the stage in venues of mythical proportion, while elsewhere a flurry of young, passionate, highly creative musicians, thespians and artists make the city's fascinating fringe art scene what it is.

Music alone is a major draw. Big-name artists headline annual festivals like Solidays, Rock en Seine and We Love Green. Up-and-coming musicians perform at smaller clubs, while the jazz scene is still going strong with destinations like Duc des Lombards and Caveau de la Huchette. If classical music is more your thing, check out the Philharmonie de Paris and the Seine Musicale, where conductor Laurence Equilbey's Insula Orchestra reigns supreme.

Opera & Dance

France's Opéra National de Paris and Ballet de l'Opéra National de Paris perform at Paris' two opera houses: the Palais Garnier and Opéra Bastille. **Théâtre National de Chaillot** dance is in the Trocadéro area. The season runs between September and July – buy tickets well in advance. Check out what modern dance and hip-hop spectacles are on while you're in town…they're a direct route to current French culture.

Live Music

Street music is a constant in this busker-filled city, with summer adding open-air concerts along the Seine and in city parks to the year-round serenade of accordions. The rue des Lombards (p120) near Chatelêt is the best for jazz, with three iconic clubs. Sainte-Chapelle holds gorgeous classical concerts (p215).

Theatre

Theatre productions, including those originally written in other languages, are invariably performed in French. Non-French speakers should check out **Theatre in Paris** *(theatreinparis.com)*, which works with playhouses on performance accessibility.

Cabarets

Whirling lines of feather-boa-clad, high-kicking dancers at grand-scale cabarets like Moulin Rouge (p133) are a bit retro to modern eyes, but – for visitors –

remain a quintessential fixture on Paris' entertainment scene. **Crazy Horse**, a legend for classic Paris burlesque, stages shows that are steamy and salacious. A favourite drag queen venue is Madame Arthur (p133), for exuberant, light-hearted shows.

Cinema

Foreign films (including English-language films) screened in their original language with French subtitles are labelled 'VO' (*version originale*). Films labelled 'VF' (*version française*) are dubbed in French.

Tickets

Purchase most concert, theatre and other cultural and sporting-event tickets from electronics and entertainment megashop **Fnac** (*fnactickets.com*), whether at the *billeteries* (ticket offices) throughout Paris or online, or directly from the venue.

Discount Tickets

On the day of performance, theatre, opera and ballet tickets are sold for half price (plus €3.50 commission) at the **Kiosque Théâtre Madeleine** (*kiosqueculture.com*).

LONELY PLANET'S TOP...

Entertainment Listings

L'Officiel des Spectacles (*offi.fr*) Paris' top listings guide is in French but is easy to navigate online. The print booklet is available from newsstands on Wednesday, and is crammed with everything on in the capital, including concert, theatre and cinema listings.

LYLO (*lylo.fr*) Short for Les Yeux, Les Oreilles ('eyes and ears'); offers the low-down on concerts, festivals and more.

Le Figaro (*lefigaro.fr/culture*) Music, cinema and theatre listings.

Paris Nightlife (*parisnightlife.fr*) All-encompassing listings site.

Paris Bouge (*parisbouge.com*) Comprehensive listings site.

Sortir à Paris (*sortiraparis.com*) Click on 'Soirées & Bars', then 'Nuits Parisiennes'.

Fnac Spectacles (*fnacspectacles.com/city/paris-369*) Browse and book concert and show tickets.

ENTERTAINMENT BY NEIGHBOURHOOD	
Eiffel Tower & Western Paris	Visit Palais de Chaillot's Théâtre National de Chaillot or the nearby Maison de la Radio, with their many dance and live music performances.
Champs-Élysées & Grands Boulevards	Famous revues and Paris' palatial 1875-built opera house take top billing here.
Louvre & Les Halles	Swinging jazz clubs, centuries-old theatres and cinemas mix it up with pumping nightclubs. Seek out buskers at Place Georges Pompidou.
Montmartre & Northern Paris	Show-stopping cabarets, legendary concert halls and cutting-edge cultural centres. Place du Tertre, Montmartre's original main square, is Paris' busiest busker stage.
Le Marais, Belleville & Ménilmontant	Rockin' live-music venues, old-style chansons and arts centres.
Bastille & Eastern Paris	Opera, old-time tea dancing and France's national cinema institute are big drawcards.
The Islands	Look for buskers on Pont St-Louis, the bridge linking Paris' two islands.
Latin Quarter	Swing bands, cinema retrospectives and jam sessions.
St-Germain & Les Invalides	Atmospheric cinemas, cultural centres and theatres inhabit this chic, sophisticated neighbourhood.
Montparnasse & Southern Paris	Some of this area's most happening venues are aboard boats moored on the Seine.

Galeries Lafayette (p95)

SHOP

Paris has it all, from designer fashion houses to fabulous markets. Stroll the city's backstreets to find unique speciality shops and boutiques.

Fashion is Paris' forte. Yet although its well-groomed residents sometimes make the city look and feel like a giant catwalk, fashion here is about style and quality first and foremost, rather than status or brand names. A good place to get an overview of Paris fashion is at the city's famous *grands magasins* (department stores). Le Bon Marché (p252) was the world's first when it opened in the 19th century.

Paris is also an exquisite treasure chest of gourmet food, wine, tea, books, stationery, art and original gifts. Ask for *un paquet cadeau* – free (and very beautiful) gift wrapping, offered by most shops.

When it comes to antiques, browse and buy one-off conversation pieces and collectibles. Just over the city limits in the north and south respectively, the Marché aux Puces de Saint-Ouen and Marché aux Puces de la Porte de Vanves are places of pilgrimage for both interior designers and everyday Parisians. Paris' twice-yearly *soldes* (sales), lasting four weeks, start in mid-January and again in late June.

Vintage Fashion, Deals & Shows

Parisian fashion doesn't have to break the bank: find fantastic bargains at secondhand and vintage boutiques and outlet shops (like **La Piscine**) selling previous seasons' collections, surpluses and seconds by top-line designers.

Thrift stores are known as *friperies*, while *dépôt-ventes* ('deposit and sale', or consignment shops) offer incredible treasure hunting, including high-quality French couture brands like Chanel, Hermès and Yves Saint Laurent. **Paris Good Fashion** aims for sustainability by improving sourcing and making processes more ecofriendly.

Although tickets for Paris' high-profile fashion shows are tough to get, you can still see some runway action: reserve ahead to attend shows at Galeries Lafayette. People-watching during Paris Fashion Week (PFW) is a great source of entertainment, and you can get a peek at the action at always-buzzing place Vendôme (p110).

Street Markets

Paris' street markets are social gatherings for the entire neighbourhood, and visiting one will give you a true appreciation of Parisian life. Nearly every little quarter has its own (never on Monday), where tarpaulin-topped tables bow beneath fresh, cooked and preserved delicacies. Some are all-organic (*marchés biologique*), and many markets also sell clothes, homewares and more.

Flea markets brim with bric-a-brac, antiques, retro clothing, cheap brand-name clothing, footwear, African carvings and electronic gear.

Every Parisian market is listed on paris.fr/pages/les-marches-parisiens-2428, including speciality markets for flowers or ephemeral (*brocantes* – secondhand markets) and *vide-greniers* ('empty the attic' sales).

Souvenirs

For distinctive souvenirs, such as rooftop-produced honey and metro-inspired ceramics, visit **Paris La Boutique** (*paris.fr/lieux/paris-la-boutique-17644*) at the Hôtel de Ville. Many items are created locally, part of the city's Fabriqué à Paris ('Made in Paris') initiative. At major museums, the **Boutiques de Musées** (*boutiquesdemusees.fr*) have high-quality replicas and a digital framing service: browse masterpieces, choose a frame and have it mailed home.

LONELY PLANET'S TOP...

Independent Shops

Marin Montagut (p265) Stock up on whimsical gifts for home at this housewares shop.

Calligrane (p167) Ogle exquisite handmade stationery and works of art made of paper.

Empreintes (p161) Choose between French-made wares from artisans all over the country.

Plastic Soul Records (p190) Browse vinyl in the oldest record store in Paris.

Lorette & Jasmin (p75) Find designer boutique deals on consignment or rent a handbag.

Candora (p164) Take a workshop in making your signature scent in the Marais.

Merci #2 (p109) Source anything from clothes to beauty products and homewares.

SHOPPING BY NEIGHBOURHOOD	
Eiffel Tower & Western Paris	Top brands and couture mingle with independent boutiques.
Champs-Élysées & Grands Boulevards	*Haute couture* houses and famous department stores.
Louvre & Les Halles	Cookware shops, high-street chains and covered arcades.
Montmartre & Northern Paris	Gourmet food shops, art and quintessential souvenirs.
Le Marais, Belleville & Ménilmontant	Quirky homewares, art galleries and up-and-coming designers in Haut Marais.
Bastille & Eastern Paris	Great markets, Viaduc des Arts workshops.
The Islands	Enchanting gift shops and gourmet boutiques. Tourist tat on Île de la Cité.
Latin Quarter	Late-opening bookshops and music shops.
St-Germain & Les Invalides	Art, antiques and chic designer boutiques.
Montparnasse & Southern Paris	Discount fashion outlets, Asian groceries.

Bassin de la Villette

TRIP PLANNER

OUTDOOR THRILLS

In Paris, *plein-air* pastimes are part of the culture. It's easy to get outside and get sporty – or simply unwind in the parks and on the river quays that act as a giant backyard for apartment-dwelling Parisians. New green spaces are adding to the allure. As part of its mission to become Europe's greenest city by 2030, Paris is totally transforming its urban fabric.

New Green Spaces

Paris is undergoing a green revolution, with reduced car traffic, eliminated parking spaces, new pedestrian zones and massive landscaping projects. The 2024 Summer Olympics and Paralympics showed Paris' commitment to cutting its carbon footprint – it was effectively halved compared to London 2012 and Rio 2016. City initiatives to combat global warming include the greening of major landmarks and squares in Paris, such as the forecourt of Notre Dame.

The Hôtel de Ville will soon be shaded by a new 'urban forest' and the Trocadéro is getting a makeover. The garden will soon stretch across the Pont d'Iéna to the Eiffel Tower and the Champ de Mars beyond. The place de la Concorde is also going green, with new lawns and plants to deflect the heat during hot summer days. The busy square, transformed to cater to pedestrians, will link the Jardin des Tuileries and the Champs-Élysées into a single green corridor, which Mayor Anne Hidalgo calls an 'extraordinary garden'.

🏖 SUMMERTIME BEACHES

Each summer, the Paris Plages (Paris Beaches) see *pétanque*, pop-up bars and cafes, sun lounges, parasols, water fountains and sprays line the river from around mid-July to early September (exact dates vary year to year). Established in 2002 for Parisians who couldn't escape to the coast to cool off in the summer months, they now typically set up at the Parc Rives de Seine (between the Pont Neuf and the Pont au Change on the Right Bank), as well as along the Bassin de la Villette in the 19e, where there's also a zip line and water sports.

Urban Hiking

The city known for its *flâneurs* is paradise for walkers. Slip on your sturdiest shoes and see where your feet take you – it's only two hours to traverse the city in its entirety. The Seine's quays and bridges are an invitation to stroll, as are the former train tracks of the Petite Ceinture (p200).

Feeling more ambitious? Long-distance hiking trails, part of France's famous *grande randonnée* (GR) network, criss-cross the capital. The GR1, also known as the 'Tour de Paris', is a 540km loop. Created in 2017 as part of the city's Olympic bid, the GR75 charts a 50km course around Paris, while also incorporating nine urban *arrondissements*. Also keep a lookout for the **Sentier de Grand Paris**, a 615km trail network that invites adventurers to discover the often overlooked and misunderstood suburbs. **La Panamée** *(rando-paris.org/panamée)* is a guided cultural walk organised on the third Thursday of every month between 7pm and 10pm – the outings are free and cover a distance of 7.5km.

For a forest fix, try Fontainebleau (p300) or the hilly suburb of Meudon, also home to a Rodin museum.

GETTING OUT ON THE WATER

Swimming
- The Bassin de la Villette offers three clean-water-zoned swimming pools during Paris Plages. The pools are patrolled by lifeguards and are typically open 11am to 9pm.
- The colossal clean-up project succeeded in opening the Seine to swimming for the 2024 Summer Olympics. (It had been banned for a century because of maritime traffic and water quality.) Now three open-air swimming areas are open to the public in the summer: Bercy, Bras Marie and Bras de Grenelle.
- There's also a floating swimming pool, **Piscine Joséphine Baker**, near Bercy.
- Paris' vintage swimming pools add a dash of style to your paddle. The art deco **Piscine Pontoise** in the Latin Quarter dates from the 1930s and has night openings – particularly moody, or try the minimalist, white Piscine de la Butte aux Cailles (p273) or the maximalist Piscine Molitor (p77). **Piscine Georges-Vallerey**, which was built for the 1924 Olympic Games, got a makeover for the 2024 Games.

Paddling
- **Nautic Paddle**, the biggest paddle race in the world, takes place annually on the Seine in central Paris. There's also **La TraverSeine**, an event that brings together canoes, kayaks, paddleboards and dragon boats on the river. If you're itching to get on the water, consider signing up for a session with outfitter Le Grand Huit, situated on the Marne right outside Paris.

Petite Ceinture (p286)

Sports

Paris hosts a great variety of sporting events throughout the year, from tennis' French Open and Paris Masters to local football matches. There's a handful of stadiums in the city – Stade Jean-Bouin (rugby), Adidas Arena (basketball), Parc des Princes (home to football team Paris Saint-Germain). Catch France's national football team, Les Bleus (fff.fr), at the Stade de France.

The city's three horse-racing tracks can make for a thrilling afternoon. The **Hippodrome d'Auteuil** and the **Hippodrome de Longchamp** are in the Bois de Boulogne. **Hippodrome de Paris-Vincennes** is in the Bois de Vincennes. Every October the **Prix de l'Arc de Triomphe** (prix arcdetriomphe.com), Europe's most prestigious horse race, is held at the Hippodrome de Longchamp.

The city of Paris website (paris.fr/sport) has info on everything from skating and badminton to climbing walls and equipment rental.

Boules

You'll often see groups of earnest Parisians playing *boules* (aka *pétanque*, France's most popular traditional game, similar to lawn bowls) in the Jardin du Luxembourg and other parks and squares with suitably flat, shady patches of gravel. The Arènes de Lutèce *boulodrome* in a 2nd-century Roman amphitheatre in the Latin Quarter is a fabulous spot to absorb the scene. There are usually places to play at Paris Plages.

If you want to try out the sport indoors, head to **Chez Bouboule**, which has a packed-sand *boulodrome* and a bar.

Cycling

Everyone knows that the Tour de France races up the Champs-Élysées at the end of July every year, but you don't need Tadej Pogačar's leg muscles to enjoy Paris on two wheels. Between the Paris bike-share scheme **Vélib'**, and the hundreds of kilometres of urban bike paths, cycling around the city has never been easier. In fact, as part of the city's plan to become 100% bikeable, City Hall has accelerated infrastructure development with secure lanes, bike racks and safety measures. The investment is paying off – a study by urban planning agency Institut Paris Region (IPR) indicates that bike use surpassed car trips in 2023.

Sign up for one of the great city bike tours or hire a bike yourself. Some streets are closed to vehicle traffic on Sundays (see paris.fr/pages/paris-respire-2122), great news for cyclists! Bring your own helmet.

French Open

TOP PARKS

Jardin du Luxembourg (p256) Tennis courts, puppet shows and coveted picnic benches by a palace-museum with ponds.

Jardin des Tuileries (p108) Stately royal gardens on the banks of the Seine are now open to all. You can see some of Monet's waterlily paintings at the Musée de l'Orangerie.

Parc Monceau Beautiful 18th-century English-style park with whimsical follies in the 8e.

Jardin des Plantes (p236) The city's beautiful botanic gardens and 18th-century glass and metal greenhouses shelter rare plants.

Bois de Boulogne (p70) A vast forest including gardens, horse-racing arenas, the French Open tennis complex and more.

Bois de Vincennes (p196) A forest to the east of the city that offers an easy escape from the concrete into nature.

Parc de la Villette (p142) Urban oasis of greenery, waterways, concert venues, bars and a science museum.

Sailing boats in Jardin du Luxembourg (p54)

TRIP PLANNER

FAMILY FUN

Parisians adore *les enfants* (children) and the city's residential density means you'll find playground equipment in parks and squares throughout the city. Families have an overwhelming choice of creative, educational, culinary and 'pure old-fashioned fun' things to see, do and experience. Plan ahead to get the best out of kid-friendly Paris.

Science Immersion

Cité des Sciences et de l'Industrie *(cite-sciences.fr)* If you have time for just one museum, make it this one. Book interactive Cité des Enfants sessions (for children aged two to 12) in advance to avoid disappointment.

Musée des Arts et Métiers *(arts-et-metiers.net)* Crammed with instruments and machines, Europe's oldest science and technology museum is fascinating. Activity- and experiment-driven workshops are top-notch.

Palais de la Découverte *(palais-decouverte.fr)* A superb science museum at the Grand Palais has a new lease on life after a renovation.

Galerie des Enfants *(mnhn.fr)* Natural history museum for six- to 12-year-olds within the Jardin des Plantes.

Art Exploration

Musée d'Orsay *(musee-orsay.fr/en)* The world-famous museum goes all out with its family programme, from concerts and giant games to podcasts and painting classes.

Musée en Herbe *(museeenherbe.com)* Thoughtful art museum for children with an excellent bookshop and art workshops for kids aged two to 12.

Palais de Tokyo *(palaisdetokyo.com)* Palais de Tokyo offers interactive installations, art workshops (for kids aged five to 10 years old) and storytelling sessions (for three- to

⚓ OUTDOOR FUN

Sailing Boats in Jardin du Luxembourg Playgrounds, puppet shows and a carousel: this legendary park has pandered to children for generations. But its vintage toy sailing boats are the real heart-stealers.

Treasure Hunts Follow the footpath medallions indicating the Chemin de St-Jacques pilgrimage route, another for the underground Bièvre river and another for the Paris Meridian.

Skating Rent a pair of in-line skates at Nomadeshop and join the Friday evening skate, Pari Roller, or the more laid-back Sunday afternoon skate, Rollers & Coquillages.

Parc Floral de Paris Easily the best playground for kids eight years and older: concerts, puppet shows, giant climbing webs, 30m-high slides and a zip line.

Locks on Canal St-Martin Watching canal boats navigate the many locks is fun, fascinating and free.

Riverside Play on Parc Rives de Seine Giant board games, a climbing wall, a 20m-long blackboard, tepees and events galore line this expressway-turned-promenade.

Boat Cruising on the Seine The Seine is also a perfect venue for family adventures (p67).

Local Walking Tour Paris Greeters (greeters.fr) guides walking tours with local volunteers, invariably in their own 'backyard' and well away from the madding crowd.

---

five-year-olds) as well as family activities for everyone.

Musée d'Art Moderne de Paris (mam.paris.fr) The city's modern-art museum offers activities and workshops for kids as young as three to tweens and teens.

Hands-On Activities

Crafty Happenings at the Musée du Quai Branly – Jacques Chirac (quaibranly.fr) Mask making, boomerang hurling and experimenting with traditional instruments – the workshops (for three-year-olds to teenagers) at this Seine-side museum, devoted to African, Asian and Oceanic art and culture, are diverse and creative.

Music at Philharmonie de Paris (philharmoniedeparis.fr) Concerts, shows and instrument workshops are part of the world-music repertoire at the city's cutting-edge philharmonic hall in Parc de la Villette.

RAINY-DAY IDEAS

- **Cirque d'Hiver Bouglione** (cirquedhiver.com) Clowns, trapeze artists and acrobats have entertained children of all ages at the city's winter circus since 1852. The season runs from October to March and performances last around 2½ hours.
- **Musée des Arts Forains** (arts-forains.com/en) Check for seasonal events at this nostalgic fairground museum, such as its Christmas season during Le Festival du Merveilleux.
- **Musée des Égouts de Paris** (musee-egouts.paris.fr) Romping through sewerage tunnels, learning what happens when you flush a loo in Paris and spotting rats are all part of the kid-cool experience at this quirky museum.
- **Les Catacombes** (catacombes.paris.fr) Teens generally get a kick out of Paris' most macabre sight, but be warned: this skull-packed underground cemetery is not for the faint-hearted.
- **An Afternoon at the Theatre** Paris' diverse theatre scene stages bags of spectacles (shows), théâtre classique (classical theatre) and other performances for kids, some in English; weekly entertainment mag L'Officiel des Spectacles (offi.fr) lists what's on.
- **Musée de la Magie** (museedelamagie.com) This museum is pure magic!
- **Metro Line 4** Grab a spot at the front of the driverless train and gape through the glass window as you zoom through the tunnels.

Parc Astérix

Cooking class at Le Cordon Bleu (cordonbleu.edu/paris-hoteldelamarine/home/en) Inside the Hôtel de la Marine, the legendary culinary institute offers kid-friendly workshops.

Dance at Centquatre (104.fr) The cool cultural centre in the 19e has a jam-packed calendar, including dance and theatre, for kids of all ages.

Musée National de la Marine (musee-marine.fr) Explore interactive exhibits at the newly remodelled marine museum with all things nautical.

Model Building at Cité de l'Architecture et du Patrimoine (citedelarchitecture.fr) Workshops at Paris' architecture museum see kids (aged four to 16 years) build art deco houses, *châteaux* and towers in miniature form.

Animals & Other Creatures

Equestrian Shows at Versailles (chateauversailles.fr) World-class equestrian shows at Château de Versailles are mesmerising. Show tickets and training sessions include a stable visit.

Sharks at Aquarium de Paris (aquariumdeparis.com) Centrally located, the aquarium has a shark tank and 500-plus fish species, and screens ocean-themed films.

Albino alligators at Aquarium Tropical (aquarium-tropical.fr) This charming aquarium is situated in the basement of the Palais de la Porte Dorée.

Ménagerie du Jardin des Plantes (mnhn.fr) The collection of animals in Jardin des Plantes includes snow panthers and red pandas.

Parc Zoologique de Paris (parczoologiquedeparis.fr) Observe lions, cougars, white rhinos and a whole gaggle of other beasties at this state-of-the-art zoo in Bois de Vincennes.

Dazzling Screentime

Histopad at the Conciergerie A tablet loaded with 3D reconstructions and interactive features allows you to step back in time and visualise the medieval rooms of what was once a royal palace – treasure hunt included.

Digital Exhibitions at Gaîté Lyrique (gaite-lyrique.net) La Gaîté Lyrique features digital-driven exhibitions, video games for older children and teens, laptops to use in the digitally connected cafe and a library with desks shaped like ducks for kids under five to sit at and draw while older siblings geek.

Special-Effect Movies at Cité des Sciences (cite-sciences.fr) La Géode is a special-effect cinema equipped with IMAX, 4DX and Dolby Cinema technologies. The wow factor is real. You can also take a cinematic trip through the solar system in the planetarium.

Behind-the-Scenes Tour at Le Grand Rex (legrandrex.com) Whizz-bang special effects stun during behind-the-scenes tours at this iconic 1930s cinema. Stand behind the big screen and muck around in a recording studio.

Art Illuminations at Atelier des Lumières (atelier-lumieres.com) Artworks projected on this former foundry's bare walls dazzle kids and adults alike.

Practicalities

Babysitting Hotels can often organise sitters for guests.

Equipment Rent strollers, scooters, car seats, travel beds and more while in Paris from companies like Baby'tems or the Kidlou app (kidlou.fr).

Paris Mômes (parismomes.fr) Covers Parisian kid culture (up to 12 years); print off playful kids' guides for major art exhibitions before leaving home.

AMUSEMENT PARKS

Parc Astérix Shuttle buses run from central Paris to this summer-opening theme park, 35km north of the city, which covers prehistoric through to the 19th century with its six 'worlds', adrenaline-pumping attractions and shows for all ages.

Disneyland Resort Paris A magnet for families, this park 32km east of Paris incorporates both Disneyland itself and the cinema-themed Walt Disney Studios Park.

Jardin d'Acclimatation The Bois de Boulogne's popular amusement park with rides, a small train, petting zoo, playgrounds, puppet shows and paddling pool.

PARIS
THE GUIDE

Chapters in this section are organised by neighbourhood. Neighbourhoods are delineated by a specific local character or identity, where you'll find unique specific experiences, local insights, insider tips and expert recommendations.

Eiffel Tower & Western Paris
p60

Champs-Elysées & Grands Boulevards
p80

Louvre & Les Halles
p96

Montmartre & Northern Paris
p126

Le Marais
p150

Belleville & Ménilmontant
p168

Bastille & Eastern Paris
p184

The Islands
p204

Latin Quarter
p222

St Germain & Les Invalides
p240

Montparnasse & Southern Paris
p268

Day Trips from Paris
p288

Jean-Baptiste Carpeaux's *Les quatre parties du monde soutenant la sphère céleste*, Musée d'Orsay (p250)
PYTY/SHUTTERSTOCK

NEIGHBOURHOODS AT A GLANCE

Find the neighbourhoods that tick all your boxes.

Champs-Elysées & Grands Boulevards (p80)

Grandiose and glamorous, luxury shopping and historic department stores, entertainment hub since the Belle Époque.

Eiffel Tower & Western Paris (p60)

Elegant residential district packed with museums, glorious architecture and opportunities to get up close and personal with the iconic tower.

St Germain & Les Invalides (p240)

Rub shoulders with Sartre's and de Beauvoir's ghosts at the cafes in this mythical quarter, also packed with chic boutiques.

Montparnasse & Southern Paris (p268)

Village charm, Paris' largest Chinatown, Seine-side action and legendary brasseries in this underrated, local-loved area.

The Islands (p204)

Washed by the Seine, Paris' geographic and historic heart is dominated by Notre Dame.

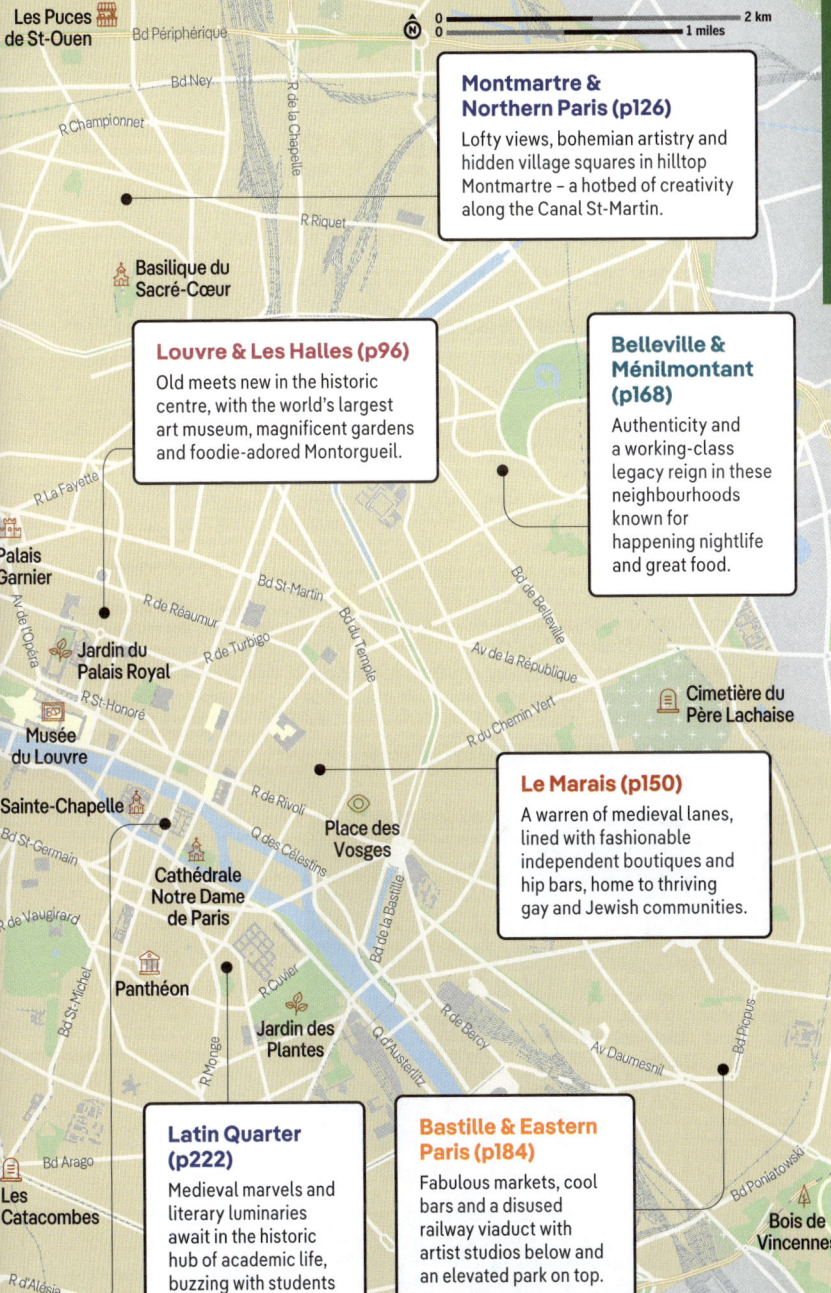

Researched by Mary Winston Nicklin

EIFFEL TOWER & WESTERN PARIS

BIG HITS, HIDDEN TREASURES AND UTTER ELEGANCE

With its hourly sparkles that illuminate the evening skyline, the Eiffel Tower needs no introduction.

Ascend the Eiffel Tower and all of Paris is at your *pieds*. To your west, the panoramas unfurl past the Trocadéro to the elegant 16e *arrondissement,* flanked by the Seine and the glorious green Bois de Boulogne. In centuries past, Passy village was home to luminaries such as Benjamin Franklin and Balzac, before it was annexed to the city in 1860. Nowadays, must-try restaurants and food markets vie for your attention alongside standout museums – the most of any Paris district. The 16e's architecture is another draw, with nature-inspired art nouveau residences, art deco buildings, and modernist villas commissioned by well-heeled residents. Above it all, the scene-stealing tower sets even the most hardened hearts aflutter.

TOP TIP

Though excellent top-end restaurants dot the 16e, it's more affordable to picnic in one of the many green spaces. build a feast with goodies from bakeries, markets and shops.

Porte Dauphine metro entrance (p77)

See p307 for places to stay in the Eiffel Tower and western Paris area.

Highlights

① Eiffel Tower
Ascend the icon at dusk to watch its sparkling lights blink across Paris. **p64**

② Bois de Boulogne
Explore Paris' green oasis: from bike rides to rowboats, an art foundation to an amusement park. **p70**

③ Musée Marmottan Monet
Revel in the world's largest collection of Monet canvases. **p69**

④ Musée du Quai Branly – Jacques Chirac
Find inspiration in exquisite art and craftwork from around the world. **p79**

⑤ Cité de l'Architecture et du Patrimoine
Wander by cathedral portals, gargoyles and intricate models at this standout museum. **p76**

Getting Around

Metro/RER
To reach the Eiffel Tower, take the metro line 6 to Bir-Hakeim, or RER C to Champ de Mars–Tour Eiffel. The 16e is served by metro lines 2, 6, 9, 10 and RER C.

Walking
This is the easiest way to appreciate the 16e's village ambience. Plus, you can admire the architecture as you stroll.

Bicycle
Numerous bike lanes, plus the Vélib' bike-share scheme, make cycling easy and convenient in the 16e. Travel from Trocadéro to Auteuil in just 10 minutes.

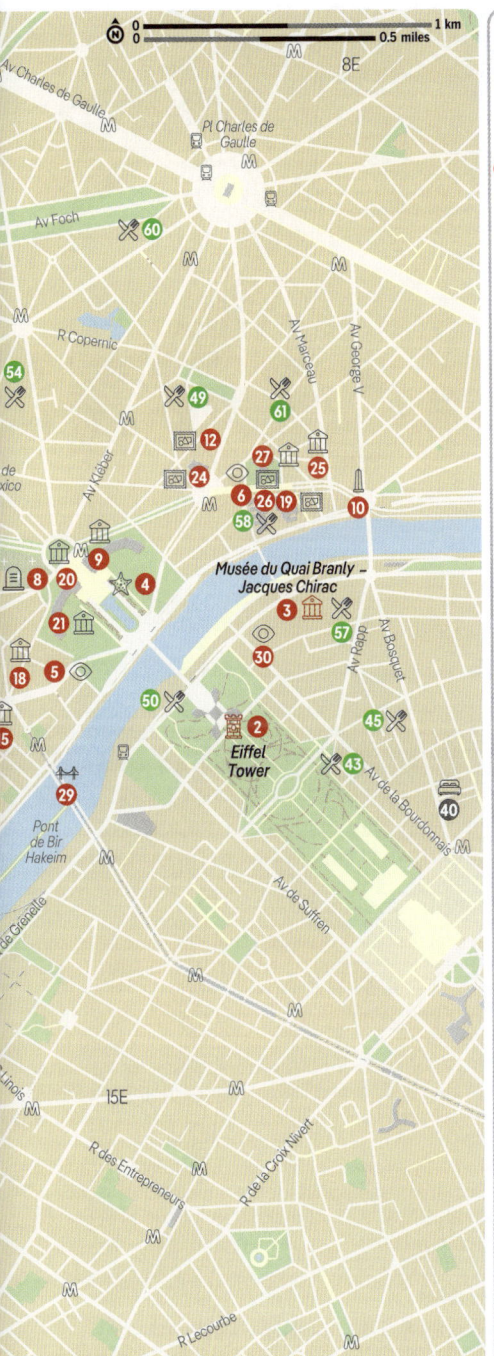

EIFFEL TOWER & WESTERN PARIS

★ HIGHLIGHTS
1. Bois de Boulogne
2. Eiffel Tower
3. Musée du Quai Branly – Jacques Chirac

● SIGHTS
4. Aquarium de Paris
5. Av de Camoens
6. Av du Président Wilson
7. Château de Bagatelle
8. Cimetière de Passy
9. Cité de l'Architecture et du Patrimoine
10. Flame of Liberty Memorial
11. Fondation Louis Vuitton
12. Hôtel d'Heidelbach
13. Jardin des Serres d'Auteuil
14. Jardin Shakespeare
15. M Musée du Vin
16. Maison de Balzac
17. Maison La Roche
18. Musée Clemenceau
19. Musée d'Art Moderne de la Ville de Paris
20. Musée de la Marine
21. Musée de l'Homme
22. Musée d'Ennery
23. Musée Marmottan Monet
24. Musée National des Arts Asiatiques Guimet
25. Musée Yves Saint Laurent Paris
26. Palais de Tokyo
27. Palais Galliera
28. Parc des Princes
29. Pont de Bir-Hakeim
30. Rue de l'Université
31. Rue Raynouard
32. Stade Roland Garros
33. Villa Windsor

● ACTIVITIES
34. Lac Inférieur Boat Hire

● SLEEPING
35. Brach Paris
36. Hôtel Beauséjour Ranelagh
37. Hôtel Botaniste
38. Hôtel Molitor
39. Hôtel Villa Nicolo
40. Rayz Eiffel
41. St James Paris
42. Villa du Square

● EATING
43. Arnaud Nicolas
44. Auberge du Mouton Blanc
45. Bistrot des Fables
46. Boulangerie Basil
47. Chocolaterie Servant
48. Comice
49. Ducasse Baccarat
50. Francette
51. Fromagerie Laurent Dubois Auteuil
52. Ken Yamamoto
53. La Rotonde de la Muette
54. Le Petit Rétro
55. Le Pré Catelan
56. Les Coltineurs
57. Les Deux Abeilles
58. Les Marches
59. Marché Couvert de Passy
60. Prunier par Yannick Alléno
61. Substance

● DRINKING & NIGHTLIFE
62. Cravan
63. Le Belair
see 49 Midi-Minuit
see 41 St James Paris

● ENTERTAINMENT
64. Jardin d'Acclimatation
see 9 Théâtre National de Chaillot

● SHOPPING
65. La Grande Épicerie Rive Droite
see 46 Lorette & Jasmin
see 6 Marché Président Wilson
66. Passy Brocante
67. Philippe Conticini

TOP EXPERIENCE

Eiffel Tower

Piercing the city skyline, Paris' icon beckons. Experience the Eiffel Tower in myriad ways, from a daytime trip or an evening ascent amid twinkling lights to a stroll in the gardens at its base. Even though nearly seven million people visit annually, few would dispute that each time is unique – it's something that simply has to be done once.

DON'T MISS

Second-floor panorama

Top-floor vertigo enhanced by the Champagne bar

Pavillon Ferrié

Tactile descent down the stairs

Strolling the gardens under the tower

Catching the nightly twinkle-show as the tower illuminates

Exploring an Icon

Named after its designer, Gustave Eiffel, the Tour Eiffel was built for the 1889 Exposition Universelle (World's Fair). It took 300 workers, 2.5 million rivets and two years of nonstop labour to assemble. Upon completion, the tower became the tallest human-made structure in the world (324m) – a record held until the 1930 completion of New York's Chrysler Building. A symbol of the modern age, it faced opposition from Paris' artistic and literary elite, and the 'metal asparagus', as some snidely called it, was originally slated to be torn down in 1909. It was spared only because it proved an ideal platform for the transmitting antennas needed for the newfangled science of radiotelegraphy. Now a local nickname for the tower is *La dame de fer* (Iron Lady).

PRACTICALITIES

● toureiffel.paris/en ● 9.15am-11.45pm (opening hours change seasonally) ● adult tickets from €14.50 for stair access; under 4s free

TOP TIPS

- Book tickets well in advance.

- Ascend as far as the 2nd floor (on foot or by lift), where a separate lift on the mezzanine serves the top floor (closed during heavy winds).

- The top floor and stairs aren't accessible to people with limited mobility.

- The stairs to the very top are closed to the public. You must book (or buy at the tower base) a lift ticket.

- Minimise queuing for lifts by descending via the stairs from the 1st or 2nd levels.

- Bring a jacket as it can be breezy at the top.

First Floor

Of the tower's three floors, the 1st (57m) has the most space, with a broad wooden deck for lounging, but the least impressive views. The glass-enclosed **Pavillon Ferrié** houses an immersion film along with a small **cafe, pizza bar** and **souvenir shop**. On the outer walkway follow a discovery circuit to learn more about the tower's ingenious design and history. Check out the sections of glass flooring that offer a dizzying view of the ant-like people walking on the ground far below. This level also hosts the restaurant **Madame Brasserie**. The 1st floor's commercial areas are powered by two sleek wind turbines within the tower.

Second Floor

Views from the 2nd floor (115m) are grand – impressively high but still close enough to see the details of the city below. Pinpoint locations in Paris and beyond using telescopes and panoramic maps placed around this level. Story windows give an overview of the lifts' mechanics, and the vision well allows you to gaze through glass panels to the ground. Also up here are toilets, **souvenir shops**, a **macaron bar**, and Michelin-starred restaurant **Le Jules Verne** (accessible by a dedicated lift in the south pillar).

Top Floor (Summit)

Views from the wind-buffeted top floor (276m) stretch up to 60km on a clear day. At this height the sweeping panoramas are more thrilling than detailed. You'll exit the lift onto a glass-enclosed level with directional panels orienting many of the world's cities. Then take one of the two small sets of metal stairs to the highest tier, which is open-air. Celebrate

NIGHTLY SPARKLES

Every hour on the hour, the entire tower sparkles for five minutes with 20,000 6-watt lights. They were first installed for Paris' millennium celebration in 2000 – it took 25 mountain climbers five months to install the current bulbs and 40km of electrical cords. For the best view of the light show, head across the Seine to the Jardins du Trocadéro.

your ascent with a glass of bubbly from the **Champagne bar** at this topmost level – or opt for mineral water, lemonade and macarons. Afterwards, peep into Gustave Eiffel's restored **office** where wax models of Eiffel and his daughter Claire greet Thomas Edison. Somewhat unbelievably, there are also toilets up here.

Guide

The Eiffel Tower's online visitor's guide (guide.toureiffel.paris) is packed with info and can be accessed by the tower's wi-fi network. There's also an information booth at the base, near the west pillar, which has brochures and information on guided tours and activities for kids.

Ticket Purchases & Queuing Strategies

Even on a good day the base of the Eiffel Tower can be a chaotic scrum of confused travellers. A bit of preparation can cut down on joining that fray, and save time waiting in often atrocious queues, especially in high season (June to September) and during holidays like Easter. Generally attendance is lowest on Tuesdays, Wednesdays and Thursdays.

External Security

Nowadays, bullet-proof glass barriers surround the tower's base. Visitors must pass through external security at one of the two entrances to the glass enclosure on av Gustave Eiffel. The two exits are on quai Branly. The security lines are divided

The Seine & the Eiffel Tower

between walk-in visitors, people with pre-booked tickets, and people with reservations at the restaurants. You are allowed through this point without a ticket if you just want to stroll the gardens directly under the tower itself.

Tickets

Once inside, there are ticket booths (with long queues) at the south pillar. It is well worth pre-booking online to reduce waiting. And, at certain times, only people with pre-booked lift tickets to the top will be allowed up there (ie sometimes there are no tickets available on the day). But most days you can buy a stairs ticket or a stairs-plus-ticket-to-the-top. If you can't reserve your tickets ahead of time, expect lengthy waits both for tickets and for lifts.

Pre-purchasing tickets online gives you an allocated timeslot and means you enter straight away to go through a second security check just before the lift or stairs. Print your ticket or show it on your phone.

Taking the Stairs

The climb consists of 327 steps to the 1st floor and another 347 steps to the 2nd floor. The stairs to the top are not open to the public for safety reasons. You must buy a lift ticket at the base or online (there are no ticket sales for the top on the 2nd floor). Plan for 10 to 20 minutes between floors, depending on your fitness level.

Top-Floor Lift

Ascend as far as the 2nd floor (either on foot or by lift), and from there a separate lift goes up to the top floor (closed during heavy winds). This lift to the top is only accessible by walking up a small flight of stairs to the 2nd-floor mezzanine where the lift is located. Note that the top floor and stairs aren't accessible to people with limited mobility. Pushchairs must be folded in lifts and bags or backpacks larger than aeroplane-cabin size aren't allowed. You will need your ticket to access the lift, after, once again, waiting in a queue.

Seine River Cruises

Taking to the Seine on a river cruise is an idyllic way to view the Eiffel Tower. **Bateaux Parisiens** runs hour-long circuits with audioguides in 14 languages and themed lunch and dinner cruises. **Vedettes de Paris** offers one-hour cruises from its base at the foot of the Eiffel Tower. The hop-on-hop-off **Batobus** stops at the Eiffel Tower. **Green River Cruises** has pontoon boats you can hire privately. Chef Alain Ducasse oversees the floating restaurant **Ducasse sur Seine** on a luxurious electric boat, where both lunch and dinner are served. The only Michelin-starred cruise is aboard the **Don Juan II**, an art deco–style yacht kitted out with a fireplace, wooden panelling and brass fixtures. The multicourse dinner menu is by chef Frédéric Anton of Le Jules Verne fame.

CHAMP DE MARS

Running southeast from the Eiffel Tower, the grassy green jewel of the Champ de Mars – an ideal summer picnic spot – was originally used as a parade ground for the cadets of the 18th-century École Militaire (Military Academy). This school in the vast French-classical building commissioned by Louis XV at the southeastern end of the park counts Napoléon Bonaparte among its illustrious graduates.

PAINT JOB

Painting the Eiffel Tower is a herculean task. Every seven years, a 50-person crew works at night to strip the old paint and then repaint the entire structure. The tower has sported six different colours throughout its lifetime. The most recent golden hue, unveiled for the 2024 Olympics, was the yellow-brown shade originally conceived by Gustave Eiffel.

WATER & WINE

Before the 16e was a chic Parisian neighbourhood, this swathe of countryside was covered with vineyards and agricultural fields. Wine production dates back to antiquity, but it really flourished in the Middle Ages, when the Auteuil vineyards, cultivated by monks, produced wines that were prized as far away as Denmark. (Locals also loved the libations because they were outside the city limits, hence tax-free.) In Passy, the wine museum **M Musée du Vin** occupies the vaulted cellars of the Couvent des Minimes de Chaillot, whose medieval monks tended grapes. Nearby, the narrow rue des Eaux recalls another claim to fame: Passy was renowned for its springs in the 18th century, and cure-seeking visitors would imbibe this therapeutic elixir at a dedicated thermal establishment.

Cimetière de Passy

A Tale of Two Hamlets
Village vibes in Passy and Auteuil

Swing by the **Cimetière de Passy**, just opposite the Trocadéro, to get a sense of the illustrious residents who've called Passy home. Among the elaborate tombs carved by sculptors like Rodin and Zadkine, you'll find artist Edouard Manet, composer Claude Debussy, perfumer Guerlain and industrialist Renault. The boutique-lined rue de Passy is the central artery – look for treasures at the antiques store **Passy Brocante** at the end of the impasse des Carrières, a cobbled lane named for the quarries that once provided stone for construction. Passy's beating heart is the vibrant **Marché Couvert de Passy** – at this covered market browse stinky cheese at Androuet, lunch at the fishmonger's counter, admire the *cave de maturation* where the butcher ages prime cuts of meat, then head to the pedestrian market street rue de l'Annunciation to pick up dessert at **Philippe Conticini**.

Parisians cross town for the lemon meringue pie.

 EATING NEAR THE EIFFEL TOWER: OUR PICKS

Arnaud Nicolas: The charcuterie maestro artfully stocks a boutique and runs this restaurant. *noon-2.30pm & 7-10pm Tue-Sat* €€	**Bistrot des Fables:** A zinc bar contributes to the old-world charm, along with the menu's traditional classics like herring potato salad, devilled eggs and beef stew. *hours vary* €€	**Francette:** Toast the tower from the deck of this floating restaurant moored right on the quay. For the best views, reserve an outside table. *noon-1am* €€	**Les Deux Abeilles:** Homemade delights await at this old-fashioned tea room that's adored by regulars. *9am-7pm Tue-Sat* €

In adjacent Auteuil, go gaga for Guimard (some of the art nouveau pioneer's buildings are clustered on rue Jean de La Fontaine, including cocktail bar Cravan – see p73), or ease into local life by taking a seat at a *café terrasse* in front of the Église d'Auteuil. A market pops up on Wednesday and Saturday mornings in the middle of the village – the charming square on the rue d'Auteuil faces Hôtel de Verrières, the mansion that hosted 18th-century literary salons and glittering soirées for the royal court. American president John Adams resided here when he served as an ambassador.

Monet Mania
A sublime setting for art

Housed in the duc de Valmy's former hunting lodge (well, let's call it a mansion), the **Musée Marmottan Monet** *(marmottan .fr/en; adult/child €14/free)* is home to the world's largest Claude Monet collection. Take this unique chance to immerse in a real cross-section of the artist's work, beginning with paintings such as the seminal *Impression, soleil levant* (1873) and *En promenade près d'Argenteuil* (1875), passing through numerous waterlily studies, before moving on to considerably more abstract pieces dating to the early 1900s. Masterpieces to look out for include *La barque* (1887), *Cathédrale de Rouen* (1892), *Londres, le Parlement* (1901) and the various *Nymphéas* – many of these were smaller studies for the works now on display in the **Musée de l'Orangerie**. This varied collection – a bequest by Monet's last direct descendant – is showcased in a dedicated downstairs gallery designed for that purpose.

With acres of gilt and plush Empire-style furnishings, the mansion almost eclipses the art collection. Head-turning decor includes a bed that once belonged to Napoléon, an enormous wood desk sculpted with winged lions and a splendid geographic clock by porcelain powerhouse the Manufacture de Sèvres. Upstairs, don't miss the ensemble of paintings by Berthe Morisot, the famed female Impressionist. The illuminated manuscripts are also worth a gander, though the room is (understandably) dim. Temporary exhibitions, included in the admission price, are usually superb.

WHY I LOVE THE 16E

Mary Winston Nicklin, Lonely Planet writer

Stubborn stereotypes cling to this refined western district. So it's often neglected by Parisians from across town who assume it's bourgeois and boring. (A longtime Left Banker, I was guilty as charged!) *Au contraire*. The 16e is far from sleepy. There are so many museums, it's almost criminal. Top chefs open gastro destinations next to bistro institutions (**Auberge du Mouton Blanc** fed the likes of Molière). But what I love most is the village vibe. Far from the tourist crowds, this is an authentic pocket of Paris. Whether slurping oysters in the Passy market or admiring art nouveau architecture in Auteuil, I find the 16e has retained the spirit of the country villages that once populated the scenic hillsides above the Seine.

 EATING IN THE 16E: GOURMET DELIGHTS

Boulangerie Basil: Drool-worthy goods here include braided cinnamon brioche and hearty loaves of bread made with local flour. *7am-7pm Tue-Sat, 7.30am-noon Sun €*

La Grande Épicerie Rive Droite: Le Bon Marché department store's foodie emporium is a wonderland of groceries, with divine pastries. *9am-8.30pm Mon-Sat, to 12.45pm Sun €€€*

Fromagerie Laurent Dubois Auteuil: This award-winning cheesemonger takes great care in selecting high-quality *fromage*. *11am-8pm Mon, 9.30am-8pm Tue-Fri, 9am-8pm Sat €€*

Chocolaterie Servant: A family-owned candy shop brimming with gourmet chocolates and glass jars filled with traditional *bonbons*. *2.30-7pm Mon, 10am-7pm Tue-Sat, 11am-1pm Sun €€*

Jardin des Serres d'Auteuil

TOP EXPERIENCE

Bois de Boulogne

On the western edge of Paris, the vast Bois de Boulogne, the remnant of a royal hunting preserve, was once the province of kings. Now it welcomes one and all for verdant strolls and picnics, rowboat rides on ponds, an array of formal gardens and greenhouses, plus a famous art foundation, children's amusement park and the clay courts of Roland Garros. Indeed, something for everyone.

DON'T MISS

Parc de Bagatelle

Fondation Louis Vuitton

Jardin des Serres d'Auteuil

Jardin d'Acclimatation

Lac Inférieur rowboats

Jardin Shakespeare historical plantings

Playground for All

The 845-hectare Bois de Boulogne (Forest of Boulogne) was originally part of the forest of Vouvray and changed hands from kings to monks and back again. At times it was the home of castles and a convent, at other times a haunt of brigands and a site of robberies and battles. The British and Russian armies camped here after the defeat of Napoléon.

The park as you see it now owes its informal layout to Baron Haussmann, who, inspired by London's Hyde Park, planted 400,000 trees here in the 19th century. Along with its myriad gardens and other sights, the park has 15km of cycle paths and 28km of bridle paths through 125 hectares of forested land.

PRACTICALITIES

● Bois: free, 24hr (sites within the park have seasonal opening hours and sometimes charge entry fees)

Fondation Louis Vuitton

Designed by Frank Gehry, this striking **contemporary-art centre** in the northwestern corner of the park opened its doors in late 2014. It's next to the Jardin d'Acclimatation, and the soaring glass-panelled building hosts one or two temporary shows at a time, from pop art to *Basquiat × Warhol*. A shuttle runs between the Arc de Triomphe and the museum.

Jardin d'Acclimatation

Inaugurated by Emperor Napoléon III as France's first leisure park, the **Jardin d'Acclimatation** is a longtime family favourite, offering a host of attractions including a petting zoo and trampolines. It was fully renovated in 2018 but it's still delightfully old school, with rides like the Enchanted River (1928) still in service.

Parc de Bagatelle

Few Parisian parks are as romantic as this one, punctuated with waterfalls and a Chinese-style pagoda. The newly restored **château**, slated to open to the public for the first time in 2025, was built as the result of a 1775 wager between Marie Antoinette and her brother-in-law, the Count of Artois. Part of Paris' Botanical Gardens, the park blooms with irises, peonies and the famous 10,000 roses in summer.

Villa Windsor

Home to Charles de Gaulle and his family after WWII, this **legendary mansion** was where the Duke and Duchess of Windsor lived after Edward VIII abdicated the British throne. Fans of TV series *The Crown* will recognise the pad later owned by Mohamed Al-Fayed.

Pré Catelan

In this area of the Bois de Boulogne, the **Jardin Shakespeare** is lush with plants, flowers and trees mentioned in Shakespeare's plays. Watch for summer performances in the attached **open-air theatre**. The restaurant here, also called **Le Pré Catelan**, is a gastronomic temple, helmed by Frédéric Anton to the tune of three Michelin stars.

Lac Inférieur

On the eastern side of the park, rent an old-fashioned **rowboat** to explore Lac Inférieur, the largest of Bois de Boulogne's lakes – romance guaranteed.

Jardin des Serres d'Auteuil

It's worth the pilgrimage to the southeastern end of the Bois de Boulogne for this manicured **garden** with impressive conservatories, which opened in 1898. Amid the humidity, browse a luxuriant collection of rare tropical plants – you'll even find an aviary and carp-filled pool in the *palmarium*.

FRENCH OPEN TENNIS & LOCAL SPORTS

The park's **Stade Roland Garros** is the home of the sizzling clay-court French Open (held late May to early June). At other times, the tennis museum – newly inaugurated as the Tenniseum in 2024 – traces the history of the sport and the tournament. Nearby **Parc des Princes** hosts Paris Saint-Germain (PSG) football and **Paris La Défense Arena** hosts rugby.

TOP TIPS

- Dogs must be kept on a leash.

- Buy picnic supplies outside of the park and bring them with you. Amenities are thin on the ground inside.

- Vélib' bike-share stations are near most park entrances, but not within the park itself.

- Metro lines 1 (Porte Maillot, Les Sablons), 2 (Porte Dauphine), 9 (Michel-Ange-Auteuil) and 10 (Michel-Ange-Auteuil, Porte d'Auteuil), and the RER C (Avenue Foch, Avenue Henri Martin) serve the park.

- Be warned that the area can be a distinctly adult playground day and night, especially along allée de Longchamp and allée de la Reine Marguerite, where sex workers cruise for clients.

TREASURES AT TROCADÉRO

Guillaume Le Roux, the expert tour guide behind Le Vrai Paris and food site 716lavie.com, shares recommendations for lesser-known sites in the 16e. @levraiparis

At place du Trocadéro, it's the Eiffel Tower that draws our gaze across the river. But if you turn your back to it, you'll find two fascinating sites: Cimetière de Passy, filled with monumental tombs, and the Jean Fidler building at 1 av Paul Doumer, considered one of the finest examples of luxury buildings built in Paris between the world wars. It's perched above the square de Yorktown, named for the famous battle of the American Revolutionary War won by George Washington and French General Rochambeau against the British. A statue of Benjamin Franklin stands at the centre.

Palais de Tokyo

Politics & Prose
Revel in the lives of historical icons

Transport yourself back in time at the pretty, three-storey house where realist novelist Honoré de Balzac (1799–1850) hid from his creditors to live and work from 1840 to 1847. (He used a pseudonym, and visitors had to pronounce a special password.) This is a small pocket of old-school Passy streets, and you can look over the wall at the rue Berton, a cobbled lane that served as Balzac's secret exit. The **Maison de Balzac** *(maisondebalzac.paris.fr/en; adult/child €9/free)* is perfect for fans of literature and letters – you can peruse rooms of memorabilia, correspondence and prints. Decorated with an ornamental wood fireplace, the study contains the armchair and table where Balzac conceived the *Comédie Humaine*. You'll also spy the porcelain coffee pot, painted with his initials, that famously fuelled his all-nighters. The app (there's wi-fi on-site for downloading) is crammed with

The edible flowers are grown on a Paris rooftop.

EATING IN THE 16E: WORTH THE SPLURGE

Comice: A friendly husband-and-wife team run this Michelin-starred favourite. Don't miss the signature roasted cauliflower *à la grenobloise*. 7-9pm Mon-Fri, sometimes Sat €€€

Prunier par Yannick Alléno: Behind a turquoise mosaic façade, in art deco surroundings, a caviar and seafood extravaganza awaits. noon-2.30pm & 7-10.30pm Mon-Fri, 7-10.30pm Sat €€€

Ken Yamamoto: The Tokyo-born chef imbues French classics with Japanese flavours like dashi. The carte blanche menu changes every month. noon-2pm & 7.30-9.30pm Tue-Sat €€€

Substance: Let yourself be wowed by Chef Matthias Marc's multicourse tasting menu. The lunch *formule* is excellent value. noon-1.30pm & 7.30-9pm Mon-Fri €€€

audio commentary, including fascinating details about how Balzac maintained his manically intense work habits. Settle in at the on-site **Rose Bakery cafe** for fresh-baked treats, soups and quiche – garden tables with the Eiffel Tower high in the distance make for the perfect setting to contemplate your next great work.

After lunch, walk 10 minutes to the **Musée Clemenceau** *(musee-clemenceau.fr; adult/child €6/free),* housed inside the apartment where the statesman lived the last years of his life. Enter through a courtyard and buzz the door to get access. Known for negotiating the Treaty of Versailles that ended WWI, Georges Clemenceau – nicknamed 'The Tiger' – was also a writer and art-loving globetrotter who championed friend Claude Monet. Upstairs, a mini museum traces his life and work, while the downstairs apartment is preserved exactly as he left it – complete with a bedside water carafe, the books he was reading at the time of his death (the library has 5000 volumes), and sacks of sand, collected from the beaches of his native Vendée, used to blot letters.

Modern Art Fest

Play at Palais de Tokyo and Paris' modern-art museum

Soaring columns, art deco friezes…what exactly is that palace on the Seine? Palais de Tokyo was created for the 1937 Exposition Internationale des Arts et Techniques dans la Vie Moderne (International Exposition of Art and Technology in Modern Life). Nowadays the western wing, also called **Palais de Tokyo** *(palaisdetokyo.com; adult/child €13/free),* is Europe's largest contemporary-arts centre. The concrete-and-steel interior is a slick host for interactive exhibitions and installations. (There's no permanent collection.) Eating, drinking and entertainment options are fun: Bambini and Forest, with tables in the central courtyard over a reflecting pool with the Eiffel Tower in the distance, and basement nightclub Yoyo.

In the east wing, **Musée d'Art Moderne de Paris** *(mam.paris.fr)* displays a vast collection representative of just about every major artistic movement of the 20th and 21st centuries, with works by Modigliani, Braque, Chagall and Soutine. The real jewels, though, are monumental installations: an entire room of murals by Henri Matisse, and Raoul Dufy's *La Fée électricité,* a fresco depicting the history of electricity. The room is so dazzling that visitors sit on stools, transfixed, losing themselves in the effervescent colours. These permanent exhibitions are all – somewhat unbelievably – completely free,

WORLD'S FAIR LEGACY

Starting in the 19th century, world's fairs drew massive crowds to gape at exhibitions designed to showcase the latest in technology, culture and industry. Paris played host to seven such events, for which staggering architectural monuments were constructed – many later dismantled, including a flamboyant Moorish-style palace that once dominated the Trocadéro. Taking its place for the 1937 International Expo was the Palais de Chaillot, perched above fountain-bedecked gardens facing the Eiffel Tower. Today the eastern wing houses the Cité de l'Architecture et du Patrimoine (p76), devoted to French architecture, as well as the **Théâtre National de Chaillot**, staging dance and theatre. The Musée National de la Marine (p75) and the **Musée de l'Homme** (tracing human evolution) are housed in the western wing.

DRINKING IN THE 16E: BEST COCKTAILS

Cravan: Sip some of the city's best drinks inside an art nouveau building by Hector Guimard – the mirror-lined interiors haven't changed since 1911. *6-11pm Wed-Sat*

St James Paris: In a wood-panelled library, or on the dreamy terrace, try creative drinks highlighting ingredients from the hotel's garden. *7pm-midnight*

Midi-Minuit: The bar at Ducasse Baccarat, inside a stunning mansion, is run by mixologist Margot Lecarpentier of Combat fame. *noon-midnight*

Le Belair: Retro glamour at this hip spot at the Maison de la Radio, with a dance floor and DJ sets. *6.30pm-2am Thu-Sat*

Fish for sale, Marché Président Wilson

THE CITY'S BIGGEST GARDEN

Europe's mostly densely populated city, Paris has historically lacked green space. Under Mayor Anne Hidalgo, who took office in 2014, city hall has been on a mission to reinvent Paris as a green capital with myriad environmental initiatives, including the planting of so-called urban forests and new areas of vegetation. One of the most emblematic is the transformation of the Trocadéro–Pont d'Iéna axis into the city's largest garden. The idea is to add greenery to the place du Trocadéro, prioritising pedestrians and bikes – essentially extending the park through the Jardins du Trocadéro, across the Pont d'Iéna (the bridge will become pedestrianised), to the Eiffel Tower and the Champ de Mars beyond. Construction began after the 2024 Summer Olympics. At the time of writing, the Jardins du Trocadéro is a construction zone.

not to mention superbly peaceful compared to the slammed Orsay and Louvre. Look out for excellent temporary exhibitions (not free). Download the free multilingual app online.

To Market, To Market
Feast on fresh delicacies

Stroll the open air **Marché Président Wilson** across from Palais de Tokyo, where fresh-cut flowers crowd vendors of heirloom vegetables, fish and artisanal charcuterie. Adored by the city's top chefs, this lively market brims with the highest-quality products: poultry from Maison Priolet, Normandy-grown fruit from Moulin de l'Abbaye and cheese from Les Fromages de Sophie. Looking for lunch? You'll also find food stands with ready-made meals you can pack up for a picnic, including Japanese street food, spice-topped Lebanese flatbread, crêpes and Turkish sandwiches. The many temptations are available Wednesday and Saturday mornings, and it's one of the most convenient options to reach in the 16e.

EATING IN THE 16E: CLASSIC FRENCH

Les Coltineurs: This bistro's name is a nod to the workers who once loaded heavy goods onto Seine boats when there was a port nearby. *hours vary Wed-Sun* €€

La Rotonde de la Muette: This celebrated brasserie is a local institution, with velvet banquettes, wood panelling and brass light fixtures. Don't miss the Grand Marnier soufflé. *7am-midnight* €€

Le Petit Rétro: An art nouveau time capsule from 1904, classified a historic monument, serving traditional treats like steak-frites. *noon-2.30pm & 7.30-10.30pm* €€

Les Marches: Red-chequered tablecloths on bistro tables set the scene at this classic joint beneath the Palais de Tokyo, with a €20 lunch menu. *noon-2.30pm & 7.30-10.30pm* €€

Riding the Waves
Epic maritime museum and popular aquarium

Get both above and below sea level at the Trocadéro. Located in the western wing of Palais de Chaillot, the **Musée de la Marine** *(musee-marine.fr/en.html; adult/child €11/free)* doesn't just celebrate France's grand naval adventures from the 17th century until the present day (with model ships galore). This maritime museum is a sensory immersion in all things related to the sea, from cargo routes to open-ocean sailing races, from pollution to the mysterious shipwrecks that have fuelled the human imagination. It all comes to life thanks to interactive touchscreens, movies and more. A massive six-year makeover unveiled in 2023 completely transformed a fusty old museum into a must-visit cultural attraction that makes Parisians keep coming back for more. Kids can't get enough. In a first for a Paris museum, there's even a special 'zen' room for autistic children.

Younger visitors also love the **Aquarium de Paris** *(aquarium deparis.com; adult/child aged 3-12 €27.50/20)* on the eastern side of the Jardins du Trocadéro, where a shark tank and 500-odd fish species entertain families on rainy days. On Saturday nights, nocturnal visits are made festive with a glass of bubbly or a soft drink included with your ticket.

Fashion Forward
Browse couture then shop for your own

Housed in the studios of the legendary designer, the **Musée Yves Saint Laurent Paris** *(museeyslparis.com/en; adult/child €10/free)* holds retrospectives of YSL's avant-garde designs, from early sketches to finished pieces. Temporary exhibitions give an insight into the creative process of designing a *haute couture* (high fashion) collection and the history of 20th-century fashion. An example: a popular past show about flowers as an exuberant theme in the designer's work, inspired by the blooms in his gardens.

The marvellous upstairs studio is a window into the designer's world – peer at the open books on his memento-strewn desk, the fabric samples and mannequins draped in finery. The building can only accommodate a small number of visitors at a time, so buy tickets online or expect to queue outside. Note that a renovation launched in mid 2025 is expected to conclude in autumn 2027.

A few minutes away, Paris' fashion museum, **Palais Galliera** *(palaisgalliera.paris.fr/en; adult/child €15/free),* showcases over 200,000 outfits, spanning royal costumes to contemporary *haute couture* by designers such as Jean Paul Gaultier, in rotating shows. Enjoy a picnic on the elegant grounds of the sumptuous Italianate palace dating from the mid-19th century (the gardens are free to enter).

These spots are perfect inspiration for shopping in the neighbourhood's many top boutiques: from **Agnès B** to **Mouty**, with its slick, cheerful streetwear, and vintage- and couture-consignment cool **Lorette & Jasmin**.

BEST MUSEUM GIFT SHOPS

Forget mugs and overpriced totes. In Paris, the museum gift shops are brimming with unique items, often made in France.

Musée de la Marine
A destination in its own right, the boutique is full of fun finds including sea-inspired ceramics, stylish sailor belts and umbrellas made of recycled plastic by Paris brand Smati.

Musée National des Arts Asiatiques Guimet (p79)
A tasteful array of porcelain teapots, calligraphy pens and Japanese masks complements the fine arts books.

Musée du Quai Branly – Jacques Chirac (p79)
Everything from African woven baskets to Mayan-inspired jewellery.

Palais de Tokyo (p73) An art- and design-focused bookshop that could keep you browsing for hours.

Palais Galliera
Swedish stylist Susan Szatmáry created a line of leather goods exclusively for Paris' fashion museum.

Cité de l'Architecture et du Patrimoine

Architectural Glory

Walk through the history of architecture in France

You'd be hard-pressed to find a grander setting to show off France's architectural achievements. Housed in the eastern wing of the Palais de Chaillot at the Trocadéro, the **Cité de l'Architecture et du Patrimoine** (citedelarchitecture.fr/en; adult/child €9/free) is a standout museum with thrilling views of the Eiffel Tower framed through enormous windows. On the ground level, the light-filled galleries showcase 350 gobsmacking plaster casts taken from the country's greatest monuments. This collection was started following the desecration of many buildings during the French Revolution, and indeed, some of the original art pieces, such as sculptures from the Reims Cathedral, were destroyed in later wars. The museum itself was established in 1879 by Eugène Viollet-le-Duc, the architect famous for restoring masterpieces including Notre Dame and the medieval walled city of Carcassonne.

Wandering through this magnificent collection of church portals, gargoyles, saints and sinners is an incomparable experience for anyone interested in the elemental stories and craftwork of the country.

Head upstairs for a tête-à-tête with modernism and contemporary architecture. Among the drawings and models, a highlight is the reproduction of a Le Corbusier apartment, the famous unité d'habitation in Marseille. You'll also find reproduced murals and stained-glass windows from France's most important monuments. Exhibitions are real crowd-pleasers – past hits include shows on Notre Dame's restoration and the architectural history of department stores.

Architecture buffs can continue their study of Le Corbusier's work in the 16e. A dedicated **foundation** (fondationlecorbusier.fr/en; adult/child €10/free), headquartered inside the **Maison La Roche** at the end of a leafy cul-de-sac, offers guided visits

LA DÉFENSE

From its genesis in the 1950s as Europe's first purpose-built business district, La Défense will soon host a major new transport hub, as part of the Grand Paris Express project that's adding new regional transport lines. La Défense's soaring skyscrapers are immediately recognisable on the skyline west of Paris. The landmark edifice is the marble **Grande Arche** – an extension of the historic axis of Paris from the Arc de Triomphe. Construction required four years and 2000 workers; it was inaugurated in 1989 for the 200th anniversary of the French Revolution. A lift whisks you up for spectacular rooftop views. More than just office space, La Défense is an open-air art gallery. Calder, Miró and Torricini are among the artists behind colourful and surprising pieces peppering the central 1km promenade.

CELEBRATE ARCHITECTURE

Take a walk around the Passy and Auteuil areas of the 16e *arrondissement,* a festival of gorgeous art nouveau, art deco and modernist masterpieces.

START	END	LENGTH
Porte Dauphine metro	Le Corbusier studio apartment	7km; 2½ hrs

Start a study of art nouveau designs by famed Hector Guimard (1867–1942) at ❶ **Porte Dauphine metro** with its fanning entrance. Stately, tree-lined ❷ **av Georges Mandel** was opera star Maria Callas' last home (No 36), and look for No 59 with its elaborate glass awning and ironwork balconies. Continue on to ❸ **39 rue Scheffer**, an art nouveau stunner from 1911.

Then, get your architecture orientation at ❹ **Cité de l'Architecture et du Patrimoine**. Upstairs in the museum, find the maquette of ❺ **25 bis rue Benjamin Franklin** (named for the fellow who lived at 66 rue Raynouard) – it's just down the street with an elaborate inlaid floral façade. Guimard's glory, ❻ **Castel-Béranger** at 16 rue Jean de la Fontaine, won the award for Paris' best façade in 1898. Guimard built his home and studio, an asymmetrical celebration, in 1909 at ❼ **122 av Mozart**. His ❽ **Hôtel Jassedé** at 41 rue Chardon Lagache showcases elaborate brickwork.

Swing by ❾ **Gustave Eiffel's 1912 aerodynamic lab** at 67 rue Boileau, the first of its kind. Pop into the ❿ **Hôtel Molitor pool complex**, an art deco icon built in 1929. If you've timed it correctly, visit UNESCO-listed ⓫ **Le Corbusier studio apartment**. Designed between 1931 and 1934, the world's first glass-fronted apartment building was the renowned architect's home.

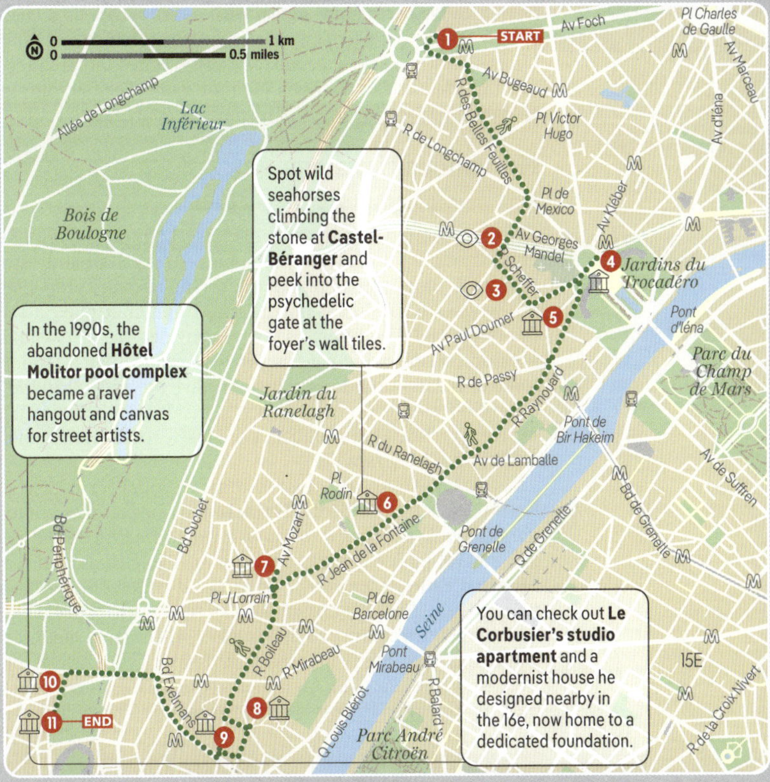

Spot wild seahorses climbing the stone at **Castel-Béranger** and peek into the psychedelic gate at the foyer's wall tiles.

In the 1990s, the abandoned **Hôtel Molitor pool complex** became a raver hangout and canvas for street artists.

You can check out **Le Corbusier's studio apartment** and a modernist house he designed nearby in the 16e, now home to a dedicated foundation.

FLAME OF LIBERTY MEMORIAL

The bronze **Flame of Liberty Memorial** above the northern end of the Pont de l'Alma, now called place Diana, is a replica of the one topping the Statue of Liberty in New York. It was placed here in 1987 as a symbol of friendship between France and the USA, but even more famous is its location above the place d'Alma tunnel where, on 31 August 1997, Diana, Princess of Wales, Dodi Fayed and their driver, Henri Paul, were killed in a car wreck. The statue is usually surrounded by tributes.

Musée National des Arts Asiatiques Guimet

of the house, which is an official UNESCO World Heritage Site. Built between 1923 and 1925 for a wealthy art collector friend, the experimental house with a free façade is a clever conceptual achievement that broke away from traditional building codes. Experience what Le Corbu called the 'architectural promenade' in the open-plan interiors. The foundation also oversees guided tours of his nearby apartment-studio.

Marvellous Mansions
Museum-hopping inside privileged pads

The vast terrain that's now the 16e was a historic playground for aristocrats to build dream homes. In the 17th and 18th centuries, the powerful pull of the Versailles court propelled the westward exodus of nobles. The trend continued after the Industrial Revolution as the wealthy fled the smoke and pollution of the Seine-side factories in eastern Paris. Today some of these sumptuous mansions have morphed into museums, offering you a chance to step inside gilded gates that are usually closed to the public. The Musée Marmottan Monet (p69) is the most famous.

Lesser known are two extraordinary properties overseen by the Guimet: the **Hôtel d'Heidelbach** *(guimet.fr/en/hotel-dheidelbach; free with admission to the Guimet)*, a Belle Époque marvel with a Japanese pagoda in the garden, and the **Musée d'Ennery** *(guimet.fr/en/musee-d-ennery; Sat guided tour in French €9)*, a mansion built by actress Clémence d'Ennery in the 19th century to show off her collection of Japanese and Chinese art. The bourgeoisie was obsessed with Asia at the time, and all of Parisian high society (including Jules Verne) lined up to ogle d'Ennery's demon masks and ivory netsuke sculptures. Left unchanged, it's a time capsule lined with custom wood cabinets that are inlaid with mother-of-pearl.

Nearby on the place des États-Unis, Maison Baccarat is housed inside a sprawling mansion that once belonged to influential 20th-century arts patron Marie-Laure de Noailles. One glimpse of the grand staircase and frescoed ballroom and you can imagine the legendary parties that she and her husband Charles threw for avant-garde artists and high society. Nowadays it's called **Ducasse Baccarat** *(ducasse-baccarat-paris.com)*, as a partnership between the luxury crystal brand and the iconic chef. There's a showroom-boutique, restaurant and bar, all filled with contemporary art, including a giant vase by designer Marcel Wanders. Artistic and cultural events are held in the ballroom once a month.

A Trip Around the World
Transport yourself to faraway lands

On the banks of the Seine, the **Musée du Quai Branly – Jacques Chirac** *(quaibranly.fr/en; adult/child €14/free)* provides boundless inspiration for travellers, armchair anthropologists and those who simply appreciate traditional craftwork. Presenting indigenous art from around the world, it's a tribute to the incredible diversity of human culture. The museum's layout adds to the feeling that you're embarking on a voyage – to access the collections, ascend a spiral ramp illuminated with a visual 'river' of words calling out the collection's people and places. Unique interiors don't have rooms or high walls.

Highlights include remarkable carvings from Papua New Guinea (Oceania); clothing, jewellery and textiles from India to Vietnam (Asia); an excellent collection of masks (Africa); and art from great American civilisations – the Mayas, Aztecs and Incas. Numerous aids on hand help you navigate the vast collection and delve deeper. Multimedia touch screens provide context, while tailored walks (available online and upon request at the entrance) focus on specific themes. Temporary exhibitions and performances are also generally excellent. Café Jacques is pleasantly set in the gardens (check out the enormous 'green wall'), while fine-dining restaurant Les Ombres offers Eiffel Tower views from the rooftop.

Across the river, **Musée National des Arts Asiatiques Guimet** *(guimet.fr/en; adult/child €13/free)* is France's foremost Asian arts museum, and entices with a superb collection from all corners of the continent. It's possible to observe the gradual transmission of both Buddhism and artistic styles along the Silk Road in some of the museum's pieces, from the 1st-century Gandhara Buddhas from Afghanistan and Pakistan to the later Central Asian, Chinese and Japanese sculptures. Above all, it's a place where you'll want to get lost in beauty – from the neoclassical rotunda in the historical library to the Khmer courtyard. In this elegant space there are delights at every turn. Keep an eye out for Tibetan mandalas, centuries-old terracotta horses from China and the world's largest collection of Khmer artefacts outside Cambodia.

BEST SPOTS TO PHOTOGRAPH THE EIFFEL TOWER

Facing the iconic monument, the popular place du Trocadéro offers sublime photo ops. Here are some less crowded alternatives.

Pont de Bir-Hakeim
Professional photographers stage wedding photos on the end of this bridge. Metro line 6 zips over the Seine.

Av de Camoens
The end of this cobbled street lined with elegant Haussmannian buildings serves as an open-air balcony overlooking the tower.

Av du Président Wilson
Next to the Palais de Tokyo, a staircase leading down to the Seine has great views.

Rue Raynouard
From the street above the Maison de Balzac, the tower rises in the distance above the charming garden and perfectly preserved house.

Rue de l'Université
This street runs at the perfect angle from the Champ de Mars for close-up photos of the landmark.

Researched by Nicola Leigh Stewart

CHAMPS-ÉLYSÉES & GRANDS BOULEVARDS

GRAND MONUMENTS AND LES GRANDS MAGASINS

On first impressions, the Champs-Élysées and Grands Boulevards areas might not seem to have all that much in common but they are home to some of the city's most historic and majestic monuments.

The world's most famous avenue, home to designer shops and surrounded by palace hotels, sits quite at home in the prestigious 8th *arrondissement,* while next door in the 9th, the streets around Grands Boulevards offer a more down-to-earth slice of Parisian life.

Within their boundaries you'll find the Arc de Triomphe, the Petit Palais, La Madeleine to name just a few. All of which tell some of Paris' most fascinating stories; tales of various kings, both Napoléons, and one very big and bloody revolution. You'll also find two of Paris' top shopping destinations here, thanks to *haute couture* boutiques and the Printemps and Galeries Lafayette department stores, as well as a great place for ending your day with a drink, a film, or an extravagant night at the opera.

TOP TIP

As the metro exit brings you out to the right of the Arc de Triomphe, this is where you'll find most tourists snapping their pics and Instagramming – cross over to the other side of the street to get a quieter shot. And in case you need them, there are also public toilets on this side.

See p307 for places to stay in Champs-Élysées & Grands Boulevards

Arc de Triomphe (p85)

Highlights

❶ Palais Garnier
Architectural masterpiece among Paris' most storied addresses, famously home to the mythical phantom. **p90**

❷ La Galerie Dior
Fashion fans will swoon over this stunning collection of Dior's loveliest creations. **p89**

❸ Arc de Triomphe
Napoléon's victorious arch comes with one of the city's best views. **p85**

❹ Petit Palais
This magnificent museum houses a wonderful collection of fine art set around a leafy courtyard. **p88**

❺ Hôtel de la Marine
Step back in time as you wander through the Hôtel de la Marine's 18th-century gilded apartments. **p86**

Getting Around

Walking
Paris is an easy city to walk around, and and strolling up the famed Champs-Élysées is the best way to see it.

Metro
There are a few key metro stations along the Champs-Élysées, and the Grands Boulevards stop is right on, as the name suggests, Grands Boulevards.

Taxi
If you're visiting some of the fancier addresses around the Champs-Élysées you might want to arrive by taxi (or Uber or Bolt).

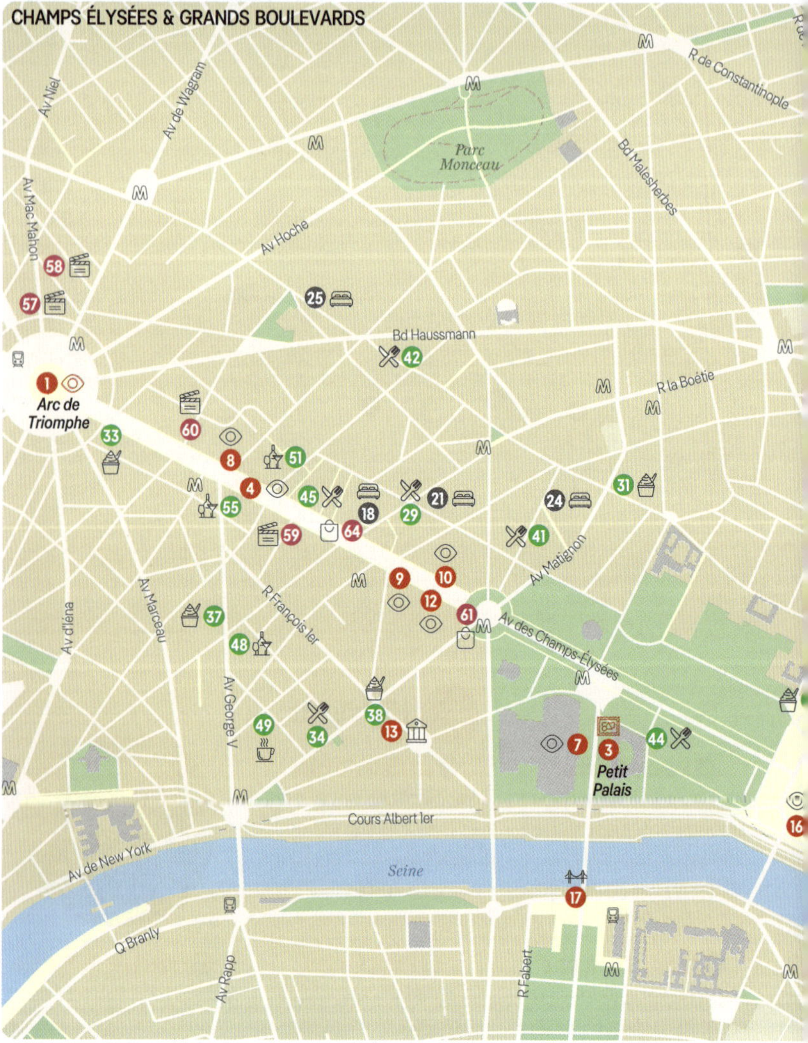

CHAMPS ÉLYSÉES & GRANDS BOULEVARDS

★ HIGHLIGHTS
1. Arc de Triomphe
2. Palais Garnier
3. Petit Palais

● SIGHTS
4. Avenue des Champs-Élysées
5. Chapelle Expiatoire
6. Folies Bergère
7. Grand Palais
8. Home of Alberto Santos-Dumont
9. Home of Colette
10. Home of the Count of Monte Cristo
11. Hôtel de la Marine
12. Hôtel de la Païva
13. La Galerie Dior
14. Musée Grévin
15. Musée National Gustave Moreau
16. Place de la Concorde
17. Pont Alexandre III

● ACTIVITIES
see 11 Le Cordon Bleu

● SLEEPING
18. CitizenM Paris Champs-Élysées
19. Grand Boulevards Experimental
20. Hôtel Chopin
21. Hôtel de la Boétie
22. Hôtel Panache
23. Hôtel Pulitzer
24. Nuage
25. PLEY Hotel

● EATING
26. Ardent
27. Bob de Tunis
28. Bouillon Chartier
29. Brasserie Baroche
30. Butterfly Pâtisserie
31. Café Antonia at Le Bristol
32. Canard & Champagne
33. Fou de Pâtisserie
see 30 Jardin d'Hiver at Hôtel de Crillon
34. Jean Imbert au Plaza Athenee
35. Jeanne-Aimée
36. Juste

- **SHOPPING**
- see **67** À la Mère de Famille
- **61** Avenue Montaigne
- **62** Boutique Maille
- see **38** Dior
- see **53** Galeries Lafayette
- **63** Galeries Lafayette Le Gourmet
- **64** Guerlain
- **65** La Maison de la Truffe
- see **69** Mariage Freres
- **66** Passage des Panoramas
- see **14** Passage Jouffroy
- **67** Passage Verdeau
- **68** Patrick Roger
- **69** Place de la Madeleine
- **70** Printemps
- see **56** Printemps du Goût
- see **33** Publicisdrugstore

- **37** La Galerie at Four Seasons Hotel George V
- see **34** La Galerie at Hôtel Plaza Athénée
- **38** La Pâtisserie Dior
- **39** Le Bon Georges
- **40** Le Comptoir Opéra Le Chocolat Alain Ducasse
- see **37** Le George at Four Seasons Hotel George V
- **41** Le Mermoz
- see **30** L'Écrin at Hôtel de Crillon
- see **31** L'Épicerie du Bristol
- **42** Maison Mathieu Pacaud
- **43** Miznon
- **44** Pavyllon
- **45** Pierre Herme
- see **32** Racines
- **46** Raviolis Nord Est
- **47** Ronnie Bakery

- **DRINKING & NIGHTLIFE**
- **48** Bulgari Bar at Bulgari Hotel Paris
- **49** Café Nuances
- **50** Certified Panoramas
- **51** CopperBay at Hotel Lancaster
- **52** Coutume
- **53** Créatures at Galeries Lafayette Haussmann
- **54** Ibrik
- see **37** Le Bar at Four Seasons Hotel George V
- **55** Le Joy at Le Fouquet's Paris
- **56** Le Picnic by Veuve Clicquot at Printemps
- see **30** Les Ambassadeurs at Hôtel de Crillon
- see **19** The Shed at Grands Boulevards Experimental

- **ENTERTAINMENT**
- **57** Cinéma Mac-Mahon
- **58** Club de L'Étoile
- **59** Elysées Lincoln
- **60** Le Balzac
- see **33** Publicis Cinémas

Avenue des Champs-Élysées

HISTORIC ADDRESSES ON THE CHAMPS-ÉLYSÉES

Although it's now Paris' most famous shopping street, the Champs-Élysées' long and rich history means there are plenty of notable addresses to look out for beyond the shops.

Home of the Count of Monte Cristo

Fans of Alexandre Dumas' novel should pass by No 30, the site of the Count's Parisian home.

Home of Colette

No 31–33 is where the writer Colette lived briefly before moving to the Palais Royal.

Hôtel de la Païva

No 25 is the former *hôtel particulier* (private mansion) of courtesan Esther Lachman, aka La Païva.

Guerlain

The French beauty brand was one of the first stores to open on the avenue, at No 68.

Home of Alberto Santos-Dumont

No 114 is the former home of pilot Alberto Santos-Dumont, where he landed his airship in 1903.

Meander the Avenue des Champs-Élysées

The world's most famous avenue

Often called the most beautiful avenue in the world, the **Avenue des Champs-Élysées** is now largely avoided by Parisians, other than those who work in the area, but its worldwide fame often makes it a bucket-list sight for tourists, particularly for first-time visitors to Paris.

Although it does live up to its shopping street reputation and that is what most people are here to do (even if you can find the same stores back home), the avenue has some beautiful architecture and a richer history than the high-street shops would lead you to believe. If you're in the area it's worth strolling up the famed Champs-Élysées for yourself, although to get the most out of the experience avoid the chain stores and try and find somewhere more French. The historic Guerlain store is particularly beautiful, or you can pick up beauty products from cult French brand Biologique Recherche, or stop by department store Galeries Lafayette. Another tip is to skip the overpriced touristy restaurants. There are better places to eat in the area; just stop somewhere for coffee.

WHERE TO EAT CLASSIC FRENCH FOOD

Bouillon Chartier: Expect to queue for an hour (or more) but the classic dishes are great value at this Paris institution. *11.30am-midnight* €

Le Bon Georges: One of the more expensive bistros in Paris, but every dish is delicious and portions are generous. *noon-2.30pm & 7pm-10.30pm* €€€

Brasserie Baroche: A perfect spot for people-watching with a slice of the signature *pâté en croûte* and a glass of wine. *7am-12.30am Mon-Sat* €€

Canard & Champagne: The name describes exactly what this restaurant specialises in. There's a good value set menu. *noon-2pm & 7-10.30pm* €

Marvel at the Arc de Triomphe
A symbol of both military power and peace

Now one of the most famous monuments in the world, Napoléon commissioned the **Arc de Triomphe** *(paris-arc-de-triomphe.fr; €16/free for under 18s)* after his victory at the Battle of Austerlitz in 1805, but by the time it was finished in 1836, the emperor had abdicated, then died, and the monarchy had made its brief return.

Although it was built as a symbol of military power, it now stands more as a symbol of peace and remembrance at the site of the Tomb of the Unknown Soldier, where the eternal flame has been burning continuously since 1923. A committee is in charge of making sure it is rekindled at 6.30pm each day; you can come and watch the event or catch it on the live video inside the museum.

The 200 original steps (although they have been restored over the years) will take you up to the museum and a further 40 lead up to the terrace, also original. Although tourists snapping photos probably wasn't what the designers had in mind at the time, it's easily one of the best views in Paris, partly because it also includes a clear view of the Eiffel Tower. However, due to its high up, open terrace, the Arc de Triomphe is closed during adverse weather conditions and when it is hosting various official ceremonies, so it's worth checking opening hours online.

As one of Paris' most visited monuments it does get very crowded, and first thing in the morning is usually your best chance for a quiet moment. The most beautiful time, however, is sunset, and although you're likely to be caught up in an even bigger crowd of tourists, it's worth it to catch the view at its prettiest. Two days a year, you can even see the sun fall right through the Arc's centre, usually on or around 10 May and 1 August (the exact date isn't posted on the website but you can find it through a Google search). To get the ultimate shot you need to be on the Champs-Élysées.

Oui Chef!
Learn to cook the French way

The world-famous **Le Cordon Bleu** *(cordonbleu.edu/paris-hoteldelamarine; from €35)* cooking school now has a day school for culinary enthusiasts who want to learn how to whip up their own French dishes and desserts at home. The school can be found hidden away in an 18th-century apartment in

---

PONT ALEXANDRE III

Another monument built for the 1900 Universal Exhibition, along with the Petit Palais and Grand Palais, the gilded gold **Pont Alexandre III** is one of the city's art nouveau masterpieces and Paris' most emblematic bridge. Named after Tsar Alexander III, who finalised the Franco-Russian alliance in 1892, it was Alexander's son Nicholas II who laid the bridge's foundation stone in 1896. Its opulent design features four imposing columns, two at each end, topped with golden bronze sculptures of winged horses that represent Arts, Sciences, Commerce and Industry, accompanied by a series of sculpted fantastical creatures such as nymphs, cherubs, and sea monsters. The opulent backdrop and Eiffel Tower view make it a popular spot for photos.

 **THE BEST HOTEL BARS**

There's a DJ playing vinyls on Thursday nights

Le Bar at Four Seasons Hotel George V: Cocktails are crafted with the latest techniques at this elegant and cosy gentlemen's club-style bar. *5pm-1am*

Bulgari Bar at Bulgari Hotel Paris: The sleek black bar hidden at the back of Bulgari Hotel makes a cool and sexy setting for after-dark cocktails. *10am-midnight*

Les Ambassadeurs at Hôtel de Crillon: One of Paris' most palatial hotels of course has an equally opulent bar: the gilded gold Les Ambassadeurs. *5pm-1am*

CopperBay at Hotel Lancaster: The cool 10th *arrondissement* cocktail bar CopperBay has opened up a third outpost inside the historic Hotel Lancaster. *5pm-1.30am*

FOLIES BERGÈRE

You can't miss the gold art deco façade of the **Folies Bergère**, one of Paris' most iconic music halls. It's passed through various owners since its 1869 inauguration as the Folies Trévise, and each had their turn switching up the entertainment programme, but the venue will forever be associated with Joséphine Baker; it's here she danced on stage in her famous banana skirt – and not much else. Charlie Chaplin, Dalida and Vanessa Paradis are some of the other big names to have graced its stage over the years.

the Hôtel de la Marine (guests enter through the gift shop) which makes a beautiful and appropriately very French setting with the original 1743 parquet flooring, coving and curved windows overlooking the place de la Concorde. This brings to mind the film *Sabrina* when Audrey Hepburn's character was learning to cook at the Cordon Bleu with an Eiffel Tower backdrop. There's a mix of savoury and sweet masterclasses where you'll get hands-on, 30-minute demonstrations where you'll watch a chef in action (and take the recipe to try it at home), classes for children, wine workshops and gastronomic lunches and dinners with wine pairings and explanations.

Crowning Glory at Hôtel de la Marine
An architectural masterpiece reborn

The beautiful **Hôtel de la Marine** (*hotel-de-la-marine.paris; from €9*) museum tells the story of the building's former life as the home of La Garde-Meuble de la Couronne ('Royal Furniture Depository' in English), which was responsible for conserving the crown's collection of furniture, tapestries, arts, jewels and weapons, as well as crafting new furnishings on demand. Following the abolition of the monarchy, and also of course La Garde-Meuble de la Couronne, some of the most important events in French history took place in this building, including the signing of Marie Antoinette's death warrant (she was executed just outside on place de la Concorde) and the signing of the bill to abolish slavery in France. Make sure to get an audio guide when purchasing your ticket to understand what you're looking at as you move through the various rooms, which were once the gilded apartments of Marc Antoine Thierry de Ville d'Avray, La Garde-Meuble's last intendant (high official). In a separate part of the building, two rooms are dedicated to the Al Thani Foundation, a non-profit organisation that brings together incredible works of art from antiquity to the modern day. The signs aren't in English, but the audio guide provides some fascinating information.

BEST SWEET TREATS: OUR PICKS

Ronnie Bakery: The owners took inspiration from an English grandmother for treats such as scones, cinnamon rolls and brownies. *8.30am-5pm Tue-Sat* €

Butterfly Pâtisserie: A taste of Matthieu Carlin's desserts in a relaxed setting. The ultra-creamy flan is the signature. *11am-7pm Mon-Fri, to 7.30pm Sat & Sun* €€

Fou de Pâtisserie: Pastries and desserts from the best names in Paris. Find a small counter at Publicisdrugstore. *8am-2am Mon-Fri, 10am-2am Sat & Sun* €

La Pâtisserie Dior: Fashionistas can find Dior's patisserie inside its flagship boutique. *11.30am-7.30pm* €€

Pierre Hermé: Macaron master Pierre Hermé has a cafe on the Champs-Elysées and a few boutiques in the area. *hours vary* €

Maison Mathieu Pacaud: Classic French patisserie from chef Mathieu Pacaud, who oversees a collection of Michelin-star restaurants in Paris. *8.15am-7.30pm Mon-Fri* €€

L'Épicerie du Bristol: Stop by Le Bristol's boutique to pick up delicious cakes, pastries and chocolates made in the hotel's own ateliers. *10.30am-5.30pm Wed-Sun* €€

Le Comptoir Opéra Le Chocolat Alain Ducasse: Alain Ducasse's Opéra boutique handily sells all Ducasse's specialities: chocolates, ice cream and biscuits. *10am-8pm* €€

Luxor Obelisk, place de la Concorde

Off With Their Heads!
Place de la Concorde – home of the guillotine

Created in 1772, **place de la Concorde** sits on what was once a dry moat and fields surrounding the Jardin des Tuileries and the former royal palace, Le Louvre. It's famously where Louis XVI and Marie-Antoinette were guillotined in 1793 during the French Revolution, along with many others, gaining the square the name place de la Révolution. It was renamed place de la Concorde in 1795 and redesigned between 1836 and 1846 to add the two fountains, Fontaine des Mers and Fontaine des Fleuves, and the statues representing various French cities, which sit around the edge of the square. But its most famous monument is the 3300-year-old Egyptian Luxor Obelisk, erected in 1836 after France received it as a gift from the King of Egypt and capped with a gilded pyramidion, gifted by the President of Egypt in 1998.

Step Inside the Home of Gustave Moreau
A beautiful 'House Museum' dedicated to the artist

Gustave Moreau spent the last years of his life converting his home and studio at 14 rue de La Rochefoucauld into the **Musée National Gustave Moreau** (musee-moreau.fr/en; adult/concession €8/6, first Sun of the month free) before leaving all his belongings to the state upon his death in 1898. France honoured his dying wishes and the museum is now a unique time capsule of 19th-century design (there's an identical copy of the painter's apartment on the 1st floor) and a full immersion into Moreau's work, which was full of Greek mythology, biblical stories and religious allegory. It's also

BEST GOURMET SHOPS FOR SOUVENIRS

In addition to the shops around La Madeleine, there are a few other places which are great for picking up foodie souvenirs.

À la Mère de Famille
Beautifully packaged chocolates and traditional French *confiseries* (confectionery) in a historic listed building.

Publicisdrugstore
This fashionable concept store sells a selection of ultra-luxe French products, including food and drink at its *épicerie fine* (delicatessen).

Galeries Lafayette Le Gourmet
Here you'll find a separate store dedicated to food with three floors of fresh produce, cakes, chocolates, wines and spirits.

Printemps du Goût
Printemps department store has its own *épicerie fine*, Printemps du Goût, which spans the whole of the 7th floor.

Petit Palais

CHAMPS-ÉLYSÉES FILM FESTIVAL

Founded in 2012, the Champs-Élysées Film Festival builds on the avenue's rich cinema history to showcase both French and American independent films (great for English-speaking cinephiles) across all of the Champs-Élysées' movie theatres. The festival takes place every June and screens a mix of feature films, shorts, previews and more, supporting independent productions and emerging filmmakers, and showing off some more daring films. While it's not quite Cannes, you can catch some high-profile films and actors here – the multi-Oscar winning *Everything Everywhere All at Once* was the closing film at the 2022 edition of the festival, and past guests have included Jeff Goldblum, Christopher Walken and *Paddington* actor Ben Whishaw.

home to one of the most Instagrammable staircases in Paris. Note that while some museums in Paris close on Mondays, this one doesn't but it is closed on Tuesdays.

Magnificent Fine Arts at Petit Palais

The museum of Paris

Commissioned by the city of Paris to showcase fine arts at the 1900 Paris Exposition (Exposition Universelle in French), the **Petit Palais** *(petitpalais.paris.fr; permanent collection free/ temporary exhibitions from €12)* was one of the monuments built for the event which, for the first time, was designed to remain a permanent fixture after the World Fair had ended.

Designed by architect Charles Girault, the idea was to create a crowd-pleasing, classical monument that everyone would like (involving plenty of marble and moulding) but which also drew inspiration from Greek classical influences (note the grand columns) and the fashionable art nouveau style. Girault's stint as an ironmonger also influenced the design, as seen in the gold ironwork entrance and the main curved staircase in the permanent collection, where floral motifs reference art nouveau.

The freshly made babkas are delicious!

 WHERE TO GRAB A COFFEE

| **Ibrik**: This Balkans-inspired cafe makes a great pitstop for Turkish coffee and a doorstop slice of pistachio cake. *8.30am-4pm Mon-Fri* € | **Coutume**: One of the original and still the best artisan coffee roasters and coffee shops in Paris. *8.30am-5.30pm* € | **Certified Panoramas**: A sleek and stylish espresso bar hidden at the back of the Passage des Panoramas. *8.30am-6pm* € | **Café Nuances**: Brothers Charles and Raphaël Corrot are sourcing and roasting some of the best coffee beans in Paris. *8am-7pm* € |

Outside, Girault added a central garden to offer a moment of tranquillity away from the city's crowds, especially during the hugely popular Exposition Universelle. It's now a particularly lovely spot to stop for a coffee from the museum's cafe.

Notable works include *Les Halles* by Léon Lhermitte; *The Sleepers* by Gustave Courbet, a commission from a Turkish diplomat who then kept it hidden behind a curtain due to its racy subject matter (and who also commissioned Courbet's most famous work, *Origin of the World,* now in the Musée d'Orsay); and the recently restored *Portrait de l'Artiste en Costume Oriental (Self-Portrait in Oriental Attire)* by Rembrandt, who later added the dog to his only full-length self-portrait to hide his legs as he wasn't happy with the final result.

Downstairs you'll find an Arts and Crafts collection intended to shine a light on the works as an art form in their own right, a collection of art nouveau treasures, including Hector Guimard's (the man behind the now iconic Paris metro entrances) entire dining room, and a collection of Monets. Unfortunately, the information is all in French, but excellent guided tours are available with an English-speaking guide, or you can find more about the works on the website.

Sashay La Galerie Dior

An haute couture celebration

Sitting next to Dior's huge flagship boutique, **La Galerie Dior** *(galeriedior.com; adult/concession €14/10)* is a fabulous fashion museum which takes you through the history of the famed French brand as you walk through 13 beautifully designed rooms. The visit starts on the museum's immaculate white curved staircase, a popular photo spot, which highlights the colourful backdrop of 1874 miniature Dior creations, all 3D printed except for the 452 dresses, which have been hand sewn in the Dior workshops. From here you'll wander into an enchanted garden, past a Paris skyline and through a mini atelier where Dior's artisans can be found showcasing their savoir-faire before finishing the grand tour with the pièce de résistance, a room full of glittering Dior ball gowns. A visit also includes a chance to briefly visit the famed 30 av Montaigne where Monsieur Dior opened his couture house in 1946, and where you can see the original changing rooms used by the Dior models before they sashayed out in the latest *haute couture* collection. The exhibition changes twice a year (and is closed during this time) so the delicate dresses can return to storage, and to tempt you back to see more of

GRAND PALAIS

Erected for the 1900 Exposition Universelle (World Fair), the glass-roofed **Grand Palais** reopened in 2025 after a painstaking restoration which returned it to its original art nouveau splendour. The four-year project enlarged the exhibition space and capacity, while adding a buzzy brasserie, called the Grand Café, with one of the prettiest terraces in Paris. Bedecked in cast iron and glass, the soaring Nef (nave) hosts major events, art shows, and even DJ-led soirées throughout the year. In the winter, there's even a massive ice-skating rink set up – considered the world's largest such temporary rink – with glittering disco balls adding to the party vibes.

 WHERE TO SPLASH OUT ON FINE DINING

Pavyllon: Yannick Alléno's haute cuisine; the set lunch menu offers a more affordable taste of his Michelin-star cooking. *noon-2.30pm & 7-10.30pm* €€€

Le George at Four Seasons Hotel George V: Sustainable, Mediterranean-inspired cuisine with one Michelin star and vegetarian tasting menus. *12.30-2.30pm & 7-10.30pm* €€€

Jean Imbert au Plaza Athénée: Chef Jean Imbert serves up Michelin-star cuisine in one of the most beautiful dining rooms in Paris. *7.15-10.15pm Tue-Sat & 12.30-2.15pm Fri & Sat* €€€

L'Écrin at Hôtel de Crillon: Based around two unusual ideas: the food matches the wine, not vice versa, and you say what you don't like, and the chef will surprise you. *7.30-9.30pm Mon-Fri* €€€

THE MANY STORIES OF AVENUE MONTAIGNE

Avenue Montaigne is another of Paris' famed streets with plenty of stories to tell. It was nicknamed 'allée des Veuves' back in the 18th century, a reference to the lonely widows who strolled the street looking for company, and in the 19th century, high society flocked to the open-air dance hall Le Bal Mabille, where the polka and cancan were reportedly created. Fashion *couturiers* arrived in the 1920s and, later, the most famous of them all, Christian **Dior**, who opened his flagship at No 30 in 1946. Other notable addresses include the **Théâtre des Champs-Elysées**, where Joséphine Baker made her Paris debut in 1925, the **Hôtel Plaza Athénée**, where courtesan and spy Mata Hari was arrested outside in 1917, and the hotel's restaurant **Le Relais Plaza**, which was once a haunt of Yves Saint Laurent.

Dior's incredible archives. Book tickets in advance to avoid the long queues outside (and try to get the first slot to have more of the museum to yourself). As well as exiting through the gift shop, you can also revive yourself at Café Dior before you leave, which comes with Dior prices, *bien sûr*, but it's a great spot for people-watching.

Another Napoléon-Approved Monument
Place de la Madeleine is a must visit for gourmands

The Greek-inspired **L'église de la Madeleine** dominates the centre of **place de la Madeleine**, the square named after it, with an imposing façade of Corinthian columns that makes it one of Paris' most unusual churches. It received its distinctive neoclassical looks from Napoléon, who changed the design originally commissioned by Louis XV to create a pantheon that would honour his armies. After starting in 1764, construction wasn't finished until 1842, by which time the royal family had returned (albeit briefly) and Louis Philippe I was ruling from the reinstated throne. But like the Arc de Triomphe – another Napoléon-approved monument that was completed under the king's reign – the emperor's design plans held strong, even if his plans for world domination didn't. It's open every day for visitors and also holds classical music concerts; check the church website for more information. Before or after a visit, make sure to browse the prestigious gourmet flagships that sit around the square, some of which have been here for nearly 100 years. There's also a flower market every day except Sunday.

Napoléon III's Great Palais Garnier
Garnier's sumptuous celebration of music and dance

In an emperor power move, Napoléon III commissioned a new Paris **opera house** *(operadeparis.fr; adult/concession/children under 12 €15/10/free)* to his liking after an assassination attempt at the former opera house on nearby rue Le Peletier. Charles Garnier was just 35 years old, and as yet unknown, when he won the commission to build it. He surprised everyone including Empress Eugénie, who was less than impressed when Garnier presented his designs. Napoléon III died before he ever got to see it and it's now visitors who use what would have been a private entrance to protect him from would-be attackers.

Inside, the 'show' starts not in the auditorium but on another stage: the grand staircase. With its sweeping steps and numer-

 AFFORDABLE EATS

Miznon: A Middle Eastern restaurant with some of the best falafel in town. The mezze plates are great for sharing. *11am-11pm* €

Juste: Affordable and good oysters. The lunchtime prix fixe menu of *moules frites* also comes with a bonus glass of wine. *hours vary* €

Raviolis Nord Est: This down-to-earth restaurant is known for its tasty dumplings (ravioli in French) and noodles. *hours vary* €

Bob de Tunis: Octogenarian Bob is still making his Tunisian sandwiches himself at this tiny sandwich shop which has only four tables. *8am-6pm* €

L'église de la Madeleine

ous balconies to observe who was sashaying up them, Garnier purposefully designed it for posing. In the auditorium, he flattered high society again by choosing red velvet seating to complement the gold leaf, saying that the pink tinge reflected on women's faces helped them look 'more youthful and radiant'. Crowning the space is a ceiling fresco by Marc Chagall, a recent design addition, and the opera house's impressive chandelier, which inspired an event in Gaston Leroux's *The Phantom of the Opera* when it fell from the ceiling in 1896.

Aside from the auditorium, one of the Palais Garnier's most prestigious rooms is the Grand Foyer, inspired by the Hall of Mirrors at Versailles and recently restored to its full splendour. You can wander around just admiring all of this grandeur but it really is worth taking a tour of some kind: the audio tour is excellent and cheaper than taking a private group tour (bookable on the website), but with the latter you'll be able to actually sit in the auditorium, unless it's in use for practice. And make sure to reserve a ticket in advance online – due to the high number of visitors, it's not guaranteed you'll get a ticket on the day at the box office.

FOOD SHOPS NEAR PLACE DE LA MADELEINE

Patrick Roger
The minimalist boutique mirrors the pared-back collection of chocolates, which focuses on the purity of chocolate and praline.

La Maison de la Truffe
The luxurious truffle-infused range runs from affordable truffle crisps to the chance to splurge hundreds on whole white and black truffles.

Mariage Frères
With more than 800 tea references from 36 countries Mariage Frères has the largest tea selection in the world, but a canister is almost worth buying for the iconic packaging alone.

Boutique Maille
While you can buy jars of France's most famous brand of Dijon mustard in the supermarket, the mustard-obsessed will love the choice at the dedicated Maille boutique.

 BEST CONTEMPORARY CUISINE & NATURAL WINES

Le Mermoz: This elegant neobistro serves up a produce-driven menu that puts a modern riff on French classics. *12.15-2pm & 7.15-10pm Mon-Fri* €€

Ardent: Large sharing plates of meat cooked over fire are the focus here but there are great veggie options too. *12-2.30pm & 7-10.30pm Mon-Fri* €€

Jeanne-Aimée: This hidden-away restaurant serves up a seasonal and creative menu (and a great-value lunch menu) under a lovely large glass verrerie. *hours vary* €€

Racines: It might be Italian not French, but tables are always in demand at Racines thanks to the contemporary, elevated cuisine. *12.15-2pm & 7.15-10pm* €€€

WALKING TOUR

Arc de Triomphe to Palais Garnier

You'll take in some of Paris' most famous sites and most beautiful architecture on this one-hour (4.8km) walk, which has plenty of coffee and shopping breaks along the way.

1 Arc de Triomphe
Start at the Arc de Triomphe (p85), and try to hit it early to avoid the crowds.

2 Champs-Élysées
From here, stroll down the 2km of the tree-lined Champs-Élysées (p84) with its many designer and luxury stores. The avenue might be the most famous in the world, but not for its food. If you need a pitstop, try Ladurée and L'Occitane x Pierre Hermé (for macarons) and Flora Danica (for coffee and a cinnamon roll).

3 Petit Palais
When you reach the Champs-Élysées Marcel Dassault roundabout turn right down av Winston Churchill to visit the art nouveau Petit Palais (p88), built as a fine-art museum for the 1900 Paris Exposition. Look out for the Statue of General Charles de Gaulle on your way, and the Winston Churchill statue past the entrance, on the corner of the museum towards the Pont Alexandre III. Opposite the museum, you'll find the grand glass-roofed Grand Palais (p90).

Palais Garnier (p90)

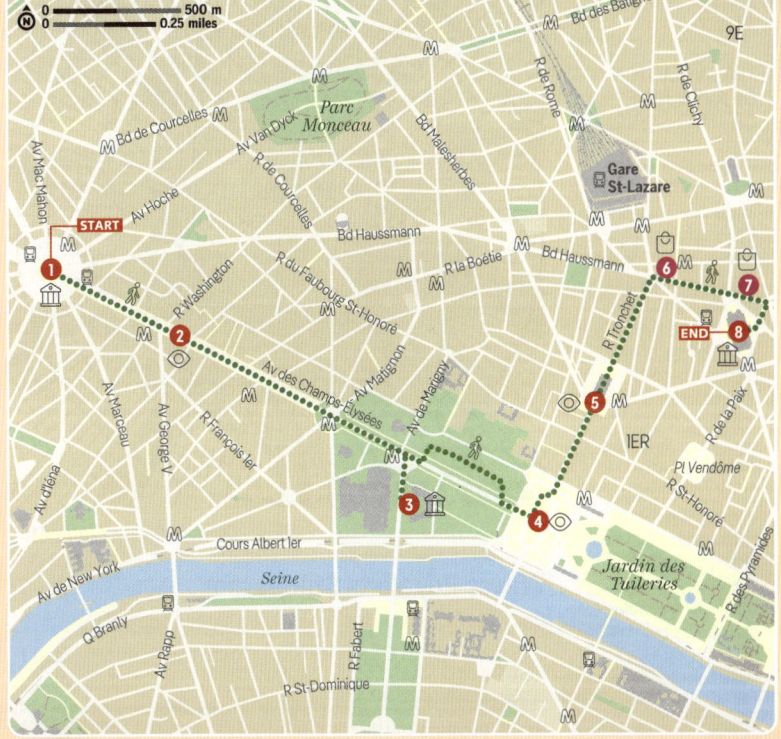

4 Place de la Concorde

Once you've got your art fix, walk back to join the Champs-Élysées and cross over the road to find the path allée Marcel-Proust in the gardens, where you'll continue east to place de la Concorde (p87).

5 Place de la Madeleine

Wander round to see if you can spot which major French cities are represented by the sculptures on the edge of the square and in the middle, just by the gold-tipped Egyptian obelisk, look for the plaque that marks the execution site of King Louis XVI and Marie-Antoinette. Cross the street and take rue Royale towards place de la Madeleine (p90); it sits in between the twin buildings designed by Louis XV's chief architect, Ange-Jacques Gabriel, that now house the Hôtel de Crillon and Hôtel de la Marine (p86).

6 Printemps

From place de la Madeleine continue north along rue Tronchet to bd Haussmann. You'll know you've arrived when you spot the golden and mosaic *coupoles* (cupolas) of Printemps (p95).

7 Galeries Lafayette

Next door is another department store, Galeries Lafayette (p95). Both *grands magasins* also have grand terraces (p94) where you can take in the view, or wander across the street in search of the finest French foods at the delicious Galeries Lafayette Le Gourmet (p87).

8 Palais Garnier

From here, head down rue Halévy to reach the magnificent Palais Garnier (p90). If you don't mind paying to sit where the likes of Victor Hugo, Ernest Hemingway and Émile Zola sat before you, you can finish with a coffee on the terrace of the historic Café de la Paix.

THE EVOLUTION OF AVENUE DES CHAMPS-ÉLYSÉES

It's hard to imagine now, but the world-famous avenue sits on what was once fields just outside the city limits. It was Louis XIV who decided to develop the area, with the help of his principal gardener André Le Nôtre, who also designed the gardens at Versailles. The avenue was further developed by Haussmann in the 19th century and later when aviation was taking off (literally), it became a popular place to try out the latest technology. Based on this, many car manufacturers opened showrooms in the early 19th century. In the 1930s, it became better known for its movie theatres, giving it the nickname, 'Avenue de Cinéma'. It's now better known as a shopping street but amazingly, around 40 to 80 people still live here, surrounded by around 80 shops and 20 restaurants.

Coupole, Galeries Lafayette

Where Royalists Still Gather
Chapelle Expiatoire in the heart of a hidden square

The neoclassical **Chapelle Expiatoire** was commissioned by Louis XVIII when the monarchy made a brief, post-Revolution reappearance and so, perhaps unsurprisingly, it's dedicated to the memory of the royal family. It sits on the site of the former Madeleine cemetery, the burial place for those executed during the Revolution, including King Louis XVI (Louis XVIII's brother) and Marie Antoinette, before they were moved to the Basilica of St-Denis. For royalists, it's still one of France's major commemorative sites. For everyone else, its setting in place Louis XVI makes a tranquil haven away from the noise of the boulevards and the often-packed *grands magasins*.

Browse Les Grands Magasins
Paris' monuments to commerce

In true Paris style, the city's *grands magasins* ('department stores' in English) are more than simply a shopping destination, they're also historical monuments and architectural feats

BEST ROOFTOP BARS

Le Joy at Le Fouquet's: Paris Le Fouquet's Paris takes its bar Le Joy outside for summer, and sometimes also opens up a rooftop pop-up with a view of the Champs-Élysées. *hours vary*

Le Picnic by Veuve Clicquot at Printemps: The Veuve Clicquot rooftop pop-up comes with an Eiffel Tower view but the department store has various other summer terraces. *hours vary*

Créatures at Galeries Lafayette Haussmann: Anyone can access the terrace for a free view, but if you want to soak it up with a drink in hand, stop by the bar and restaurant Créatures. *hours vary*

The Shed at Grands Boulevards Experimental: This rooftop bar is tucked away from the buzz of the street and serves up drinks from the cocktail connoisseurs. *hours vary*

of their time. The 9th *arrondissement* is home to two of the grandest, the flagships of **Galeries Lafayette** *(haussmann. galerieslafayette.com)* and **Printemps** *(printemps.com)* which sit nearly side by side as neighbours (and competitors) on bd Haussmann. Both specialise in high-end luxury, whether you're looking for womenswear or kitchenware, but with nearly everything for sale under their stained-glass and gilded roofs, there's pretty much something for everyone.

If you're not here to shop, they're worth a visit for the architecture alone. The stained-glass art nouveau *coupole* (cupola) is the most famous sight of the 19th-century Galeries Lafayette Haussmann, and all of Paris visits at Christmas when it crowns the store's annual festive installation.

Printemps has its own *coupoles* to match, four in fact, shimmering with gold and mosaics on the outside and housing cafes and a fantastic vintage section on the inside. If you're interested in its history, Printemps offers tours booked through **Cultival** *(cultival.fr)*, with after-hours tours also available. Galeries Lafayette brings the store to life through guided visits, as well as fashion shows, cooking and pastry classes. As with most shopping expeditions, avoid going on weekends if you want to dodge the crowds. And if you can't decide on something to buy, a drink from one of the panoramic terraces or bars admittedly costs more than what you'd pay on the ground, but is worth the splurge for the view.

Les Passages Couverts

Hunt for secondhand treasures in these 19th-century arcades

Paris' 19th-century *passages couverts* were originally shopping arcades for wealthy Parisians to shield them from the noise, rain and dirt of the city, and are now among the most charming architectural features in Paris, with three located around Grands Boulevards. Built in 1800, **Passage des Panoramas** is the oldest and the liveliest, full of good restaurants and secondhand shops. **Passage Jouffroy** is just opposite on the bd Montmartre and opened in 1847. It's most famous for housing the **Musée Grévin** *(grevin-paris.com; from €14.50)*, a Parisian Madame Tussauds, but there's also a good selection of secondhand shops selling books and vintage posters. A three-minute walk away is **Passage Verdeau**, which dates to the same year as Jouffroy and shares some of the same architectural details – note the large glass roofs. It's definitely the quieter of the three for browsing vintage and antique shops away from the crowds.

WHERE TO SEE FILMS

You'll find some of Paris' most iconic cinemas around the Champs-Élysées and Grand Boulevards:

Publicis Cinémas
The group behind Le Drugstore also owns a cinema next door. Look out for international films, and cult classics screening on Sundays.

Club de L'Étoile
This 1920s one-room cinema, designed in the style of an Italian theatre, is open to the public at weekends.

Elysées Lincoln
Sitting just off the Champs-Élysées, this independent cinema reopened in 2025 after receiving a more modern restoration, while still retaining its art-house programme.

Cinéma Mac-Mahon
Dating back to 1938 this is another historic address for cinephiles with a fantastic programme of classic films and retrospectives.

Le Balzac
This art-house cinema (screenings mainly in French) opened just off the Champs-Elysées in 1935.

 WHERE TO TAKE AFTERNOON TEA

La Galerie at Hôtel Plaza Athénée: World Pastry Champion Angelo Musa puts a contemporary twist on classic French cakes. *2-7pm* €€€

Jardin d'Hiver at Hôtel de Crillon: The gorgeous Jardin d'Hiver is one of the most opulent and historic rooms in Paris for tea and cakes. *3-6pm Fri-Sun* €€€

Café Antonia at Le Bristol: Palace hotel famed for its gastronomy serving tea in the 18th-century-style Café Antonia or in the lush garden in summer. *3.30-6pm* €€€

La Galerie at Four Seasons Hotel George V: La Galerie makes an elegant setting for afternoon tea, surrounded by 19th-century works of art. *3-5pm* €€€

Researched by Fabienne Fong Yan

LOUVRE & LES HALLES

BLENDING HISTORY AND PARISIAN LIFESTYLE

Immerse yourself in the vibrant historical heart of Paris, where the Louvre and Les Halles commercial hub take centre stage.

Stretching over the 1st and 2nd *arrondissements*, this quarter might have the highest concentration of historical landmarks and architectural wonders in the city. Once the residence of kings, with the most visited museum in the world at its heart, it perfectly embodies Paris' urban evolution through the ages. While Baron Haussmann's urban planning largely defines its present-day layout – with vast squares and high-end venues – the district's essence is also found in its narrow cobblestone streets and well-preserved 19th-century covered passages, offering glimpses into the past. Near former palaces, Les Halles and its surroundings – once described as 'the belly of Paris' by French writer Émile Zola – remain a vibrant hub of movement and commerce, stretching all the way up to Sentier.

INCLUDES

LOUVRE & PALAIS ROYAL
p98

MONTORGUEIL, LES HALLES & SENTIER
p116

Musée du Louvre (p100)

See p308 for places to stay in Louvre and Les Halles.

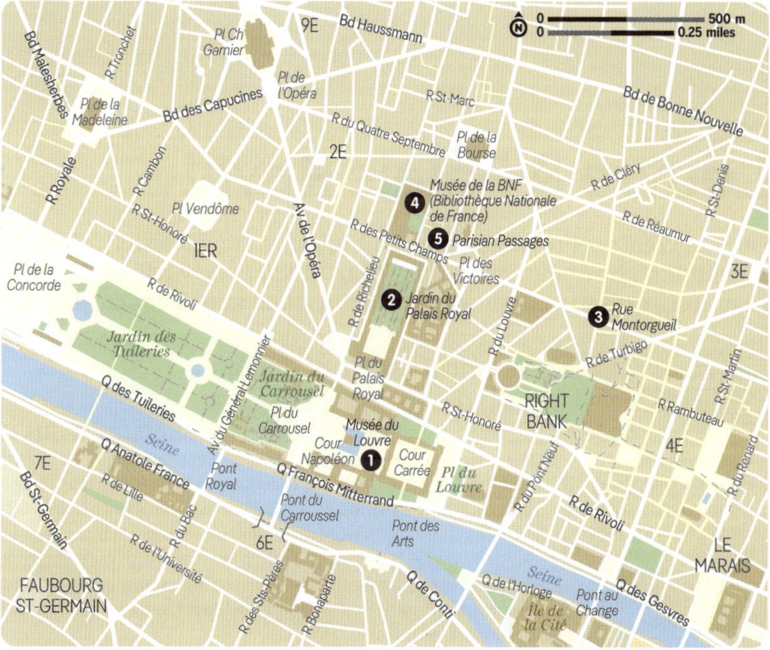

Highlights

❶ Musée du Louvre
Explore the countless masterpieces housed within one of the world's largest museums. **p100**

❷ Jardin du Palais Royal
Wander beneath the arcades of this former royal palace, now an open-air museum. **p98**

❸ Rue Montorgueil
Discover the vibrant market scene, where cafes and restaurants create a lively atmosphere. **p116**

❹ Musée de la BNF
Go through centuries of archives and books, preserved for the sole purpose of advancing human knowledge. **p111**

❺ Parisian Passages
Stroll beneath the sheltered 19th-century galleries, each with their own atmosphere. **p112**

Getting Around

Walking
The area doesn't cover much ground but offers many cultural attractions, activities, and food venues. Therefore, it is easiest and best explored on foot to navigate all the landmarks.

Underground
It is easily accessible by metro, with Châtelet as Paris' most central hub for metro and suburban train lines. Other convenient stations include Palais Royal – Musée du Louvre (Line 7) and Sentier (Line 3).

Cycling
Cycling is becoming increasingly convenient in the area, as car traffic is becoming more restricted and cycle lanes are being better implemented. Rental bike stations are common.

Louvre & Palais Royal

Once the centre of royal power and a beacon of French history, the area around the Musée du Louvre and Palais Royal is now one of the most beautiful, ready to impress with its architectural grandeur and glamour.

THE PALAIS ROYAL CONTEMPORARY ART

'Les Confidents', Michel Goulet Usually found around the central fountain, these green metal chairs celebrate moments of daydreaming in Paris' public gardens.

'Les Deux Plateaux', Daniel Buren Widely known as Buren's columns, this zebra-striped installation enhances the building's former car park.

'Fontaine des Spheres', Pol Bury Made of giant silver spheres, this fountain is a children's favourite.

'Poetry-benches' Eighteen benches engraved with quotes by writers such as Colette and Cocteau.

Historical Cradle of Culture

Stroll in the Palais Royal

A serene haven adored by locals, the **Jardin du Palais Royal** *(domaine-palais-royal.fr)* is tucked between the Louvre and the bustling av de l'Opéra. It is one of those historical places in Paris where tourists and Parisians seamlessly merge, both enjoying the magnificence of centuries-old architecture in their own way. It is true that there's something mesmerising about strolling beneath its impeccably trimmed trees and long arcaded galleries – their depth and symmetry creating an illusion of infinity.

Built in 1624 by Cardinal de Richelieu, King Louis XIII's Prime Minister, Palais Royal has long been at the heart of Paris' political and cultural life. However, its characteristic galleries date back to the late 18th century, initiated by Louis-Philippe d'Orléans. By then, they had become home to shops, cabarets and residences.

Some landmarks have endured the test of time. Beneath the Galerie de Beaujolais for instance, a 200-year-old iconic restaurant still stands: it is said that Napoléon Bonaparte and his wife Joséphine used to lunch at Le Grand Véfour, as did artists such as Victor Hugo.

The building also houses the Conseil Constitutionnel and part of the Ministry of Culture's offices, but it is best known as the home of the Comédie-Française, France's National Theatre (entrance located on Pl Colette), and most notably, for the contemporary artworks displayed in the southern part of the garden – like an open-air museum.

EATING NEAR PALAIS ROYAL: OUR PICKS — MAPS P99, P118

Daroco: Pair a Neopolitan pizza with a glass of wine under the mirror ceiling of this chic Italian restaurant, in the romantic covered passage Galerie Vivienne. *noon-3pm & 7-11.30pm Tue-Sat, to 11pm Sun-Mon* €€

Jantchi: Whether you're into bulgogi, kimchi soup, or traditional *yukkaejang* (vermicelli soup), you will find your favourite dish at this Korean restaurant housed in an old building. *hours vary* €€

Eats Thyme: A Lebanese restaurant with vegan, vegetarian and meat options, with plenty of side choices. Don't miss the manoush flatbread. *11am-10.30pm Mon-Sat, to 4.30pm Sun* €€

Comme un bouillon: A small spot serving French popular classics, including the *steak-frites* and *oeufs-mayonnaise*, hidden in a street near the Palais Garnier. *11.45am-10pm Mon-Fri, noon-10pm Sat* €

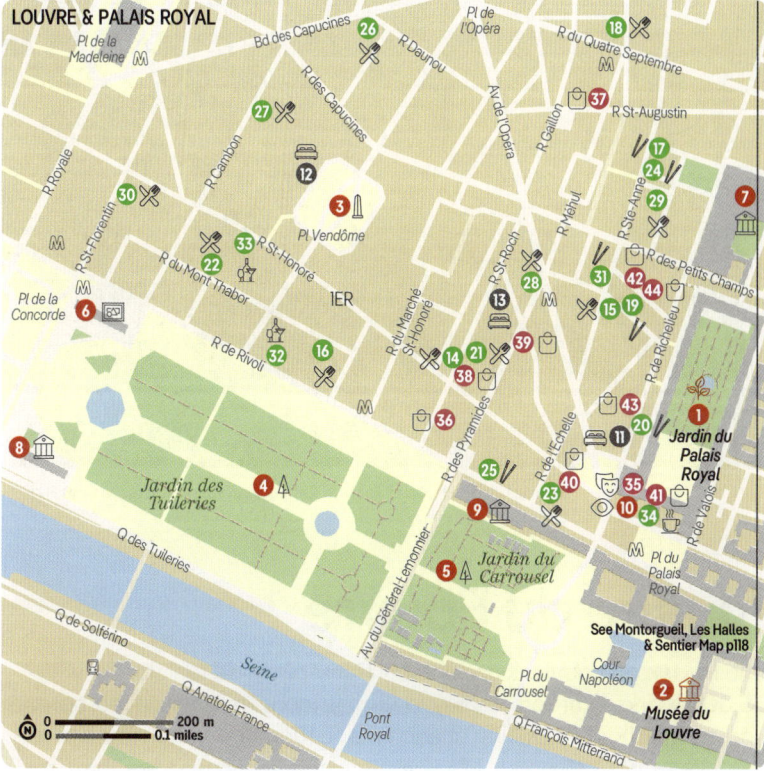

LOUVRE & PALAIS ROYAL

★ HIGHLIGHTS
1 Jardin du Palais Royal
2 Musée du Louvre

● SIGHTS
3 Colonne Vendôme
4 Jardin des Tuileries
5 Jardin du Carrousel
6 Jeu de Paume
7 Musée de la BNF (Bibliothèque Nationale de France)
8 Musée de l'Orangerie
9 Musée des Arts Décoratifs
10 Place Colette

● SLEEPING
11 Drawing Hotel
12 Hôtel Ritz Paris
13 Le Roch Hotel & Spa

● EATING
14 19 Saint Roch
15 Aki Boulangerie
16 Au Petit Bar
17 Chez Miki
18 Comme un bouillon
19 Jantchi
20 Kodawari Ramen Tsukiji
21 La Cordonnerie – Chez Yvette & Claude
22 Le Soufflé
23 Matin des Oliviers
24 Michi
25 Nodaïwa
26 Public House
27 Ritz Paris Le Comptoir
28 Takumi Patisserie
29 Tomo
30 Toraya
31 Udon Jubey

● DRINKING & NIGHTLIFE
32 Bar 228
33 Bar 8
see 12 Bar Hemingway
34 Le Nemours

● ENTERTAINMENT
35 Comédie Française

● SHOPPING
36 Au Nain Bleu
37 Book Off
38 Brigitte Tanaka
39 Junku
40 Kure Bazaar
41 Les Drapeaux de France – Noxa
42 Maison Wa
43 Merci #2
44 Nishikidori – Le Comptoir des Poivres

Above: lion frieze, Near Eastern Antiquities collection; right: Cour Marly

TOP EXPERIENCE

Musée du Louvre

The Musée du Louvre is undeniably Paris' pièce de résistance, with 35,000 works of art on display, including iconic masterpieces, spread across four floors. Looking at each piece for one minute would take 24 days without sleeping. Plan carefully to fully experience the world's largest art museum.

DON'T MISS

Mona Lisa

Winged Victory of Samothrace

Venus de Milo

Ballroom's Cariatides

Salon Carré

Sphinx' Crypt

Cour Khorsabad

Great Pyramid

First Time at the Louvre?

Entering the museum for the first time can be intimidating. The key to approaching the vast collections of the Louvre is to consider them from two significant perspectives: Western art spanning from the Middle Ages to the mid-19th century, and the art and crafts of five ancient civilisations that preceded and influenced it. Simultaneously, immerse yourself in the museum's captivating architecture shaped by multiple sovereigns. To navigate the museum, just remember that there are three wings: Sully (East) and the parallel Richelieu (North) and Denon (South).

The Louvre can be both awe-inspiring and overwhelming. Maybe the best way to visit it is to allow yourself to choose, explore and be pleasantly surprised. Don't worry about seeing every masterpiece – enjoy the journey itself.

PRACTICALITIES

● louvre.fr/en ● 9am-6pm, to 9pm Wed & Fri, closed Tue ● €22

Guided by Ancient Civilisations

The antiquities department showcases pieces dating from the Neolithic period to the decline of the Roman Empire.

Exploring chronologically, the treasures of ancient civilisations will primarily lead you through the ground floor, with additional areas dedicated to Egyptian antiquities on Level 1. Begin your journey in the Richelieu Wing, exploring Mesopotamian art (from what is considered the earliest human civilisation). Continue to the Sully Wing to descend into the Sphinx' Crypt and uncover Egyptian art. Proceed to the Denon Wing to see Greek, Etruscan and Roman art.

Gardens of Sculptures

Sculpture enthusiasts should not miss the **Cour Marly** and **Cour Puget**, on Level -1 of the Richelieu Wing. These indoor courtyards bathed in natural light house French masterpieces created under Louis XIV. The Cour Marly provides an atmospheric setting reminiscent of its original location in one of the king's residences. Interestingly, in an arrangement that may seem counterintuitive, ascending to the upper level will transport you back in time to medieval French sculpture. Moving through the Richelieu Wing on the ground floor, you'll then encounter more sculptures from the 17th to the 19th centuries.

A European Tour of Masterpieces

The top floors showcase European paintings and decorative arts from the Middle Ages to the mid-19th century. Many visitors explore these floors towards the end of their visit, following the sequential order of the rooms. If you're a painting enthusiast, it's advisable to prioritise them. They are must-visit areas for iconic artworks like the *Mona Lisa,* as well as monumental

TOP TIPS

● Make sure you book your ticket online in advance, as you won't need to queue at the museum desk and there may be discounts available.

● The website (louvre.fr/en) is a valuable resource for finding inspiration and planning your visit, with thematic itinerary ideas and room closure information.

● Arriving early will give you the opportunity to explore the galleries with fewer crowds.

● Remember to wear comfortable shoes, as the museum comprises 403 halls and nearly 15km of corridors.

● If you're visiting with children, you can take a break at the Studio (Richelieu Wing, Level -1), which provides creative materials for them to enjoy.

FROM FORTRESS TO MUSEUM

Initially built as a stronghold by King Philippe-Auguste in the 12th century, the Louvre remained mostly untouched for three centuries. But from 1546 onwards, no less than 20 phases of destruction, reconstruction and enhancements took place. The Louvre became a museum after the French Revolution, and the Cour Carrée was added. IM Pei's Great Pyramid was erected in 1989. More changes are expected by 2030 to welcome the annual 8 million visitors.

paintings such as *The Wedding Feast at Cana* and *The Raft of the Medusa*. In addition, don't miss the impressive **Great Gallery**, the historic **Salon Carré** (the precursor to exhibition salons) and the opulent **Galerie d'Apollon**, adorned with stunning murals and golden embellishments, and home to the French royal jewels.

Around the Louvre, Around the World

Like no ordinary museum, the Louvre takes you on a journey to different eras and continents. Don't miss the **Napoleon III Apartments**, almost untouched for nearly 150 years, at the end of the Richelieu Wing on Level 1. For a broader cultural experience, explore the small section dedicated to American, African, Asian and Oceanic arts, situated in a remote part of the Denon Wing (access through Level 1).

Louvre Itineraries

There are different ways to experience the museum, whether you have particular artworks in mind or prefer to wander freely. Here are some itinerary ideas to make the most of your time.

A Couple of Hours for the Essentials

If you're short on time, you can approach the Louvre by focusing on some iconic pieces. Start with a face-to-face with the **Great Sphinx of Tanis**, and explore the **Egyptian Antiquities** in the Sully Wing. On Level 1, view the **Seated Scribe** (Room 635), then proceed to the lavishly decorated **Rooms 600-622**, showcasing the 18th-century royal court lifestyle. Head to the ground level using the central staircase and head directly to Room 345 to admire the **Venus de Milo**. From here,

Great Gallery

make your way up again via the magnificent staircase, where the **Winged Victory of Samothrace** awaits you.

Once on Level 1 again, continue your journey through the Denon Wing. Take a glance at the golden **Galerie d'Apollon** (Room 705) before immersing yourself in the painting galleries. Start with the **Salon Carré** (Room 708), which leads to the impressive **Great Gallery**, featuring masterpieces by renowned Italian artists, including Leonardo da Vinci's **Mona Lisa** (Room 711), at least until it is moved to a dedicated room, as part of the museum renovation plans.

If you have extra time, visit the **Cour Marly** and **Cour Puget** in the Richelieu Wing to bask in the light through the glass roof and marvel at their imposing sculptures, including the Marly horses.

Half a Day at the Louvre

With additional time, you can further explore the magnificent Renaissance sections of the Sully and Denon wings: discover the **Greek and Roman Antiquities** displayed across the Ballroom and the Salle du Manège. These rooms showcase the imported style from Italy, with notable features like the gate supported by the Cariatides, originally designed for hosting musicians. Molière himself performed in front of King Louis XIV in this very space.

Ascend the grand Mollien staircase to Level 1, where you'll find the Red Galleries, housing masterpieces by French artists including Delacroix' **Liberty Leading the People** (Room 700). For a refreshing break, head to **Café Mollien**, offering a splendid view of the Carrousel du Louvre from its terrace.

To end your visit with a spectacular experience, head to **Cour Khorsabad** (Room 229 in the Richelieu Wing) and admire the monumental vestiges of the Assyrian city and palace of King Sargon II at Dur-Sharrukin (now Khorsabad).

The Full Louvre

Are you up for a more extensive exploration? If you came in from the Carrousel's entrance, you might have seen some of the medieval remains, dating to 1190 when King Philippe-Auguste decided to build the Louvre fortress around Paris. Descend beneath the Cour Carrée to witness the surviving elements of the **original moats and drawbridge**.

Then, make a jump in time and walk up to the impressive **Napoleon III Apartments** in the Richelieu Wing (Rooms 535-49) for a taste of lavish Second Empire style. Visit the **Café Richelieu** if you need a break. It is run by the Angelina team: you can sample its famous hot chocolate.

Last but not least, art enthusiasts shouldn't miss the top floor of the Sully Wing, which showcases two centuries of **European and French masterpieces**. If you're more into **decorative arts**, you will prefer to spend time wandering the Richelieu Wing galleries on Level 1.

Alternatively, discover a small collection of **artworks from Asia**, **Africa**, **Oceania** and **the Americas** in a more intimate section (Pavillon des Sessions, Rooms 424–33). Note that these regions are better represented in other dedicated museums in Paris, like the Musée du Quai Branly – Jacques Chirac (p79).

ANTIQUE MYSTERY

The oldest displayed piece is the statue of Aïn Ghazal (Room 303 – Sully Wing), unearthed in the 1980s in Jordan. Its subject is still a mystery: was it a man, a child or a god?

In comparison, the *Winged Victory of Samothrace* and the *Venus de Milo* date to the 3rd and 1st century BCE, which means more than 8000 years separate them from the enigmatic statue.

LAVISH LOUVRE: A PEEK AT GALERIE D'APOLLON

If you think you've seen it elsewhere, it's because it served as a model for the Hall of Mirrors in Versailles. Louis XIV, the 'Roi-Soleil' had this gallery made by the greatest painters, gilders and sculptors. It is filled with references to everything influenced by the sun: time, seasons, zodiac signs, continents. The ceiling shows Apollo driving his chariot from dawn to night.

The Louvre

Three-day exploration

Successfully visiting the Louvre is a fine art. Its complex labyrinth of galleries and staircases spiralling across three wings and four floors renders discovery a snakes-and-ladders experience. Initiate yourself with this three-hour itinerary – a playful mix of Mona Lisa–obvious and up-to-the-minute unexpected.

Arriving in the **1 Cour Napoléon** beneath IM Pei's glass pyramid, pick up colour-coded floor plans at an information stand, then ride the escalator up to the Sully Wing and swap passport or credit card for a multimedia guide (there are limited descriptions in the galleries) at the wing entrance.

The Louvre is as much about spectacular architecture as masterful art. To appreciate this, zip up and down Sully's Escalier Henri II to admire **2 Venus de Milo**, then up parallel Escalier Henri IV to the palatial displays in **3 Cour Khorsabad**. Follow signs for the escalator up to the 1st floor and the opulent **4 Napoléon III apartments**. Next traverse 25 consecutive galleries (thank you, floor plan!) to flip conventional contemplation on its head with Cy Twombly's **5 The Ceiling**, and the hypnotic **6 Winged Victory of Samothrace**, which brazenly insists on being admired from all angles. End with the impossibly famous **7 Raft of the Medusa**, **8 Mona Lisa** and **9 Virgin & Child**.

LOUVRE EVENTS & ACTIVITIES

Concerts, dance shows, talks and conferences are regularly scheduled at the Louvre Auditorium or sometimes even in the museum galleries. Check the online quarterly program.

TOP TIPS

➡ Floor plans for navigating the Louvre's maze of galleries are free from the information desks in the Hall Napoléon.

➡ Visit on late nights (Wednesday or Friday) for a less packed museum. Late night entry on the 1st Friday of the month is free of charge.

4 Napoléon III Apartments
Rooms 544 & 547, 1st Floor, Richelieu
Napoléon III's gorgeous gilt apartments were built from 1854 to 1861, featuring an over-the-top decor of gold leaf, stucco and crystal chandeliers that reaches a dizzying climax in the Grand Salon and State Dining Room.

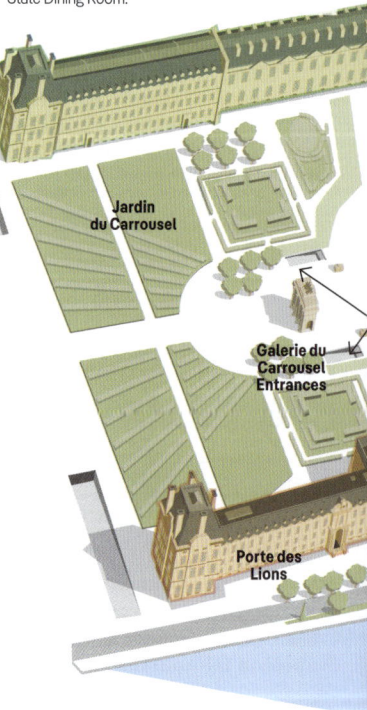

8 Mona Lisa
Room 711, 1st Floor, Denon
No smile is as enigmatic or bewitching as hers. Da Vinci's diminutive *La Joconde* hangs opposite the largest painting in the Louvre – sumptuous, fellow Italian Renaissance artwork *The Wedding at Cana*.

❼ The Raft of the Medusa
Room 700, 1st Floor, Denon

Decipher the politics behind French romanticism in Théodore Géricault's *Raft of the Medusa*.

❸ Cour Khorsabad
Ground Floor, Richelieu

Time travel with a pair of winged human-headed bulls to view some of the world's oldest Mesopotamian art. **Detour»** Night-lit statues in Cour Puget.

❺ The Ceiling
Room 663, Sully

Admire the blue shock of Cy Twombly's 400-sq-metre contemporary ceiling fresco. **Detour»** The Braque Ceiling, Room 662.

❾ Virgin & Child
Grande Galerie, 1st Floor, Denon

In the spirit of artistic devotion save the Louvre's most famous gallery for last: a feast of Virgin-and-child paintings by Da Vinci, Raphael, Domenico Ghirlandaio, Giovanni Bellini and Francesco Botticini.

❷ Venus de Milo
Room 346, Ground Floor, Sully

No one knows who sculpted this seductively realistic goddess from Greek antiquity. Naked to the hips, she is a Hellenistic masterpiece.

❻ Winged Victory of Samothrace
Room 703, 1st Floor, Denon

Draw breath at the aggressive dynamism of this headless, handless Hellenistic goddess. **Detour»** The razzle-dazzle of the Apollo Gallery's crown jewels.

WALKING TOUR

The Louvre Inside Out

The experience of the Louvre isn't complete without an outdoor exploration. Landmark after landmark, history unfolds as you walk from the mesmerising Cour Carrée to the Jardin des Tuileries. Beyond the iconic Great Pyramid, you discover a magnificent perspective of Paris, beginning with the smaller Arc de Triomphe. It continues with the Grand Obélisque, the Champs-Élysées and the bigger Arc de Triomphe. These monuments guide the eye towards the towering Grande Arche de La Défense.

1 Cour Carrée
You're standing on the hidden medieval remains of the original Louvre, which once occupied only the current courtyard's southwest corner. Over 250 years, this square courtyard underwent multiple construction phases. If you observe the buildings closely, you'll notice the engraved monograms of the various kings and rulers who successively commissioned parts of the palace.

2 Pavillon de l'Horloge
As you move to the Clock Pavilion, which separates the Cour Carrée from the grand Cour Napoléon, you'll be amazed by the exceptional acoustics under the arches, often attracting talented street musicians, especially cellists. Notable characteristics here include a prominent clock, the imposing Cariatides supporting its frontispiece, and a domed roof that served as a model for all other domes in the Louvre. Inside, this section of the museum's exhibition focuses on the history of the building.

3 Great Pyramid
The main entrance to the museum (until 2030) was designed by Chinese American architect IM Pei. Despite initial controversy

Louis XIV Statue

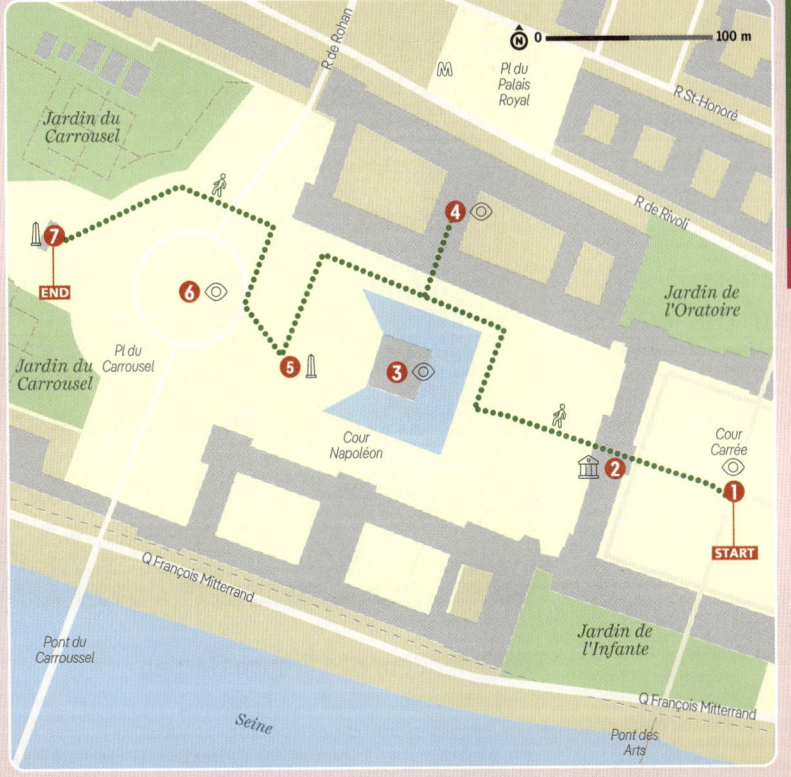

over its contrasting appearance, it has become an integral part of Paris' landscape and the museum's third-most visited artwork after the *Mona Lisa* and *Venus de Milo*. Standing at 21m high, it's made of 675 glass lozenges and 118 triangles. Esoteric rumours have suggested the presence of 666 triangles since Dan Brown's bestselling novel *The Da Vinci Code*.

4 Passage Richelieu

The Richelieu Wing houses three stunning courtyards covered by glass roofs: Cour Marly, Puget and Khorsabad. These are impressive sources of natural light. As you cross towards the Palais Royal through the central passage, you can catch a glimpse of these indoor sculpture gardens.

5 Louis XIV Statue

Peculiarly positioned in a non-central location within the Cour Napoléon, this statue was intentionally placed here by architect IM Pei, in order to accommodate the non-alignment of the Great Pyramid with the rest of the 'Great Axis of Paris' envisioned by Baron Haussman.

6 Inverted Pyramid of the Carrousel

An architectural tour de force, the inverted pyramid is visible from underground as you pass through the Carrousel du Louvre shopping mall. From the surface, its base is concealed by the vegetation of the central roundabout.

7 Arc de Triomphe du Carrousel

This smaller version of the famous Arc de Triomphe represents Napoléon's victories. Look down and you'll discover that it's also the central point of a giant sundial, formed by lines of paving stones on the ground. Walk beyond here into the Jardin des Tuileries to catch a glimpse of the Great Axis. Once in the garden, check out André Maillol's bronze statues, which seem to play hide-and-seek amid the meticulously trimmed bushes.

PERFECT BACKDROP FOR THE PARIS 2024 CAULDRON

For two months in 2024, the rise of the Olympic's flying cauldron was a spectacular sight in Paris' sky. Watching the hot-air balloon cradling the Olympic Flame soar every evening had become a ritual, and looking for the best viewing spots, a real sport! We admired not only the cauldron's original design, but also the perfect illusion of fire created by electricity and vapour, 'burning' against the sunset.

Seeing the cauldron go at the end of the summer was heart-wrenching for many…so much so that the city of Paris announced that it would be back every summer until the opening of the 2028 Los Angeles Games. Two recommended viewing spots: the **Jardin du Carrousel** and rue du 29 Juillet, on the Tuileries' northern side.

The Splendour of a French Garden
Wander through Jardin des Tuileries

It's the sense of infinite perspective that first meets the eye when walking into the **Jardin des Tuileries**. It owes its design to royal gardener André Le Nôtre, hence some resemblance to Versailles. Structured like a traditional French garden, the first part formed by flowerbeds is best enjoyed from the windows of the Louvre. In the middle, lines of perfectly trimmed trees offer some shade to joggers. Contemporary and classical sculptures play hide-and-seek in the garden's alleyways, surprising strollers at times. The two long, stonewashed 19th-century buildings spotted at the Concorde end now host renowned museums: Musée de l'Orangerie and the Jeu de Paume gallery.

During summer and winter holidays, the garden hosts one of the most popular Parisian fairs, with dozens of rides and food stalls. A 70m-high big wheel offers a chance for a bird's-eye view of Paris on clear days.

EATING NEAR THE LOUVRE: OUR PICKS

MAPS P99, P118

Nodaïwa: An elegant Japanese restaurant specialising in traditional grilled eel (unagi) served in various refined – and surprising – ways. *noon-2.30pm & 7-10pm Wed-Sat* €€€

Matin des Oliviers: A great pick for a tasty Mediterranean brunch or snack break. Choose from Turkish eggs to revisited avocado toast. *9am-6pm Mon-Thu, to 8pm Fri, 8am-8pm Sat-Sun* €€

Public House: British food comes to Paris: have a Scotch egg and meat pie, or good fish and chips in an elegant pub atmosphere. Pair with wine, beer or cocktails. *8am-2am* €€

Boutique yam'Tcha: Take a regenerating break at this Hong Kongese tearoom offering soft bao buns with original fillings – stilton and cherry jelly anyone? *hours vary* €€

Jardin des Tuileries

Beyond the Louvre
A visual-art museum trip

Modern- and contemporary-art enthusiasts should not miss **Musée de l'Orangerie** (*musee-orangerie.fr; adult/child €12.50/8.50*) and the **Jeu de Paume** (*jeudepaume.org; adult/child €12/free*), both in the Jardin des Tuileries, as well as **Musée des Arts Décoratifs** (*madparis.fr; adult/under 26 years €15/free*) in the Louvre's northern wing. They offer complementary approaches, allowing art-lovers to dig deeper into specific periods or media, perhaps in a slightly less overwhelming atmosphere than at the Louvre.

For those interested in Impressionism, the Musée de l'Orangerie provides an absolutely unique immersive experience into Monet's water lilies, the culmination of the painter's life work. Housed in specially designed oval rooms, the immense

BEST CONCEPT STORES FOR SOUVENIRS

Brigitte Tanaka: One French and one Japanese designer teamed up to create a tiny shop where you will find only delicately embroidered organza bags, all inspired by Paris.

Au Nain Bleu: A traditional toy shop with a beautiful selection of quality plush toys, including several made-in-France teddy bears.

Kure Bazaar: Following a French manicure at its relaxing beauty salon facing av de l'Opéra, don't leave without your selection of nail polish in a Paris-themed box.

Merci #2: Paris-themed books, fruit-shaped candles, designer accessories and homewares you didn't know you needed – this Parisian concept brand has it all.

Junku: It's a little bit more than a mere Japanese bookstore. People interested in this culture will love shopping for stationery, a few tableware items, small toys and accessories.

 EATING NEAR THE LOUVRE: FRENCH MEALS — MAP P99

Au Petit Bar: This quaint tiny bar still serving traditional Parisian ham-and-butter baguette sandwiches is a surprisingly rare, very affordable find in this high-end area. *7am-9.30pm Mon-Sat* €

19 Saint Roch: Near the Tuileries, this creative restaurant offers refined French dishes with seasonal products, designed by a chef who's worked in high-level kitchens. *12.15-2pm & 7-11pm Tue-Fri* €€€

Le Soufflé: Difficult to make it may be, but traditional soufflé cake has been this house's successful speciality for years. Sweet or savoury, enjoy it in a convivial setting. *noon-4pm & 7-10pm Tue-Sat* €€

La Cordonnerie – Chez Yvette & Claude: Enjoy French home-style dishes such as pepper steak, andouille and creamy scallops in this discreet, somewhat old-style establishment. *noon-2pm & 7.30-10pm Mon-Fri* €€

Musée de la BNF (Bibliothèque Nationale de France)

PLACE VENDÔME: HIGH FASHION IN THE CITY

At the centre of place Vendôme, the 44m-high **Colonne Vendôme** – a Napoléonic commemorative monument – resembles a gem in a jewel case. One of the five royal *places* in Paris, place Vendôme is famous for its classical architecture and exquisite jewellery store windows – it is home to high-end jewellery houses like Cartier, Van Cleef & Arpels, Boucheron and Chaumet. The *place* has long been associated with elegance and fashion. The stopper of the Chanel N°5 perfume bottle, for instance, is inspired by the square's distinctive octagonal shape. It pays tribute to Coco Chanel, who resided here for decades. During Paris Fashion Weeks (twice a year), Pl Vendôme becomes a show of fashionistas and celebrities invited to the *haute couture* catwalks, echoing its fashionable past.

canvases completely draw the viewer in. Arriving early usually allows for a more tranquil viewing.

The Tuileries' other museum, Jeu de Paume, stands in contrast with its Impressionist counterpart: it primarily focuses on contemporary photography and the exploration of new media. To complete this innovative approach, some projects are only featured on a dedicated digital platform, so don't hesitate to check its website prior to your visit.

Last but not least, the Musée des Arts Décoratifs provides a rich testament to the French *art de vivre* (art of living) and history of decorative arts. Its extensive collection pays tribute to artists and craftspeople who have brought beauty and functionality into our daily lives, through the art of furniture making, glassware, ceramics, jewellery, fashion, graphic design and even advertising. Don't miss the museum shop, in which design lovers will revel.

Teatime at a Palace Hotel

Ritz Hotel indulgence

With rich wood panelling and delicate seasonal flowers on each table, the Proust Salon at the **Hôtel Ritz Paris** *(ritzparis.com)* provides an opulent setting to a classic French teatime, curated by renowned pastry chef François Perret. Madeleines, small cakes and traditional biscuits, the selection is meant to evoke memories of a French childhood. You can pair this with a delicate cup of tea or even Champagne.

For a less luxurious alternative, book a slot at Bar Vendôme. Beneath the glass roof, particularly pleasant on sunny days, you can order Perret's pastries *à la carte,* from his delicate vanilla mille-feuilles to the pear-almond *entremet.* Don't leave the hotel without gazing at its luxury shop gallery, designed in the spirit of a Parisian covered passage.

Royal Swing
Take a few dance steps at Palais Royal

What better backdrop than Palais Royal to put on a dancing show? On **Place Colette**, it is not rare to hear live music or bump into local performers, who like taking advantage of the convenient location. But the place truly comes alive at weekends, when dozens of regulars gather to show off their swing and rock 'n' roll dance steps. **Le Nemours** *(lenemours.paris)*, a traditional high-end cafe-restaurant, is the ideal viewpoint for dance-watchers. But if you're a dancer yourself – amateur or professional – don't hesitate to join the swinging crowd, who will warmly welcome your moves.

More Than a Historical Reading Room
Inside the national library's collections

Initiated by Cardinal de Richelieu, the **Musée de la BNF (Bibliothèque Nationale de France)** *(bnf.fr/en/the-bnf-museum; €24)* is also the house of the Dépôt Légal (legal depot), where any published work in France is registered. Therefore, a staggering 40 million documents are preserved here and across a few other Parisian sites. We are not only talking about books: they include all sorts of objects, manuscripts, photographs and even costumes: each catalogued piece must serve a purpose in advancing human knowledge.

To make this extensive archive more accessible, the Richelieu site was ingeniously transformed into a rotating museum. In Galerie Mazarin, a remarkable corridor boasting a 280-sq-metre Italian-style painted ceiling, 900 objects from antiquity to modern times, including rare manuscripts and maps, and religious artefacts are exhibited and changed every four months. It's like a constantly changing mini-Louvre!

Continues on p114

WHY I LOVE THE LOUVRE & PALAIS ROYAL AREA

Fabienne Fong Yan, Lonely Planet writer

After moving to Paris as a young adult, I immediately developed the habit of strolling in the centre of the city, from Palais Royal to the Tuileries, to take in all the beauty of this quarter. I started to notice little details: sculptures in gardens, engravings on frontispieces, hidden fountains...they sparked my curiosity and led me to uncover the various layers of Paris' history. But what charms me the most, even today, is how as Parisians, we seamlessly integrate all this beauty and art into our daily lives: I worked in a heritage-listed edifice, and ate countless takeaways from the Japanese quarter seated on one of the Palais Royal benches, and never once got tired of it at all.

🍸 DRINKING NEAR THE LOUVRE-PALAIS ROYAL: HOTEL BARS — MAPS P99, P118

Bar Hemingway: American writer Ernest Hemingway frequented this bar during his time in Paris. It's renowned for its vintage decor reflecting the style of the 1920s and 1930s. *5pm-midnight*

Bar 228: In the prestigious Le Meurice hotel, this Philippe Starck–designed bar is primarily known for its extensive selection of premium spirits, wines and skilfully prepared cocktails. *noon-1am*

Bar 8: Offering a sophisticated atmosphere at the Mandarin Oriental, where guests can enjoy original cocktails crafted at the central oval marble bar. *noon-midnight, to 1am Thu-Sat*

ROOF: The best thing about the Madame Rêve hotel bar, besides its large outdoor terrace, is, of course, its wonderful panoramic view over Paris, best enjoyed on summer days. *4pm-1am*

WALKING TOUR

A Sheltered Walk Back in Time

The area's covered galleries were inspired by the success of those at the Palais Royal, where shops, cabarets, and other businesses thrived in the late 18th century. Landlords soon started constructing their own covered passages. They quickly gained popularity, as they offered the revolutionary experience of shopping indoors, sheltered and in a comfortable environment.

1 Galerie Beaujolais & Passage du Perron

The northern gallery of the Palais Royal, housing a few luxury shops, is connected to Passage du Perron, which used to be a meeting place for speculators due to its proximity to the stock exchange.

The Walk: Exit north and look for stairs on your right.

2 Passage des Deux Pavillons

Check out Olympia Le Tan's shop, famous for her original 'book clutch' concept. Exiting the passage, you'll be right across from Galerie Vivienne. Its owner bought and rebuilt Passage des Deux Pavillons, directing people from Palais Royal into his gallery, much to the annoyance of his rival, the owner of Galerie Colbert next door.

The Walk: Don't be tricked by this rivalry. Walk a few steps left and enter Galerie Colbert.

3 Galerie Colbert

At the heart of Galerie Colbert's rotunda stands a statue depicting the nymph Eurydice being bitten by a snake. You can stop and have lunch at Le Grand Colbert and admire its art nouveau decor.

The Walk: Head left onto rue des Petits Champs, then right towards the entrance of passage Choiseul.

Passage des Panoramas

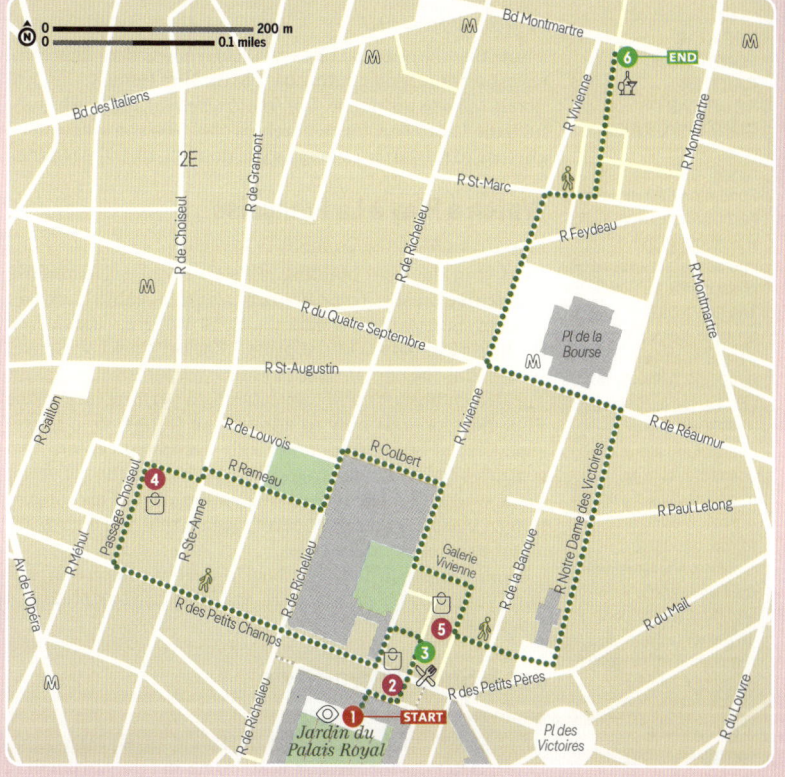

4 Passage Choiseul

Restored in 2007, this passage is one of the longest in Paris and used to have strong associations with literature and theatre. This heritage is still evident at Lavrut, a magnificent stationery store. Old upscale shops coexist with newer cafes and concept stores.

The Walk: Exit at the north end of passage Choiseul. Enjoy square Louvois and its ornamental fountain as you head to 6 rue Vivienne.

5 Galerie Vivienne

One of the most stunning covered galleries in the area, Galerie Vivienne transports you to another world. It's bathed in light and adorned with a mosaic floor, beautifully decorated shopfronts and illuminated windows. Treat yourself to coffee and cake at Le Valentin Vivienne, appreciate the fine fabrics at Wolff and Descourtis, discover vintage postcards at Librairie Jousseaume and find a gift at the pretty Si tu Veux toy store.

The Walk: Leave through the rue de la Banque exit and walk up north towards Palais Brongniart. Make a detour to the charming place des Petits-Pères before continuing to rue St-Marc.

6 Passage des Panoramas

Opposite 7 rue St-Marc, this passage is interconnected with other galleries. Despite being a bit darker, it has its own picturesque charm, filled with vintage shop signs hanging overhead. If you're in a hurry, visit Culottées cafe near the entrance for a quick takeaway. With more time, sit down at Caffè Stern, housed in the former workshop of renowned engraver Stern.

You can finish here or continue the tour further north through Passage Jouffroy and Passage Verdeau.

> **THE NEW FONDATION CARTIER POUR L'ART CONTEMPORAIN**
>
> At the time of research, Fondation Cartier pour l'Art Contemporain was about to move into new premises on place du Palais Royal. The new location is rather iconic: a Haussmannian landmark, formerly the Louvre des Antiquaires – a 1970s antique department store. Jean Nouvel, who had already designed the much-admired former (modern) building, has remained the Fondation's architect and worked on the long-awaited renovation of the new building's interior.
>
> The contemporary art exhibitions commissioned by the Fondation will take place on three levels, some parts being designed as mobile platforms to be able to modify the exhibition spaces at will. This new addition reinforces the artistic footprint in the area, already hosting the most famous Parisian museums and galleries.

Continued from p111

Note that the National Library is also renowned for its breathtaking reading rooms dating back to the 19th century: the Oval Room, open to the public *(bnf.fr/en/richelieu)*, and the beautiful Salle Labrouste, for researchers only. You can still catch a glimpse of the latter as long as you don't disturb the readers.

Watch a Play à La Française
Theatre night at the Comédie Française

Housed in the front building of Palais Royal, the **Comédie Française** theatre *(comedie-francaise.fr)* usually showcases plays by classical playwrights, such as Molière – considered the historical patron of the place – Racine, Chekhov, Shakespeare. It is the only theatre in France with its own company. Theatre enthusiasts will love catching a performance in the Richelieu room, if only to admire the Italian-style horseshoe-shaped auditorium and richly decorated ceiling. Two centuries ago, Parisians would have sat here in the red velvet seats, waiting for the three blows on the stage. This convention in classical French theatre signals that the actors are about to enter the stage.

If you simply wish to visit, book a weekly guided tour, but don't forget to check if they're available in your preferred language.

Eat & Shop Tokyo-Style
Explore Paris' Japanese quarter

Just a stone's throw away from the Palais Royal, Paris' Japanese quarter has thrived on rue Ste-Anne and the surrounding streets since the 1900s, forming today a vibrant neighbourhood beloved by Parisians who appreciate Japanese, and more recently Korean, cultures.

Foodies will love wandering around, trying a matcha *melonpan* (bun) from **Aki Boulangerie** *(akiparis.fr)* or the *anko dorayaki* (red bean paste-filled pancake) from **Tomo** *(patisserie tomo.fr)*, one of the first Japanese tearooms in the area. Although these two have been around a long time, the area is now home to all sorts of food concepts imported from Japan: from the traditional seafood omelette *(okonomiyaki)* to matcha-only tearooms, and yuzu cheese tarts or crepes served in cones in the tradition of Harajuku, a popular area in Tokyo.

 EATING NEAR THE LOUVRE-PALAIS ROYAL: FINE PASTRIES —— MAPS P99, P118

| **LV Dream:** Live an experience designed by Louis Vuitton, and taste chef Maxime Frédéric's creations at this high-end riverside cafe. Ask for a river view. *11am-8pm* €€€ | **Toraya:** Tearoom adepts will enjoy choosing among an exquisite selection of 'wagashi' wake (Japanese fine-pastry) at this minimalist cafe. *11am-6.30pm Mon-Sat* €€ | **Takumi Patisserie:** Known for the cheese tarts, this Japanese pastry shop also offers 'fluffy' cheesecake. *9.30am-8pm Tue-Sun, 10.30am-7.30pm Mon* €€ | **Ritz Paris Le Comptoir:** At chef François Perret's takeaway counter, grab one of his iconic pastries. A few tables are available. *8am-8pm Mon-Sat, 9am-7pm Sun* €€€ |

Kodawari Ramen Tsukiji

If you're more into finding souvenirs for a Japan-enthusiast and less about eating (although it is much of the experience in this quarter), stop by **Nishikidori – Le Comptoir des Poivres** (nishikidori.com), a high-end delicatessen shop specialising in pepper, and **Maison Wa** (maisonwa.com), where you'll find a tasteful selection of Japanese ceramics and decoration. Book lovers will enjoy **Book Off** (lingonbook.fr), one of the largest bookshops dedicated to Japan, which started with secondhand books, where you're sure to find every sort of manga, including old editions.

The most passionate foodies shouldn't miss **iRASSHAI** (irasshai.co), although it is a bit further away, towards Les Halles. It is the biggest concept store dedicated to Japanese food in Paris, and includes a well-stocked grocery store, a cafe and a restaurant.

PART SHOP, PART CURIOSITY CABINET

Some unconventional shops in the area could stock the best curiosity cabinets.

Les Drapeaux de France – Noxa This workshop has been specialising in the art of miniature soldiers and figurines since 1949.

Design & Nature Discover the fascinating art of taxidermy in this gallery specialised in naturalised animals and entomology.

Athanase A treasure trove of etchings and ancient maps. Entering this shop is like entering the mind of an explorer.

Rickshaw This store abounds in Indian-style decorative objects, tableware, furniture as well as smaller curiosities.

Mokuba This discreet Japanese haberdashery provides elegant ribbons to some of the greatest fashion designers.

HARPO A jewellery store specialised in Native American art, sustainably sourced directly from different tribes in New Mexico.

 EATING NEAR THE LOUVRE-PALAIS ROYAL: JAPANESE MEALS —— MAP P99

| **Kodawari Ramen Tsukiji:** Popular ramen venue, not only for its original immersive fish-market decor, but also for its fusion recipes. *11.45am-11pm* € | **Udon Jubey:** Enjoy light udon noodles served in extra creamy broth or cold refreshing dishes, ideal for hot summer days. *11.30am-9.45pm* € | **Michi:** Here, the chef serves high-quality delicate sushi, in the style of tiny Tokyoite venues. You can sit at the counter to admire his skills. *noon-2pm & 7-10pm Tue-Sat* €€ | **Chez Miki:** An elegant Japanese canteen offering small bites as well as more hearty rice bowls topped with grilled or freshly sliced fish. *noon-2.30pm & 6-10pm Thu-Mon* €€ |

Montorgueil, Les Halles & Sentier

Formerly home to tradespeople and grocers, the area spreading from Les Halles-Montorgueil to Sentier remains one of the most diverse and busy in Paris, where residents, workers and tourists cross paths.

CENTRE POMPIDOU

What happens when the largest collection of contemporary art in France closes for renovation for five long years? Until 2030, the Centre Pompidou, which for decades has hosted some of Paris' most avant-garde exhibitions, will be closed to the public. The renovation aims to rethink the space for new generations of art enthusiasts. During this time, travelling exhibitions will take place in Paris and other cities. By the end of 2026, a gallery curated by the Centre Pompidou, dedicated to creation and conservation, will be opened in Massy, a 40-minute train ride from Paris.

Montorgueil's Food Delights
A historical market-street food tour

Vintage shop signs hanging overhead remind us of **rue Montorgueil**'s past as the main supply lane to Les Halles' food market. Now a pedestrian area, it is a busy market street, on which many establishments have an old story to tell.

Don't miss the oldest bakery in Paris, **Stohrer** (*stohrer.fr*) open since 1730 and renowned for its rum baba and mirrored walls, and buy some chocolate at **À La Mère de Famille** (*lameredefamille.com*). Cheese lovers will adore **La Fermette's** (*la-fermette-paris.com*) selection, and you will find the tastiest *saucissons* (dry sausages) at **Cul de Cochon** (*culdecochon.com*).

Although they are a better feast for the eyes, note that **Au Rocher de Cancale** (*instagram.com/aurocherdecancale*) has been serving oysters since the early 1800s, and **L'Escargot Montorgueil** (*escargotmontorgueil.com*) specialises in buttered snails. For a hearty meal, try a pig's trotter at the iconic brasserie **Au Pied de Cochon** (*pieddecochon.com*), open all night. On Thursdays and Sundays, get your fresh groceries from the outdoor market around Église St-Eustache.

Mesmerising Rotunda of Art
Explore the Bourse de Commerce

The circular walls, the glass roof creating a vast well of light, the windowed indoor walkway and the dome ceiling, all create a vertiginous impression when you enter the **Bourse de Commerce** (*pinaultcollection.com*; adult/child €15/free).

EATING NEAR LES HALLES: OUR VEGETARIAN PICKS — MAP P118

BrEAThe: Creative vegan kitchen serving a great variety of sushi and Japanese-style dishes. Try the 'Discovery' plate to share and pair with a sesame latte. *12-2.30pm & 6.30-10pm Mon-Sat, from 11.30am Sun* €€

Kitchen Izakaya: Don't be afraid to order three to four small plates among the refined 'tapas-style' options at this charming canteen, tucked behind rue Montorgueil. *noon-3pm & 7-11pm Tue-Sat, noon-2.30pm Mon* €€

Maslow: A welcoming vegetarian restaurant by the river, advocating for hearty, creative meals and slow living. Pair one cocktail, with or without alcohol, with your meal. *noon-11pm Mon-Sat, 11.15am-9pm Sun* €€

Eric & Lydie: In this hybrid place in Passage du Grand Cerf, locals often go for the vegetarian bento box (meat options are available). For a snack, try the cakes. *11.30am-7pm Wed-Fri, to 6pm Sat, from 1pm Tue* €-€€

Au Rocher de Cancale

It's hard to imagine that this place was once a bustling hub for commercial trades or even a wheat warehouse.

It is now an increasingly admired contemporary art gallery showcasing the collection of its patron, French billionaire François Pinault. But beyond his already impressive collection, the Bourse du Commerce welcomes both well-established and emerging contemporary artists, who are invited to create temporary exhibitions tailored to the specific shape of the building. Its central room is therefore usually dedicated to an installation, while more traditional exhibitions are hosted on the floors above.

When visiting this unique space, have a look at the compelling circular mural, depicting international trade during an era of extensive colonial expansion: it deserves both an admiring and a critical eye. Daily guided tours in English are available (no additional charge), and provide insightful commentary on the site's heritage.

AN ODE TO MONTORGUEIL'S LIVELINESS

Noémie Bourrié (@noemiebourrie), culinary author and podcaster

Les Halles/Montorgueil is a place of convergence that impresses with its crowds, labyrinthine transport network, and hundreds of shops... But as a local, I've managed to find some gems in places that have existed for ages! Among the specialities dearest to my heart are the os à moëlle (marrow bone) and generous pieces of beef, in restaurants specialising in meat. The soul of these places is still anchored in the late 19th century, when Les Halles was Paris' central market. On the sweet side, I cannot resist either a tasty *religieuse au café* from my traditional bakery, or a dessert at the bistro: profiteroles are my go-to. Once you've filled up, there are many shops to explore.

 EATING NEAR MONTORGUEIL-LES HALLES: SWEET TREATS — MAP P118

Tartelettes: An intimate tearoom creating indulgent fruit tarts and other cakes – perfect for enjoying on cold winter days. It also serves savoury tarts for lunch. *9am-7pm Mon-Fri, from 10am Sat & Sun* €

Baltis: A Lebanese ice-cream parlour where you can try traditional halwa with crushed pistachios, along with creative flavours like olive oil and basil. *12.30-7.30pm Sun-Fri, to 11pm Sat* €

Cloud Cakes: A vegan bakery offering colourful mouth-watering cupcakes and pastries. Savoury plant-based options are also available for brunch. *9am-7pm Mon-Sat* €

PLAQ Chocolat: Chocolate-lovers will fall head over heels for this specialised shop, where the chocolate is made right before your eyes. Try its no-milk hot chocolate. *11am-7.30pm Mon-Fri, from 10am Sat, 10am-6.30pm Sun* €€

MONTORGUEIL, LES HALLES & SENTIER LOUVRE & LES HALLES

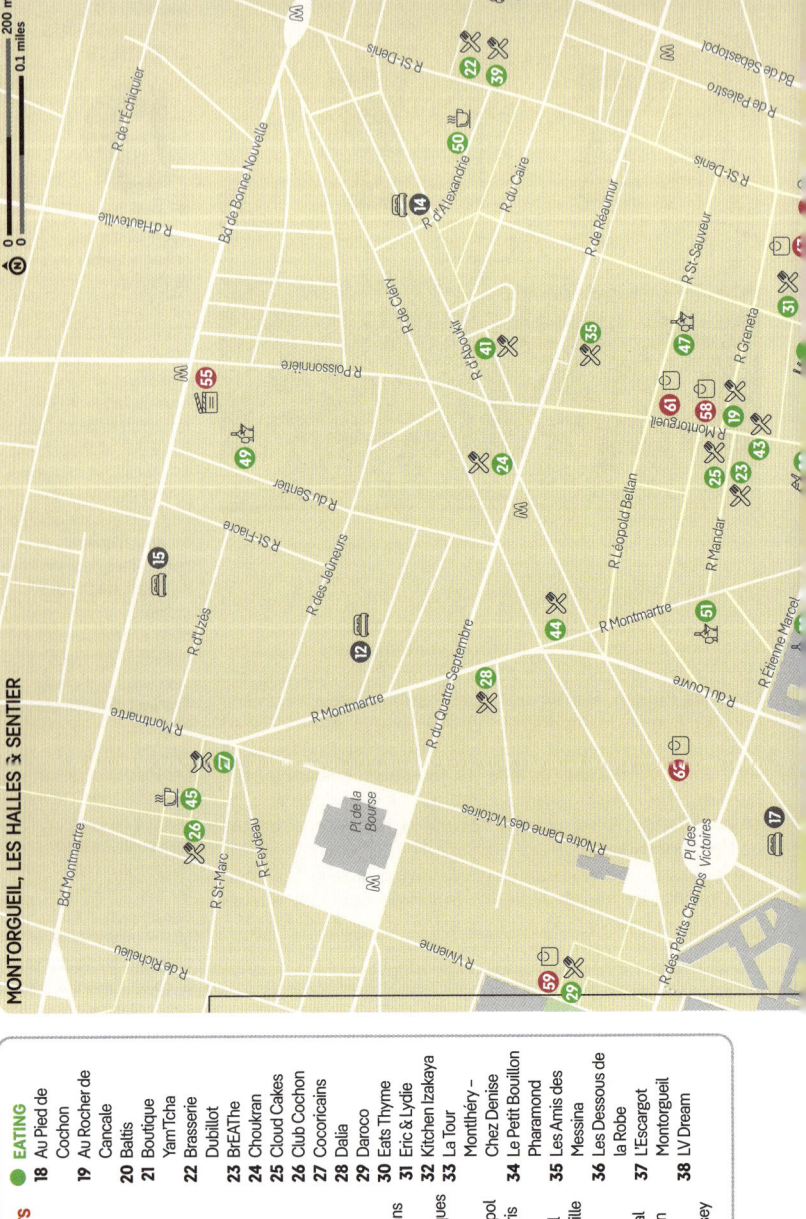

MONTORGUEIL, LES HALLES & SENTIER

★ HIGHLIGHTS
1 Rue Montorgueil

● SIGHTS
2 59 Rivoli
3 Bourse de Commerce
4 Église St-Eustache
5 Fontaine Stravinsky
6 Forum des Halles
7 Musée en Herbe
8 Passage Molière
9 Tour Jean sans Peur
10 Tour St-Jacques

SLEEPING
11 1 2 3 Sebastopol
12 CitizenM Paris Opéra
13 Dandy Hotel
14 Edgar & Achille
15 Grand Boulevards Experimental
16 Hôtel Crayon Rouge
17 Hôtel Odyssey

● EATING
18 Au Pied de Cochon
19 Au Rocher de Cancale
20 Baltis
21 Boutique YamTcha
22 Brasserie Dubillot
23 BrEAThe
24 Choukran
25 Cloud Cakes
26 Club Cochon
27 Cocoricains
28 Dalia
29 Daroco
30 Eats Thyme
31 Eric & Lydie
32 Kitchen Izakaya
33 La Tour Monthléry – Chez Denise
34 Le Petit Bouillon Pharamond
35 Les Amis des Messina
36 Les Dessous de la Robe
37 L'Escargot Montorgueil
38 LV Dream

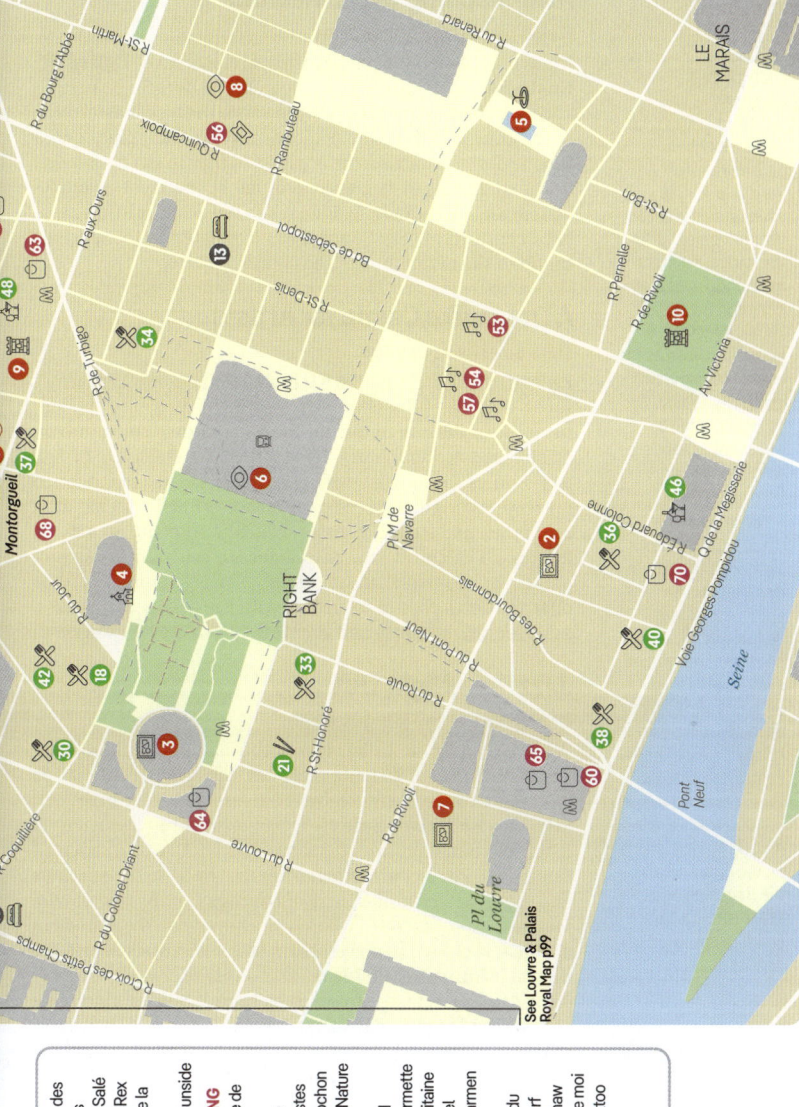

- 39 Maison Constantine
- 40 Maslow
- see 27 Mûre
- 41 PLAQ Chocolat
- 42 Postiche Bistrot
- 43 Stohrer
- 44 Tartelettes

● **DRINKING & NIGHTLIFE**
- 45 Culottées
- 46 Dernier Bar avant la Fin du Monde
- 47 Experimental Cocktail Club
- see 41 Frenchie Bar à Vins
- 48 Golden Promise Whisky Bar
- 49 Jacques' Bar
- 50 KICK Café
- 51 Le Cœur Fou
- 52 ROOF
- 53 Duc des Lombards

- see 6 Forum des Images
- 54 Le Baiser Salé
- 55 Le Grand Rex
- 56 Maison de la Poésie
- 57 Sunset/Sunside

● **SHOPPING**
- 58 À La Mère de Famille
- 59 Athanase
- 60 Bouquinistes
- 61 Cul de Cochon
- 62 Design & Nature
- 63 HARPO
- 64 iRASSHAI
- see 58 La Fermette
- 65 La Samaritaine
- 66 Lit'Weasel
- 67 Louise Carmen
- 68 Mokuba
- 69 Passage du Grand Cerf
- see 31 Rickshaw
- see 67 Tricote moi un Tattoo
- 70 Vilmorin

● **ENTERTAINMENT**
- 53 Duc des Lombards

Awe-inspiring Organ Recitals
Music by stained-glass light

Known for its impressive Gothic architecture, **Église St-Eustache** *(saint-eustache.org)* attracts visitors for its breathtaking stained-glass windows. However, the true masterpiece of the church is its renowned organ. With 8000 pipes and a unique design allowing the organist to play in the nave (close to the audience), it is considered one of the most beautiful instruments in France. St-Eustache's musical tradition dates back centuries. Every Sunday, you can listen to the glorious sound of the organ during the church service.

A Dreamlike Castle for Artists
Take an artistic voyage

Known as an 'aftersquat', **59 Rivoli** *(59rivoli.org)* is a former squat that was fully embraced and integrated into the cultural life of the city in the 2000s. It has transformed into an established contemporary-art venue and a collective of artists' studios. Despite its evolution, the space has managed to preserve its original essence: the façade is filled with hanging art pieces, and stepping inside feels like entering an artistic fortress. The spiral staircase, adorned with artworks and paintings, creates a mesmerising effect. The open studios offer visitors a chance to engage with the artists themselves. Additionally, concerts and events are hosted every weekend.

Jazz Your Night Out
One street, many jazz bars

Whether you're an ardent jazz enthusiast or simply seeking an evening of soul stirring melodies, the jazz bars along rue des Lombards are your gateway to an unforgettable night out. Step into **Le Baiser Salé** *(lebaisersale.com; prices vary)* to listen to contemporary or fusion jazz, with Afro-Caribbean influences. For a contrasting ambience, head to the spacious and sophisticated atmosphere of **Duc des Lombards** *(ducdeslombards.com; €29-41)*, where you can savour the sounds of classical jazz, swing or even Latin jazz with two concerts per night. At **Sunset/Sunside** *(sunset-sunside.com; €20, prices can vary)*, get a taste of two clubs in one. Sunset highlights acoustic and traditional jazz styles, while Sunside showcases more contemporary jazz and improvisation. There's something to satisfy every jazz lover along this street.

UNDER THE CANOPY

Once described as 'the womb of Paris', Les Halles underwent significant redevelopment after the relocation of the fresh-food market to Rungis in the 1970s. Today, it remains a gathering place as the central transport hub in the city, recently complemented by a vast green space welcoming people from all walks of life.

The remarkable metal 'canopy' now sheltering the **Forum des Halles** is an architectural tour de force. It houses a popular underground mall, along with cultural venues such as the **Forum des Images**, a multimedia centre dedicated to the art of cinema, and popular with Parisians. Among notable shops on the ground floor, the flagship **Lego store** attracts both children and adults with its displays of monumental brick constructions, including representations of Paris monuments.

 EATING NEAR MONTORGUEIL-LES HALLES: FRENCH MEALS — MAP P118

La Tour Montlhéry – Chez Denise: A favourite among locals, this traditional restaurant serves classic and regional dishes. Go for meaty meals. *noon-12.30am* €€	**Le Petit Bouillon Pharamond:** Try all the French classics in this old-style house, from bœuf bourguignon to duck confit. Then pick from the dozens of desserts on the menu. *11.45am-midnight* €	**Les Dessous de la Robe:** By day, have an affordable three-course meal paired with an excellent wine; by night, enjoy a tapas-style dinner. *noon-2.30pm & 7-10.30pm Tue-Sat, 7-10.30pm Mon* €€	**Postiche Bistrot:** A beloved bistro among locals for dinner, offering occasionally audacious French dishes. *6.30-10.30pm Mon-Fri, noon-3.30pm & 6.30-10.30pm Sat* €€

Église St-Eustache

Take 300 Steps to Heaven

A panoramic embrace of Paris

Who would suspect that the most incredible, panoramic view in Paris is also the starting point of the St-Jacques de Compostelle pilgrimage? Just steps away from Châtelet, in a small patch of green, the **Tour St-Jacques** *(boutique.toursaint jacques.fr; €12)* looms above the city. However, few people, including locals, are aware that it opens seasonally to the public, giving visitors the unique opportunity to discover the history of what was once part of the Church of St-Jacques-de-la-Boucherie, dating back to the 16th century. Following your guide, you will ascend 300 steps on a narrow spiral staircase to finally marvel at a breathtaking 360-degree view of Paris and hear stories about the tower's intriguing connections to alchemist Nicolas Flamel. Try to book in advance, online or at the kiosk at the foot of the tower, and wear comfortable shoes for the climb.

FONTAINE STRAVINSKY

At the foot of the Centre Pompidou, you might notice a vast fountain with quaint moving and rotating monumental sculptures, looking like they're dancing on the surface of the water. The **Fontaine Stravinsky** is a modern art landmark in Paris. Created in 1983 by French sculptors Nikki de Saint-Phalle (to whom we owe the colourful figures) and Jean Tinguely (who designed the darker ones), the dream-like sculptures were inspired by Igor Stravinsky's music. The figures represent various aspects of Stravinsky's music. The combination of darker industrial creations and more colourful, curvy ones evokes a certain duality in life, a form of harmony. The movement and ever-flowing water symbolise constant change, but also the innovative character recognised in Stravinsky's music, who composed extremely varied pieces during his career.

 DRINKING NEAR MONTORGUEIL-LES HALLES: OUR PICKS ──── MAP P118

| **Dernier Bar avant la Fin du Monde:** Fantasy and science-fiction fans will enjoy grabbing a drink at this themed bar, where pop culture references bring all the fun. *hours vary* | **Le Cœur Fou:** A small bar mainly frequented by locals who like to enjoy its summer terrace. Its simplicity makes it the perfect apéritif spot. *4pm-2am* | **Experimental Cocktail Club:** A bar with a speakeasy vibe and skilled mixologists, offering a sophisticated experience for cocktail enthusiasts. *7pm-2am Mon-Thu, to 4am Fri & Sat, from 8pm Sun* | **Golden Promise Whisky Bar:** Comfortably seated in a stone vault, learn about whisky with expert bar staff and taste some of the 400 bottles at this bar. *6pm-1am Tue-Thu, 6pm-2am Fri & Sat* |

CENTRAL RIVERBANK RECOMMENDATIONS

Julia Chican (@maslow_restaurants), co-founder of the Maslow low-impact restaurants.

Rue Montorgueil is a must-visit. The thought of it once being a hub for fresh food products, with oysters delivered by horse carriage to Rocher de Cancale, fascinates me. With kids, take a stroll along the quayside: they will enjoy the football cages and climbing walls. On sunny days, it's perfect for a picnic. As for historical landmarks, I have two favourites: **La Samaritaine**, and **La Conciergerie**, where part of the monument is dedicated to the French Revolution. It's one of my highlights. For a unique souvenir, head to **Vilmorin**, the oldest seed shop in France. If your home country allows it, buy some seeds and grow them when you return home.

See the World Through a Child's Eyes
An art museum for children

Musée en Herbe (musee-en-herbe.com; €8) is the only museum dedicated to children as young as three years old. It's a must-do if you're travelling with kids. It takes a unique approach with artists offering exhibitions meaningful to children and specifically tailored to their height. So no motionless frames or 'Don't touch!' panels there. Children can experience art through interactive, engaging and educational works.

The museum's exhibitions often fill the space with vibrant colours, patterns, shapes and textures. What better way to reconnect with your inner child? It can be a fun moment for adults, too. The museum also offers workshops to enhance creative expression, and adult storytellers can sometimes accompany the visits, creating a dynamic experience.

A Riverside Stroll for Book Lovers
Read an ancient book along the Seine

How about taking a leisurely stroll along the quayside, picking up an ancient edition of a French classic, or buying a vintage print as a souvenir of Paris?

The **bouquinistes** (secondhand booksellers) lining up on quai du Louvre represent just a fraction of the 3km of ancient books, engravings and vintage posters sold along the Seine. They have become as iconic as the metro entrances and Wallace fountains, and have the same 'wagon green' colouring. Today, they are even part of UNESCO's Intangible Cultural Heritage.

Once your souvenir shopping is done or you've found your book, find a spot at one of the various summer bars along the pedestrian riverbanks. They can be great spots to admire the sunset behind the Eiffel Tower on clear days.

Shop at a Parisian Icon
A timeless feast for the eyes

First opened in 1869, **La Samaritaine** (dfs.com/fr/samaritaine) revolutionised shopping with the concept of offering a wide range of goods under one single roof. This 'Grand Magasin' (department store) embraced modern merchandising and was known for its quality products and exceptional service. Although it used to offer affordable goods to the public, it's worth noting that the shopping experience nowadays is more high-end, even luxurious. However, La Samaritaine has always

---

 EATING NEAR MONTORGUEIL-SENTIER: OUR PICKS — MAP P118

Brasserie Dubillot: Designed by the Nouvelle Garde team, set on modernising the French brasserie experience. French classics with a modern twist. *9am-midnight* €€

Cocoricains: What if an American diner met a French brasserie? It would serve the tastiest chicken in an artfully decorated restaurant. *noon-3pm & 6-11pm Tue-Sat, 11am-3pm Sun, noon-3pm Mon* €€

Club Cochon: Hidden in narrow Passage des Panoramas, this wine bar offers many charcuterie options, and hearty pig-based meals. *noon-2pm & 7-11pm Tue-Fri, 7-11pm Sat* €€

Mûre: Brunch or breakfast is the best time to enjoy this canteen serving seasonal and organic products, mostly sourced from its own local farm. *9am-3pm Mon-Fri* €

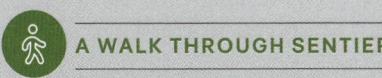

A WALK THROUGH SENTIER

Discover a multifaceted neighbourhood often overlooked by tourists, yet possessing its own charm for travellers seeking a more lived-in side of Paris.

START	END	LENGTH
Passage du Bourg l'Abbé	Combo's mural	1.1km; one hour

Begin at ❶ **Passage du Bourg l'Abbé** on rue de Palestro. Exiting it, you'll find yourself in the contrasting ❷ **Passage du Grand Cerf**, bathed in light. Continue around the cobblestoned and narrow streets to make your way to ❸ **Rue Saint-Denis**, one of the oldest streets in Paris. Leaving the Montorgueil area, you'll enter Sentier, whose character was shaped by its history as a hub for merchants and craftspeople. It has been undergoing a more recent transformation, with the presence of start-ups and digital companies, earning it the nickname 'Silicon Sentier'. As you walk north, take a quick look at ❹ **Passage de la Trinité** before reaching ❺ **Passage du Caire**.

If the passage is closed, walk through rue du Caire towards ❻ **2 place du Caire**, where the building features heads of the Egyptian goddess Hathor. Turn left to head towards ❼ **Rue du Nil**, where foodies will find a surprisingly high concentration of French delicatessens and restaurants. Go find some food for thought this time at bookshop ❽ **Petite Égypte**, before lending a curious eye to ❾ **L'Oasis d'Aboukir**, a vertical wall of plants bringing a refreshing touch to this village-like area. End your tour below ❿ **Combo's mural of Tintin & Captain Haddock kissing**, an icon of Parisian street art.

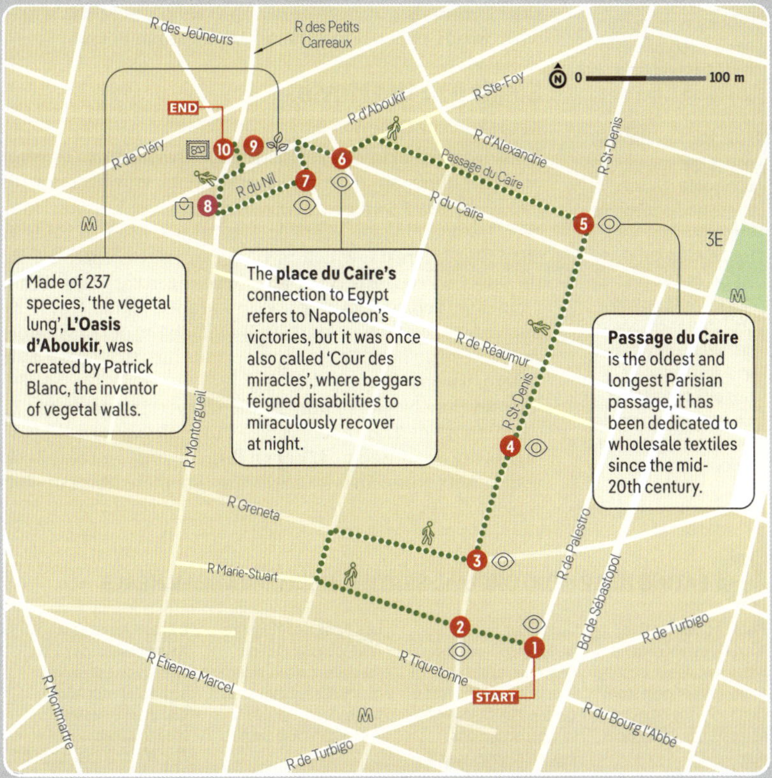

Made of 237 species, 'the vegetal lung', **L'Oasis d'Aboukir**, was created by Patrick Blanc, the inventor of vegetal walls.

The **place du Caire's** connection to Egypt refers to Napoleon's victories, but it was once also called 'Cour des miracles', where beggars feigned disabilities to miraculously recover at night.

Passage du Caire is the oldest and longest Parisian passage, it has been dedicated to wholesale textiles since the mid-20th century.

A MEDIEVAL VESTIGE AT THE HEART OF PARIS

There are very few traces of the Middle Ages in Paris, and it is all the more surprising to find one in Sentier, right on one of the axes made during the great Haussmannian transformations (1853–1870). **Tour Jean sans Peur** *(tourjeansanspeursite.wordpress.com; adult/child €6/free)*, named after King Charles VI's cousin Jean de Bourgogne, who had it erected in the 15th century, is more than easily overlooked. In fact, it's completely absorbed in the urban landscape, but the attentive traveller will notice the sometimes open gate. Those interested in medieval lifestyle might want to spend an hour inside, to discover the well-preserved sculpted vault, some historical costumes, and an annual exhibition hosted in the basement, usually tackling an aspect of European medieval life.

held a special place in Parisian hearts, especially for its iconic façade looking out at the Seine.

Reopened in 2021 after decades of uncertainty, it now showcases the splendour of both art nouveau and art deco styles. Whether you're there to shop or not, don't miss its grand geometrical staircase, the top floor's meticulously restored murals, and the expansive glass roof.

A Secret Passage
Poetry night at Passage Molière

You stumble upon **Passage Molière** by chance more often than you head there on purpose, and there's something poetic about getting lost in a city. Maybe that's why the **Maison de la Poésie** *(maisondelapoesieparis.com; €25)* is located in this discreet passage tucked between Centre Pompidou and Le Marais. French-speaking poetry enthusiasts will be delighted by its program. You can attend readings and literary performances almost every evening.

The passage itself was revitalised by local shopkeepers, who dedicated it to literature and all things related to reading and writing, so while you're there, browse **L'Ecritoire** *(lecritoireparis.com)* for selected cards, posters and pens – a great place to get souvenirs – and don't miss Japanese bookbinder **Misaki Iinuma's** *(misakiiinuma.com)* shop where she works with 'washi' paper, a traditional Japanese paper technique.

Singing at the Movies
Karaoke at Le Grand Rex

Known for its art deco aesthetics, **Le Grand Rex** *(legrandrex.com)* offers an amazing experience for moviegoers with one of the most well-equipped auditoriums in Europe. However, beyond cinema, it offers cultural activities to cater to changing interests, which in turn can reignite passion for the silver screen, especially among younger Parisians. From a cinema-themed escape game to karaoke nights featuring musicals (like *Mamma Mia!*, *We Will Rock You* or *Dirty Dancing*), Le Grand Rex offers many opportunities to unleash your inner performer.

So say goodbye to singing in the shower and get ready to shine alongside 2799 other people – fancy dress allowed! These nights are organised by **L'Ecran Pop** *(lecranpop.com)*. Book your tickets online in advance as they are incredibly popular.

EATING NEAR MONTORGUEIL-SENTIER: MEDITERRANEAN MEALS — MAP P118

Maison Constantine:	Choukran:	Les Amis des Messina:	Dalia:
A hybrid establishment with a restaurant, beauty salon and concept store. Don't miss the brunch at weekends. *10am-6pm Tue-Sun* €€	Expect well-thought-out decor, generous tajines and specialities of Moroccan cuisine. Mouth-watering vegetarian options available. *hours vary* €	A welcoming Sicilian restaurant with a selection of antipasti, pasta and pizza. *noon-2.30pm & 7-10.30pm Mon-Sat* €€	A restaurant with a summer-holiday vibe, where you can share small plates or family dishes with eastern Mediterranean influences. *12-2.30pm & 7pm-12am* €€

Passage Molière

And don't worry, all this said, you can still enjoy a regular movie screening at the theatre.

Shop Beneath Glass Ceilings
A passage with pretty craft shops

Bridging the districts of rue St-Denis and rue Montorgueil, this covered passage is not only a pretty shortcut for locals, but also a remarkably well-preserved gallery, with a high glass roof and vintage shop signs adding to its appeal. Unlike its more upscale counterparts near Palais Royal, **Passage du Grand Cerf** possesses two levels of fully glazed façades, which suggests that it was originally designed for production and craftwork (with shop below and workshop above).

The current stores remain faithful to this heritage. Each of them contributes to the essence of this not-so-hidden treasure. Don't miss **Lil' Weasel** *(lilweasel.com)* to find the right wool or ribbon, **Louise Carmen** *(louisecarmen.com)* to make your own customised diary, and **Tricote moi un Tattoo** *(tricote moiuntatto.com)* for personally designed embroidery.

To get a glimpse of what the passage looks like from its top floor, stop at Eric & Lydie's (p116; *ericetlydie.com*) jewellery store and restaurant, where you can sit upstairs to enjoy a homemade meal or a piece of cake.

FAVOURITE SPOTS IN SENTIER

Kenza Otmani (@ maison.constantine), founder of Maison Constantine.

Welcome to Sentier, also called 'Little Egypt', one of the most charming neighbourhoods in Paris, full of passages bridging large avenues. Its architecture and streets were influenced by the French exploring Egypt since 1798. Start at **Place du Caire** to admire Egyptian façades then wander through **Passage du Caire**: it's a labyrinth of old clothing manufacturers. Exit on rue St-Denis, one of the oldest in the city, and take a stroll through enchanting Passage du Grand Cerf. Visit Tricote moi un Tattoo, an eccentric shop specialising in customised fun embroidery. Come back and walk towards the St-Denis gate. On the same pavement as Maison Constantine, stop by **Nawak**, a thrift shop with an amazing vintage selection.

 DRINKING IN SENTIER: COCKTAILS & COFFEE — MAP P118

Jacques bar: In the Hoxton hotel, climb the stairs to access this intimate cocktail bar with a long list of options. *6pm-2am, Thu-Sat, to 1am Tue-Wed*

KICK Café: This cafe was born from a passion for k-pop culture: you can order colourful drinks and homemade biscuits while listening to your favourite band. *11am-7pm*

Frenchie Bar à Vins: One of the four establishments of the Frenchie group, this wine bar has a relaxed vibe and pairs your wine with refined French dishes. *6.30-11pm*

Culottées Panoramas: This small coffee shop is perfect to take a break from the crowds, sipping your latte. Also serves food. *9am-4pm Mon-Fri, 10am-5pm Sat-Sun*

Researched by Rooksana Hossenally

MONTMARTRE & NORTHERN PARIS

BOHEMIAN HILLTOP VILLAGE AND ARTY WANDERINGS

Once bypassed en route to Montmartre, the north is now a patchwork of evolving neighbourhoods drawing travellers in with creativity, charm and renewed energy.

Perched on a hill in the 18th *arrondissement,* Montmartre has long stood apart, first as a rural village, then as a bohemian stomping ground for artists like Picasso and Toulouse-Lautrec. Its winding streets, once home to windmills and cabarets, drew creatives seeking inspiration and escape from central Paris. Meanwhile, the surrounding northern neighbourhoods evolved as working-class enclaves, shaped by waves of immigration and cultural fusion. Over time, gentrification, artistic revival, and a renewed interest in authentic, local experiences have transformed the area. Today, this corner of Paris blends grit and charm, and is the most exciting place to get under the surface of the city.

INCLUDES

MONTMARTRE, PIGALLE & BATIGNOLLES
p128

BARBÈS, LA CHAPELLE & CANAL ST-MARTIN
p138

JAURÈS TO LA VILLETTE
p143

ST-DENIS, ST-OUEN, PANTIN & AUBERVILLIERS
p146

La Maison Rose (p132), Montmartre

See p309 for places to stay in Montmartre and northern Paris.

Highlights

❶ Basilique du Sacré-Cœur
Gaze on the gleaming white basilica atop Montmartre and its bohemian winding streets. **p129**

❷ Marché aux Puces de St-Ouen
Hunt for bargains in the world's largest flea market, offering antiques, vintage finds, and a lively, local atmosphere. **p148**

❸ Canal Walks
Stroll from La Villette park to St-Martin's trendy waterside bars and boutiques. **p140**

❹ La Villette
Wander the park and pocket of concert venues and cabarets, from cult spots to more intimate, indie spaces. **p143**

❺ Yoyaku
Listen to vinyl at Paris' largest record store, part of the wave of new stores and listening bars bringing fresh energy. **p140**

Getting Around

Metro
Your best bet is taking Line 2 (Anvers, Barbès-Rochechouart), Line 4 (Château Rouge, Porte de Clignancourt), and Line 12 (Abbesses, Jules Joffrin).

Walking
Essential here, as it's the only way to soak up Montmartre's hills, hidden stairways and cobblestone lanes. Wear good shoes and bring a rain jacket.

Bus/tram
Offers a slower, scenic ride: try Bus 85 or 31 for local hops, or Tram T3b to reach the Saint-Ouen flea market and La Villette with ease.

Montmartre, Pigalle & Batignolles

Montmartre, Pigalle and Batignolles each embody Parisian charm with distinct flavours. Pigalle thrives with cabarets, cocktail bars and music venues. Montmartre enchants with its artistic legacy, while Batignolles offers a serene village atmosphere.

> **WHERE TO STAY**
>
> Book a hotel in Montmartre or just at the bottom of the hill in lively Pigalle, which has some great options, like Elysée Montmartre Hotel, Le Pigalle or HOY. That way, you can dip in and out of Montmartre as you like, but also explore beyond, including the nightlife at music venues Le Trianon, Elysée Montmartre, La Cigale or La Boule Noire, as well as the area's numerous cocktail bars and restaurants. Thanks to great transport links (metro lines 2 and 12), it's also easy to get to the city's main sites from here, like the Louvre or the Seine River, reachable in 20 minutes on the metro, or 30 minutes on foot via the Opéra Garnier.

Take a Deep Dive into Montmartre
The village's arty hangouts live on

Visitors are often busy admiring the standalone houses and quaint cafes that look like they are stuck in a time past, but look beyond and you'll see that Montmartre's arty side still lives on in the form of street-art-splashed walls, small artist ateliers and galleries, a handful of caricature artists on the very top of the hill on Place du Tertre, as well as more formal venues like the **Théâtre des Abbesses** (*theatredelaville-paris.com/fr/lieux/les-abbesses*), which puts on plays and contemporary ballets. There is also a small **Dalí Museum** (*daliparis.com*) with more than 300 of his artworks, from paintings to sculptures and etchings. A local favourite for its glass-and-iron-clad art nouveau structure, don't miss the **Halle St-Pierre** (*hallesaintpierre.org*), which used to house a market and is now an atmospheric venue for contemporary art shows, with a cafe and a book shop, surrounded by fabric markets, down towards the Barbès end of the hill. Try to time your visit with an event at the **Cité des Arts de Montmartre** (*citedesartsparis.net*) on rue Girardon, when the artists in residency at the cluster of ateliers hidden behind the stone wall in the leafy garden, open their doors to the public and you get to explore this secret village.

 EATING IN MONTMARTRE: OUR PICKS

Le Bon, La Butte: A cosy bistro serving French staples with a contemporary twist in laid-back surroundings. *dinner Tue-Thu, lunch & dinner Fri-Sun* €€

Aléa: Terrific, simple market-led cuisine in a light-filled spot. There's a three-course lunch menu for under €30 during the week. *lunch & dinner Wed-Sat, lunch Sun* €€

La Part des Anges: A relaxed local spot off the radar for its exposed stone walls and great traditional food like *magret de canard*. *dinner only Tue-Fri, lunch & dinner Sat* €€

Le Progrès: A typical Parisian cafe open all day for coffee and wine, and the day's specials, as well as snails and steak tartare à la carte. *9am-2am* €€

TOP EXPERIENCE

Basilique du Sacré-Cœur

Rising above Montmartre (the hill of martyrs), the Basilique du Sacré-Cœur, dedicated to the Sacred Heart of Jesus, is more than a landmark; it's a vantage point, a sanctuary, a Parisian rite of passage, and one of the city's most visited landmarks. From its gleaming domes to one of the world's largest mosaics, it stuns with grandeur. Below, the streets buzz with artists and cafes, but up here, the sweeping views and quiet reverence offer a moment apart.

Christ in Majesty mosaic

Get Behind the History

Perched at the highest point in Paris, Montmartre officially became part of the city's 18th *arrondissement* in 1860. The Basilique du Sacré-Cœur, whose luminous white dome hovers above Paris like a celestial apparition, was built later, rising as close to the heavens as possible to atone for the city's sins, particularly after the Revolution.

See One of the World's Biggest Mosaics

Designed in a striking Roman-Byzantine style, the basilica took five architects over four decades to complete (1875–1919). Its brilliant white façade comes from calcite-rich stone that naturally cleans itself with rain. Inside, the apse features Christ in Majesty, one of the world's largest mosaics, while the Blessed Sacrament remains the heart of the basilica's spiritual devotion.

Climb Up for Sweeping City Views

The north-facing campanile houses the 19-ton Savoyarde bell, one of the world's heaviest, cast in Annecy in 1895 to honor Savoy's union with France. Visitors can climb the 300 steps to the dome for breathtaking panoramic views of Paris, while inside, chapels, stained-glass windows, and a crypt bathed in natural light create a contemplative atmosphere. The basilica's perpetual adoration prayer cycle, which began in 1885, continues uninterrupted, and on Sundays, the grand organ resonates through the sacred space during mass and vespers.

TOP TIPS

● You can spend the night at the Basilica from 11pm to 7am if you pray for at least an hour, as part of the continuous prayer cycle, unbroken since 1885 (sign up on the Basilica website).

● Arrive early to avoid the crowds; as it's a sunset spot, it gets overcrowded around then.

● Visit on weekdays to avoid the crowds

PRACTICALITIES

● Map p130 ● sacre-coeur-montmartre.com ● 10am-7pm, but check the site before your visit as times may vary according to Basilica events ● adult/child/groups €8/5/6, all tickets available onsite only

MONTMARTRE, PIGALLE & BATIGNOLLES

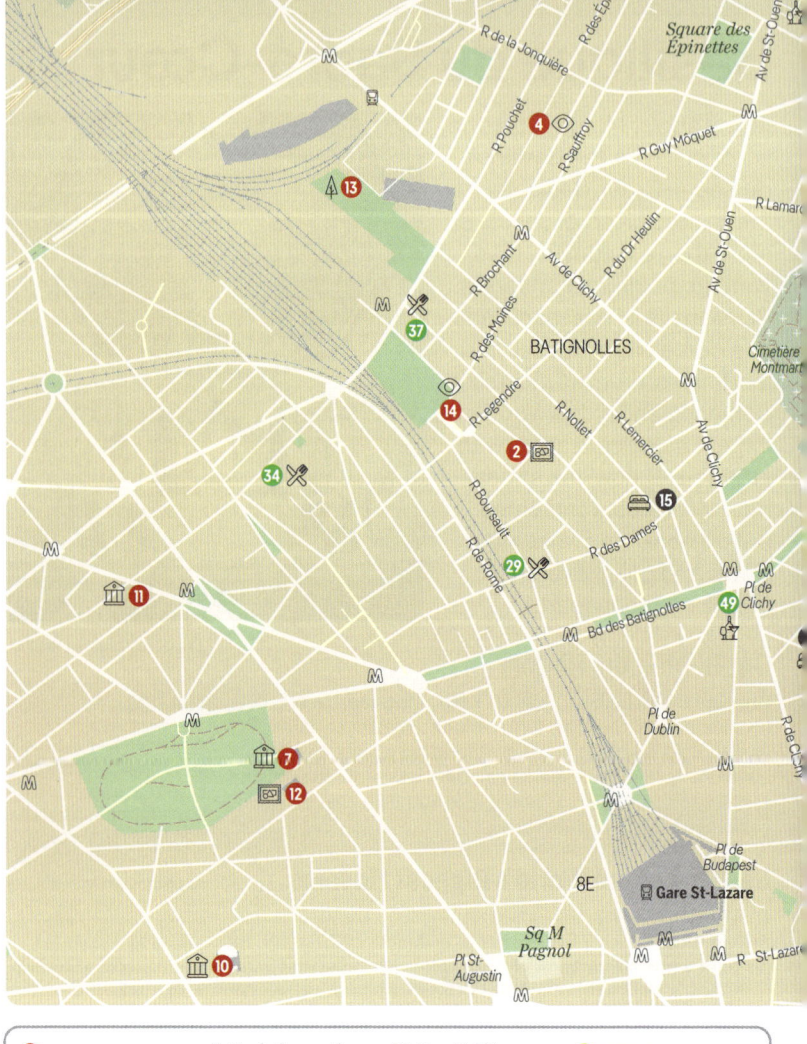

★ HIGHLIGHTS
1 Basilique du Sacré-Cœur

● SIGHTS
2 Atelier Marie La Varande
3 Cité des Arts de Montmartre
4 Cité des Fleurs
5 Dalí Museum
6 Halle St-Pierre
7 Musée Cernuschi
8 Musée de la Vie Romantique
9 Musée de Montmartre
10 Musée Jacquemart-André
11 Musée Jean-Jacques Henner
12 Musée Nissim de Camondo
13 Parc Clichy-Batignolles – Martin Luther King
14 Place Dr Félix Lobligeois

● SLEEPING
15 Hôtel Eldorado
16 Hotel Élysée Montmartre
17 Hôtel HoY
18 Hotel Le Ballu
19 Le Pigalle
20 Le Relais Montmartre
21 Le Village Montmartre by Hiphostels

● EATING
22 Aléa
23 Bouillon Pigalle
24 Buvette Gastrothèque
25 Caillebotte
26 Cuisine
27 Fana
28 Fantomas
29 Gare au Gorille
see 15 Hotel Eldorado
30 La Part des Anges
31 L'arpaon

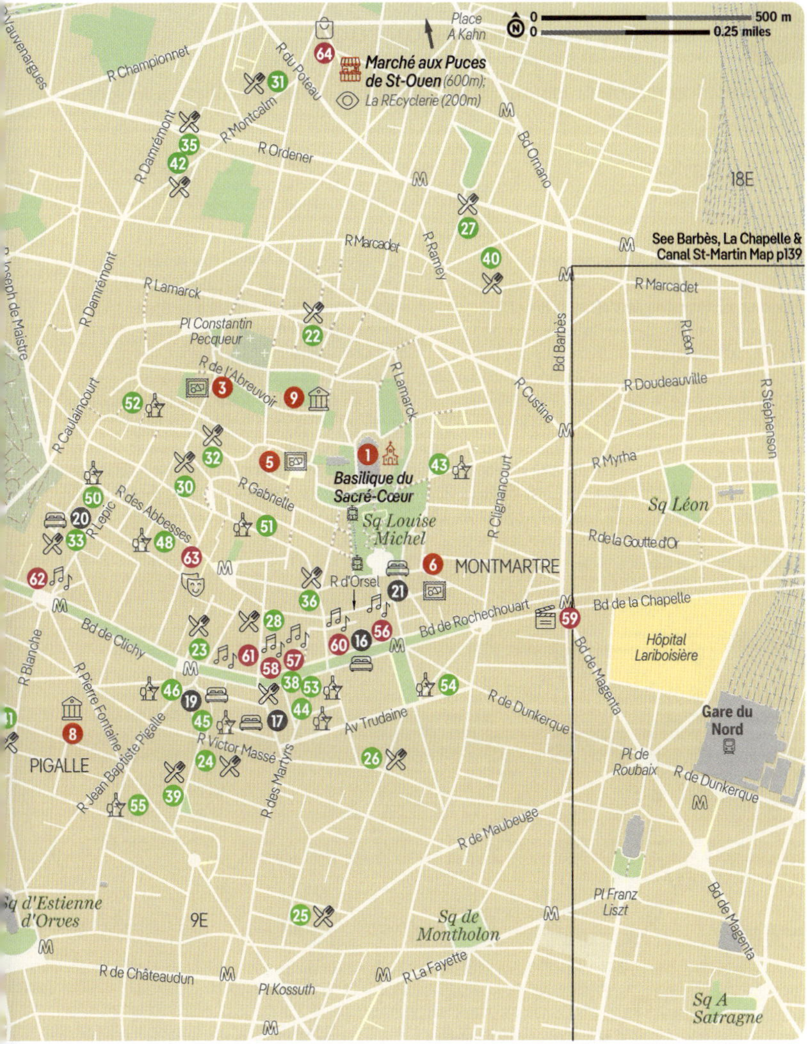

MONTMARTRE & NORTHERN PARIS — MONTMARTRE, PIGALLE & BATIGNOLLES

- 32 Le Bon, La Butte
- 33 Le Café des Deux Moulins
- 34 Le Faham
- 35 Le Maquis
- 36 Le Progrès
- 37 Le Truffaut
- 38 Maggie
- 39 Magnolia
- see 17 mesa de HOY
- 40 Pantobaguette
- 41 Perception
- 42 Restaurant Montcalm

DRINKING & NIGHTLIFE
- 43 Au Soleil de la Butte
- 44 Classique
- 45 Dirty Dick
- 46 Folies Pigalle
- 47 Hasard Ludique
- 48 La Cave des Abbesses
- 49 La Fête
- see 62 La Machine du Moulin Rouge
- 50 Le Petit Café de Montmartre
- 51 Le Tagada
- 52 Le Très Particulier
- 53 Mikado Dancing
- 54 Minore
- see 44 Sister Midnight
- 55 Stéréo

ENTERTAINMENT
- 56 Elysée Montmartre
- 57 La Boule Noire
- 58 La Cigale
- 59 Le Louxor
- 60 Le Trianon
- 61 Madame Arthur
- 62 Moulin Rouge
- 63 Théâtre des Abbesses

SHOPPING
- 64 Dizonord

ESSENTIAL MONTMARTRE ON FOOT

Discover Montmartre's main sights and delve into its history with this walking tour.

START	END	LENGTH
Pigalle	Halle St-Pierre	2.5km; 1½ hours

Start on ❶ **Rue des Abbesses**, with its shops and cafes to rue des Trois Frères. Pass the ❷ **Mur des Je t'aime** (Wall of 'I Love Yous') and ❸ **Spree Café Galerie** and the ❹ **Fotoautomat**, which usually has a queue but takes great snaps. At rue Androuet you'll pass ❺ **Au Marché de la Butte**, featured in the film *Amélie*, and then to place Emile Goudeau and ❻ **Le Bateau-Lavoir** artist studios, where artists like Picasso once lived. Take rue d'Orchampt, passing singer Dalida's former home, ❼ **Maison de Dalida**, then walk to ❽ **rue de l'Abreuvoir**, one of the most scenic streets in the city. Pass by ❾ **La Maison Rose**, ivy-clad houses and the vineyard, continue along rue des Saules, onto rue St-Vincent to ❿ **Parc de la Turlure**, for a magnificent view of the back of the Sacré-Cœur. To reach the front of the basilica take ⓫ **rue du Cardinal Guibert** and admire the dome and panoramic rooftop views. Make a detour west to ⓬ **place du Tertre** to see the crowded square of artists and restaurants. Back at Sacré-Cœur, walk left down the stairs through the ⓭ **square Louise Michel** to the ⓮ **Halle St-Pierre** in the area's textile neighbourhood. You can see the basilica from the bottom of its pedestal.

The **Clos Montmartre vineyard** is the heart of the annual Fête des Vendanges, celebrating the village's grape harvest in October.

Place du Tertre still buzzes with artists sketching portraits, cafés, and a nostalgic charm that recalls Montmartre's bohemian heyday.

Fotoautomat

Where Cabaret Meets Cocktails
Glamour and after-dark revelry

Since the Belle Époque, Pigalle has been Paris' playground of after-dark pleasures. Its reputation truly took shape after WWII, when it became a hub for neon-lit sex shops, cabarets and smoky bars. While many of its infamous establishments are fading, Pigalle's spirit endures in legendary venues like the **Moulin Rouge** *(moulinrouge.fr; adult €103)*, where, since 1889, high-kicking dancers and extravagant sets bring the cancan to life in nightly shows at 9pm and 11pm. Cabaret **Madame Arthur** *(madamearthur.fr)* is a fun evening out of live music and gender-bending performances, keeping Pigalle's legacy of spectacle and seduction alive. Beyond the show lights, Pigalle's warren of small spaces has always been central to its illicit charm, once home to shadowy dens, opium-fuelled escapades, and whispered rendezvous. Today, these tight quarters have found a new life as cocktail bars, where locals and visitors mingle over expertly crafted drinks. Spots like **Sister Midnight**, **Dirty Dick**, **Minore** and **Classique** shake up inventive cocktails, blending Pigalle's hedonistic past with a squeakier-clean present.

WHY I LOVE MONTMARTRE

Rooksana Hossenally, Lonely Planet writer

Like many Parisians, I too dismissed Montmartre as overrated, frozen in time, with little contemporary clout. But living here for six months changed that. Beyond the weekend crowds and the tourist-heavy place du Tertre, I discovered a neighbourhood with a true local pulse; bars, cafes and boutiques where residents actually gather. Whether you are catching an arthouse film at the retro Studio 28, buying wine from the owner at **La Cave des Abbesses**, sipping a drink in pocket-sized bars like **Fantomas**, **Le Petit Café de Montmartre**, the no-name Cafe Bar on rue Véron (nicknamed Chez Momo), or the quirky Marlusse et Lapin, Montmartre reveals itself as a real living place. Its spirit isn't just nostalgia; it's a fiercely local way of life, hidden in plain sight.

AFTER-DARK IN MONTMARTRE: OUR PICKS

Le Tagada: This family-run bar is named after a red 1970s strawberry-flavoured sweet and is good for pre-dinner drinks. *5pm-2am Tue-Sat €*

Au Soleil de la Butte: The perfect spot to keep the night going. There's a small bar at ground level, but the real action is on the basement dance floor. *8am-2am €*

Le Café des Deux Moulins: Featured in the film *Amélie*, this is the place to hang out at a typical Parisian cafe for a glass of wine against a retro backdrop. *9am-2am €*

Le Très Particulier: Known for its cocktails, this bar is a must for its picturesque setting, hidden in the garden of a fancy hotel. *6pm-2am Mon-Sat, 4pm-midnight Sun €€*

GHOSTS OF ARTISTS PAST

Pigalle has long been a stage for Paris' most electrifying performers and artists. In the late 19th century, Toulouse-Lautrec immortalised its cabarets, painting La Goulue and Jane Avril, the high-kicking stars of the Moulin Rouge. The district pulsed with bohemian energy, drawing poets and painters. By the 1920s, Joséphine Baker mesmerised crowds at the Folies Bergère, while Édith Piaf sang in Pigalle's streets before becoming the soul of French *chanson*. Jazz musician and writer Boris Vian added his avant-garde flair to the area's clubs. After WWII, Pigalle's neon glow lit up a world of jazz, burlesque and underground culture. Today, its music halls, cabarets and cocktail bars keep the spirit of its legendary artists alive.

Musical Past to Present
From cabaret to global sounds

Pigalle's transformation from a cabaret hub to a diverse musical landscape reflects its enduring creative spirit. While the district remains synonymous with the legendary Moulin Rouge and intimate drag performances, its **music shops** selling instruments and concert venues have become key destinations for both emerging talent and established acts. **La Cigale** (*lacigale.fr*) hosts indie and alternative concerts, **Le Trianon** (*letrianon.fr*) offers a blend of world music and rock, **Elysée Montmartre** (*elyseemontmartre.com/fr*) draws large crowds for rock and electronic shows, and **La Boule Noire** (*laboule-noire.fr*) caters to underground genres. These venues draw artists from all over the world, showcasing an eclectic mix of sounds, from jazz and blues to electronic and experimental music. There are also a couple of notable clubs, including one of Paris' biggest venues, **La Machine du Moulin Rouge** (*lamachinedumoulinrouge.com*), below the Moulin Rouge, **Folies Pigalle** (*instagram.com/foliespigalle.fr*) and the smaller newcomer **Mikado Dancing** (*orsohotels.com/hotel-rochechouart/mikado-dancing*).

Artist Ateliers & Villa Museums
Artists' homes turned hidden museums

In Montmartre, the **Musée de Montmartre** (*museedemontmartre.fr; adult/child €15/free*) occupies a 17th-century house where Renoir once lived, immersing visitors in the area's vibrant artistic past. Down the hill in Pigalle, the **Musée de la Vie Romantique** (*museevieromantique.paris.fr*) offers a glimpse into the life of Dutch painter Ary Scheffer and his illustrious guests, including Dickens and Chopin. Nearby, the Musée National Gustave Moreau (p87), housed in the symbolist painter's former home, invites visitors to explore his evocative works and charming studio via a creaky wooden spiral staircase. Beyond these iconic spots, other northern

EATING IN PIGALLE: OUR PICKS

Bouillon Pigalle: Terrific value, this *bouillon* is one of several in the city not to miss for escargot and *steak-frites* at teeny prices. *noon-midnight* €	**Maggie**: This vintage-style dining space with vestiges of its days as a 1920s dancing hall serves traditional French food. Don't miss the rooftop bar. *7-10pm Tue-Sat* €€	**Caillebotte**: A local neo-bistro favourite with an unbeatably priced lunch menu (week lunchtimes only) in contemporary surroundings. *12.30-3pm & 7.30-11.30pm Mon-Sat* €€€	**mesa de HOY:** A fantastic option for flavours rooted in Latin American *savoir-faire*, rustled up with top-notch vegetarian produce. *7.30am-10pm Tue- Sat, to 6.30pm Sun & Mon* €€
Magnolia: A light-filled French bistro with a nod to the '70s and French staples with a twist. *lunch & dinner Thu-Fri, dinner Tue, Wed & Sat* €€	**Cuisine:** The chef leans into influences from his home country of Japan and Paris to create heartwarming dishes. *dinner Mon & Tue, lunch & dinner Wed-Fri* €€	**Perception:** The Michelin-approved South Korean cuisine combining Korean and French influences makes this spot a top choice. *lunch & dinner Tue-Fri, dinner Sat* €€€	**Buvette Gastrothèque:** A great spot inside an old bistro with easy bites like croque monsieur and shepherd's pie made with fresh produce. *hours vary* €€

A PIGALLE WANDER THROUGH THE AGES

This short walking tour takes you through the area, from the Moulin Rouge to tucked-away villa museums as well as local landmarks.

START	END	LENGTH
Moulin Rouge	Hotel Ballu	3km; one hour

From the ❶ **Moulin Rouge**, turn into the tangle of streets known as SoPi (South Pigalle). Walk along bd Rochechouart and make a stop at the ❷ **Phono Museum**, with its collection of more than 100 fully working phonographs and thousands of records. Walk to the south end of the ❸ **square d'Anvers Jean-Claude Carrière** for a view of the Sacré-Cœur towering above the city. Head southwards and stop at 9 rue de Douai, which was ❹ **Henri de Toulouse-Lautrec**'s last abode, and ❺ **Villa Frochot** (renamed Villa Yora) with its Hokusai-inspired stained-glass window. Continue to ❻ **Hôtel Amour**, where you'll be lured by its hot-pink neon; the service and food are very average, but it draws creative types from major film stars to artists, giving the place an insider vibe. Then head to the atmospheric artist-atelier museum ❼ **Musée Gustave Moreau**. Stroll the streets lined with restaurants and bars to ❽ **St-Georges** and the bucolic ❾ **Musée de la Vie Romantique**. Then head a couple of minutes west to rue Ballu and the ❿ **Villa Ballu**, where Impressionist painter Edgar Degas is said to have lived, among other spots in Pigalle. Across the road, make sure you drop in at the intimate ⓫ **Hotel Le Ballu** and its tucked-away courtyard.

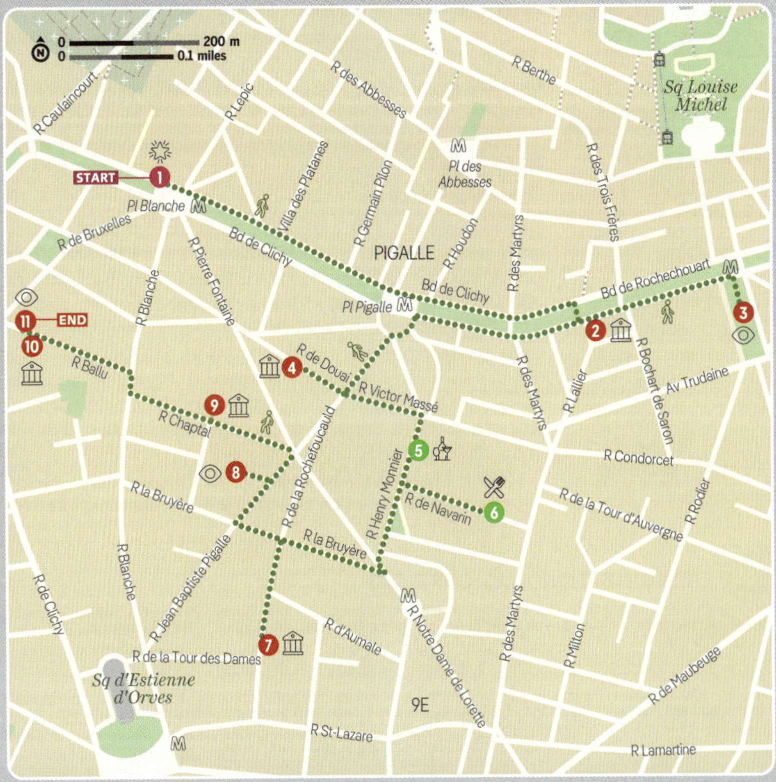

THE GUIDE

MONTMARTRE & NORTHERN PARIS MONTMARTRE, PIGALLE & BATIGNOLLES

135

OFFBEAT ART SCENE

Alexandra Weinress (@theseenparis), a Californian expat, helps visitors navigate Paris' offbeat art scene through her bespoke tours.

Le 19M Chanel's 25,500-sq-m hub brings together top artisans specialised in crafts from embroidery to feather work. There is also a gallery, a bookstore, and a cafe.

Le 104 A publicly run, multi-purpose space with diverse cultural programming, residencies, exhibitions, concerts, performances and workshops. The is a range of shops and restaurants too.

Chapelle XIV An art and design gallery showcasing emerging artists, a record store, a cafe, and an event space.

Galerie Thaddaeus Ropac Pantin A fixture of the Marais art scene, its Pantin outpost is housed in a striking former metalworking factory. The space includes a bookstore and a cafe.

Renoir Gardens, Musée de Montmartre (p134)

Paris museums like **Musée Jacquemart-André** (*musee-jacquemart-andre.com*), **Musée Nissim de Camondo** (*madparis.fr/Musee-Nissim-de-Camondo-125*), **Musée Cernuschi** (*cernuschi.paris.fr*), and **Musée Jean-Jacques Henner** (*musee-henner.fr*) are worth a visit for art lovers.

Arty Vibes

A breath of fresh air

Tucked into Paris' 17th *arrondissement,* Batignolles is a tranquil pocket of the city where leafy squares like **Place Dr Félix Lobligeois**, parks like the modern **Parc Clichy-Batignolles – Martin Luther King** with a bar and food counters packed with locals in summer, and a village-like rhythm offer a welcome pause from the urban buzz. With few tourists, it's a favourite for Parisians craving space to breathe. The Eiffel Tower was assembled nearby, and today, the neighbourhood still echoes with creative energy; pottery studios abound, many offering hands-on workshops.

Atelier Marie La Varande, nestled in the heart of the Batignolles district, is a cherished space for artistic exploration.

EATING IN BATIGNOLLES: OUR PICKS

Le Faham: Michelin-starred chef Kelly Rangama brings gentle Réunionese flavours to this elegant address. *noon-2pm & 7.30-10pm Tue-Fri, 7.30-10pm Sat* €€€

Gare au Gorille: A minimalist bistro turning heads with its inventive French plates and stellar wine list. *12.15-2pm & 7.30-10pm Mon-Fri* €€

Le Truffaut: Loved for its honest prices and seasonal French cooking, this cosy spot delivers modern tradition. *noon-3pm & 7.30pm-midnight Mon-Fri* €€

Hôtel Eldorado: Slip into the lush courtyard of this stylish hotel for laid-back Mediterranean dishes in a postcard setting. *8-10.30am, 12-3pm & 6.30-10.15pm* €€

For over 30 years, sculptor Marie La Varande, who worked on the restoration of the Château de Versailles and many other projects, has offered courses in clay modelling, wood carving, engraving, and drawing, welcoming both beginners and seasoned artists. The atelier is a beautiful, atmospheric spot with a warm, communal atmosphere, where creativity thrives. Located at 6 bis rue Bridaine, it's a real hub for those passionate about sculpture and the arts, as well as cats, as Marie has a couple at the atelier. It's worth taking a peek through the window when passing by, even if you don't end up taking a course here.

The Good Life
Local charm, minus the crowds

Batignolles is also a smart shopping alternative to Paris' busier districts, especially during the sales, when it's quieter than central districts. It's home to a mix of French high-street favourites and small indie boutiques along rue Legendre, rue des Moines and rue des Batignolles. Just steps away, stroll through the picturesque **Cité des Fleurs**, a blooming private cobblestone lane lined with grand homes and gardens. The lane was home to actress Catherine Deneuve and painter Simon Hantaï. At apéritif hour, the neighbourhood's cafe terraces fill with locals, ideal for settling in with a glass of wine and watching the world go by at a gentler pace or the **Hasard Ludique** *(lehasardludique.paris)* inside an abandoned train station.

Reclaiming the City Outskirts
A more diverse arts scene

Abandoned train stations, factories, and wastelands have been reborn as cultural playgrounds. As Paris sprawls outward, so does its creativity. Repurposed SNCF buildings like **La Gare – Le Gore** *(Map p144; instagram.com/la_gare_le_gore)* jazz club in a basement, La Station – Gare des Mines (p146; for experimental music) in Aubervilliers, and eco-cultural hub **La Cité Fertile** (Map p144) in Pantin, have brought new energy to forgotten corners. Massive art incubators like POUSH (p146) in Aubervilliers and the **Fiminco Foundation** in Romainville now house international artists. Even former universities and factories, like Césure in the Latin Quarter and an old airship hangar in Meudon, are now cultural spaces, blending performance, community and creativity.

FOOD & ART INSIDE OLD TRAIN STATIONS

The 32km **Petite Ceinture**, or 'PC', railway built around Paris some 150 years ago, is the favoured territory of social recluses, homeless people and *cataphiles* that emerge from clandestine bars hidden below ground in the city's catacombs, a network of tunnels that runs underneath the city. A number of its abandoned train stations have also been turned into bars, such as **La REcyclerie** and **Hasard Ludique**, that offer food, drinks, concerts and various other events all year round. Elsewhere in town, check out **La Gare – Le Gore** jazz club with a nightclub in the basement, La Muette restaurant and Poinçon cafe. The railway itself is slowly being reclaimed by the City Hall as a bucolic promenade.

 MORE TOP RESTAURANT PICKS IN NORTH PARIS

L'arpaon: A tiny spot with sleek retro vibes in Jules Joffrin at the foot of Montmartre, serves an excellent twist on *vols-au-vent* served with natural wines. *7.30-10.30pm Mon-Fri €€*

Fana: A warm, minimalist Michelin-approved bistro with a concise, ever-changing market menu and inventive plates that showcase French terroir. *12.15-2pm and 7.30-10pm Mon-Sat €€*

Restaurant Montcalm: On a quiet street in the 18th, Montcalm offers polished small plates and a generous wine list in an intimate, stylish setting. *12.30-2.30pm & 8-10.30pm Tue-Fri, 8-10.30pm Sat €€*

Le Maquis: This convivial favourite on rue des Cloys balances bistro classics with modern flair, drawing locals nightly for its bold tasting menu. *12.30-2.30pm & 7.30-10.30pm Tue-Fri €€*

Barbès, La Chapelle & Canal St-Martin

A crossroads of global cultures, this vibrant area hums with street markets, music venues, and bold flavours from Africa to India. Nearby, Canal St-Martin and Colonel Fabien blend industrial charm with bohemian, quietly rebellious energy.

THE AFRICA CONNECTION

Paris' African heritage is complex, runs deep and is rooted in its former colonies – Senegal, Mali, Ivory Coast, Algeria and the Democratic Republic of Congo were once part of the French colonial empire – especially in neighbourhoods like Château Rouge and La Goutte d'Or in Barbès. These areas pulse with life, from the scent of grilled meat and bissap juice to the colourful stalls of Marché Dejean selling spices, fabrics and beauty products from across the continent. Institutions like the Musée Dapper and La Colonie (now closed but influential) have spotlighted African art and thought. Music venues like Le 360 and New Morning showcase musical talent from all over Africa.

Global Sounds
Local voices and global beats

Northern Paris is rich in the number of music venues it has scattered all over. For instance, **FGO-Barbara** *(fgo-barbara.fr)* is a vibrant cultural hub in north Paris, offering 2500-sq-m dedicated to music creation, with rehearsal and recording studios and a concert venue. It supports both emerging talent and established independent artists. Nearby, **Le 360** *(le360paris.com)* is a fixture of the independent international music scene, with five floors of workshops, studios, and residency spaces, plus multiple concert venues and a restaurant, making it a cornerstone of the area's music culture. Further south, the **New Morning** *(newmorning.com)* showcases eclectic, predominantly Black artists spanning jazz to hip-hop, while **Alhambra** *(alhambra-paris.com)* hosts a varied programme from pop concerts to stand-up comedy, and the **Adidas Arena** *(adidasarena.com)* built for the Olympics, hosts concerts and sports events.

Theatrical Treasures
Creativity, history and innovation

Paris is a city where theatre thrives, with venues like the atmospheric 1800s **Théâtre des Bouffes du Nord** *(bouffesdunord.com)*. With its carved wood balconies, the theatre is a hotbed for contemporary theatre talent. Westwards along the main boulevard, **Le Louxor** *(cinemalouxor.fr)* cinema dazzles with its opulent, ancient-Egyptian art deco façade, showing a mix of arthouse films. These spots are just a glimpse into the city's dynamic stage scene, blending classic performances with cutting-edge creativity.

Paris Nightlife Is Back
The return of Paris' nightlife

After a sleepy spell, Paris' nightlife is roaring back to life, especially its electronic music scene. New clubs are opening at a dizzying pace, from the cavernous 3000-sq-m **Mia Mao** *(miamao.fr)* in La Villette to gritty, genre-blending nights at

BARBÈS, LA CHAPELLE & CANAL ST-MARTIN

● SIGHTS
1. Canal St-Martin
2. Chapelle XIV
3. Espace Niemeyer
4. Little India
5. Paris Canal Croisières

● ACTIVITIES
6. Akwa Experience
7. Canauxrama
8. La Montgolfière

● SLEEPING
9. Bloom House Hotel
10. Generator Hostel

● EATING
11. Café les Deux Gares
12. Casimir
13. Côté Canal
14. Early June
15. Krishna Bhavan
16. Le Canon d'Achille
17. Les Enfants Perdus
18. Neni

● DRINKING & NIGHTLIFE
19. Comptoir Général
20. Essaim
21. La Cave à Michel
22. Le Renard
23. Martha

● ENTERTAINMENT
24. Alhambra
25. FGO-Barbara
26. Le 104
27. Le 360
28. New Morning
29. Point Éphémère
30. Théâtre des Bouffes du Nord

● SHOPPING
31. Artazart
32. Jamini
see 32 La Trésorerie
33. Thanx God I'm a V.I.P.
34. Yoyaku

LISTENING BARS

The concept of listening bars, originally popularised in Japan, has inspired the opening of new bars that play vinyl records. Gone are the days of music merely as background noise.

Favourite bars in the north of Paris include wine bar **Stéréo** (*stereoparis.com*), near Pigalle, and tapas bar **Pantobaguette** (*pantobaguette.fr*), close to Montmartre. Elsewhere in town, check out **Le Discobar**, **Montezuma Café**, **Bambino**, **Fréquence**, and original vinyl bar **Les Disquaires**, among others.

Essaim (*instagram.com/essaimparis*) near Gare du Nord. Over in Place de Clichy, **La Fête** (*instagram.com/paris.lafete*) is drawing stylish crowds, while **Fawa Wafa** (p145; *fawa-wafa.org*), tucked under a 19th-*arrondissement* flyover (formerly Le Péripate), offers a raw, DIY energy. Across the city, underground parties and pop-up sets are multiplying, with lineups spanning house, techno, afrobeat, and experimental sounds. It's a good time to be a night owl in Paris, if you can keep up.

Record Revival
Paris Loves Vinyl

Vinyl is having a serious moment in Paris, and the city's revival is best felt in its old and new generation of record shops. **Yoyaku** in La Chapelle is one of Paris' top independent record stores and labels, known for its tightly curated selection of vinyl spanning house, techno, minimal, electro and acid. It also distributes music for over 500 labels and 500 shops worldwide. In 2020, the team opened **Chapelle XIV**, a sleek cultural space in the 20th *arrondissement* that blends a record shop, cafe, art gallery, and creative workshop under one roof. Open daily, it's a great spot to browse records, catch an art show, or soak up Paris's growing vinyl and bar scene. **Dizonord**, near Montmartre, is a playful, eclectic space offering new and secondhand vinyl, books, tapes and kid-friendly events. Over by Canal St-Martin, **Record Station** is a crate-digger's dream, packed with original pressings and imports spanning soul, funk, punk, jazz, reggae and more. There are lots of other spots across the city though; check out the Instagram account **@grooovz.paris** for a map and general vinyl record news in the city.

Canal Strolls
Bohemian chic Paris by the water

A short walk from Gare de l'Est, **Canal St-Martin** offers a slower, stylish side of Paris. The **tree-lined waterway**, spanned by iron **footbridges** and flanked by cobblestone

EATING IN NORTHERN PARIS: OUR PICKS

Krishna Bhavan: A really well-priced vegetarian restaurant mixing South Indian and Sri Lankan flavours and serving excellent thalis. *11am-11pm* €

Neni: This cosy, stylish spot is great for flavourful Middle Eastern plates like roasted cauliflower, baba ganoush and warm pita. *7-10.30am & 12-10.30pm* €

Casimir: Recently refitted, this bistro is still a favourite with the locals for its fantastic food with flair, like chunky *pâté en croûte* and perfectly crisp rib of beef. *9am-11pm* €€

Café les Deux Gares: A bistro that was reimagined by designer Luke Edward-Hall. Serves dishes where vegetables shine as brightly as meat. *9am-midnight Mon-Fri, from 10am Sat* €€

Le Canon d'Achille: Natural wines and Mediterranean-inspired small plates are the mainstays at this relaxed spot. *noon-2pm & 5-11pm Mon-Fri, 5pm-12am Sat* €€

Early June: A globally minded chef-in-residence concept where each visit offers a new, creative tasting menu, in a cosy, minimalist setting. *6pm-midnight Wed-Sun* €€

Comptoir Général: Tropical cocktails, Afro-Caribbean snacks, and an overgrown, eclectic decor make this canal-side bar feel like an urban jungle. *hours vary* €€

Les Enfants Perdus: A romantic neobistro with vintage charm, serving refined French fare and one of the best brunches in the area. *noon-2.30pm & 7-10.30pm* €€

Canal St-Martin

A FEAST OF INDIAN FLAVOURS & FABRICS

The inception of this enclave traces back to post-1947, following India's independence, when many South Asians, particularly Tamils from Sri Lanka, sought refuge from civil unrest. In La Chapelle district, **Little India** has heaps of well-priced restaurants like Krishna Bhavan, colourful sari shops and temples like **Manicka Vinayakar Alayam Temple**, the epicentre of the annual **Ganesh Chaturthi** procession (August), when the neighbourhood transforms with lively celebrations.

pavements comes to life in warmer months when locals settle along the banks with wine, snacks and portable speakers. It's the kind of place where **picnics** stretch into impromptu dinners at a nearby restaurant. It's a favourite area with locals because its cluster of **street-art-covered thoroughfares** are packed with creative boutiques, trendy bars and restaurants. Browse the beautiful Indian homeware at **Jamini** *(jaminidesign.com)*, the carefully curated homeware at **La Trésorerie** *(latresorerie.fr)* and the treasures at thrift store **Thanx God I'm a V.I.P.** *(thanxgod.com)*, where you might be able to dig out a Dior sports jacket or designer dress at a bargain price. If you're here to work and you want to work out, then the glass-roof **La Montgolfière** *(lamontgolfiereclub.com)*, inside an old hot-air-balloon workshop, should be your go-to. Pop into bookshop **Artazart** *(artazart.com)* to leaf through the fantastic children's books and design magazines from all over the globe.

Paris Off the Radar

Politics and underground culture

A few blocks northeast, Colonel Fabien anchors a lesser-known patch of the city with an edge all its own. The neighbourhood takes its name from a WWII resistance fighter and is home to the striking **Espace Niemeyer**, the Communist Party headquarters, a swooping glass-and-concrete landmark designed by Oscar Niemeyer. While the building opens to the public only during France's annual Heritage Days, its presence sets

GRANGE AUX BELLES

In the early 1980s artists congregated at the Grange aux Belles club, off square du Colonel Fabien, for Sunday afternoon parties with DJ Chabin that mixed reggae, jazz-rock, zouk, funk and hip-hop. Music and graffiti came together here with breakdancing, and artists from Afrika Bambaataa to NTM passed through. The creative energy of the early days was documented by photographer, TV presenter and journalist Sophie Bramly, who recently published *Yo!*, a fanzine that includes some of her best photography from that time. The venue has long since closed but the memories are still very much alive.

Canal St-Martin cruise

the tone: bold, unconventional, and proudly local. Around it, narrow backstreets brim with casual, creative restaurants and unpolished bars that feel lifted from Berlin or Brooklyn. Walk to the **rue Ste-Marthe**, a quiet square with laid-back bars, and nearby, try **La Cave à Michel** for the wines and **Le Renard**, a fun, casual bar with floor seating, as well as **Martha**, usually packed with locals who come for a nightcap.

Canal Cruise

Exploring northern Paris on the water

As well as a cruise along the River Seine (p67), it's also possible to explore northern Paris on a canal cruise. Make a booking to explore the **Canal St-Martin** and **Parc de la Villette** and watch the locals sitting canalside enjoying drinks, and pass through swing bridges and banks covered in street art. Several companies offer cruises, such as **Canauxrama** *(canauxrama.com)* in Jaurès, **Paris Canal Croisières** *(pariscanal.com)* from Porte de Pantin, and **Akwa Experience** *(akwa-experience.com)*, from whom you can hire a self-drive boat with a group of people and putter along the Canal de l'Ourcq, bookended by Jaurès and La Villette.

Jaurès to La Villette

In summer, Canal St-Martin and La Villette buzz with life – people picnic by the water, lounge on terraces, or explore La Villette's vast park, with kid-friendly fun by day and vibrant clubbing scenes by night.

The Creative Edge of Paris
Music, art, clubs and culture

This last pocket of Paris, just before the *périphérique* (ring road) spills into the suburbs, is an eldorado for **night owls** and culture seekers. Along the canal between Stalingrad and Jaurès, iconic venues like **La Rotonde**, housed in a grand 18th-century rotunda, and **Point Ephémère** *(point ephemere.org)*, a hub for alternative music and visual arts, pulse with activity year-round. Keep walking towards Riquet and you'll find **Le 104** *(104.fr)*, a multidisciplinary space that's part gallery, part community center, and part dance-floor for the city's youth. If you're there in summer, then plan an evening at the **Cinéma en Plein air**, an annual open-air film festival in the Parc de la Villette, which is a beloved summer tradition; just bring a blanket and some snacks and you're set. **Festival 100%** in spring is also worth popping by for the cutting-edge performances, installations, and art by emerging talents. Another festival worth adding to your diary is also the **Mondial du Tatouage** (the World Tattoo Convention) which brings together tattoo artists from all over the world under one roof at the Grande Halle; there are a number of talks, exhibitions and events too.

Life Along the Canal
Cruises, cafes sun and sand

Hop on a canal boat for a leisurely ride from Villette to Bastille, drifting through locks and even an underground tunnel, a surprising adventure for both adults and kids. Back on land, stroll the canal banks and take your pick from casual cafes, craft beer terraces, and waterside restaurants. In summer, the area transforms for Paris Plages (July to September), with lounge chairs, boules, pedal boats, pop-up bars, and beach games turning this little patch of the city into an urban holiday escape.

Science, Sound & Silver Spheres
Family fun and futuristic vibes

The city opens up at **Parc de la Villette** *(lavillette.com)*, a green sprawl anchored by the **Cité des Sciences et de l'Industrie** *(cite-sciences.fr)*, one of Paris's best museums for immersive, kid-friendly learning. Don't miss the recently reopened

LA VILLETTE: PARIS' PLAYGROUND

Spanning 55 hectares in northeast Paris, **La Villette** is the city's largest park and a bold blend of modern design and cultural ambition. Created by architect Bernard Tschumi, it hosts exhibitions, performances, and workshops year-round. With over 20 themed gardens and open lawns, it's also a space for play, sport, and relaxation. Highlights include the eco-friendly Jardins Passagers and a small urban farm for children. There are also a number of concert venues and clubs, as well as exhibition spaces. Make sure to book ahead of time on the website.

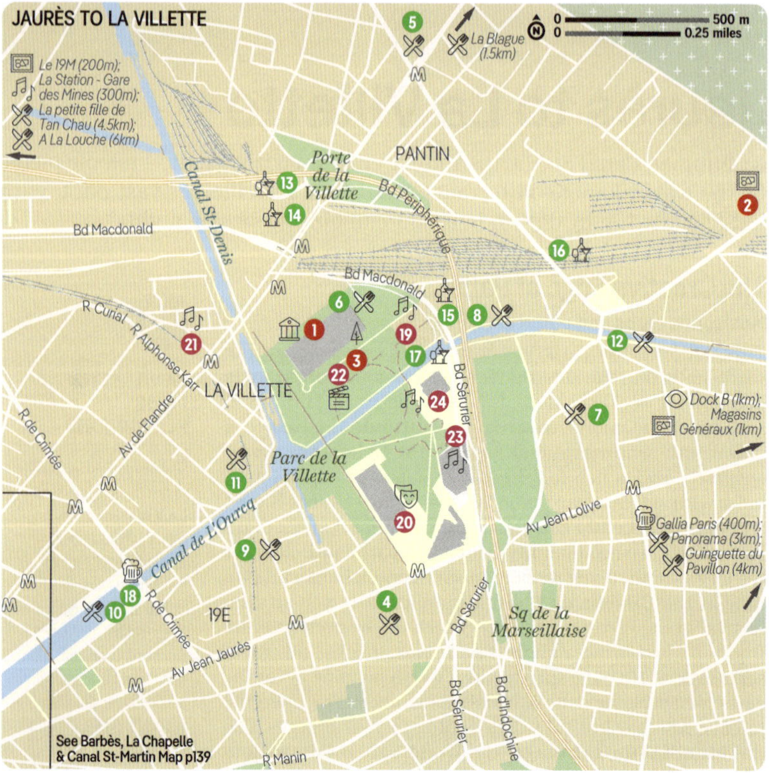

JAURÈS TO LA VILLETTE

SIGHTS
1. Cité des Sciences et de l'Industrie
2. Galerie Thaddaeus Ropac Pantin
3. Parc de la Villette
   see 2 Thaddeus Ropac Pantin

EATING
4. Au Boeuf Couronné
5. Auberkitchen
6. Boom Boom Villette
7. Chéri Coco
8. Jardin21
9. La Cantine Bretonne
10. Le Pavillon des Canaux
11. Les Bancs Publics
12. Les Pantins

DRINKING & NIGHTLIFE
13. Fawa Wafa
14. Glazart
15. Kilomètre25
16. La Cité Fertile
17. La Péniche Cinéma
   see 8 Mia Mao
18. Paname Brewing Company

ENTERTAINMENT
19. Cabaret Sauvage
20. Grande Halle de la Villette
21. La Gare - Le Gore
22. La Géode
23. Le Trabendo
24. Le Zénith

EATING & DRINKING IN LA VILLETTE: OUR PICKS

Le Pavillon des Canaux: A whimsical cafe-bar styled like a cosy home. Enjoy coffee in the 'bathtub' or work from the 'bedroom'. Situated by the canal, it's a favourite among creatives and remote workers. *hours vary* €€

Paname Brewing Company: This canal-side microbrewery attracts a lively crowd with its house-made beers and expansive deck overlooking the water – ideal for sunset pints and people-watching. *11am-1pm* €€

Les Bancs Publics: A straightforward, charming bistro that sets up tables along the canal during warmer months. Expect affordable wine, classic French dishes, and a relaxed, local atmosphere. *8am-2am Mon-Sat, 9am-6pm Sun* €

Au Boeuf Couronné: The last vestige of the old Villette meat halls, this Belle Époque gem serves top-quality steaks in a chic, throwback dining room, like a rediscovered monument to Parisian tradition. *noon-midnight* €€

and refurbished **La Géode** *(lageode.fr)*, a huge mirrored dome and 3D cinema that catches the sky in its curves. By night, nearby venues like **Le Zénith** *(le-zenith.com)*, **Le Trabendo** *(letrabendo.net)*, **Cabaret Sauvage** *(cabaretsauvage.com)*, and newcomer Mia Mao (p138) take over, offering everything from indie gigs to global club nights. On the water, **La Péniche Cinéma** *(penichecinema.com)*, a floating club-bar, and the **Grande Halle de la Villette** *(lavillette.com)*, a former abattoir turned events hall, complete the vibrant scene.

Beats Beneath the Flyover
Open-air parties and raw energy

For a grittier, underground vibe, head east to **Kilomètre25** *(kilometre25.fr)* and **Fawa Wafa** *(fawa-wafa.org)*, open-air house and techno venues tucked beneath a flyover. Here, the party often stretches into the morning, with pop-ups, DJ sets, and eclectic visuals. Long-standing favorite **Glazart** *(glazart.com)* mixes genres like techno, rap, and metal, and even has a beach in summer. Whether you're club-hopping or lounging canalside with a drink, this stretch of northeast Paris proves the city's cultural scene is anything but sleepy.

While quieter, Pantin has also seen a revival around its canal, starting with an offshoot of prestigious gallery **Thaddeus Ropac Pantin** *(ropac.net)*, along with iconic French fashion brand Hermès transferring its ateliers to the area. Subsequently, a cultural hub on the site of an old train depot, **La Cité Fertile** (p137; *citefertile.com*), opened its doors here too and hosts various events and festivals. The striking **Magasins Généraux** *(magasinsgeneraux.com)*, a former warehouse turned creative campus, now houses agencies and artists, while nearby you'll find **Dock B** *(dockbpantin.com)*, a space for contemporary art and club nights, and **Gallia Paris** *(galliaparis.com)*, a homegrown brewery and bar you can visit on set days.

Just south of Pantin, east of the suburb of Les Lilas, Romainville, with its small detached houses, has attracted families looking for more space at reasonable prices. Hosting various exhibitions, concerts and residencies inside a former heating plant, is **Fondation Fiminco** *(fondationfiminco.com)*, set to become Europe's biggest cultural quarter.

LA VILLETTE UNCOVERED

This guide is not meant to deter visitors from exploring another side of the city – coming to La Villette is a wonderful opportunity to discover a less-polished, more industrial area that is full of surprises. Here, families will find plenty to do, from clubs and concerts to unique events and children's attractions. However, a word of caution: although the area offers pleasant canals and expansive parkland, it can feel somewhat unsafe at night. It is wise to remain extra vigilant when walking the canals alone after dark. During the day, La Villette bustles with picnicking families and friendly, energetic crowds enjoying its vibrant, diverse atmosphere.

 EATING ALONG OURCQ CANAL: OUR PICKS

La Cantine Bretonne: Proper buckwheat galettes made just like your Breton grandma would, including classics like *la complète* with artisanal ham, cheese and an egg, sunny side up. *8am-11.30pm* €

Boom Boom Villette: Located inside the Villette complex, this newish industrial-style market has street food from sushi to banh mi at over 20 kiosks, with long tables to sit at in the middle. *9am-1am* €

Jardin21: A 1850-sq-m outdoor bar on the banks of the canal, where locals come for the concerts and events while grabbing a drink or a bite to eat – like the giant ham and cheese boards. *hours vary* €€

Côté Canal: A low-key cafe right on the canal, serving well-priced staples like steak tartare. It's a handy spot for meeting friends when you don't have a reservation. *9am-2am Mon-Fri, 10am-2am Sat & Sun* €

St-Denis, St-Ouen, Pantin & Aubervilliers

Once cast-off suburbs, they are slowly becoming eclectic cultural hubs where raw nightlife, avant-garde art incubators and high-end players, including names like Chanel, merge with a richly mixed urban community.

The 'Grand Paris' Expansion
Hidden gems, culture and wild partying

Paris is expanding beyond the confines of the ring road, through an extension of its metro lines, which has accelerated due to the Olympic Games in 2024. 'Grand Paris' includes areas of the 93 department, which has suffered a bad rap due to reports of gangs, and ghettos, like St-Ouen, St-Denis, Aubervilliers and Pantin, originally small industrial towns on the tram line. Young Parisian families wanting more space for their money have flocked to these areas, driving up prices and bringing trendy restaurants, bars and boutiques.

The star attractions remain the Marché aux Puces de St-Ouen (p148) flea market and the **Basilique de St-Denis** *(saint-denis-basilique.fr)*. Dating from the 1100s, it is France's largest royal necropolis (42 kings and 32 queens are buried here). The tombs in the crypt, adorned with lifelike *gisants* (recumbent figures) carved from death masks, are Europe's largest collection of funerary art and the main reason to make the trip out here.

In Aubervilliers, check out events at **POUSH** *(poush.fr)*, the city's biggest contemporary art incubator, located inside a repurposed factory. Also in the area you'll find **La Station – Gare des Mines** *(lastation.paris)*, a platform for emerging musical artists. Lately, clubbing spots like **Le Point Fort d'Aubervilliers** *(lepointfort.com)* have been offering parties, concerts and family events in the day, surrounded by tall residential blocks.

EATING IN ST-DENIS & AUBERVILLIERS: OUR PICKS

La petite fille de Tan Chau: A Vietnamese canteen in St-Denis with a striking vermilion façade near Musée Paul-Eluard, its menu features pho, bo bun and banh mi under €15. *11.30am-2.30pm Mon-Fri* €

A la Louche: This charming new spot in St-Denis blends vintage style with serious culinary chops. Chef Julien Attal serves up inventive, well-sourced dishes in a warm space that welcomes all generations. *hours vary* €

La Blague: In a 1970s brutalist landmark, it serves creative, organic veggie dishes for €14, with coffee, books, and even homework help, making it a rare community cafe that feeds both body and soul. *hours vary* €

Auberkitchen: A bright, light-filled canteen; dishes are all made using local organic seasonal produce from nearby farms, which you can also buy to take home. *10am-4pm Mon & Tue, to 11.30pm Wed-Sat* €

Swan on the Ourcq Canal, Pantin

Present Day Vibe
Often overlooked or unfairly labelled

The northern suburbs of Paris – think St-Denis, Aubervilliers, Pantin – are quietly redefining the city's cultural edge. Here, brutalist architecture meets buzzing canteens, cutting-edge art spaces, underground clubs, and experimental kitchens. While gentrification unfolds at a slower, patchier pace than in central Paris, it's precisely this mix, rough and refined, old and emerging, that makes the area so compelling. From Chanel's fashion workshops (Le 19M) in Aubervilliers to natural wine bars in Romainville, the 93 is full of surprises. Come for the food, stay for the energy – and maybe rethink your Paris map while you're at it.

LOOKING BACK

Once an industrial powerhouse, Pantin, located just northeast of Paris, has undergone a remarkable transformation. What was once a gritty manufacturing district has bloomed into a vibrant cultural enclave. The area's industrial roots still show through its canals and historic buildings, but today, the likes of Hermès have made their mark, relocating their ateliers to Pantin. With artistic spaces like La Cité Fertile and galleries springing up, the area is buzzing with creativity. A place where old Parisian charm meets modern design, Pantin now offers an exciting blend of culture, innovation and just the right amount of edge.

EATING IN PANTIN & ROMAINVILLE: OUR PICKS

Les Pantins: A relaxed restaurant serving modern high-end French food rustled up with well-sourced produce and great natural wines. *noon-2pm & 7.30-10pm Tue-Fri* €€

Chéri Coco: Pantin's first vegan canteen, it offers a vibrant Afro-Caribbean menu. Expect oyster mushrooms, plantain croquettes, and a daily lunch special. *lunch Mon-Wed, lunch & dinner Thu* €

Panorama: The chefs here bring bold, seasonal dishes and wild wines to their Romainville bistro, with a menu featuring marinated zucchini, roasted aubergine, and confit pork belly. *hours vary* €€

Guinguette du Pavillon: Offers homemade dishes at affordable prices, featuring a seasonal, plant-based menu. The cosy space, ideal for families, serves coffee, pastries, and hearty meals. *9am-6pm Tue-Fri* €

Above: antique kitchen utensils for sale; right: homewares, Marché Vernaison

TOP EXPERIENCE

Les Puces de St-Ouen

Founded in 1885, the Marché aux Puces de St-Ouen (*pucesdeparissaintouen.com*) is the world's largest antiques market, located just beyond Paris' northern edge. Spanning 12 distinct markets, it's a treasure trove of antiques, vintage furniture, rare collectibles, fashion and curiosities. Whether you're a serious collector or a curious wanderer, the maze-like alleys offer endless inspiration and irresistible old-world charm.

A Storied Legacy of Treasure Hunting

Just beyond Paris' northern edge, Les Puces unfolds like a village within a village, equal parts treasure trove and time capsule. What began as an informal sprawl of rag pickers selling secondhand wares, has evolved into the largest antiques market in the world, a labyrinthine network of more than a dozen markets spread across seven hectares. At weekends, some 180,000 visitors descend upon its narrow alleys, hunting for everything from gilded mirrors and art deco light fixtures to vinyl records and timeworn furniture. With its mix of museum-grade galleries and showrooms, dusty bric-a-brac

DON'T MISS

Marché Paul Bert Serpette

Marché de L'Entrepôt

Marché Vernaison

Marché Dauphine

Mob Hotel

Mains d'Oeuvres

PRACTICALITIES

- pucesdeparissaintouen.com
- 8am-noon Fri, 10am-6pm Sat & Sun, 11am-5pm Mon

stalls and discreet ateliers, it offers more than shopping: it's a window into the layered, eclectic soul of Paris.

A Maze of Markets

The allure of Les Puces lies in the diversity and distinct rhythm and charm of each market. Marché Vernaison, the oldest, is a warren of open-air lanes lined with vintage postcards, embroidered linens and costume jewellery. Marché Paul Bert Serpette, the crown jewel, draws a discerning crowd of interior designers and collectors who come for 20th-century design icons, museum-worthy antiques and impeccably curated vignettes. Inside the vaulted glass pavilion of Marché Dauphine, the atmosphere is more freewheeling; think vinyl records, retro cameras, tribal artefacts and the occasional taxidermied bird. L'Entrepôt is one of the smallest markets but it's mighty and has a bunch of old zinc-top brasserie bars and spiral staircases from houses all over the country. The joy, of course, is in the serendipity: a meandering stroll, a spontaneous chat with a vendor, and a find you never knew you needed.

A Weekend Ritual of Culture, Food & People-Watching

A visit here is as much about ambience as it is about the hunt. Open Fridays, Saturdays, Sundays and Mondays, the market comes alive with a mix of locals, designers, tourists and curious *flâneurs*. Live music often spills out of cafes, while dealers chat with regulars over espresso and wine. You'll find locals tucking into couscous at Le Coq d'Or on rue des Rosiers, or enjoying a hearty bistro meal at a bargain price at nearby Le Bouillon du Coq, opened by Michelin star chef Thierry Marx. There's also the stylish Mob Hotel designed by Philippe Starck (not Mob House, which is a little drab), a cult favourite for pizza and cocktails. The flea market isn't just a shopping destination, it's a cultural experience of history, art, and everyday Parisian life, regardless of whether you're buying or just browsing. In fact, La Chope des Puces, an old bistro that puts on jazz concerts, is an ode to the unique spirit of this sprawling village of stalls and showrooms. And if you have time, take in a show or a DJ night at indie arts hub Mains d'Oeuvres, nearby.

HAGGLING

Haggling is part of the charm at Les Puces. Approach vendors with a smile, and you might knock 10-20% off the price. While some accept cards, cash is often preferred for smaller items or better deals. Vendors are relaxed, often found reading, napping, or chatting, and expect you to take your time, happily sharing details about their goods.

TOP TIPS

● The easiest way to reach the market, without having to wade through tens of stalls peddling cheap designer knock-offs, is to get metro line 4 to Porte de Clignancourt. Don't be put off by the unpolished surroundings. Cross the ring road and enter the market on rue des Rosiers. Maps and lots of background information to help you plan your trip here are available on the Puces website.

● Sunday morning is the best time to visit. Vendors are all open, the crowds are manageable, and there's a lively local buzz.

GIMAS/SHUTTERSTOCK

Researched by Rowan Twine

LE MARAIS

INTERSECTION OF HISTORY, LUXURY AND ART

Le Marais has an atmosphere that feels both timeless and cosmopolitan, with a rich variety of architectural styles, fashion and a thriving bar scene.

The 4e *arrondissement* is the only district in Paris that escaped the Haussmannian redesign of Paris, with almost all of its narrow streets and occasionally crooked buildings from the pre-Revolutionary era. Today Le Marais also offers a plethora of activities. Admire stunning 17th- and 18th-century *hôtels particuliers* (private mansions) as you explore, or while visiting the museums, which many *hôtels particuliers* now house. Enjoy falafel in a historically Jewish district, then stretch your budget in trendy boutiques, designer stores and art galleries. An LGBTIQ-friendly attitude welcomes the community to rainbow-hued bars and clubs. Le Marais invites exploration of its winding lanes and never fails to satisfy.

TOP TIP

Don't underestimate the time and walking needed to fully appreciate Le Marais. It may not cover much ground in Paris, but this district is particularly dense, with its narrow, winding streets, and it isn't well connected by the metro. Note that the area can be particularly busy on weekends.

Musée Carnavalet (p157)

See page p310 for places to stay in Le Marais.

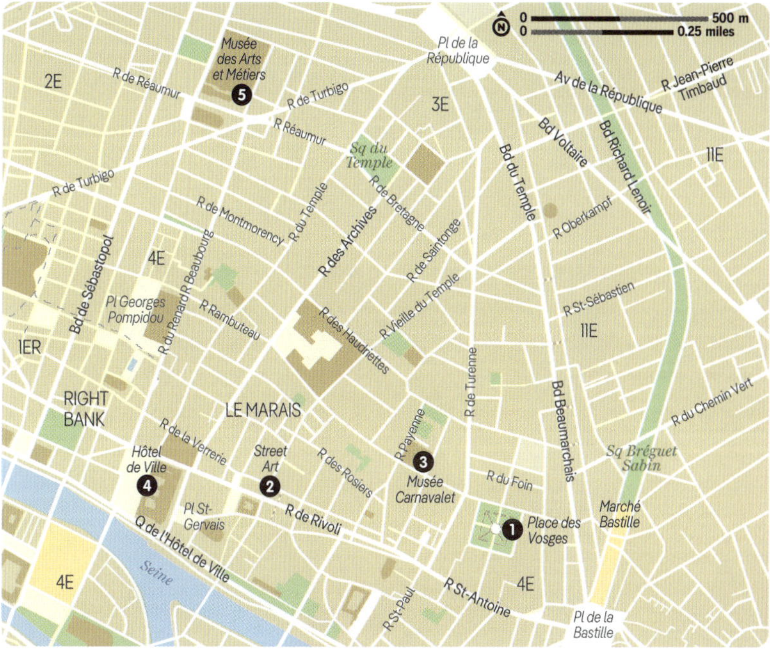

Highlights

❶ Place des Vosges
Picnic in the most elegant former royal square in the city. **p155**

❷ Street Art
Explore a pixelated world of street art adding whimsy to buildings throughout Le Marais. **p159**

❸ Musée Carnavalet
Discover the varied layers of life in Paris' throughout history. **p157**

❹ Hôtel de Ville
Admire the stunning neoclassical façade of Paris' old institutional heart. **p155**

❺ Musée des Arts et Métiers
Be inspired by the breadth of human ingenuity at this richly diverse museum. **p157**

Getting Around

Walking
Le Marais is best explored on foot to navigate the crowds, browse boutiques and admire the architecture. Don't underestimate how long it can take to explore all the side streets.

Bicycle
Flying down the rue Rivoli bike lanes is a great way to access Le Marais, but weekend crowds can be frustrating, so it's easiest to save the bike for larger streets.

Underground
For the lower Marais, the best stop is St-Paul, but it can get crowded on weekends. Metro stations Filles du Calvaire and Arts et Métiers are both good alternatives.

LE MARAIS NORTH

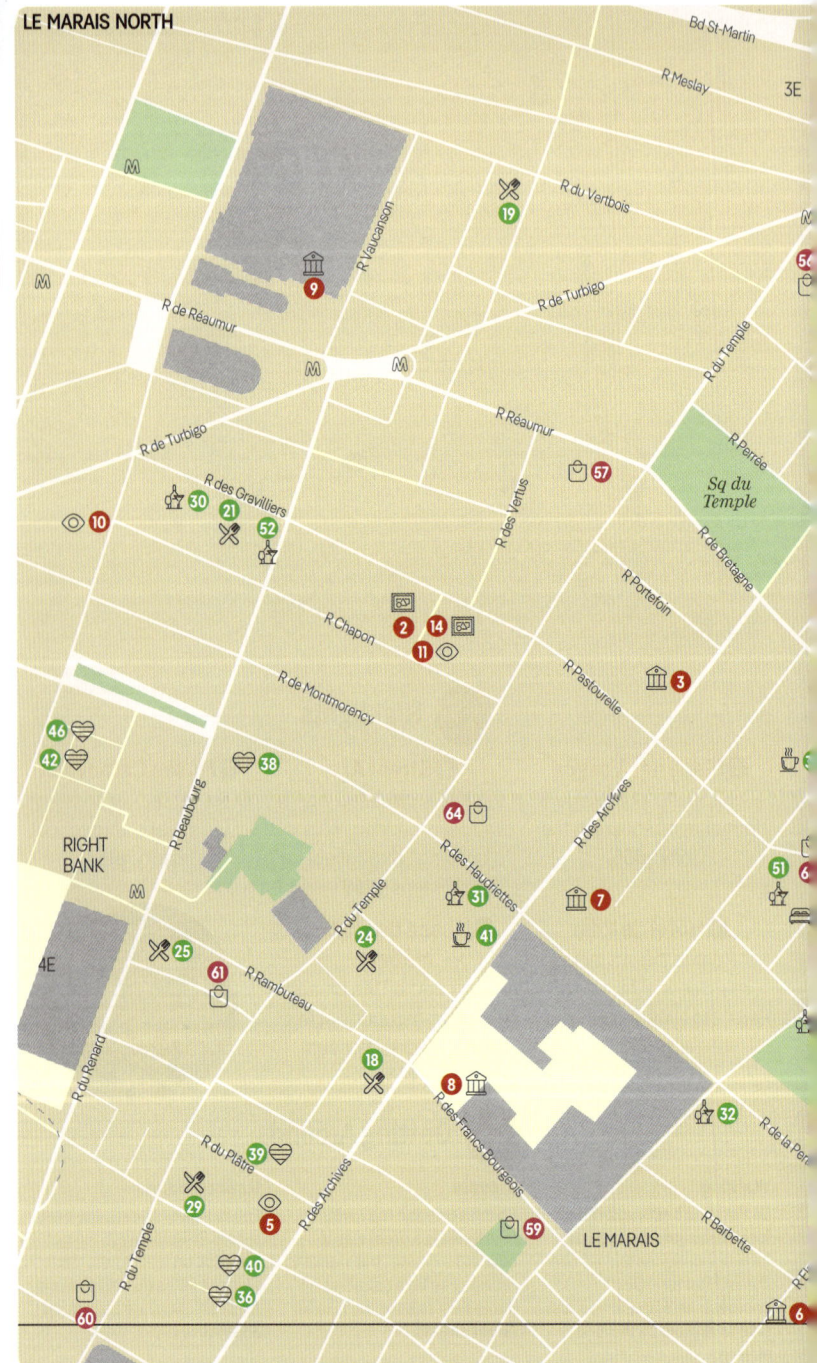

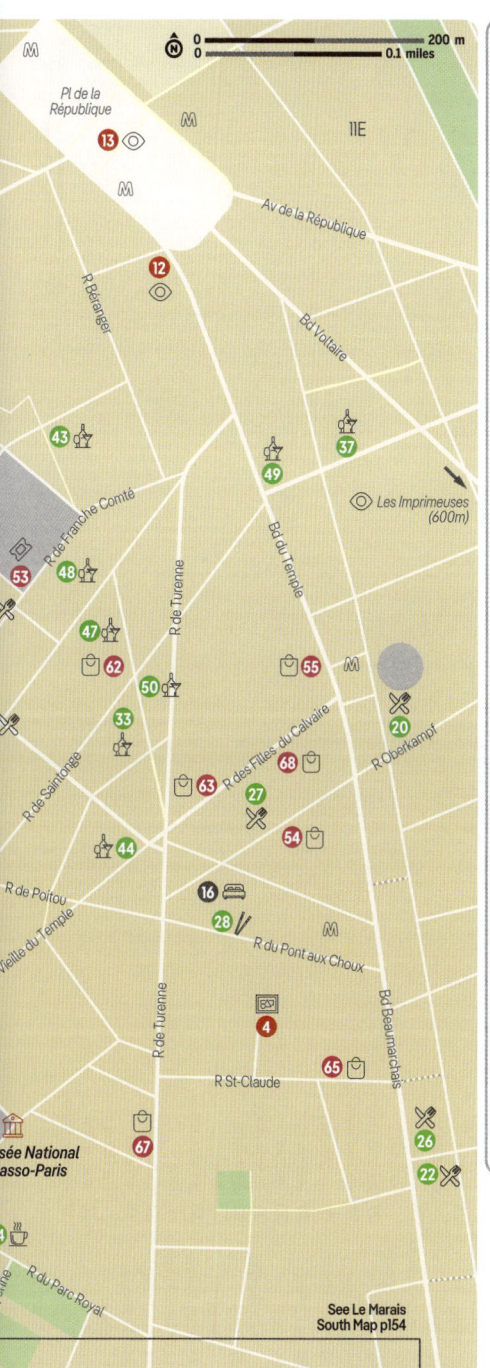

★ HIGHLIGHTS
1. Musée National Picasso-Paris

● SIGHTS
2. Christian Berst
3. Fondation Henri Cartier-Bresson
4. Galerie Emmanuel Perrotin
5. Lafayette Anticipations
6. Musée Cognacq-Jay
7. Musée de la Chasse et de la Nature
8. Musée des Archives Nationales
9. Musée des Arts et Métiers
10. Passage de l'Ancre
11. Passage des Gravilliers
12. Passage Vendôme
13. Place de la République
14. Sator

● SLEEPING
15. Boudoir des Muses
16. Suzie Blue

● EATING
17. Bistrot Instinct
18. Carré Pain de Mie
19. Chez Eating
20. Keili
21. Kitchen
22. Land&Monkeys
23. Le Marché des Enfants Rouges
24. Le Reflet
25. Legay Choc
26. Moon Croissant
27. Petite Île Boulangerie
28. Pontochoux
29. Tata Burger

● DRINKING & NIGHTLIFE
30. Andy Wahloo
31. Bar Nouveau
32. Café La Perle
33. Candelaria
34. Causeries
35. Cortado
36. Cox
37. Delicatessen Place
38. Duplex Bar
39. Elles Bar
40. freedj
41. Ha Noi 1988 Flowers & Archives
42. La Mutinerie
43. Le Barav
44. Le Progrès
45. Le Saint-Gervais
46. Les Aimant·e·s
47. Little Red Door
48. Maison Proust
49. Martin
50. Mesures
51. Sotto
52. Spootnik Bar
see 21 Terra bar à vins

● ENTERTAINMENT
53. Le Carreau du Temple

● SHOPPING
54. Alix D. Reynis
55. BIS Boutique Solidaire
56. Bobby
57. BRUT
58. Empreintes
59. Fragonard
60. Free 'P Star
61. Les Cahiers de Colette
62. Liquides Bar à Parfums
63. Papier Tigre
64. Praline
65. RSVP
66. Sabre
67. The Room
68. Yvon Lambert

THE GUIDE — LE MARAIS

LE MARAIS

LE MARAIS SOUTH

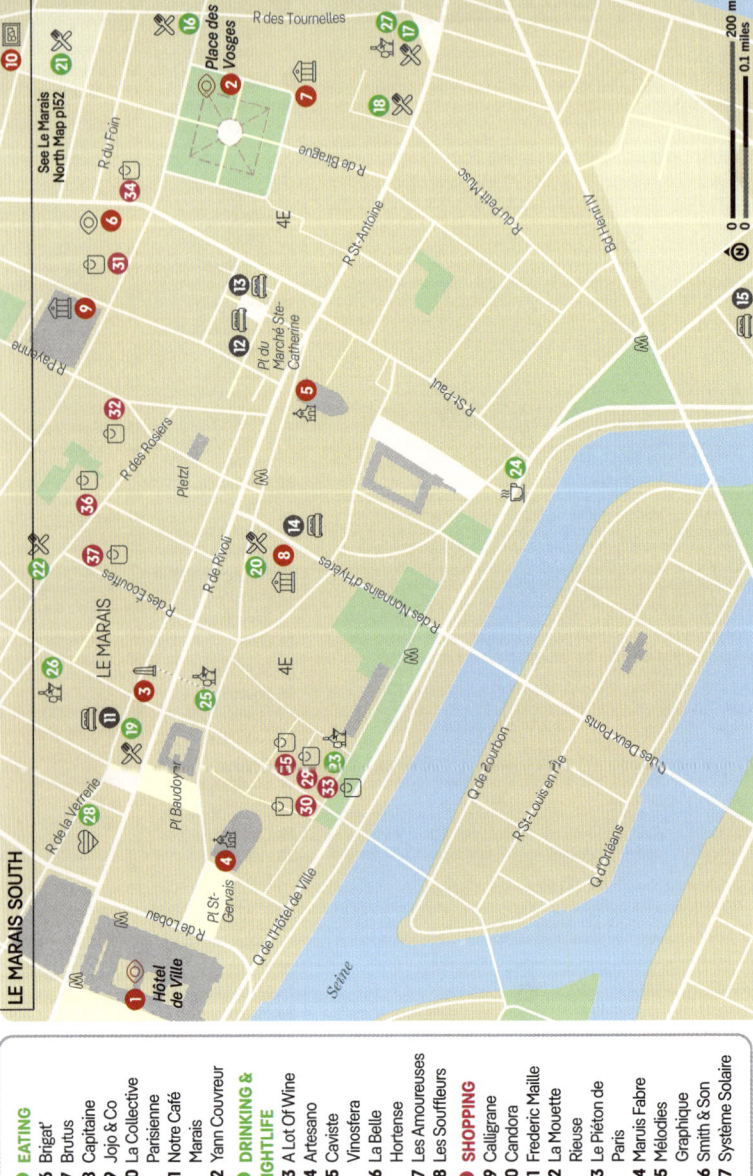

★ HIGHLIGHTS
1 Hôtel de Ville
2 Place des Vosges

● SIGHTS
3 Cheshire Cat
4 Église St-Gervais-St-Protais
5 Église St-Paul St-Louis
6 MAIF Social Club
7 Maison de Victor Hugo
8 Maison Européenne de la Photographie
9 Musée Carnavalet
10 Polka Galerie

● SLEEPING
11 Hôtel 9Confidentiel
12 Hôtel de JoBo
13 Hôtel Jeanne d'Arc le Marais
14 MIJE Fourcy
15 The People Marais

● EATING
16 Brigat'
17 Brutus
18 Capitaine
19 Jojo & Co
20 La Collective Parisienne
21 Notre Café Marais
22 Yann Couvreur

● DRINKING & NIGHTLIFE
23 A Lot Of Wine
24 Artesano
25 Caviste Vinosfera
26 La Belle Hortense
27 Les Amoureuses
28 Les Souffleurs

● SHOPPING
29 Calligrane
30 Candora
31 Frederic Maille
32 La Mouette Rieuse
33 Le Piéton de Paris
34 Marais Fabre
35 Mélodies Graphique
36 Smith & Son
37 Système Solaire

THE GUIDE

154

An Enduring Royal Square   MAP P154
Relax in the place des Vosges

Place des Vosges has truly stood the test of time. The vision of King Henry IV, who wanted a grand square in Paris, this iconic landmark was constructed in 1605 and has remained a social hub and one of the most elegant squares in the city throughout the centuries.

Today visitors and locals alike still converge upon the spacious lawns beneath the shade of trees. The square is ideal for picnicking, so consider stopping into **Brigat'** *(brigat.paris)* to buy some tiramisu to enjoy on the grass. Later, stroll the arcades to admire art galleries and *hôtels particuliers*, including the former residence of writer Victor Hugo, or have coffee at one of the traditional French restaurants sitting under the arcades.

The Intersection of History & Politics   MAP P152
Admire Place de la République

Place de la République has become one of Paris' most renowned squares, largely due to the years of social unrest that have marked recent decades in France. Symbolising democracy and the collective spirit of the people, the square serves as a gathering point for demonstrations and marches, with groups often gathering around the statue of Marianne in the centre. Criss-crossed by commuters during the week, at the weekend this expansive square becomes a space frequented by skateboarders, dancing clubs, street performers and locals who come together to socialise and participate in civic activities.

Admire Paris' Old Institutional Heart   MAP P154
Visit the Hôtel de Ville

The intricate neoclassical façade of Paris' town hall can evoke a sense of awe. The **Hôtel de Ville** features numerous statues representing notable figures from Paris' history, including politicians, scientists, artists and industry pioneers, as well as allegories of the arts.

The esplanade, now known as place de la Libération, was called place de Grève until President Charles de Gaulle delivered his 'liberation of Paris' speech at the Hôtel de Ville in

MARIANNE

In the centre of place de la République you're greeted by a woman standing tall on a richly decorated plinth. This triumphant statue depicts Marianne, the personification of the French Republic. She has been its emblem since the First Republic in 1792, but this statue was created in 1883 by sculptor Léopold Morice. In this depiction she holds aloft an olive branch in her right hand, symbolising peace, and rests her left hand on a tablet inscribed with *les droits d'hommes*, the rights of men. Encircling the plinth at her feet are three stone statues that represent *La Liberté, La Fraternité* and *L'Égalité* – liberty, brotherhood and equality – the values of the French motto. A lion proudly guards an urn labelled *suffrage universel* (universal suffrage).

Get bottles from its sister location, Delicatessen Cave!

 DRINKING IN LE MARAIS: BUZZING WINE BARS   MAP P152

Le Barav: The perfect neighbourhood bar for great prices and an excellent playlist. If the terrace is full, get your name on the waiting list. *5pm-midnight Tue-Sat*

Martin: This sprawling terrace is always full of conversation and cigarette smoke; they serve fresh small plates with a lengthy natural-wine list. *4pm-2am Tue-Sat*

Terra bar à vins: A modern wine bar where well-dressed patrons enjoy wine and a bite to eat in minimalist surroundings. *7pm-1am Tue-Sat*

Delicatessen Place: Get comfy in this wine bar decorated straight from a vintage market and enjoy glasses of wine served by recommendation. *5-10pm*

PARTICULIER MUSEUMS

Discover a variety of topics while exploring magnificent former *hôtels particuliers*.

Musée Cognacq-Jay (Map p152) Housed in the Hôtel Donon are the collections of Ernest Cognacq and Marie-Louise Jay, founders of La Samaritaine.

Musée National Picasso-Paris (Map p152) Dating to the 17th century, the Hôtel Salé's classic architecture contrasts with 5000 artworks by Picasso.

Maison de Victor Hugo (Map p154) The residence of this icon of French literature showcases his manuscripts and memorabilia.

Musée de la Chasse et de la Nature (Map p152) This unusual museum explores the historical relationship of humans and animals with a focus on the hunt.

Musée Carnavalet (Map p154) A vast museum that spans Paris' history as well as the 16th-century Hôtel des Ligneris and 17th-century Hôtel Le Peletier de Saint-Fargeau.

Hôtel de Ville (p155)

1944. It now regularly welcomes cultural events and street performers, but these kinds of shows replaced another – for five centuries it had been the site where criminals were executed.

Delve Into the Archives

MAP P152

Reading at the Musée des Archives

Most locals frequently appreciate the **Musée des Archives Nationales** *(archives-nationales.culture.gouv.fr; free)* for its gardens, some of which were closed at the time of writing, hidden behind the walls of the Hôtel de Soubise. But it is also the custodian of precious documents forming the foundation of the French republic.

The mission of the National Archives is to preserve and safeguard not only legislative acts but also significant objects that represent the establishment of the republic, such as seals and the Constitutional Act. The museum showcases its collections through a regularly updated exhibition that explores their different types of documents, from papyrus scrolls to coded letters.

EATING IN LE MARAIS: MODERN FRENCH RESTAURANTS — MAPS P152, P154

Brutus: Enjoy crisp *galettes* and artisanal cider on a sun-soaked *terrasse*. Leave room for the house speciality, the chocolate hazelnut *galette*. *hours vary* €€

Le Reflet: A convivial French bistronomy restaurant that employs people living with Down syndrome. *hours vary* €€

Bistrot Instinct: Creative seasonal menus from Chef Maximilian Wollek – his *œuf mayonnaise* is a permanent fixture, with good reason. *noon-2pm & 6.30-9.30pm Mon-Sat* €€€

Capitaine: This cosy modern brasserie has a regularly changing menu with a seafood focus. *noon-2pm & 7.30-10.30pm Wed-Sat, 7.30-10.30pm Tue* €€€

Journey Through Paris' History
MAP P154
Discover the Musée Carnavalet

At the **Musée Carnavalet** *(carnavalet.paris.fr; free)*, you're first welcomed by a grand hall adorned with old shop signs, reminders of Paris' vibrant commercial life throughout the centuries. As you wander through the museum's spacious rooms, you'll encounter artworks, artefacts and historical finds that recount the layered history of Paris.

The city is showcased in all its forms and across all eras through numerous scale models, paintings, architectural remnants and modern masterpieces. Murals, entire shops and even a hotel ballroom were all moved to the Hotel Carnavalet to testify to their enduring magnificence. Our favourite floor is dedicated to the French Revolution and includes a pair of guillotine earrings, complete with dangling severed heads.

Embrace Parisian Style
MAP P152
Go vintage shopping in the fashion capital

Every year Paris Fashion Week brings hordes of stylishly attired attendees to Le Marais, but the cost of buying a new Parisian wardrobe can add up quickly. Fortunately, Le Marais boasts a range of vintage and secondhand boutiques to suit all manner of budgets and styles. Wander in and out of boutiques along rue Turenne or head straight to these favourites: Less curated and more affordable are **BIS Boutique Solidaire** *(bisboutiquesolidaire.fr)* and the boutiques of **Free 'P Star** *(instagram.com/freepstar_officiel)* on rue Verrière; **Bobby** *(bobbyparis.com)* stocks more current styles; **Système Solaire** *(Map p154; systeme-solere.com)* and **The Room** *(theroom.fr)* focus on luxury items with matching prices; finally, **BRUT** *(brut-clothing.com)* offers military deadstock and reworked original designs.

Be Inspired By Human Ingenuity
MAP P152
Explore Musée des Arts et Métiers

The immersive collection of the **Musée des Arts et Métiers** *(arts-et-metiers.net; adult/child €12/free)* includes scientific instruments, mechanical devices, vehicles, communication equipment and much more. It features iconic inventions such as Blaise Pascal's Pascaline (an early mechanical calculator), the original model of the *Statue of Liberty* designed by Bartholdi, Foucault's pendulum (with daily demonstrations at

PARISIAN POP-UP MARKETS

The food markets, *brocantes* (flea markets) and *vide-greniers* (garage sales) of Paris offer a wide range of products, from vegetables to antique mirrors. *Brocantes* tend to have higher-quality items, while *vide-greniers* can be more of a mix, with a better chance of finding a well-priced treasure. They often reflect the tastes of their *arrondissement*, so expect more high-quality goods in Le Marais, especially around rue de Bretagne, and lots of clothing. You can find fresh-food markets along the bd Beaumarchais and in place Baudoyer. The dates and locations for all markets are listed online and most happen at weekends. Arrive early and bring cash to get the widest choice, and take your time strolling between stalls to admire the goods on offer.

 DRINKING IN LE MARAIS: HIDDEN BARS — MAP P152

| Sotto: This cellar-like bar hidden underneath Italian restaurant Carboni's is the ideal spot for a fruity cocktail and a tiramisu. 7pm-2am | Little Red Door: A speakeasy with talented mixologists, accessible through a small, discreet entrance. Expect queues. 5pm-1.30am | Candelaria: A hidden cocktail bar accessed through a taco restaurant, it's one of Paris' original speakeasies and still highly regarded. 4pm-2am | Spootnik Bar: If a futuristic cosmonaut met an audiophile in Berlin this is the delicious cocktail bar that they would open. 7pm-2am Tue-Sat |

EXPLORING JEWISH TRADITIONS & HISTORY

Le Marais has been home to Jewish communities since the Middle Ages; explore its Jewish history in places where this heritage is still visible today.

START	END	LENGTH
Musée d'Art du Judaïsme	Mémorial de la Shoah	1.4km; 2½ hours

Discover Jewish history and practices in ❶ **Musée d'Art et d'Histoire du Judaïsme**, housed in the historic Hôtel de St-Aignan. Established in 1948 by Holocaust survivors, this institution showcases a diverse collection of artworks depicting Jewish history and culture, encompassing European and Maghreb communities.

Exit along rue des Archives and head to ❷ **rue des Rosiers**, renowned for its culinary delights and cultural importance. Visit ❸ **Librairie du Temple**, a bookshop dedicated to Jewish books and culture. The most curious will take a peek at ❹ **Joseph Migneret Garden**. Named after a professor who played a vital role in rescuing Jewish children during WWII, this hidden garden is a peaceful sanctuary. Continue to rue Pavée, where you'll find a striking ❺ **synagogue** designed by Hector Guimard, famous for his art nouveau metro station entrances. Guimard created this synagogue as a tribute to his Jewish wife. You're now at the former location of the Pletzel ('small square' in Yiddish).

Conclude your tour at the ❻ **Mémorial de la Shoah**, accessible via the Allée des Justes de France. This narrow street often hosts open-air exhibitions that shed light on different aspects of Jewish history. The memorial itself comprises a museum and document centre dedicated to the Shoah, providing a solemn and contemplative setting, including the Tomb of the Unknown Jewish Martyr in the crypt.

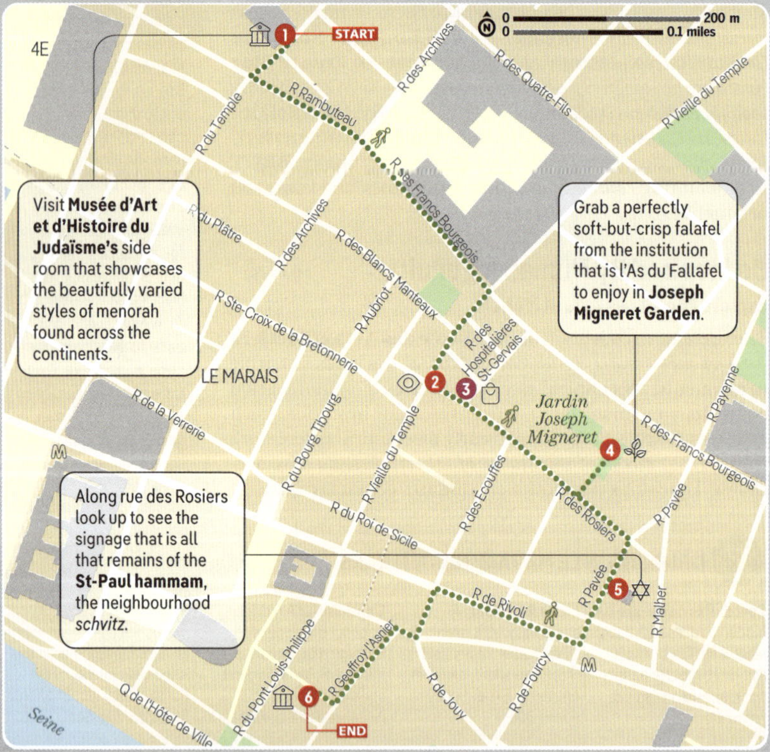

Visit **Musée d'Art et d'Histoire du Judaïsme's** side room that showcases the beautifully varied styles of menorah found across the continents.

Grab a perfectly soft-but-crisp falafel from the institution that is l'As du Fallafel to enjoy in **Joseph Migneret Garden**.

Along rue des Rosiers look up to see the signage that is all that remains of the **St-Paul hammam**, the neighbourhood *schvitz*.

noon and 5pm), and even a reconstruction of the laboratory of chemist Antoine Lavoisier. There is even a disconcerting darkened room dedicated to automata; it includes videos of their movements complete with discordant music. Additionally, the museum offers educational opportunities for children through regular workshops that familiarise them with the spirit of invention and pioneering innovation. Visit on a weekday morning to enjoy having the museum largely to yourself.

Go Flashing in Le Marais
MAP P154
Find French street art

Invader is a French street artist known internationally for his pixelated mosaic creations and there is a particularly dense concentration of them in Le Marais. Track which ones you've spotted by downloading his free app, **Flash Invaders**, and photographing or 'flashing' them as you explore. Pay attention to building façades as you wander, starting your collection with his **Cheshire Cat**. Immortalise the experience by creating your own Invader-inspired T-shirt to wear home with **Les Imprimeuses** *(lesimprimeuses.com; per person €50)* – their child-friendly workshop is a fun and memorable family activity.

Brunch from the Stalls
MAP P152
Dine in the oldest Parisian covered market

Le Marché des Enfants Rouges, dating back to the 17th century, still exudes plenty of charm after undergoing renovations in the 1990s. It has become a vibrant gathering place for both locals and visitors. The market is home to a diverse array of food stalls and small eateries. Whether you're passing by or looking to sit down, take a moment to immerse yourself in the lively atmosphere and explore the generous, typically French market stalls offering fresh food, fruit, flowers, cheese and charcuterie products. As the market is open on Sundays as well, one of the best experiences is to indulge in brunch at one of the numerous local or international food stalls surrounding the market. You can enjoy vegetarian delights at **Au Coin Bio** *(aucoinbio-restaurant.fr)*, order a Japanese bento at **Chez Taeko**, or tuck into Levantine pitas at **Chez Jeanphi** *(instagram.com/chez_jeanphi)*. You can do a culinary world tour!

A STEAMPUNK STATION

If you come to the museum on metro line 11, you will emerge into the Arts et Métiers station and its steampunk ambience, created by copper plaques covering the platform walls and ceiling. These plaques were added in 1993 to celebrate the Conservatoire des Arts et Métiers bicentenary and designed by François Schuiten. He was inspired by the writing of Jules Verne, the author of *Around the World in Eighty Days,* and particularly influenced by Verne's description of Captain Nemo's submarine, the *Nautilus*, which appears in the novel *Twenty Thousand Leagues Under the Sea.* If you peek into the port-like display cases you'll spot some of the exhibits from the Musée des Arts et Métiers.

 EATING IN LE MARAIS: QUICK BITES — MAPS P152, P154

Pontochoux: Enjoy a warming platter of Japanese curry made from scratch; even its marinated vegetables are homegrown. *11.30am-7pm €*

Notre Café Marais: This bright cafe with a sunny terrace serves simple, classic fare while employing people with Down syndrome. *8.30am-3pm Tue-Fri €*

Carré Pain de Mie: Combining the best of Japan and France, these cloud-like sandwiches include fillings like *tonkotsu* and croque monsieur. *10am-8pm €€*

La Collective Parisienne: This social-enterprise cafe serves wholesome seasonal lunches from a four-item menu plus a dessert. *noon-3pm Mon-Fri €*

WHAT'S IN A NAME?

The etymology of the name 'Le Marais' gives insight into this *quartier*'s less glamorous origins, even if it's brimming with luxury today. 'Le Marais' literally means 'the swamp', and is a name dating back 30,000 to 40,000 years ago when the Seine had a second arm that encircled a northern semicircle of the city centre from the Bassin de l'Arsenal to the Pont d'Alma. As the climate changed, this arm disappeared, leaving behind a large swampy area. By the 9th century the right bank had been drained and the rich, swampy land was a fertile resource for agriculture. The area came to be known for its pastures, market gardens, and *maraîcher* (vegetable growers), before becoming a more desirable area during the Renaissance.

In the Footsteps of the Templars   MAP P152
Enjoy events at Le Carreau du Temple

Street names like rue du Temple, rue Vieille-du-Temple and rue du Trésor in Le Marais hint at the Templars' presence here. While their treasure remains a mystery, the Templars' historical influence is undeniable. In the 12th century they were granted lands by the king, transforming the marshy area into what it is today. The Templar enclosure and dungeon are long gone, leaving only a blue trace on the ground outlining their previous location near the town hall of the 3e *arrondissement*. **Le Carreau du Temple** *(lecarreaudutemple.eu)*, once a market for various household and fashion goods, now hosts a range of cultural and sporting events, including the Food Temple Culinary Festival, the much-appreciated Paris Café Festival and the Salon du Vintage.

DRINKING IN LOWER MARAIS: WINE BARS — MAP P154

La Belle Hortense: For lovers of wine and literature this bookshop–wine bar is the place to while away a cosy afternoon. *5.30pm-2am Wed-Sun*

Les Amoureuses: Modern and sleek, this is the perfect spot for a romantic date night of wine and artfully crafted small dishes. *6pm-midnight Tue-Sat*

Caviste Vinosfera: Pair wine tasting with history at this well-stocked wine bar inside one of Paris' oldest buildings, which has a stunning medieval cellar. *11.15am-8pm*

A Lot Of Wine: Ideally situated facing the Seine, this wine bar has an exciting range of natural wines and the expertise to help you choose. *hours vary*

Le Carreau du Temple

Savour French Savoir-Faire

MAP P152

Buy the best products made in France

Dining has always been an important part of French culture, which is why creating your own set of cutlery at **Sabre** (*sabre.fr*) is a perfect way to bring Paris home to your table. **Empreintes** (*empreintes-paris.com*) showcases some of the best French designers, with a focus on artisanal decorative objects, jewellery and home goods. **Alix D. Reynis** (*alixdreynis.com*) designs elegant ranges of porcelain goods that are handmade in Limoges. For traditional cubes of green Marseille soap, try **Maruis Fabre** (*Map p154; marius-fabre.com*). Finally, if you need something to fit all your goodies, stop into **RSVP** (*rsvp-paris.com*) to pick out a handmade leather bag, or **Praline** (*pralineparis.com*) for bags stitched in Paris using sofa material from Strasbourg.

THE REAL PHILOSOPHER'S STONE

Thrust into the pop-culture canon by author JK Rowling in her novel *Harry Potter and the Philosopher's Stone*, Nicolas Flamel did exist, but his relationship to alchemy and the Elixir of Life are a little more dubious. During his lifetime Flamel worked as a successful notary and scribe, running two shops in Paris. Flamel and his wife, Perenelle, were also active philanthropists who donated money to churches and the poor. Texts that describe discovering the Philosopher's Stone have been attributed to Flamel, but have been dated too long after his supposed death in 1418. Although his gravestone can be found near the Musée de Cluny, some claim that the headstone was erected as a ruse to fake his death after his discovery of everlasting life.

 EATING IN LE MARAIS: PATISSERIES — MAPS P152, P154

Petite Île Boulangerie: Fusing Taiwanese and French baking, this *boulangerie* (bakery) excels at sweet treats with black sesame. *8am-6pm Tue-Sat, 9am-2.30pm Sun* €

Moon Croissant: These croissant specialists use the finest ingredients to handcraft their goodies, creating delicious explosions of buttery flakes and filling. *7.30am-5pm Wed-Sun* €€

Yann Couvreur: The renowned French pastry chef's store, featuring his best creations, such as vanilla millefeuilles. *10am-8pm* €€

Jojo & Co: With over 13 years of experience, *pâtissière* Johanna Roques crafts delightful seasonal *pâtisseries* and unctuous flans. *11am-8pm Wed-Fri, 10.30am-7.30pm Sat & Sun* €€

WALKING TOUR

Walking Through Time in Le Marais

One of the few areas to have remained untouched by Baron Haussmann's reconstructions, Le Marais contains layers of history dating as far back as the Middle Ages. Its evolutions from marsh to aristocratic hub to insalubrious shambles are still peeking out between its present-day luxury. Unravel the city's past as you navigate through bustling streets to discover the remains of medieval life and the tranquillity of 17th-century mansions and hidden courtyards.

1 Medieval Houses on Rue François-Miron

At Nos 11 and 13 are two of the oldest houses in Paris; they date from the 14th century, although their current appearances include 16th-century additions. Further up the street at No 46 is the **Association pour la Sauvegarde et la Mise en Valeur du Paris Historique** *(1-6pm Mon-Fri, to 7pm Sat, 2-6pm Sun):* visit to learn more about the history of Paris and tour their medieval cellar. The tours (adult/child €5/2) are offered in English on Wednesdays.

The Walk: Head east along rue de Jouy, then south along rue des Nonnains-d'Hyères before walking east on rue de l'Hotel de Ville.

2 Hôtel de Sens

This remarkable Gothic mansion from the 15th century was once a residence for Sens' archbishops. History remembers the execution of one of Queen Margot's suitors, which she supposedly witnessed from a window of the mansion. Try to spot the Revolutionary-era cannonball lodged above a window: it's not as big as you might expect.

The Walk: Take rue de l'Ave Maria and reach the entrance to Village St-Paul's courtyards.

3 Village St-Paul

This densely packed neighbourhood was once home to the domestic servants that accompanied wealthy local families. As you

Hôtel de Sens

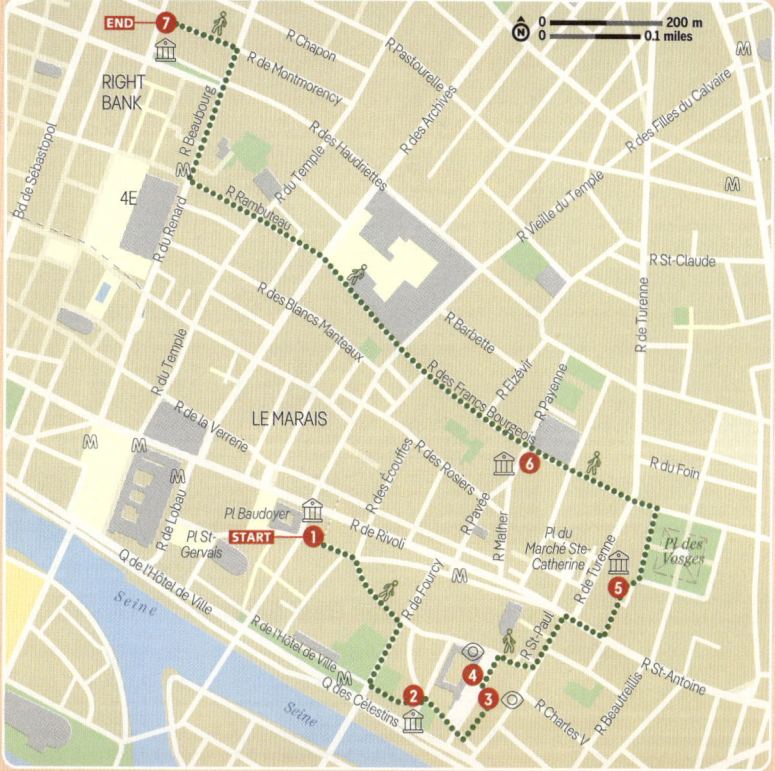

walk through, try to picture the women washing clothes and live chickens clucking in the courtyards that now house fashionable boutiques and restaurants.

The Walk: Exit through rue des Jardins St-Paul.

4 King Philippe Auguste's Wall

You'll find yourself across from the largest remnants of King Philippe Auguste's Wall, a defensive fortification built at the end of the 12th century to protect Paris from potential attacks.

The Walk: Head north to rue St-Antoine and enter the courtyard of Hôtel de Sully.

5 Hôtel de Sully

Built in 1624, this magnificent *hôtel particulier* represents the characteristic mansions of Le Marais during its fashionable era and features a passageway leading to place des Vosges.

The Walk: Exit through the passageway to place des Vosges, then head north along its western side. At the corner, turn west onto rue Francs-Bourgeois and continue to reach the entrance of the Hôtel de Lamoignon courtyard.

6 Hôtel de Lamoignon

In 1759 the last resident of this mansion bequeathed 14,000 books to the city of Paris upon his death. Four years later, this *hôtel particulier* became the first public library in Paris, open to all. Today it houses the **Historical Library of Paris** *(10am-6pm Mon-Sat)*.

The Walk: Continue along rue Francs-Bourgeois towards metro Rambuteau, then turn right onto rue Beaubourg and look for rue de Montmorency, the second street on the left.

7 Nicolas Flamel's House

Tucked away on rue Montmorency, this is believed to be the oldest house in the city. It was built by the scribe Nicolas Flamel; the detailed inscription on the façade dates its construction to 1407.

Église St-Paul St-Louis

MARCHE DES FIERTÉS

Running in Paris since 1981, the **Marche des Fiertés** has its origins in the Gay Pride marches that began in New York. In Paris the annual parade is attended by over 500,000 people and includes support from more than 200 volunteers. Organisation of the event is led by the group Inter-LGBT, who bring together around 90 organisations. Their shared mission is to 'combat discrimination based on sexual orientation or gender identity, as part of the promotion of human rights and fundamental freedoms'. Open to all, whether you identify as an ally or part of the community, the event itself is simultaneously a celebratory and political day filled with music, creative costumes, placards, floats, a final concert and dance-filled afterparties.

In Search of the Best Scent

MAPS P152, P154

Discover the art of perfumery

Le Marais is drenched in perfumeries; walking along rue de Francs Bourgeois from rue Turenne you'll be enveloped in clouds of fragrance wafting out of boutiques. There are renowned brands like **Fragonard** *(fragonard.com)*, niche independent houses such as **Frederic Maille** *(fredericmalle.co.uk)* and perfume concept store **Liquides Bar à Parfums** *(liquides-parfums.com)*. For an immersive and personalised experience, join a workshop at **Candora** *(candora-fragrance.com; from €98)*: here you can learn about the history of perfumery and create your own individual scent.

Proud Marais

MAP P152

Celebrate with all communities and orientations

Le Marais has maintained its reputation as an inclusive area and a stronghold of the LGBTIQ+ community, although rising property prices in the past decade have led to the displacement or closure of many emblematic establishments. Nonetheless,

DRINKING IN LE MARAIS: COCKTAILS WITH AMBIENCE

MAP P152

Andy Wahloo: Neon and chrome give this buzzing cocktail bar a retro glow. Lounge at a courtyard table in the summer. *7pm-1am Tue & Wed, to 2am Fri & Sat*

Bar Nouveau: Inspired by the art nouveau movement, this creative bar mixes deliciously different cocktail interpretations of their theme. *3pm-1am*

Maison Proust: A hotel bar with elegant library decor and plush armchairs, it's ideal for a late-night cocktail. *5pm-1am*

Mesures: Over 1000 vinyl records provide a soundtrack to enjoy with unusual cocktails at this bar modelled on 1920s Japanese jazz cafes. *hours vary*

the inclusive identity of the area remains, and it continues to be a traditional district that celebrates Pride all year long. LGBTIQ+ establishments are often marked by rainbow flags, indicating their connection to the community and their friendly nature. Rainbow street art can be found throughout the neighbourhood, adding to the welcoming atmosphere.

The gay-friendly vibe is concentrated mainly around rue Ste-Croix de la Bretonnerie, the southern part of rue du Temple, and hidden place des Émeutes de Stonewall. Day or night, everyone is welcome at the surrounding restaurants, with **Tata Burger** *(instagram.com/tataburger_restaurant)* number one for a suggestive burger and **Legay Choc** *(instagram.com/legaychoc)* offering phallic sweet treats.

The real excitement begins when night falls, **freedj** *(freedj.fr)*, **Cox** *(cox.fr)*, **Duplex Bar** *(instagram.com/duplex_bar_paris)* and **Les Souffleurs** *(Map p154; instagram.com/lessouffleuses)* are all vibrant bars that attract a diverse crowd. **Elles Bar** *(instagram.com/elles_bar_paris)* provides a venue for lesbians. Slightly further away on rue St-Martin are feminist venue **La Mutinerie** *(lamutinerie.eu)* and **Les Aimant·e·s** *(instagram.com/barlesaimantes)*, both open daily.

Go Beyond Notre Dame

MAP P154

Discover Le Marais' churches

With an enduring history of religion dating back to medieval times there are a host of churches to visit in Le Marais, with two in particular worth a visit.

Enter **Église St-Paul St-Louis** *(spsl.fr)* through the cherry-red side door on passage St-Paul, and look for the Revolutionary-era graffiti on one column declaiming 'République Française ou la mort' ('French republic or death'). As you leave through the main door, note the holy-water stoups donated by Victor Hugo for his daughter Léopoldine's wedding.

Église St-Gervais-St-Protais *(paris.fraternites-jerusalem.org)* is famous for its organ and singing traditions; visit for a mass to enjoy both. As you approach the church from rue des Barres, notice the steps leading up and away – the church was originally built on a rise to bring it above the marshy land.

Step Off the Beaten Track

MAP P152

Walk Paris' hidden passageways

Although many of Paris' passageways were destroyed in the 19th century, a few can still be found tucked behind

THE COMPANIONS OF DUTY

History in Le Marais isn't limited to architecture and stories; on a small corner near the Église St-Gervais-St-Protais you'll find the **Compagnons du Devoir**. This organisation traces its roots back to the medieval period when craftspeople would travel the country learning the skills of their trade, and since 1901 it has trained young people in a range of artisanal crafts. Apprentices train for three to 10 years and must undertake a personal *tour de France*, travelling around France and learning on location, in order to master their craft and become a full-fledged *compagnon*.

Traditional crafts like stone masonry are now taught alongside modern skills like precision mechanics. The rigorous training in every craft is emblematic of a national pride in the French savoir-faire.

EATING IN LE MARAIS: EAT VEGGIE

MAP P152

Kitchen: Healthy and wholesome, this friendly *cantine*-style cafe serves hearty organic dishes. *8am-2.30pm Mon-Fri, to 3.30pm Sat & Sun* €€

Land&Monkeys: Vegans can now enjoy French classics from this fully plant-based *boulangerie*, like quiche Lorraine and *jambon-beurre* baguettes. *7.30am-7.30pm* €

Chez Eating: Taiwanese-born chef and owner Yi Ting runs this one-woman show, creating East Asian dishes bursting with flavour. *noon-3pm Mon, Tue, Thu-Sat* €€

Keili: Start your day right with a vegetarian brunch from a small but perfectly executed menu at this fresh cafe. *10am-5pm Mon-Fri, 11am-5pm Sat & Sun* €

> **ALWAYS LOOK UP**
>
>
>
> **Anne Chouraki,** a guide specialising in Le Marais, shares her top tip.
>
> I tell all my tours to examine the façade of the buildings in Le Marais; the wealthy loved to include classical and astrological references that tell us a story of what they considered important and were almost a code understood by other similarly educated people of their class. The deer and moon carved on the façade of the Bibliothèque Historique de la Ville de Paris reference the Roman goddess Diana, meaning that a woman called Diana lived there. Studying the façades of the Hôtels Sully, Soubise and Musée Carnavalet we see depictions of the seasons and astrological signs. Finally, no coat of arms means that the people who built the building weren't part of the nobility.

unobtrusive doors. The **passage de l'Ancre** is one of the most charming and oldest in the city. Enter from rue St-Martin – look out for the name written above a faded blue door and step into a world of coloured façades and vegetation.

Passage des Gravilliers has bold street art and the galleries **Sator** *(galeriesator.com)* and **Christian Berst** *(christian berst.com)* are found here. The **passage Vendôme** is the least aesthetically pleasing of the passages, but it is Le Marais' only covered passageway and provides a quiet respite from the crowds around place de la République.

Find Your Inspiration

MAPS P152, P154

Explore art in Le Marais

The **Maison Européenne de la Photographie** *(MEP; mep -fr.org; adult/child €13/free)* is dedicated to contemporary photography, and through temporary exhibitions features cutting-edge international photographers. In a different vein, the **Fondation Henri Cartier-Bresson** *(henricartier bresson.org; adult/child €10/6)* preserves and promotes the work of the renowned French photographer, considered a pioneer of modern photojournalism. The foundation exhibits highlights from the archives and work by contemporary photographers. Finally, **Polka Galerie** *(polkagalerie.com)* exhibits and sells fine-art photography, both by established contemporary artists and emerging photographers.

The artistic exploration of Le Marais would not be complete without its numerous art galleries covering a diversity of artistic approaches. **Lafayette Anticipations** *(lafayette anticipations.com)* offers a hybrid experience, with cultural events, temporary exhibitions of contemporary designers, a trendy bookshop and a cafe. Additionally, numerous galleries in the area actively play with the boundaries of traditional art forms, like **Galerie Emmanuel Perrotin** *(perrotin.com)*, which exhibits artists from around the world in its spacious gallery, runs cultural events and sells art-inspired items including books and clothing. The area also supports art communities, with venues like **MAIF Social Club** *(maifsocial club.fr; free)* running a programme of exhibitions, workshops, a cafe and an ethical concept store. They have information cards in English and are always buzzing with visitors, from school groups to grey-haired drawing clubs.

Look for a copy of Arturo's self-produced newspaper!

 DRINKING IN LE MARAIS: SPECIALIST COFFEE SHOPS — MAPS P152, P154

| **Causeries:** A delicate oasis of Danish coffee and natural wine with elegant decor and a gentle vinyl soundtrack. *hours vary* € | **Ha Noi 1988 Flowers & Archives:** Discover salted-cream or egg-yolk coffee at this florally perfumed Vietnamese cafe and flower shop. *10am-7pm* €€ | **Cortado:** Step briefly into Spain at this buzzing coffee shop that offers Spanish nibbles and excellent cortados. *hours vary* € | **Artesano:** Arturo Valentino roasts his Mexican coffee weekly for this cafe filled with sun, music, photography and rich coffee. *9am-1.30pm & 2.30-5.30pm* €€ |

Le Progrès

Elevate Your Postcard Game

MAP P154

Shop for stunning stationery

France has a storied history of writing; from novelists to Marie Antoinette's coded letters in the Musée des Archives. For stationery to inspire your own writing, **Calligrane** *(calligrane.fr)* is a homage to all things paper, offering tastefully curated objects and stationery. Be sure to ease open the drawers to uncover more beautiful items. In **Mélodies Graphique** *(melodies-graphiques.com)* you'll find gilded, Baroque-inspired collections of cards, books and stamps. **Papier Tigre** *(Map p152; papiertigre.fr)* is a colourful modern French brand that designs many products just across the street from the boutique.

People-Watching Hot Spots

MAP P152

Sit and absorb Parisian life

Le Marais is a place to see and be seen, and by far the best way to do this is while sipping a glass of wine or a cup of coffee. For these more traditional spots, be sure to have cash, as many have minimum spends for cards. It can be competitive getting a seat under the awnings of **Le Progrès** *(leprogresmarais.fr)*, so arrive early for your morning coffee and settle in. **Le Saint-Gervais** *(lesaintgervais.fr)* is an afternoon suntrap and is conveniently around the corner from the Musée National Picasso-Paris. For the evening, funky **Café La Perle** *(cafelaperle.com)* is a fashion and artsy hot spot. While you're here look across the street for the regularly changing murals by Le Mur.

LITERARY BREAKS

Feel truly Parisian by enjoying a book while you sip drinks on a *terrasse*.

Le Piéton de Paris

(Map p154) This tiny bookshop is a celebration of the city across literary and visual forms.

La Mouette Rieuse

(Map p154) Browse a wide range of genres and souvenirs then enjoy their hidden cafe squeezed in the back.

Yvon Lambert

(Map p152) A gallerist since the 1960s, in 2017 Lambert established this sleek gallery and bookshop space filled with glossy international titles.

Les Cahiers de Colette

(Map p152) Immerse yourself in the heady world of French literature at this bookshop inspired by the celebrated writer herself.

Smith & Son

(Map p154) For contemporary or classic English-language books, this charming bookshop in the heart of Le Marais has stocked a well-curated range since 1870.

Researched by Fabienne Fong Yan

BELLEVILLE & MÉNILMONTANT

ARTS, VIEWS AND MULTICULTURAL WALKS

The northeastern neighbourhoods not only have a unique history of immigration, but also a festive and artistic spirit.

Stretching over the 19e and 20e *arrondissements* down to some of the neighbouring streets of the 10e and 11e, Belleville used to be a separate town outside Paris, and Ménilmontant one of its boroughs. Incorporated into the city in 1860, they maintained a strong identity, with a vibrant artistic spirit, multicultural quarters, and a somewhat rebellious nature, inherited from the historical popular movements born on their streets. Day or night, these quarters offer a dynamic scene where people seem to easily connect with each other despite a variety of backgrounds. Many locals proudly claim that Belleville is not Paris, it is Belleville! Walk its hills, explore its urban art and diverse food scene: come and discover what they mean.

TOP TIP

Belleville's streets can be winding and steep, and the landmarks are a bit spread out, so wear good shoes and take your time to explore.

Street art, Rue Dénoyez (p177)

See p310 for places to stay in Belleville and Ménilmontant.

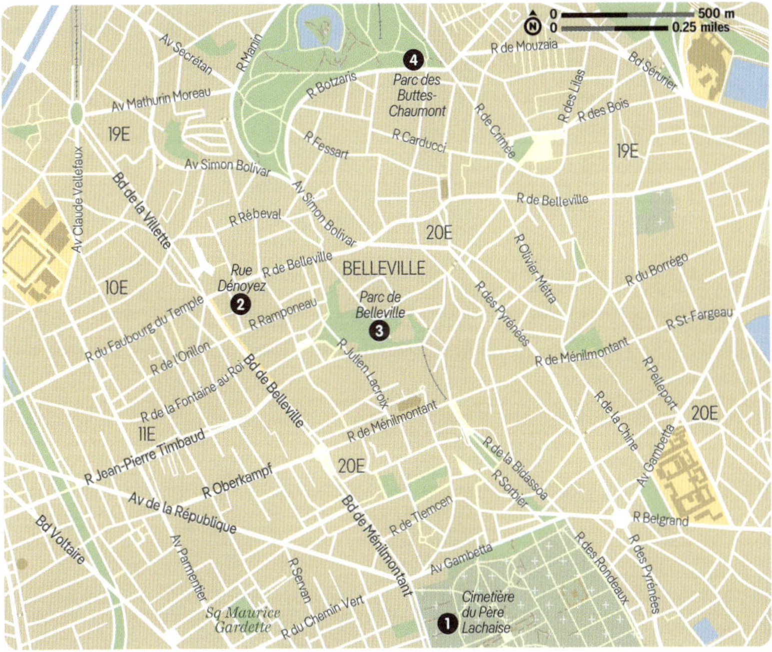

THE GUIDE

BELLEVILLE & MÉNILMONTANT

Highlights

❶ Cimetière du Père Lachaise
Visit the famous resting place for iconic figures such as Oscar Wilde, Jim Morrison and Édith Piaf. **p172**

❷ Rue Dénoyez
Stroll this ever-changing street, a sanctuary for street art in the heart of Belleville. **p177**

❸ Parc de Belleville
Don't miss the panoramic view from the Belvédère, one of the highest hills in Paris. **p179**

❹ Parc des Buttes-Chaumont
Picnic on this park's grassy slopes, admiring the romantic hill in the middle of its central lake. **p183**

Getting Around

Walking
Although it may be more challenging than other areas because of the sometimes steep streets, walking remains the best way to stumble upon the details holding the soul of Belleville.

Underground
Choose your metro station wisely, considering they can be far apart from each other and either bottom or top of the hill. Useful stations are Belleville (lines 2 and 11) and Philippe Auguste (line 2).

Bus & Cycling
Buses and electric bikes can help bridge the distance between your metro station and final destination, in this less central – slightly underserved – quarter.

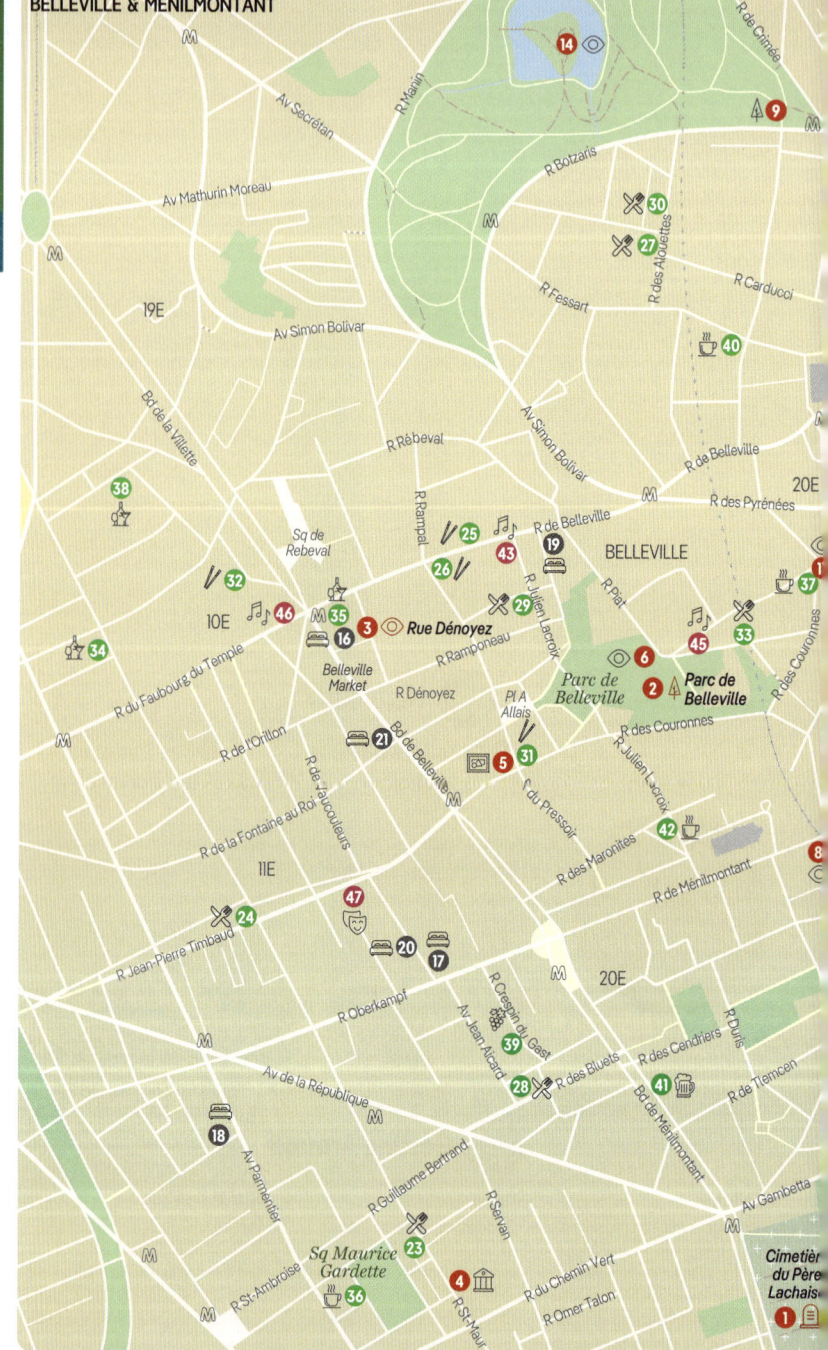

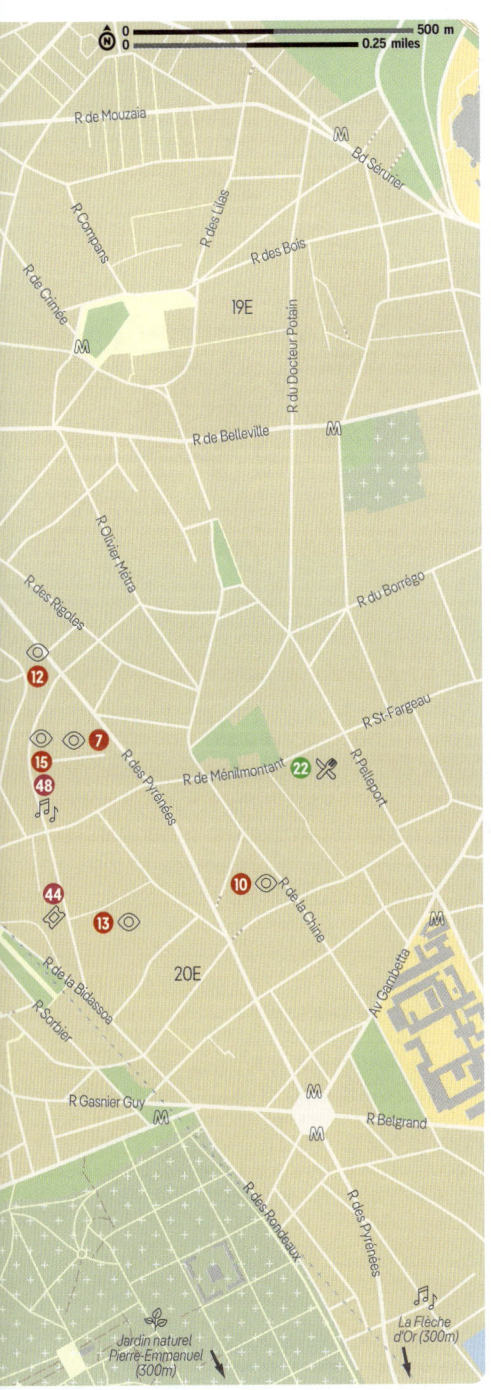

⭐ HIGHLIGHTS
1. Cimetière du Père Lachaise
2. Parc de Belleville
3. Rue Dénoyez

● SIGHTS
4. Atelier des Lumières
5. Ateliers d'Artistes de Belleville
6. Belvédère de Belleville
7. Cité Leroy
8. Jérôme Mesnager's art
9. Parc des Buttes-Chaumont
10. Passage des Soupirs
11. Place Henri Krasucki
12. Regard St-Martin
13. Rue Laurence Savart
14. Sybille's Temple
15. Villa de l'Ermitage

● SLEEPING
16. Babel Belleville
17. Fraternity Hostel
18. Hotel Les Deux Girafes
19. Hôtel Scarlett
20. La Nouvelle République
21. The People Belleville

● EATING
22. Benoît Castel – Ménilmontant
23. Chanceux
24. Demain
25. Lao Siam
26. Mian Guan
27. Milligramme
28. Oobatz
29. PALOMA
30. Patisserie Ginko
31. Pavillon aux Pivoines
32. Raviolis Nord Est
33. ROND

● DRINKING & NIGHTLIFE
34. Abricot Bar
35. Aux Folies
36. Beans on Fire
37. Candle Kids Coffee
38. La Sardine
39. Le Perchoir Ménilmontant
40. Mardi
41. Micro Brasserie Balthazar
42. Plural

● ENTERTAINMENT
43. Culture Rapide
44. La Bellevilloise
45. Le Vieux Belleville
see 21 Le Zèbre de Belleville
46. Le Zorba
47. Maison des Métallos
48. Studio de l'Ermitage

THE GUIDE

BELLEVILLE & MÉNILMONTANT

TOP EXPERIENCE

Cimetière du Père Lachaise

The prestigious Cimetière du Père Lachaise serves as Paris' necropolis, aligned with the Panthéon, where figures who shaped the French nation are honoured. However, this cemetery is not only a resting place for the renowned. Today it stands as an otherworldly space where extraordinary funerary monuments coexist with the graves of both famous and lesser-known individuals, each still cherished by someone.

DON'T MISS

- The Monument to the Dead
- Lovers Héloïse and Abélard
- Irish writer Oscar Wilde
- Rock star Jim Morrison
- French singer Édith Piaf

An Eternal English Garden

When commissioned to design the new Parisian cemetery in the early 19th century, architect Alexandre-Théodore Brongniart envisioned a space that would embody nobility without grandiosity, simplicity without neglect, and invoke religious sentiments without fear. He aimed to create a place of peaceful remembrance, with a melancholic charm based on a combination of nature and monuments. Inspired by English gardens,

PRACTICALITIES

● 8am-6pm, from 9am Sat & Sun ● the cemetery's main entrance is located on rue du Repos (metro: Philippe Auguste, line 2) ● visitors are asked to leave the cemetery 30 minutes before closing

the cemetery was meticulously planned, with winding paths and a significant portion dedicated to nature. Today, as you enter, the cacophony of the city fades away and the graves seamlessly blend into the undulating landscape, creating a feeling of beautiful strangeness, as if you were suspended between two worlds.

The Construction of a Legendary Place

Overlooked at the time of its inauguration, the cemetery faced challenges in gaining popularity due to its location far from the city. However, to enhance its appeal, the city of Paris relocated the graves of famous figures like Molière and La Fontaine (Division 25), and had an impressive sepulchre erected for the mythical medieval lovers Héloïse and Abélard (Division 7). Over time, politicians, scientists, artists and writers followed, solidifying Père Lachaise's reputation as the eternal resting place of the renowned.

Funerary Art for Posterity

The entire site is recognised for its historical heritage, with all funerary steles dating to before 1900 listed as Historical Monuments. Additionally, 14 monuments are classified – the classification is reserved for works that hold public interest from a historical or an artistic perspective. Among them, the Wall of the Federates; Godde's chapel on the former Jesuit house site; bd Ménilmontant's monumental gate; the Monument to the Dead; and 10 sepulchres. The sepulchres include Héloïse and Abélard, Molière and La Fontaine, Oscar Wilde (Division 89), Frédéric Chopin (Division 11), Antoine de Guillaume-Lagrange (Division 29), Montanier-Delille (Division 11), Cartellier-Heim (Division 53), Georges Guët (Division 19) and Yakovleff (Division 82).

Rituals & Superstitions of Père Lachaise

Like all cemeteries, where the boundaries between worlds blur, Père Lachaise has its own superstitions and esoteric rituals associated with its iconic graves. Couples renew their vows in front of Héloïse and Abélard's tomb, seeking eternal love. Oscar Wilde's tomb has long been the object of passionate kisses believed to bring luck in love. Journalist Victor Noir's effigy (Division 92) is central to erotic morbid fertility rituals. Laying hands at the dolmen of medium Allan Kardec (Division 44) is believed to grant wishes. Lastly, the ritual offerings left on Jim Morrison's grave (Division 6) perpetuate a cult (mainly based on alcohol).

A RURAL GARDEN IN THE CITY

Below Père Lachaise, **Jardin naturel Pierre-Emmanuel** hosts native plant species from the Parisian region and offers a glimpse into Paris' nature when it was still rural. With minimal mowing to respect natural cycles, the meadows allow vegetation to thrive. This true biodiversity reserve provides a habitat for frogs, newts and water lilies, and contrasts radically with the usual meticulously arranged parks of Paris.

TOP TIPS

● Download the cemetery map from a QR code at the entrance: this will help you locate specific graves and landmarks.

● Choose the right entrance: there are five different ones, but only three of them are near metro stations.

● Wear comfortable shoes: the cemetery is vast, with uneven terrain and stairs. Be prepared for walking and stay hydrated.

● Show respect: remember that this is a graveyard where people come to pay their respects to their loved ones. Don't climb on tombs and keep noise levels low.

● Plan ahead: if you have limited time or specific graves you want to visit, plan your itinerary in advance.

Cimetière du Père Lachaise

A Half-Day Tour

There is a certain romance to getting lost in this jungle of graves spun from centuries of tales. But to search for one grave amid the million in this 44-hectare land of the dead requires guidance.

Approaching the main entrance on bd de Ménilmontant, pay your respects at the **1 Monument aux Morts Parisiens de la Première Guerre Mondiale**. Inside the cemetery, head up av Principale and turn right onto av du Puits to grab a map at the **2 Bureaux de la Conservation**.

Backtrack along av du Puits, turn right onto av Latérale du Sud, scale the stairs and bear right along chemin Denon to New Realist artist **3 Arman**, film director **4 Claude Chabrol** and **5 Chopin**.

Follow chemin Méhul downhill, cross av Casimir Périer and bear right onto chemin Serré. Take the second left (chemin Lebrun – unsigned), head uphill and near the top leave the footpath to weave through graves on your right to rock star **6 Jim Morrison**. Back on chemin Lauriston, continue uphill to roundabout **7 Rond-Point Casimir Périer**.

Admire the funerary art of contemporary photographer **8 André Chabot**, av de la Chapelle. Continue uphill for energising city views from the **9 chapel steps**, then zigzag to **10 Molière & La Fontaine**, on chemin Molière.

Cut between graves onto av Tranversale No 1 – spot potatoes atop **11 Parmentier's** headstone. Continue straight onto av Greffülhe and left onto av Tranversale No 2 to rub **12 Monsieur Noir**'s shiny crotch. Navigation to **13 Édith Piaf** and the **14 Mur des Fédérés** is straightforward. End with angel-topped **15 Oscar Wilde** near the Porte Gambetta entrance.

❺ Chopin, Division 11
Add a devotional note to the handwritten letters and flowers brightening the marble tomb of Polish composer/pianist Frédéric Chopin (1810–49), who spent his short adult life in Paris. His heart is buried in Warsaw.

❻ Jim Morrison, Division 6
The original bust adorning the disgracefully dishevelled grave of Jim Morrison (1943–71), lead singer of The Doors, was stolen. Pay your respects to rock's greatest legend – no chewing gum or padlocks please.

TOP TIPS

➡ Père Lachaise is a photographer's paradise any time of the day or year, but best are sunny autumn mornings after the rain.

➡ Cemetery lovers will appreciate themed guided tours (two hours) led by entertaining cemetery historian **Thierry Le Roi** (necro-romantiques.com).

10 Molière & La Fontaine, Division 25

Parisians refused to leave their local *quartier* for Père Lachaise so in 1817 the authorities moved in popular playwright Molière (1622–73) and poet Jean de la Fontaine (1621–95). The marketing strategy worked.

15 Oscar Wilde, Division 89

Irish writer Oscar Wilde (1854–1900) was forever scandalous: check the enormous packet of the sphinx on his tomb, sculpted by British-American sculptor Jacob Epstein 11 years after Wilde died.

8 André Chabot, Division 20

Contemporary photographer André Chabot (b 1941) shoots funerary art, hence the bijou 19th-century chapel he's equipped with a monumental granite camera in preparation for the day he departs.

12 Monsieur Noir, Division 92

Cemetery sex stud Mr Black, alias 21-year-old journalist Victor Noir (1848–70), was shot by Napoléon III's nephew in a botched duel. Urban myth means women rub his crotch to boost fertility.

13 Édith Piaf, Division 97

The archbishop of Paris might have refused Parisian diva Édith Piaf (1915–63) the Catholic rite of burial, but that didn't stop more than 100,000 mourners attending her interment at Père Lachaise.

14 Mur des Fédérés, Division 76

This plain brick wall was where 147 Communard insurgents were lined up and shot in 1871. Equally emotive is the sculpted walkway of commemorative war memorials surrounding the mass grave.

BEST MUSIC BARS & CONCERT HALLS AROUND BELLEVILLE

Le Zorba Straight out of Belleville metro station, this quaint, beloved bar has become a Belleville institution. It's renowned for its lively late-night parties.

Culture Rapide This popular cabaret offers an eclectic program matching the diversity of its clients, who gather for drinks on its open-air terrace.

Le Vieux Belleville In the heights of Belleville's park, this French bistro known as the 'Singing Cafe' embraces traditional French *musette* music with accordion melodies.

La Flèche d'Or Beyond Père Lachaise, in a former train station, this performing-arts venue offers a diverse concert program throughout the year.

Studio de l'Ermitage Located on a discreet street uphill in Ménilmontant, this live music venue focuses on jazz and music from around the world.

Aux Folies

Festive Belleville

A lively quarter by day and night

With many bars, cafes and live music venues, the northeastern area of Paris, from Popincourt (with rue d'Oberkampf and rue St-Maur in particular) to Belleville and Ménilmontant, has a festive reputation. Belleville's in particular dates back to the 14th century, when the village began welcoming its first cabarets, taverns and *guinguettes* – where you could drink and dance. Why Belleville? Monks had been producing wine there for a century, on the slopes of what is now Parc de Belleville, so supply was easy!

With this heritage, the area has a long-standing tradition of festivity, one of the most famous local celebrations being the 19th-century Descente de la Courtille (Going down Courtille St) – a lively procession that marked the Paris Carnival with music, drinking and dancing.

EATING IN BELLEVILLE: OUR PICKS

PALOMA: A French midday canteen offering a daily menu with a single option for starter, main and dessert. Sit outside in summer. *8am-2pm & 7pm-midnight Mon-Sat* €

Oobatz: Sourdough pizza is prepared on the spot by a chef who has his secret recipes. Pick from six basic options or entrust him with your preferences. *6-10pm Wed-Sun* €€

ROND: Make a feast of homemade buckwheat *galettes* and sweet crêpes in this tiny bistro located on the top of Belleville's hill. *noon-10.30pm Wed-Sat, to 4pm Sun* €

Chanceux: A family-style restaurant with a refreshing countryside ambience, delicatessen and a daily menu. *8.30am-11.30pm Mon & Thu-Sat, to 5pm Tue & Wed, from 10am Sun* €

Don't miss a night at **Aux Folies**, a former cabaret turned cinema and now a beloved bar, open since 1872. Legend has it that Édith Piaf sang on stage here during her teenage years. On the other side of the boulevard, **Le Zèbre de Belleville** *(lezebre.com)* offers unique cabaret-dinner shows, an experience easily enjoyed with children. **La Bellevilloise** *(la bellevilloise.com),* a former cooperative hall created by workers, has transformed into one of the favourite music and dancing venues for Parisians. Its weekend jazz brunch is particularly appreciated.

The Cradle of Street Art
Where art transforms the public space

You could say the history and soul of Belleville and Ménilmontant are reflected on their walls. Graffiti and street art hold a prominent place in these historically rebellious neighbourhoods.

Start in Parc de Belleville (p179). At the base, a wide mural depicts scenes from the Paris Commune, a pivotal moment in the city's history that unfolded on Belleville's streets. It stands as a symbol of the neighbourhood's ongoing struggles for social change. At the top of the hill, several street artists worked with local children to paint on the Belvédère de Belleville.

Wander around place Henri Krasucki and rue des Couronnes: note Nemo's characteristic black figures chasing a red balloon (a reference to the movie *Le Ballon Rouge*, taking place in Ménilmontant) and keep an eye out for Jérôme Mesnager's people dancing hand-in-hand. Both artists are revered as 'uncles' – or godfathers – of French street art.

Downhill, stop by **rue Dénoyez**, where artists can freely showcase their art. Looking closely, you'll notice layers of painting accumulating on the walls, leading to the nickname 'the shrinking street'. Like in an ephemeral open-air gallery, you see a piece one day that might no longer be there the next.

To delve deeper into this evolutive world, seek the expertise of **Fresh Street Art Paris** *(freshstreetartparis.fr)*. Its guided tours reveal the hidden layers and meanings behind this urban form of expression, and offer an opportunity to appreciate the transformative power of street art with insiders.

PARISIAN STREET ARTISTS WHO SHAPED THE CITY

Street art, by essence a gesture of life and affirmation, has become more accepted in Paris, with a growing number of commissioned murals adorning the city. But here are a few 'first generation' artists who have shaped the city from the 1980s.

Nemo (1947–2001) His enigmatic black stencil figures often come with coloured objects: a balloon, an umbrella, a suitcase...

Jérôme Mesnager (b 1961) His white figure is 'a symbol of light, strength and peace'. He has painted them from Paris to the Great Wall of China.

Miss Tic (1956–2022) One of the first Parisian female street artists, she used stencils to paint sensual women accompanied by aphorisms advocating for freedom.

Jef Aerosol (b 1957) His most famous Parisian stencil fresco, *Chuuuttt!!!*, looms over Fontaine Stravinsky.

DRINKING IN BELLEVILLE: COFFEE SHOPS

Beans on Fire: A pioneering Parisian coffee roaster offering delicious blends in a serene setting. *8am-6pm Mon-Fri, from 9am Sat & Sun*

Plural: A spacious coffee shop with a pleasant terrace to sit on sunny days. Savoury options, including tasty empanadas, are available for lunch. *9am-5pm*

Candle Kids Coffee: Having a coffee here is like sitting in your living room, except you're looking at charming pl Henri Krasucki. *8.30am-5.30pm Wed-Fri, 10am-6pm Sat & Sun*

Mardi: Don't miss the matcha cheesecake to pair with your filter coffee at this small coffee shop; busy on weekends. *8.30am-5pm Mon-Fri, 10am-5.30pm Sat & Sun*

BELLEVILLE'S PASSAGES

Marine Sultan (@byrogers), creator of cultural media and mobile app By RogerS.

I think the best way to explore Belleville is on foot, to fully experience its cosmopolitan spirit – shaped by the many communities who have settled here over time – as well as its artistic side (French icon Édith Piaf was born here).

But one aspect I particularly love is the neighbourhood's pastoral and industrial heritage, reflected in the passages and workers' courtyards so typical of eastern Paris. Don't miss **rue Laurence Savart**, Villa de l'Ermitage (p181), **Cité Leroy**, **passage des Soupirs** and the **Regard St-Martin** – a small building that once monitored water quality dating back to when Belleville supplied Paris with water. At the end of your walk, you can stop by the Pavillon Carré de Baudouin (p181), which hosts photography exhibitions.

Living Art Meets Industrial Past
From industrial buildings to cultural centres

South of Belleville, the Popincourt district developed around metallurgy and mechanics, its working-class heritage still visible in the geometrical brick-layered edifices. As part of an initiative to repurpose Paris' 19th-century industrial buildings, two projects have thrived in the area. **Atelier des Lumières** *(atelier-lumieres.com; adult/child €18/11)*, a digital art centre housed in a former foundry, has gained popularity thanks to seasonal immersive light and sound exhibitions, particularly popular with children.

A few streets further north, a performing arts centre boasts a cast-iron gate adorned with a lyre, the building initially housing a musical instrument manufacturer. **Maison des Métallos** *(maisondesmetallos.paris)* has evolved into a multidisciplinary space with a rich program of concerts, conferences and festive performances.

 DRINKING IN BELLEVILLE: BEER & COCKTAILS

Micro Brasserie Balthazar: A 'microbrewery' where you can try local beers, and enjoy an apéritif on the terrace. Cocktails and wine also available. *hours vary*

La Sardine: A relaxed bar with a charming terrace located on a square tucked away from the bustling avenues. *9.30am-2am Mon-Fri, from 10.30am Sat & Sun*

Abricot Bar: A cocktail bar run by a woman – rare enough to mention it. Her surprising creations are plant-based and seasonal. *6pm-midnight Mon-Thu, to 2am Fri & Sat, to 11pm Sun*

Le Perchoir Ménilmontant: This is one of the first rooftop bars in Paris, providing a perfect open-air setting to party. Busy in summer. *6pm-2am Wed-Sat*

Parc de Belleville

Sunset in Belleville
Panoramic Paris

Parc de Belleville often leaves me breathless: not only are the stairs steep, but the view at the top of the hill is unexpectedly breathtaking! Take your time wandering along the park's terraced slopes, hearing a waterfall trickle between the meandering trails. Spot the vines, a reminder of Belleville's history as a winemaking village since the Middle Ages.

Going up, you'll reach the **Belvédère de Belleville**, a meeting point for street artists but also the second-highest summit in Paris! This vantage point offers an embracing view of Paris, stretching from Montparnasse to the Eiffel Tower. As you're facing west, you're arguably standing on the best sunset spot in the entire city.

Cultural events around Chinese food also take place here!

 EATING IN BELLEVILLE: ASIAN MEALS

Lao Siam: This popular Thai restaurant in Belleville has been a local favourite for years. It's easier to get a table for lunch. *12-3pm & 7-11pm Thu-Mon, 7-11pm Wed* €€

Mian Guan: A tiny spot specialising in Chinese handmade noodles served in savoury soups. Spicy and non-spicy options available. *12-3pm & 6-10.45pm Wed-Mon* €

Raviolis Nord Est: This small discreet restaurant specialises in dumplings, in the style of northeastern Chinese cuisine. *11am-11pm* €

Pavillon aux Pivoines: Recreating a traditional Chinese house, the former chef's daughters revisit classic Chinese dishes. *12-2.30pm & 7.30-10.30pm Tue-Sat, 12-3pm Sun* €€

WALKING TOUR

Exploring Belleville's Villages

With its rolling hills and winding streets, Belleville has a history as both a festive and idyllic area. Its slopes were covered in vineyards, and waterfalls ran down its hills. Wandering through former workers' courtyards, now picturesque passages, step back in time to discover Belleville's pastoral legacy. Wear good shoes for this tour, as this 3km-long walk will constantly take you up and down!

1 La Mouzaia
Begin your tour among the colourful houses and gardens of Villa Paul Verlaine and Villa des Boers. This now enchanting housing estate dating back from the 1880s was built on the slopes of a former gypsum quarry – now the Parc des Buttes-Chaumont – and was initially created to house working-class families.

The Walk: Make for rue du Général Brunet and walk all the way down to Botzaris metro.

2 Parc des Buttes-Chaumont
Try and get a glimpse of Montmartre from the highest slopes of the park (p183)! The bravest can go all the way down to the central pond, to then climb the artificial hill all the way up to Sybille's Temple.

The Walk: Exit the same way you came. Walk along the park's railings on rue Botzaris. Turn left on rue des Alouettes, left again on rue Fessart and finally right on rue Lassus.

3 St-Jean-Baptiste de Belleville
It is one of the first neogothic churches in Paris. Besides its two steeples, the 19m-high nave is particularly impressive.

The Walk: Walk on rue de Jourdain towards place des Grandes Rigoles and take the flight of stairs leading to rue Levert.

Place Henri Krasucki

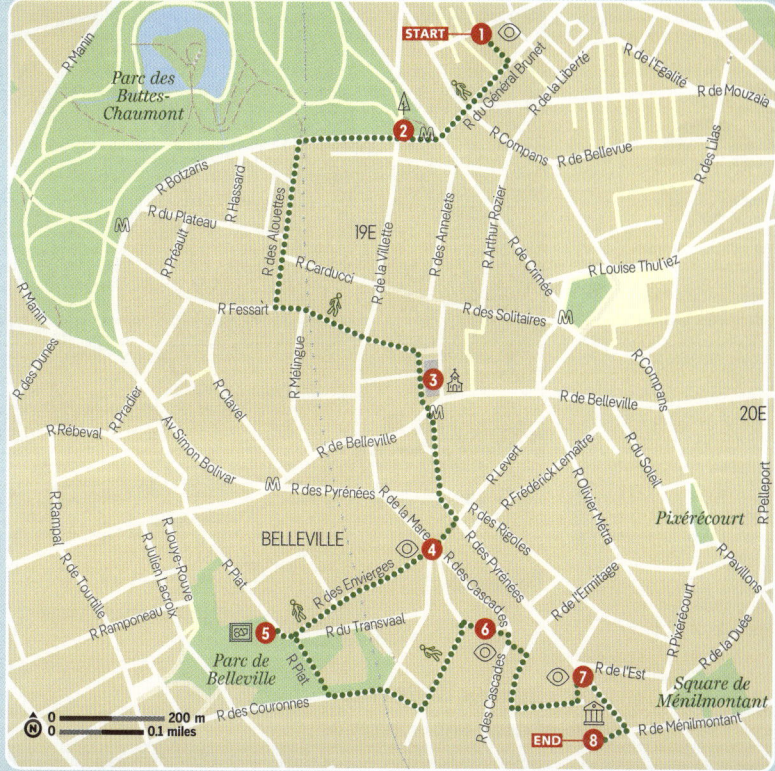

4 Place Henri Krasucki

A French *résistant,* union worker and active member of the French communist party, Henri Krasucki was a freedom activist until his last breath. The square named after him is among the most beloved among Belleville residents.

The Walk: Continue west on rue des Envierges.

5 Belvédère de Belleville

On clear days, a beautiful panoramic view of Paris opens up. Street art enthusiasts shouldn't miss the Belvédère de Belleville (p179).

The Walk: If you still have some stamina, turn left on passage Piat and walk down the stairs. Turn left on rue des Couronnes and right on rue Henri Chevreau. Make a left on rue de la Mare.

6 Rue de Savies

Covered in colourful murals, this street bears the name of the original farm that gave birth to the entire city of Belleville during the Middle Ages, 'la Ferme Savies'. Just across from it, the Regard St-Martin (p178) is a small surviving stone building that once served as a water-observation station.

The Walk: Take the stairs up, then right on rue de l'Ermitage.

7 Villa de l'Ermitage and Cité Leroy

A narrow yet picturesque vegetation-covered passage will appear on your left: it's Villa de l'Ermitage, and at the end of the cobblestoned way, another hidden passage, Cité Leroy, both vestiges of Ménilmontant's village history.

The Walk: Exit on rue des Pyrénées and turn right onto rue de Ménilmontant.

8 Pavillon Carré de Baudoin

Conclude with a cultural pause. This 18th-century building, formerly a venue for parties, has been repurposed as a contemporary arts centre.

A MULTICULTURAL & REBELLIOUS SPIRIT

Ali Lair (@alifrom pariss), a local food tour guide and a Belleville passionate, shares his approach to the neighbourhood.

Festive, welcoming, and affordable – Belleville has been shaped by its history of cultural diversity, following the arrival of various communities: Jewish, Tunisian, Chinese, Vietnamese, and more. Today, people continue to contribute to the neighbourhood's story. You come to Belleville for fun and good food! Food is a great way to approach multiculturalism. But Belleville is also, by nature, an artistic, working-class and rebellious area. The Paris Commune took place on Belleville's hill! I love stopping by Le Monte-en-l'Air, a fantastic feminist bookshop. And you shouldn't miss the many murals: they bring life to the walls and are an integral part of Belleville, where street art was born. Don't miss Belleville's Belvédère (p179), rue Dénoyez (p177) and Mesnager's dancing figures (p177) (rue de Ménilmontant), which capture the neighbourhood's revolutionary spirit.

Parc des Buttes-Chaumont

Insider Belleville
Explore with a local guide

Belleville is often seen as the newest Chinatown in Paris, but that is only one of its most recent immigration waves in the 20th century. The first foreign communities arrived in the 1920s: they were Armenians, Italians, Russian and Polish Jews, followed by German Jews in the 1930s and Moroccan Jews in the 1960s. Then Africans, Chinese and people from the West Indies came in the 1980s, and Yugoslavians and Pakistanis in the 1990s. All these communities have left a unique footprint and woven a tapestry of languages.

To unlock Belleville's nuances, insider knowledge brought by a local guide can be a plus. Join expert guide **Donatien Schramm** *(French only; exploreparis.com/fr/211_donatien-schramm)* who walks you through Belleville's historical layers thanks to themed tours, from its Revolutionary heritage to Chinese immigration history. With **Chloé Vasselin** *(French or English; Instagram @bouiboui.leblog),* spend a few hours sampling food and exploring background stories. Finally, with passionate **Ali Lair** *(French or English; in summer only; Instagram @alifrompariss),* explore three cultures – Vietnamese, Chinese and Tunisian – through carefully selected food spots from Popincourt to Ménilmontant. More autonomous travellers may prefer downloading the 'By Roger(S)' cultural app (in French), which gives additional insight through local itineraries.

Food on the Hill
Picnic in Buttes-Chaumont

With its undulating terrain, **Parc des Buttes-Chaumont** offers excellent picnic areas, highly appreciated by locals in summer. We can spend entire afternoons lying down on the steep grassy slopes with drinks, sandwiches and card games.

Yet this charming backdrop hides a more sombre story. A former landfill and then a gypsum quarry, it was finally abandoned in 1860, leaving the area neglected and prone to crime. It was only under Napoléon III that it was transformed to become today's peaceful hilly refuge.

With a bit of stamina, don't hesitate to climb the artificial hill standing in the middle of the lake: you'll discover characteristic elements of English gardens, including bridges, grottoes and a replica of a Greek ruin, **Sybille's Temple**.

Art to Heart
Open-art studios in the city

With a long tradition of inspiring and welcoming writers, painters and film directors alike, it's no wonder Belleville continues to draw contemporary artists. The **Ateliers d'Artistes de Belleville** *(ateliers-artistes-belleville.fr)* serves as a pulsating artistic hub, housing over 250 artists' studios and an art gallery.

Throughout the year, the gallery showcases regular exhibitions, but the true highlight? The annual open-studio days, typically in May or June. During four days, over a hundred artists open their workshops to visitors in the whole neighbourhood. It's a festive moment with artistic encounters, concerts and street performances, infusing the whole area with creative energy.

LA MÔME'S HERITAGE

Born in Ménilmontant, **Édith Piaf** led a remarkably romantic, eventful and successful life, ultimately becoming an icon of early-20th-century French music. Parisians continue to pay tribute to her across the hills of Belleville, from her grave in Cimetière du Père Lachaise (p174) to the steps of 72 rue de Belleville. While legend suggests she was born on these steps, she actually entered the world a few blocks away at Tenon Hospital. At the nearby place Édith Piaf, her statue with arms towards the sky perfectly captures the essence of her songs of love and sorrow. Across these emblematic places, three music boxes playing her songs are hidden – see if you can uncover them through your wanderings!

Don't miss the flans by Maison Savary when available!

 EATING IN BELLEVILLE: POPULAR BAKERIES

Patisserie Ginko: The pastries are a feast for both eyes and taste buds at this French pastry shop with Japanese and Mediterranean influences. *9am-7pm Tue-Sat* €€

Benoît Castel – Ménilmontant: A bakery-pastry shop known for its delectable all-you-can-eat brunch, popular with locals. *7.30am-8pm Wed-Fri, from 8am Sat, 8am-6pm Sun* €€

Milligramme: An infinite selection of mouth-watering bread and pastries awaits, but there's a special mention for the flan and *viennoiseries*. *7am-8pm Tue-Fri, from 8am Sat, 8am-1pm Sun* €€

Demain: This concept bakery sells top-quality bread from the day before, whole or repurposed, at a discounted price. *8am-8pm Mon-Sat, 9am-2pm Sun* €

Researched by Peter Yeung

BASTILLE & EASTERN PARIS

HISTORY, NATURE, NIGHTLIFE AND INDUSTRIAL HERITAGE

Often overlooked by tourists, this area offers a captivating blend of experiences that will reward those who enjoy travelling off the beaten path.

This lesser-known, more typically local area, which spans parts of the 11th, 12th and 20th *arrondissements,* has key historical sites and a compelling industrial heritage to complement an increasingly cool, youthful scene. Near Bastille, craft workshops that bustled in the 19th and early 20th centuries are today home to vibrant arts venues, hipster cafes, independent shops and creative restaurants. Going east, the landscape transforms. Past Nation's broad residential avenues and the city limits lies the Bois de Vincennes, one of Paris' green lungs. These neighbourhoods are distinct but most retain a village-like charm thanks to their history as faubourgs (small boroughs), representing a different, more relaxed and lived-in side of Paris.

TOP TIP

Utilise public transport effectively. While walking is a great way to explore the immediate surroundings, the distance between Bastille and Vincennes is significant. The transport system is quite efficient in the area so make extensive use of it to save time and energy.

FROM LEFT: ELISABETH SCHITTENHELM/GETTY IMAGES, PREMIER PHOTO/SHUTTERSTOCK

See p310 for places to stay in Bastille and eastern Paris.

Coulée Verte René-Dumont (p192)

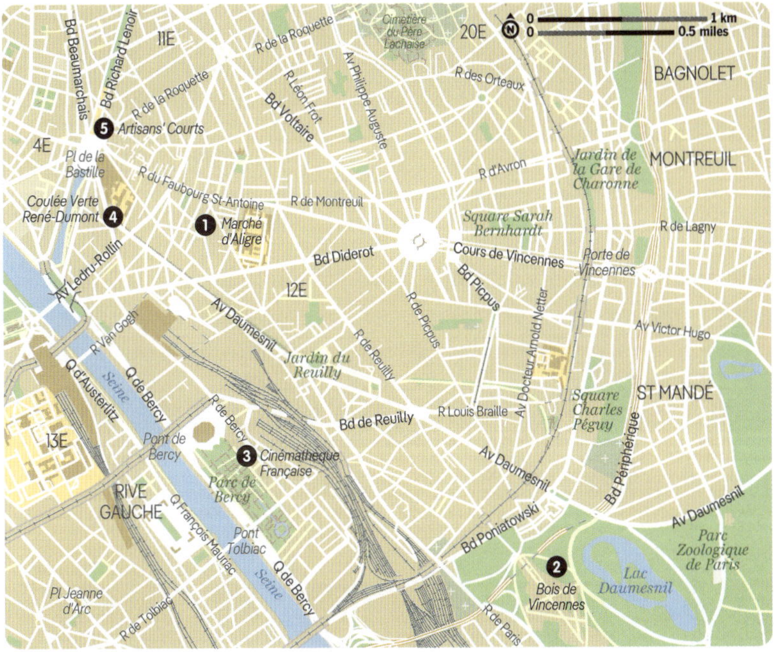

 Highlights

◀ ❶ Marché d'Aligre
Try typical French products at the indoor and outdoor stands of this vibrant, popular market. **p195**

❷ Bois de Vincennes
Join Parisians in escaping the urban frenzy at this beautiful, sprawling forest on the city's doorstep. **p196**

❸ Cinémathèque Française
This high temple of French cinema is the perfect place to pay homage to the so-called 'seventh art'. **p202**

❹ Coulée Verte René-Dumont
Stroll above the streets of Paris on this green pedestrian promenade along former train tracks. **p192**

❺ Artisans' Courts
Explore the hidden alleys and courtyards that were home to skilled craftworkers for centuries. **p191**

 Getting Around

Walking
This is the best way to explore and it's eminently possible thanks to the area's density and surfeit of green paths.

Bicycle
The area is well served by the municipal Vélib' bikes and there are many cycling lanes, even if busier streets near Bastille are trickier to navigate.

Metro
Lines 1 and 8 will likely be the most helpful if you want to save time and energy (or if the weather isn't great).

BASTILLE

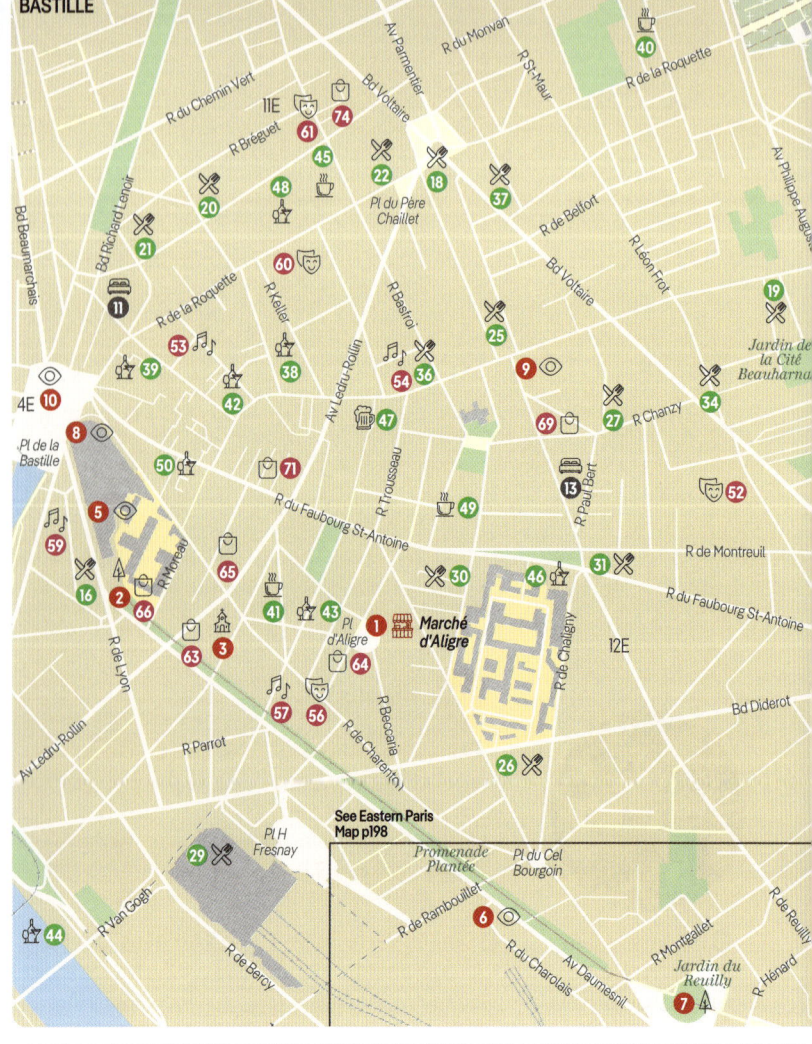

⭐ HIGHLIGHTS
1 Marché d'Aligre

● SIGHTS
2 Coulée Verte René-Dumont
3 Église St-Antoine des Quinze Vingts
4 Église St-Germain de Charonne
5 Grand Palais Immersif
6 Ground Control
7 Jardin de Reuilly
8 Opéra Bastille
9 Palais de la Femme
10 Place de la Bastille

● SLEEPING
11 Hôtel Daval
12 Hôtel du Printemps
13 Hôtel Paris Bastille Boutet
14 JO&JOE Paris – Nation
15 Mama Shelter Paris East

● EATING
16 Amarante
17 Au Levain des Pyrénées
18 Aux Bons Crus
19 Boulangerie Manobaké
20 Boulangerie MieMie
21 Café de l'Industrie
22 Chez Aline
23 Chez Tante Farida
24 KALANK
25 La Boulangerie Nouvelle
26 La Cantine Diderot
27 La Chocolaterie Cyril Lignac
28 Le Bricheton
29 Le Train Bleu
30 L'Ébauchoir
31 Les Copains du Faubourg
32 Les Rêveuses
33 Paulownia
34 Pépite
35 Peppe Pizzeria
36 Tapisserie
37 VG Pâtisserie

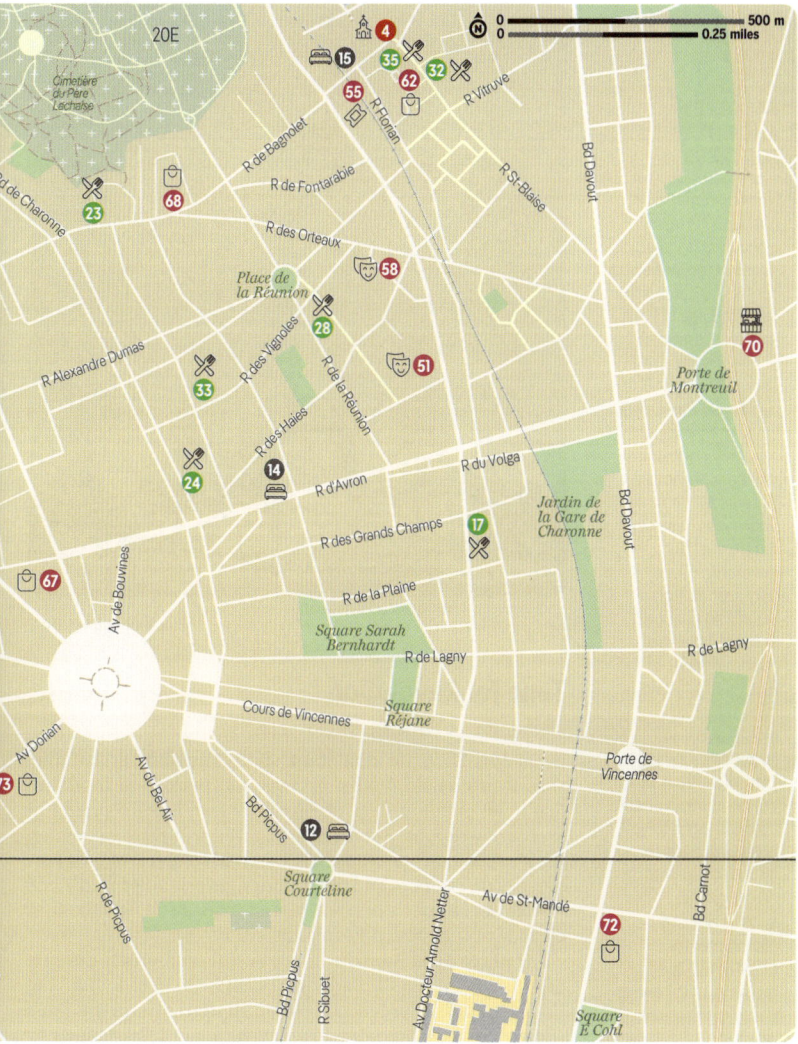

● DRINKING & NIGHTLIFE
- **38** Badaboum
- **39** Bar des Ferrailleurs
- **40** Klover Coffee Showroom
- **41** La Tropicale Glacier
- **42** L'Atelier Saisonnier
- **43** Le Baron Rouge
- **44** Le Mazette
- **45** Le Sedaine Bar
- **46** Les Blouses Blanches
- **47** Les Cuves de Fauve
- **48** Les Mauvais Joueurs
- **49** Mokochaya
- **50** Pachamama
- **see 36** Septime La Cave

● ENTERTAINMENT
- **51** Arcal
- **52** Artishow
- **53** Café de la Danse
- **54** Café de la Plage
- **55** La Flèche d'Or
- **56** Le 100
- **57** Le POPUP du Label
- **see 38** Les Disquaires
- **58** Les Rendez-Vous d'Ailleurs
- **59** Supersonic
- **60** Théâtre de la Bastille
- **61** Théâtre la Boutonnière

● SHOPPING
- **62** Chapellerie De Punta en Blanco
- **63** Confiture Parisienne
- **64** Graineterie du Marché
- **65** Guayapi
- **66** La Fabrique nomade
- **67** L'Auguste Cave
- **68** Le Merle Moqueur
- **69** Le Parti du Thé
- **70** Marché aux Puces de Montreuil
- **71** Plastic Soul Records
- **72** Temps de Terre
- **73** Un Jour, une vieillerie
- **74** Ursa Major Chocolats
- **see 63** Viaduc des Arts

● TRANSPORT
- **see 29** Gare de Lyon

BASTILLE'S ANCIENT FORTRESS

Nothing remains of Bastille's fortress, which was originally constructed in the 14th century to defend the eastern flank of Paris against the English during the Hundred Years' War. By 1417 the royal castle took on an unusual new aspect: it formally became a state prison, housing inmates for centuries until it was destroyed during the 1789 Revolution. Today, only a small sign on a building near bd Henri IV indicates the boundaries of the former stronghold, once boasting eight towers and surrounded by a 24m-wide moat. Over the centuries, various urban designs have been proposed to update the place de la Bastille, such as placing a monumental, elephant-shaped fountain at its centre, though this was never realised.

Place de la Bastille

Time for Revolution

MAP P186

Visit an iconic Parisian symbol of liberty

On 14 July 1789, the inhabitants of the Faubourg St-Antoine, sick of prolonged food shortages and periods of hardship due to an ongoing siege of Paris, stormed Bastille prison in search of weapons. But when the guards refused to surrender, the situation escalated. Rebels seized 250 barrels of gunpowder, freed prisoners and put military governor Bernard-René Jordan de Launay's head on a pike. This event was the first episode of the French Revolution.

The **place de la Bastille** is a powerful symbol of the events of 1789, but it also broadly represents the freedom of the French people. The central column commemorates the *Trois Glorieuses*, the three-day July Revolution of 1830, topped by the winged statue of the *Génie de la Liberté* (Genius of Liberty). At its base are two funerary stones: one commemorating

EATING NEAR BASTILLE: OUR BAKERY PICKS

MAP P186

Boulangerie MieMie: Top-tier baked goods include featherweight cream puffs and a mega 'anti-waste' croissant cake made with pastry scraps. *8am-8pm Tue-Sat, 8am-1pm Sun* €

Boulangerie Manobaké: Rising star in the Paris bakery scene with a charming mosaic interior and understated yet quality cinnamon rolls, apple tarts and carrot cake. *hours vary* €

VG Pâtisserie: Delicious vegan croissants and *pains au chocolat* made using organic wheat grown 80km from Paris. Gluten-free options. *1-7pm Tue, 9am-7pm Wed-Sat, 9am-6pm Sun* €

Pépite: TikTokers come for the decadent black sesame-filled croissants, but the broader pastry selection is seriously good too. *7am-8pm Tue-Sun* €

the fallen during the 1830 revolution, with 500 individuals buried underneath; the second honouring those who died in the 1848 revolution, which brought an end to the monarchy.

This symbolic political history means that Bastille, like the nearby place de la République, draws frequent protests (practically every weekend in the afternoon), so if you're in the mood for marching, join in for a quintessential Parisian experience. Otherwise, there's usually a more relaxed atmosphere, so grab a coffee at one of the many surrounding cafe terraces and gaze at this iconic symbol of liberty.

A Night at the Opera

MAP P186

See a show at Europe's largest opera house

With its striking glass and steel façade, the **Opéra Bastille** *(operadeparis.fr/en)* was inaugurated on 13 July 1989 to commemorate the bicentenary of the storming of the Bastille. Boasting Europe's largest performance stage, the 2745-seat venue hosts bold modern music and dance shows and is part of a broader effort to promote contemporary arts, in contrast with its traditional counterpart, the Palais Garnier.

Guided tours on Saturdays (adult/child €20/13, only in French) offer the chance to learn about the modernist architecture – still divisive among Parisians – designed by Uruguayan-Canadian architect Carlos Ott. Last-minute deals are available at the ticket office an hour before shows, and *'avant-premiere'* nights for people under 28 offer tickets for just €10, but usually require booking far in advance.

Immersive Arts Space

MAP P186

Visit unique multisensory exhibitions

Located in an underground section of Opéra Bastille, the **Grand Palais Immersif** *(grandpalais-immersif.fr/en; adult/child €17/12)* holds two multisensory, interactive exhibitions per year. Curated by the team of the Grand Palais, renowned for their monumental installations, the exhibitions immerse visitors in a selected artist's work or a specific artistic theme, via huge wall projections, sound installations, olfactory experiences and interactive devices. This highly Instagrammable museum, good for an hour-long diversion on rainy days or to keep kids occupied, transports visitors into a living universe of art. Note that the entrance is separate from the Opéra's.

PARIS OPERA 101

The art form that was born over 400 years ago in Renaissance-era Italy, later used in France by Napoléon as a tool of propaganda, has long been associated with the rich and elite. But these days, while going to the opera in Paris might seem like an intimidating experience, it needn't be. For one, there's a broad selection of arts, not only formal classics like Giuseppe Verdi's *La Traviata*, but also modern genres like Israeli techno dance and Japanese electronic music. Nobody will bat an eyelid at how you dress, either, as long as you're clean and presentable. And aim to arrive at least 30 minutes early, so you have time to soak in the atmosphere and admire the surroundings while sipping on a drink.

EATING NEAR BASTILLE: OUR PICKS

MAP P186

Café de l'Industrie: Fake rhino heads, plastic pink flamingos and portraits of film stars fill this fun, retro bistro delivering affordable classics. *8.30am-2am Mon-Sun* €

Chez Aline: This former butcher's shop sells the finest Parisian lunch food, with *jambon beurre* baguettes and *oeufs mimosa* (devilled eggs) on its daily blackboard. *11.30am-3.30pm Mon-Fri* €

Amarante: A carnivore's delight, with pork and veal specialities sitting along classics. Understated in plating and decor and buoyed by impeccable service. *12.30-1.30pm & 7.30-9.30pm Thu-Tue* €€

Aux Bons Crus: This throwback in the style of a French *relais routier* (truck stop), with red-and-white chequered tablecloths, is one for the gourmands. *noon-2.30pm & 7.30-10.30pm Mon-Sun* €€

PALAIS DE LA FEMME

Initially built in 1910 by the Catholic philanthropist Amicie Lebaudy as an affordable hotel, and then acquired by the Salvation Army in 1926, the **Palais de la Femme** (Map p186) has for a century been dedicated to supporting women and women's rights. The grand, five-storey art nouveau building, which was recognised as a national historic monument in 2003, has retained many of its original features, including a monumental staircase, mosaic flooring and a charming library filled with paintings and stained-glass windows. These days the space houses several nonprofits supporting vulnerable women, with services including emergency support and temporary accommodation, but it also hosts exhibitions, events and dance classes that are open to the public. Check their social media for listings.

Passage L'homme

Shop Until You Drop

MAP P186

Visit a wealth of independent businesses

The area has a plethora of unique independent shops worth patronising. Near Bastille, there's **Le Parti du Thé**, a wonderful tea shop working directly with small-scale producers across the world; **Plastic Soul Records**, the oldest and perhaps most charming record store in Paris; and **Ursa Major Chocolats**, an exquisite chocolatier run by three sisters known for their planet-inspired creations.

Around Marché d'Aligre, the **Graineterie du Marché**, which sells all kinds of seeds, herbs and spices, is one of the last few genuine Parisian *épiceries* (specialist grocers). **Guayapi** sources products like the energising *warana* plant from an indigenous community in the Amazon rainforest.

Towards Nation, **Un Jour, une vieillerie** is a treasure trove of retro collectibles full of Proustian nostalgia; **Tucked Friperie** (Map p198) is a thrift store with a curated selection of trendy clothes; and **L'Auguste Cave** offers an excellent array of natural wines to take home (along with friendly advice if you're unsure).

Don't miss **Le Merle Moqueur**, a lovely bookstore by St-Blaise with a solid offering in English; **Temps de Terre**, where you can pick up elegant teapots, mugs and plates, among other ceramics; and **Chapellerie De Punta en Blanco**, which has a wide selection of handmade headwear, notably original Panama hats.

EXPLORE THE ARTISANS' COURTS

Strolling around the picturesque passages that dot Faubourg St-Antoine provides a glimpse into its past as a centre of artisanship.

START	END	LENGTH
Cour Damoye	Passage du Chantier	1.5km; one hour

As far back as the 15th century there's been a proud tradition of artisanship among Faubourg St-Antoine's inhabitants, with their workshops lining the area's picturesque, tranquil courtyards and passages. A stroll here will immerse you in the historic atmosphere.

Start at ❶ **cour Damoye**, a site founded by an ironmonger that was previously home to ragpickers and scrap dealers, but is now a courtyard filled with charming townhouses whose large glass façades you can peek through. Exit via rue Daval and head along frantic rue de Lappe, known for its nightlife, for a few minutes. Turn left to ❷ **passage L'homme**, surrounded by nostalgic, peeling storefronts, a cute antique games shop and a furniture shop with the sign of a chair hanging out front. Follow the street's curve onto ❸ **passage Josset**, past colourful street murals, then perhaps have a coffee at Passager, before turning right onto busy rue de Charonne. Continue to ❹ **passage de la Main d'Or**, once again cobblestoned and calm, before traversing the narrow passage on the southern end. Turn right and walk to ❺ **74 rue du Faubourg St-Antoine**, formerly a 19th-century furniture factory, where you can admire its 32m brick chimney, then make a final detour through ❻ **passage du Chantier**, a tunnel-like route still home to artisans.

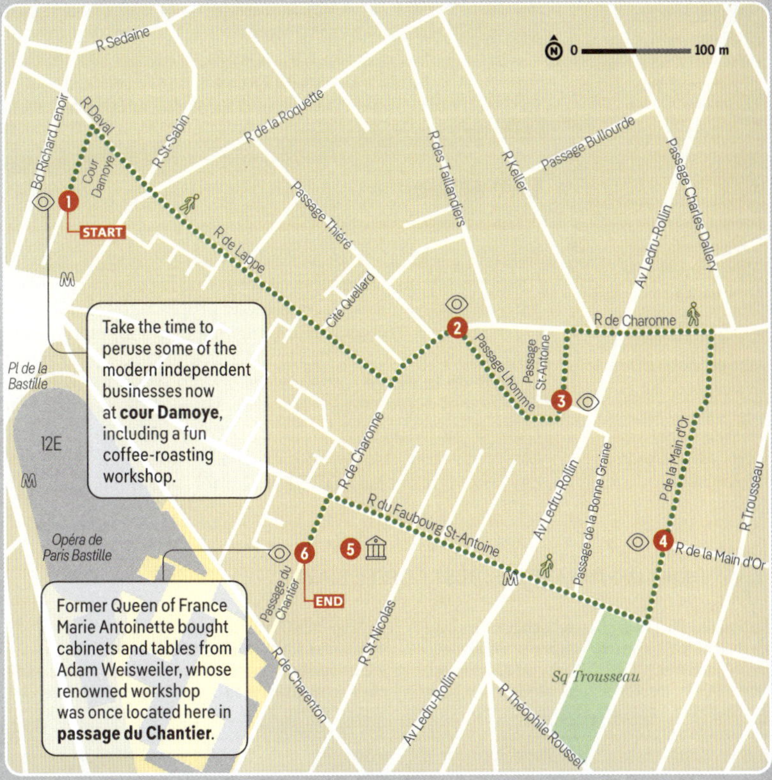

> Take the time to peruse some of the modern independent businesses now at **cour Damoye**, including a fun coffee-roasting workshop.

> Former Queen of France Marie Antoinette bought cabinets and tables from Adam Weisweiler, whose renowned workshop was once located here in **passage du Chantier**.

WHY I LOVE THE COULÉE VERTE RENÉ-DUMONT

Peter Yeung, Lonely Planet writer

There's nothing else in Paris quite like the **Coulée Verte René-Dumont**, a 4.5km elevated green walkway that inspired New York City's High Line. I usually prefer to go eastward on the flower-filled route along former train tracks, since the city gradually becomes greener and calmer with each step. Along the way there are plenty of sights: the pointed spire of **Église St-Antoine des Quinze Vingts**, Haussmannian buildings with Parisian zinc rooftops and intricate art nouveau façades, the pretty **Jardin de Reuilly**, prime for a picnic and with sparkling water on tap, and then, at the gateway to Bois de Vincennes, murals in homage to legendary female French explorer Alexandra David-Néel.

Modern Artisans
MAP P186
Buy direct from skilled producers

The grand arches of the Bastille viaduct, constructed in the 19th century to support a railway line, are these days home to a rich variety of contemporary arts and crafts workshops, also known as the **Viaduc des Arts** *(leviaducdesarts.com/en)*. About 40 artisans – including fashion designers, glassblowers, chocolate makers, shoesmiths and luthiers – inhabit the 1.5km viaduct along av Daumesnil. Glass façades let you peek in from the street, but you can enter most places to buy products, such as delicious jams made on-site by **Confiture Parisienne**, or stylish jewellery at **La Fabrique nomade**, which employs refugees.

Bottoms Up
MAP P186
A bar for every mood

The Bastille area comes alive at night and it is one of the best areas in Paris to have a merry night of drinking. Rue de la Roquette and rue de Lappe are lined with bars and clubs, so if you're looking for a rowdy time you'll inevitably end up here. Look out for **Bar des Ferrailleurs**, which has a cosy ambience and creative cocktails, and **L'Atelier Saisonnier**, which is perfect for a few glasses of wine and cheese. Further afield, **Les Mauvais Joueurs** is a fun board-game bar to spend a chill evening with friends, while the minimalist, industrial-style **Les Cuves de Fauve** is one of the best places in the city to drink craft beer, and **Septime La Cave** is a hip spot that specialises in natural wine.

Live Music
MAP P186
Intimate venues with great bands

Bastille is a great place to see live music in a smaller, more intimate setting. **Les Disquaires** *(lesdisquaires.com)* is a cafe-concert venue with an eclectic program, but largely focusing on rock and pop, before turning into a nightclub open until 5am on weekends. The Brazilian samba nights on Fridays at **Café de la Plage** *(lecafedelaplage-paris.com)*, which also holds *forró* dance classes, are a joy. Meanwhile, the 500-seat **Café de la Danse** *(cafeladanse.com)* welcomes mid-tier acts from around the world. Elsewhere, don't miss the Tuesday jazz nights at **Le POPUP du Label** *(popup.paris)*, which

---

 DRINKING IN BASTILLE: BEST COFFEE SHOPS — MAP P186

Le Sedaine Bar: This charming locals' joint run by an elderly couple is refreshingly uncool and husband Marc makes a memorable cappuccino. *6.30am-8pm Mon-Sat*

Mokochaya: This hyped Japanese-influenced space is beautiful and inventive, with offerings from hot drinks to famous cookies. *8.30am-6pm Tue-Fri, 11am-3.30pm Sat*

La Tropicale Glacier: Best known for its creative ice-cream flavours, this airy spot also serves all kinds of coffee. *10am-6pm Tue-Fri, 10am-7pm Sat & Sun*

Klover Coffee Showroom: This new minimalist space is a destination for coffee nerds and the Korean owner roasts the speciality beans himself. *hours vary*

Viaduc des Arts

hosts all kinds of emerging artists throughout the week, and **Supersonic** *(supersonic-club.fr)*, another platform for young talent, with shows every day that often have free entry.

After Midnight

MAP P186

Late-night entertainment

Clubbing around Bastille, often a rough and ready experience, is a far cry from the chic of western Paris. The city's branch of international club **Pachamama** *(pachamama-paris.com)*, spread across three storeys in a beautiful 19th-century building designed by Gustave Eiffel, is the closest you'll get to that glamour. For something more different, head to the 400-person dance floor at **Badaboum** *(badaboum.paris)*, renowned for its funk parties and neon ceiling, where the high-quality sound system pumps out a mix of house, disco and trance.

FÊTE DE LA MUSIQUE

If you are in Paris on 21 June, the longest day of the year, get ready for the **Fête de la Musique** (Festival of Music). During this jovial annual celebration, which was launched in 1982 by the French government to encourage and support amateur music, the city's streets are filled all day and night with every kind of music genre imaginable. Concerts include big-hitter names, and are even held in unique venues like the Louvre, but one of the best ways to experience the festival is to just stroll around by foot in neighbourhoods like Bastille, encountering concerts by chance.

 EATING & DRINKING NEAR ALIGRE: OUR PICKS — MAP P186

Le Baron Rouge: Grab a spot on the edge of the wooden barrels for a perfect soirée of cheese, charcuterie, bread and wine. *hours vary* €

Les Blouses Blanches: The sprawling terrace and cosy indoor sofas, overseen by house cat Maya, are perfect for a coffee or cocktail at all hours. *7am-2am* €

La Cantine Diderot: Affordable bistro classics, from *œuf mayo* to *steak-frites*, make this a reliable address to return to. *noon-3pm & 6-10.30pm* €

L'Ébauchoir: Quality seasonal produce combined with excellent cooking and a long wine list make this classy bistro perfect for wining and dining. *hours vary* €€

THEATRE OF CRUELTY

According to French avant-garde theorist Antonin Artaud, who rose to fame in the 1920s and 1930s, civilisation was undergoing what he saw as a 'psychological and human stagnation' due to the bourgeois nature of society. But Artaud argued that humanity could be liberated, awoken to the harsh realities of the world, through theatre. His Theatre of Cruelty, an experimental approach inspired by the indigenous dancers of Bali, involved shocking spectators with 'violent physical images [that] crush and hypnotise the spectator's sensibility'. In practice, that means actors screaming and dancing aggressively as well as the use of striking costumes, bright lights and piercing noise, to force audiences to realise how bizarre life really is. Artaud's influence is still seen in contemporary theatre.

Palais de la Porte Dorée

A Night at the Theatre

MAP P186

Lesser-known performance spaces

Paris is full to the brim with glorious and historic theatres, mostly clustered in the central *beaux quartiers*. But for those in search of a more intimate, local and often much cheaper experience, eastern Paris is a great place to look. **Théâtre de la Bastille** *(theatre-bastille.com)*, based in a pretty building that dates back to the early 1900s, is a brilliant place to see quality contemporary dance and theatre – and there's even the odd play in English. Not far away is **Théâtre la Boutonnière** *(laboutonniere.fr)*, a former button factory that is now an adorable theatre set in a tranquil, tree-filled courtyard, whose politically engaged programming spans theatre, dance and circus. Towards place d'Aligre, **Le 100** *(100ecs.fr)* is a 1800-sq-metre 'cultural factory' that supports emerging artists and there's usually an exciting blend of film screenings, exhibitions and innovative theatre. For opera-curious travellers, **Les Rendez-Vous d'Ailleurs** *(lesrdvdailleurs.fr)*, founded by a former opera singer, is a great local place to see less fusty performances of classical music or even musicals, from Beethoven to Édith Piaf – as is **Arcal** *(arcal-lyrique.fr)*, a national theatre company, recently turned 40, that has a goal of making opera accessible to the wider public. For a classic Parisian cabaret with all the colourful and camp trimmings, from flirty drag queens to dinner deals, look no further than **Artishow** *(artishowcabaret.com)*, a recently renovated space that's been running for over 20 years.

Market Day

MAP P186

See the district's living soul

Locals and tourists alike adore the vibrant **Marché d'Aligre**, without doubt one of the best of the more than 70 open-air fresh-produce markets in Paris. The Aligre Market, which was built in 1843 and later named after local resident Etienne François d'Aligre, the first president of the Parliament of Paris, is split into three sections. The Halle Beauvau is a covered section home to permanent vendors of cheese, wine, olives and other classic French produce. Meanwhile, the outdoor market, which runs along rue d'Aligre, features dozens of stalls with fresh fruit and vegetables, meat and fish, flowers and more, attracting early-morning grocery shoppers seeking the best goods. Closed only on Mondays, the Aligre Market offers a perfect opportunity to experience the typical French way of shopping for fresh food. Lastly, the flea-market section, in the eastern part of Aligre, is a gem. It traces its roots back to a time when royal edicts allowed anyone to sell whatever they wanted on place d'Aligre. So, antique enthusiasts, African-mask collectors, book lovers and treasure hunters will have a lot to explore. Beyond the market, Aligre forms a wider community, with many shop owners here established for decades, and the area seems to have managed to resist gentrification better than others. It even hosts its own independent radio station, Aligre FM, which has been broadcasting since 1981.

End of Empire

MAP P198

Learn about France's complicated colonial past

Set in a grandiose art deco building, the **Palais de la Porte Dorée** (Palace of the Golden Gate) is an underrated destination on the edge of Paris. Constructed for the Colonial Exhibition of 1931, a dark chapter in France's history during which racist stereotypes were perpetuated in a celebration of the French Empire, the building is nonetheless an architectural curio lined with massive columns, sprawling murals and glorious mosaics (especially those in the Marie-Curie Hall on the ground floor). Since 2007 the building has been home to the **Musée de l'Histoire de l'Immigration** (*histoire-immigration.fr/en; adult/child €12/free*), a fascinating museum that covers the often painful history of immigration in France, including the transatlantic slavery trade, in which France transported over a million enslaved Africans to the Caribbean.

Continues on p199

ANCIENT GRAINS

Maxime Bussy (@lebricheton), owner of Le Bricheton bakery.

As a baker living in the southwest of France, surrounded by countryside, it was easy to work directly with farmers. But in Paris, sourcing good local produce is more of a challenge. Most bakeries in the city today use industrial flour from varieties made to maximise output. So when I set up Le Bricheton in 2016, the idea was to build a network that could change that. We use grains that are more nutritional and sustainable to grow, like Khorasan wheat and buckwheat. All of our bread, which is 100% sourdough, is kneaded by hand. We even recently took over a 17th-century mill near Paris to make flour ourselves.

 BEST BAKERIES FOR BREAD — MAP P186

Le Bricheton: This hole-in-the-wall bakery is renowned across Paris for its delicious loaves made with rare, ancient grains and kneaded entirely by hand. *4-8pm Tue-Sat, 10.30am-1pm Sun* €

Les Copains du Faubourg: This popular spot uses top-class Rouge du Roc wheat and then grinds it using a mill in the bakery. *8am-8pm Tue-Sat, 8am-11am Sun* €

La Boulangerie Nouvelle: Non-industrial flours and long fermentations are the philosophy here, with spectacular knotted brioches (vegan) and sourdough loaves. *11am-8pm Tue-Sat* €

Au Levain des Pyrénées: French-Tamil baker Tharshan Selvarajah was winner of the 2023 'best baguette in Paris' competition. *7am-8.30pm Mon-Fri, 8am-2pm Sat* €

Lac Daumesnil

TOP EXPERIENCE

Bois de Vincennes

The wonderful Bois de Vincennes is one of the capital's two 'green lungs' along with the Bois de Boulogne. Parisians flock to this 995-hectare forest for a breath of fresh air but also for the myriad things to see and do, from boat rides on lakes to restorative nature walks, floral gardens, a zoo, a racecourse, a circus and a historic château.

DON'T MISS

Boating on the lakes

Parc Floral de Paris

Château de Vincennes

Parc Zoologique de Paris

Jardin d'Agronomie Tropicale

La Cartoucherie

Boating on the Lakes

Renting a rowboat on a sunny day is a classic Bois de Vincennes experience. Most do so at **Lac Daumesnil**, artificially built in 1860, to the west of the park. One-hour rides costs €15 for up to four people. The isles at the lake's centre, **Île de Reuilly** and **Île de Bercy**, can be accessed by a footbridge to the south. Don't miss the pretty, Greek-inspired **Romantic Temple** and the grotto below with waterfalls. Here and the surroundings are prime – and popular – for picnics and sunbathing. Just south, the **Kagyu-Dzong Buddhist temple** and the towering **Great Pagoda**, open on weekends, make for a peaceful visit. Boats can also be rented (€12 per hour for up to four) at the north edge of the smaller, lesser-known **Lac des Minimes**, in the forest's northeast. Drinks and snacks are available nearby

PRACTICALITIES

● Map p198 ● parisjetaime.com/eng/culture/bois-de-vincennes-p1017 ● 24hr; free to enter (though some activities have fees and limited opening times)

at the **Confiserie Du Lac**, or, on Friday and Saturday nights, at **Rosa Bonheur à l'Est**, which hosts live music and DJs on an island in the lake until 1am.

Fun-Packed Flower Park

Inaugurated in 1969, the 28-hectare **Parc Floral de Paris** *(adult/child €2.70/1.55)* is one of the city's best places to admire flowers, from bonsai gardens to tropical greenhouses. Come between April and September for the best sights. The site itself is also jam-packed with family-centred activities, including an 18-hole mini-golf course, zip lines, an escape game, a children's theatre and a butterfly garden. Majestic blue peacocks frequent the park and are easier to spot late morning or at lunchtime.

Château de Vincennes

To the north of the forest, **Château de Vincennes** attracts relatively few visitors. But this gleaming castle, which began in the 12th century as a hunting lodge before being transformed into a fortress, royal residence and prison, is worth an hour-long visit. Entry to the expansive courtyard is free, however a ticket is required for the site's **dungeon** *(adult/child €13/free)*, one of the tallest in Europe, allowing you to explore and ascend the tower for a panoramic view. A ticket also allows entry to Ste-Chapelle, a small version of its famed counterpart in central Paris, with its stained-glass windows and beautiful entrance door, one of the first masterpieces of the flamboyant Gothic style.

Parc Zoologique de Paris

The **Parc Zoologique de Paris** *(parczoologiquedeparis.fr/en; adult/child €22/17)* is a whole lot of fun and great for a change of pace. Divided into geographic zones such as Patagonia, the Andes and Madagascar, this triangle-shaped zoo contains more than 3000 animals and 250 species. There are daily feeding sessions with animals, including giraffes, sea lions, ostriches and baboons, so check times before going.

Jardin d'Agronomie Tropicale

The lesser-known, tranquil **Jardin d'Agronomie Tropicale** is filled with lush vegetation and has remnants of the 1931 Colonial Exhibition, including a pretty Chinese gate and Cambodian stupa. Grab lunch or a coffee at the lovely *cantine*.

École du Breuil

The municipal **École du Breuil** is yet another delightful green space to visit, with a wonderful lotus garden and the benches at this horticulture school carved out from tree trunks.

La Cartoucherie

This **cultural complex** of five theatres in the forest showcases theatre, dance and circus arts.

WE LOVE GREEN

We Love Green *(welovegreen.fr)*, held in Bois de Vincennes in June, is a festival that raises awareness about ecological issues through music and art. Hop on the metro, bus or a bike (coming by car is discouraged) to get to this three-day event, spread over five stages in the forest, including a dedicated Think Tank stage for environmental talks.

TOP TIPS

- Phone signal can be weak in parts, so bear that in mind when meeting friends. It's a good idea to download maps on your phone before you go.

- The forest is vast so it's worth considering using a bicycle to traverse it. There are a number of municipal Vélib' stations scattered throughout the forest.

- Rubbish bins are few and far between, so be prepared to carry out whatever you bring in.

- There are many water stations across the forest. Don't forget to bring your reusable drink bottle.

- Some sites are only open on the weekend, which will also be by far the busiest time to come, so choose wisely.

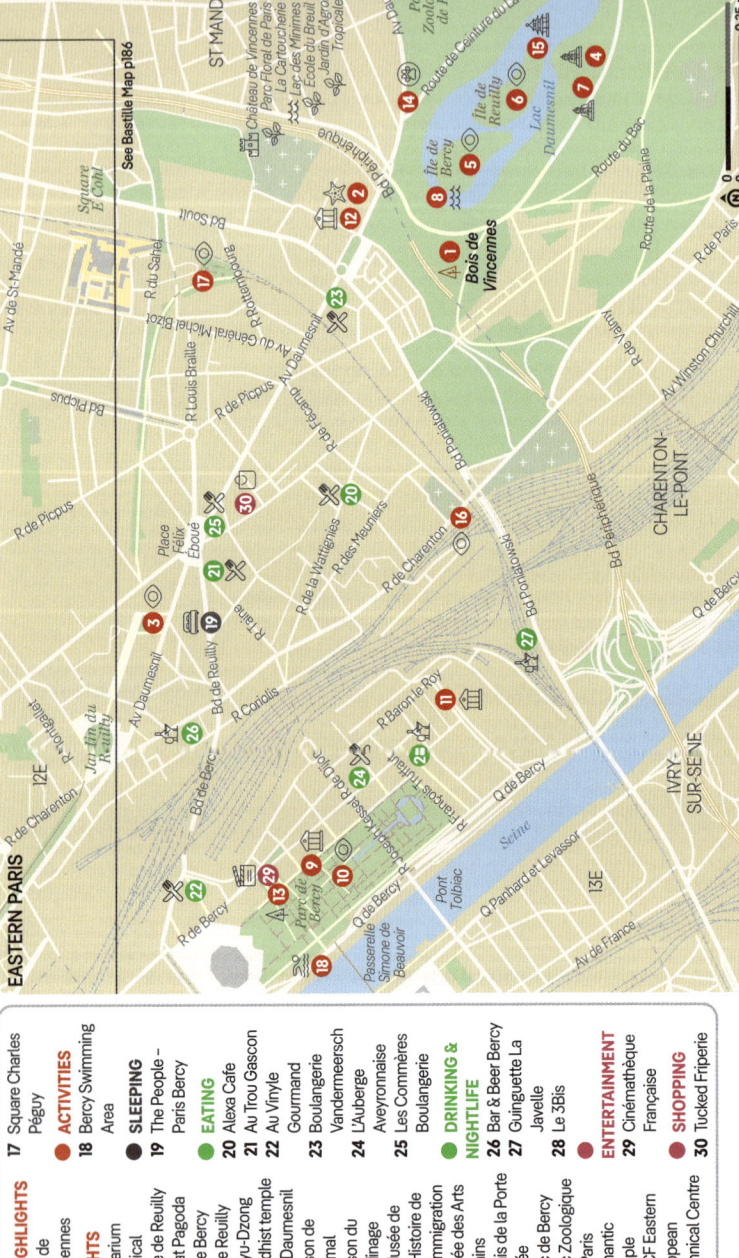

BASTILLE & EASTERN PARIS

EASTERN PARIS

★ HIGHLIGHTS
1 Bois de Vincennes

● SIGHTS
2 Aquarium Tropical
3 Gare de Reuilly Great Pagoda
4 Great Pagoda
5 Île de Bercy
6 Île de Reuilly
7 Kagyu-Dzong Buddhist temple
8 Lac Daumesnil
9 Maison de l'Animal
10 Maison du Jardinage
see 2 Musée de l'Histoire de l'Immigration
11 Musée des Arts Forains
12 Palais de la Porte Dorée
13 Parc de Bercy
14 Parc Zoologique de Paris
15 Romantic Temple
16 SNCF Eastern European Technical Centre
17 Square Charles Péguy

● ACTIVITIES
18 Bercy Swimming Area

● SLEEPING
19 The People – Paris Bercy

● EATING
20 Alexa Cafe
21 Au Trou Gascon
22 Au Vinyle
23 Boulangerie Vandermeersch
24 L'Auberge Aveyronnaise
25 Les Commères Boulangerie

● DRINKING & NIGHTLIFE
26 Bar & Beer Bercy
27 Guinguette La Javelle
28 Le 3Bis

● ENTERTAINMENT
29 Cinémathèque Française

● SHOPPING
30 Tucked Friperie

Continued from p195

It also covers the immigration linked to the world wars, France's colonisation of Algeria, xenophobia under former president Valéry Giscard d'Estaing, and, more recently, the emergence of refugee camps in Calais. Scant space is usually given to these stories in France, yet with the rise of the far right today they are more relevant than ever.

The palace also hosts the diverting **Aquarium Tropical** *(combined entry with museum €15),* part of the initial museum a century ago and home to 400 species, including small crocodiles, seahorses and stingrays, with detailed panels in English. When your legs tire, pause at the airy cafe terrace.

The Countryside in Paris

MAP P186

A slice of village life

If you're tired of the at-times intense bustle of Paris, head over to **rue St-Blaise**, whose cobblestoned street, old lampposts, tranquil cafe terraces and quaint historic churches evoke the calm of a rural village in Provence. There's a good reason for this: the surrounding neighbourhood of Charonne was once a municipality separate from Paris that was home to factories for leather, matches, candles and hats – before being merged with the capital in 1860 by Napoléon III. These days, the unique pedestrianised area to the west of rue Vitruve is the perfect place to while away a few hours, sipping a *café allongé* with a book and people watching at one of the many cafes, such as **Les Rêveuses**. It's worth taking a peek at the numerous artist studios, from potters to woodworkers, that line the street. Looking northwest, there is a postcard-worthy view of the **Église St-Germain de Charonne**, a church that dates back to at least the 12th century. A scene from the cult French movie *Les Tontons flingueurs* (1963) was filmed here. Inside, look out for the stained-glass window of St Blaise, patron saint of the rather niche subjects of wool combers, wild animals and ailments of the throat. The small, vine-leaf-covered cemetery contains an unmarked grave of revolutionary Federates shot in 1871 during the Paris Commune and Robespierre's secretary, François Begue.

LA FLÈCHE D'OR

Set in the former Charonne train station, **La Flèche d'Or** *(Map p186; flechedor.org),* or the Golden Arrow, is a vibrant alternative arts venue named after the train-boat service that ran between Paris and London via Calais and Dover from 1926 to 1972. In the 1990s, students from the École des Beaux-Arts de Paris turned the decommissioned station into a concert space, which in 2024 was the subject of urgent repairs by Paris city hall. Today, the venue remains markedly left wing, hosting concerts, cinema screenings, fundraisers, drag shows and poetry nights, often with a focus on climate issues, politics and LGBTIQ+ rights.

Pair a margherita with Barolo red wine

 EATING & DRINKING AROUND REUNION: OUR PICKS — MAP P186

Paulownia: Brilliant modern Mediterranean cooking makes for a special, good-value visit at this refined yet laid-back restaurant. *noon-2pm & 7.30-10.30pm Wed-Sat* €€

Chez Tante Farida: Algerian street food at its finest, cheap and lovingly homemade, thanks to the wonderful owner Aunty Farida. *10am-10.30pm* €

KALANK: Charming southern hospitality is in abundance at this cute spot serving Marseille cuisine in Parisian style and portion sizes. *noon-3pm & 7.30-11pm Tue-Sat* €€

Peppe Pizzeria: It's not hard to see why the *pizzaiolo* behind these fluffy, cloud-like Neapolitan pizzas is a former world champion. *noon-3.30pm & 7-10.30pm* €€

MARCHÉ AUX PUCES PORTE DE MONTREUIL

Opened in 1885, the **Porte de Montreuil flea market**, straddling the *Périphérique* (ring road) that runs between Paris and the suburb of Montreuil, is one of the oldest of its kind in Paris. Compared to its better-known cousin in St-Ouen, you're more likely to find a bargain here, whether that be vinyl records, antiques or vintage clothes. The market is rough around the edges, but part of the charm of visiting is to see today's working-class Paris. For the best chance of rare finds, go in the morning on Saturday or Sunday; it's also open on Mondays.

Petite Ceinture

Trainspotting

MAP P198

On track to discover old and new rails

The lesser-known district of Bercy is probably the best place to delve into Paris' past and indeed its ongoing links with trains. Progressively built between 1852 and 1869, a 32km-long track that encircled the city, known as the **Petite Ceinture**, served a peak of 38 million passengers during the Universal Exhibition in 1900. Gradually replaced by the more convenient and less polluting underground metro system in the early 20th century, it closed definitively in 1934. However, since 2006 Paris city hall has worked with SNCF (the French national railway company) to turn the tracks into walkable

 EATING IN BASTILLE & EASTERN PARIS: SWEET TREATS —— MAPS P186, P198

Tapisserie: Maple-syrup tarts, peanut Paris Brest and herb-infused cream puffs are the standouts at this creative pastry arm of the Septime empire. *hours vary* €€

La Chocolaterie Cyril Lignac: Enjoy a luxuriously thick *chocolat chaud* with a *pain au chocolat*, before grabbing one of the renowned chocolate bars to go. *9am-7pm Tue-Sun* €€

Les Commères Boulangerie: The pistachio cake, vanilla-infused flan and homemade jam are unmissable at this bakery. *hours vary* €

Boulangerie Vandermeersch: Try the city's best *kouglof*, a chimney-shaped brioche from the Alsace region stuffed with candied fruit. *7am-8pm Tue-Fri, 7am-7.30pm Sat* €

green spaces. The largest section open to the public is in Bercy, with the route starting at av de St-Mandé and accessible at numerous points to the south, including the pretty **square Charles Péguy**. Serious enthusiasts can follow the track southwest until reaching the sprawling **SNCF Eastern European Technical Centre**, a startlingly industrial corner of Paris where France's famed high-speed TGV trains are repaired. Otherwise, from square Charles Péguy, hike west on the Coulée Verte René-Dumont (p192), another old train line, passing the former **Gare de Reuilly**, now a cultural centre, and eventually you will reach **Gare de Lyon**, one of the six mainline stations in Paris. Inside, grab an overpriced coffee at **Le Train Bleu**, a century-old establishment with gawp-inducing neobaroque and Belle Époque decor. See p286 for information on Petite Ceinture du 14e and 15e.

Unique Green Space

MAP P198

From urban vineyards to gardening

Possibly the most underrated park in Paris, the rectangular **Parc de Bercy** houses a curious mishmash of styles across three sections. In the western area, large lawns form a somewhat plain but significant green space great for picnicking. The central area, Jardin Yitzhak Rabin, includes a pretty rose garden, a hedge labyrinth and several vibrant flowerbeds. This central zone, full of little secluded areas to sit down in, also contains the **Maison du Jardinage**, an educational place in a quaint house full of plants where gardening experts are often on hand to give advice, and the newly opened **Maison de l'Animal**, an events and exhibition space dedicated to urban biodiversity in Paris. To the east, on the other side of rue Joseph Kessel across some footbridges, is the Romantic garden, whose tranquil ponds contain turtles and gawking fish and are lined with oaks, sweet gums and willows.

The park has a curious link with winemaking: during the 19th century it was the site of enormous wine warehouses, when Paris was the world's largest hub for the wine and spirits trade. This vinicultural history, dating as far back as the Middle Ages, persisted until the 1950s when bottling on vineyards was preferred. Even today it endures through the park's 400 grapevines, still harvested annually, and you can see the train tracks that were once used to transport wine.

GROUND CONTROL

Located in a former mail-sorting hall, **Ground Control** *(Map p186; groundcontrolparis.com)* is a sprawling 6000-sq-metre culture and events space. While this isn't a place of great tradition and charm, it's modern and lively, filled with repurposed train station decor and colourful murals. There's a packed schedule, including dance and yoga classes, sports screenings, DJ sets and even an urban agriculture awareness workshop run by a local nonprofit (one of several that are based here). It's a great place to grab a drink with snacks from the many food stands, particularly during the summer at the large outdoor terrace.

 DRINKING NEAR BERCY: OUR PICKS — MAPS P186, P198

| **Guinguette La Javelle:** Open-air *guinguette* bar with a rowdy atmosphere on the industrial edge of Paris. Open spring and summer. *5pm-midnight Mon-Fri, noon-midnight Sat & Sun* | **Le Mazette:** Watch sunset with a cocktail in hand on this multistorey boat, which has a busy schedule of concerts and club nights. *6.30pm-midnight Wed-Fri, 6.30pm-6am Sat & Sun* | **Bar & Beer Bercy:** Cheerful service and several craft beers on tap, including tasting flights, make this a cosy local watering hole. *4pm-2am* | **Le 3Bis:** This board-game/karaoke bar has playful decor and a themed room inspired by the TV show *Friends*. *hours vary* |

Temple of Cinema

MAP P198

Delve into the culture of filmmaking

The French have a profound affinity for cinema, also known as the seventh art form, with many Gallic directors leaving an indelible mark on the history of filmmaking – Agnès Varda, Jean-Luc Godard, Jacques Audiard and Alice Guy, to name a few. In Paris, home to over 70 cinemas including many charming independent venues, and nearly 400 screens – the most of any city in the world – going to the movies is an unmissable experience. It's no surprise, then, that there's an entire complex in Paris dedicated to cinema culture. On the edge of the Parc de Bercy, the **Cinémathèque Française** – founded in 1936 and moved to this location in 2005 – offers a diverse program of world cinema, with screenings often introduced by film experts or directors themselves, alongside debates and workshops. The informative 800-sq-metre **museum** *(cinematheque.fr; adult/child €10/5)*, opened in 2021, recounts the birth of filmmaking in 1895 and offers a captivating journey through the following decades of cinema, showcasing vintage equipment and technologies in a way that's accessible for veteran cinephiles and young kids alike. A special focus is given to the influential director Georges Méliès. The library, accessible for a modest fee, provides access to the veritable gold mine that is the Cinémathèque's archives, including rare recordings, vintage film posters and even correspondence from movie stars.

GEORGES MÉLIÈS

Born in Paris in 1861, Georges Méliès was one of the most influential figures in the early years of cinema. Born into a wealthy shoemaking family, Méliès fell in love with magic and, at 26, bought a theatre to put on grand shows. But the silver screen beckoned in 1895, when Méliès saw one of the first-ever cinematograph screenings. Inspired, he went on to make more than 500 films, many shot at his world-first film studio. Conjuring fantastical images using technology, including in his masterpiece, *A Trip to the Moon* (1902), Méliès is still an influence on film special effects today.

Merry-Go-Round

MAP P198

Interactive fun-fair experience

Set within the impressive former wine warehouses of Bercy, the 11,400-sq-metre **Musée des Arts Forains** *(arts-forains.com/en; adult/child €18/12)* makes for a very jolly, interactive journey across the largest space dedicated to fun-fair objects in the world. The brisk, 1½-hour tours, which must be booked in advance daily, traverse three wonder-filled spaces: the Venetian Lounges, which have a mini Rialto bridge, mechanical opera singers performing from balconies and a gondola ride; the Theatre of Marvels, featuring image-warping mirrors, a 1900s self-playing Belgian organ and a hot-air balloon with an elephant-shaped basket; and the Fairground Art Museum,

Don't miss the heavenly homemade millefeuille dessert

EATING NEAR BERCY: OUR PICKS

MAP P198

Au Vinyle Gourmand: Part vinyl store, part canteen run by a friendly Franco-Vietnamese couple serving simple Viet food – *bo buns,* banh mis – to an impeccable soundtrack. *hours vary* €

Alexa Cafe: Simple, delicious French classics and generic international staples like burgers and pizzas, delivered with warm service that makes you feel at home. *hours vary* €

Au Trou Gascon: New owner Sarah Chougnet-Strudel has blown fresh life into this emblematic Parisian address with stylish modern European dishes. *noon-2pm & 7-10.30pm Tue-Sat* €€€

L'Auberge Aveyronnaise: Cosy local institution specialising in the traditional cuisine of France's southern Aveyron region, notably the fondue-like *aligot. 12.30-3.30pm & 7-11pm Tue-Sat* €€

Musée des Arts Forains

where visitors can ride a unique pedal-powered carousel and compete in a fun-fair horse-racing game, among countless other curiosities. The objects, largely from the late 19th and early 20th centuries, come from the private collection of actor and antiques dealer Jean-Paul Favand, who began amassing the marvels in the 1970s before establishing the museum in Bercy in 1996. Note that tours in English only run during the summer when demand is high, but large groups might consider a private booking. Even so, non-French speakers can easily enjoy standard tours – it's a visual experience and guides provide notes in English. In December, the museum hosts the Festival du Merveilleux, a 10-day event of dance, opera, hypnosis and more.

Urban Swimming

MAP P198

Go for a dip in the Seine

In 1900, during the first edition of the Olympic Games in Paris, swimming races took place in the River Seine. Decades of industrialisation polluted the waters until a nadir was reached in the 1970s. After a mass clean-up operation, including the construction of water-treatment plants and rainwater-storage basins, swimming was possible once again for the 2024 Games. Since the summer of 2025, the public has also been able to bathe in the iconic river, including at the **Bercy swimming area** by the Simone de Beauvoir footbridge. The area is supervised, marked with buoys and equipped with showers and lockers.

FISH THRIVING IN THE SEINE

Thousands of years ago and even up to the Middle Ages, Paris was a city of marine life. The Seine, which is over 14,000 years old, teemed with eels and salmon. But by the 1970s there were only three fish species left in the 777km river, which spans northern France and cuts through the capital, as industrial and residential pollution decimated biodiversity. However, after decades of urban water policies alongside community efforts, things are going swimmingly: there are now nearly 40 species that have been officially registered, with more turning up all the time.

Researched by Alexis Averbuck

THE ISLANDS

CHIC AND DELIGHTFUL PARISIAN LIFE MEETS HISTORY

Romance and history meet here, at Paris' geographic and spiritual heart in the Seine.

The Romans set up shop on these two inner-city islands and slowly the entire city radiated out. The larger of the two islands, Île de la Cité, is home to majestic Notre Dame, resplendent once again after its devastating 2019 fire, and Sainte-Chapelle, a symphony of kaleidoscopic 13th-century stained glass. It sits footsteps from today's functioning Palais de Justice and the dungeons in the French Revolution prison, Conciergerie. Cross Pont St-Louis to reach enchanting Île St-Louis, graced with charming boutiques and sun-bathed quays beckoning to picnickers. In the evening from Pont Neuf, with its dramatic busts of ogres and kings, appreciate the lights sparkling on the length of the Seine. Revel in it – you're in Paris.

TOP TIP

As with travel worldwide, wander just a bit off the heavily travelled routes and you'll find yourself in another, quieter universe. Same holds true on these islands.

Conciergerie (p215)

See p311 for places to stay on the islands.

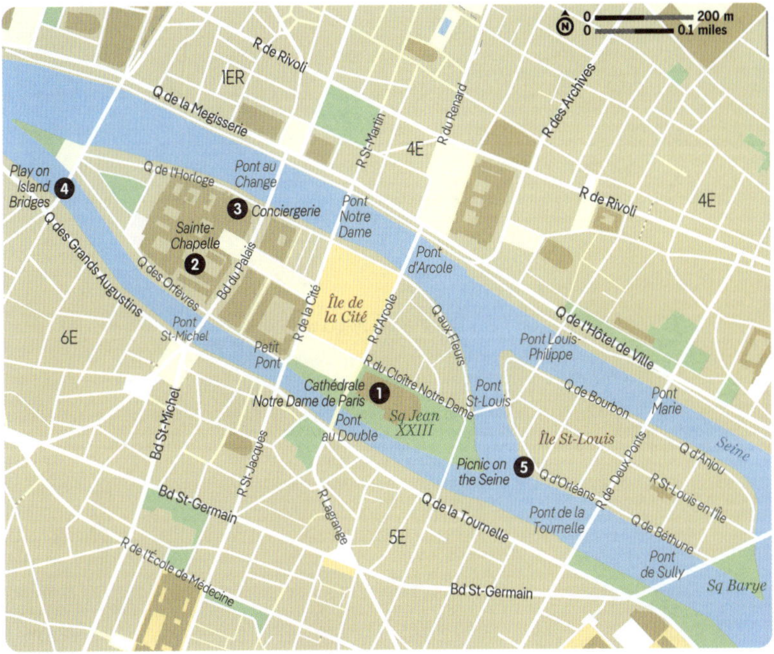

Highlights

❶ Cathédrale Notre Dame de Paris
Behold the crowning glory of medieval Gothic architecture, renewed to a high gloss. **p208**

❷ Sainte-Chapelle
Bathe in richly coloured biblical tales, exquisitely told through stained-glass imagery with 13th-century grace and beauty. **p214**

❸ Conciergerie
Learn how Marie Antoinette and thousands of others spent their final days at this 14th-century palace turned prison. **p215**

❹ Play on Island Bridges
Stroll and dance to buskers on some of Paris' most iconic bridges, like the Pont Neuf. **p217**

▲ **❺ Picnic on the Seine**
Crunch crusty baguettes and savour the sweetness of famous Berthillon ice cream on sunny riverbanks. **p215**

Getting Around

Walking
The islands are easiest on foot, and the quays are a quick descent down stairs or ramps.

Metro & Bus
Cité (line 4) on Île de la Cité is the islands' only metro station. St-Michel (line 4 and RER B and C) serves Notre Dame from the Left Bank, and Pont Marie (line 7) on the Right Bank. Buses serve the islands, too.

Boat
The hop-on, hop-off Batobus (p221) stops opposite Notre Dame on the Left Bank.

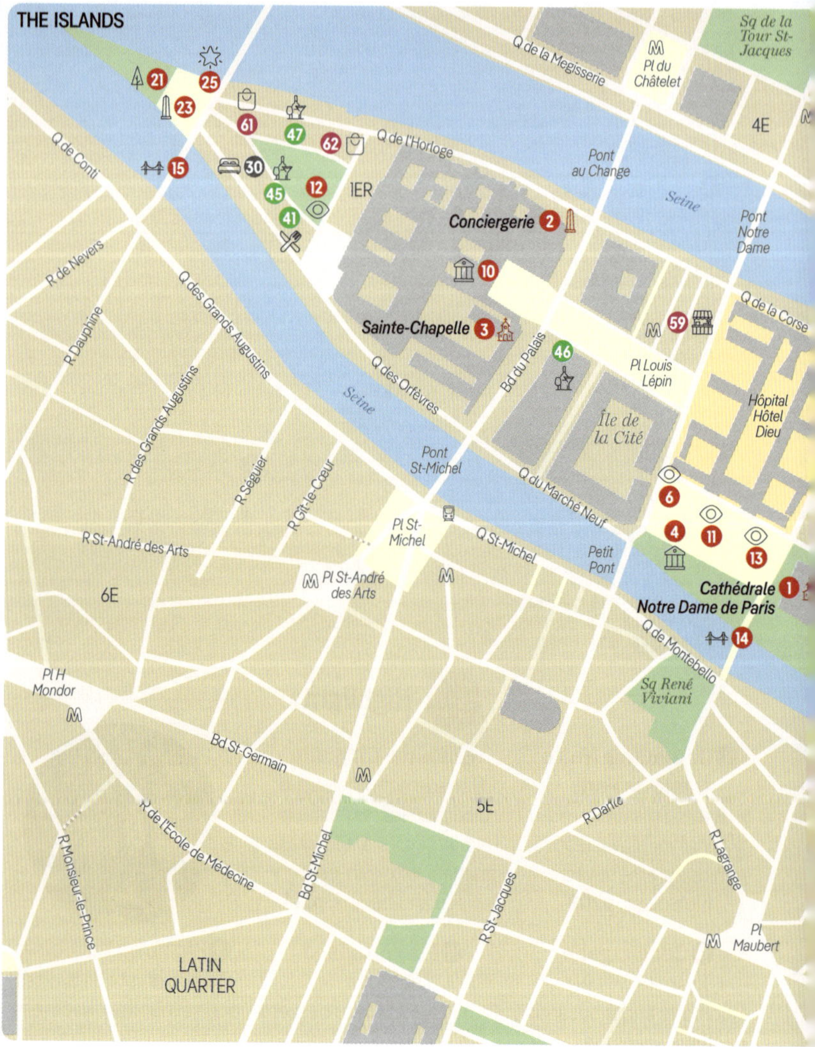

THE ISLANDS

✪ HIGHLIGHTS
1 Cathédrale Notre Dame de Paris
2 Conciergerie
3 Sainte-Chapelle

● SIGHTS
4 Crypte Archéologique
5 Église St-Louis en l'Île
6 Éternelle Notre-Dame
7 Mansion at 1 rue de Ursins
8 Mémorial des Martyrs de la Déportation
9 Musée Vivant du Fromage
10 Palais de Justice
11 Parvis Notre Dame
12 Place Dauphine
13 Point Zéro des Routes de France
14 Pont au Double
15 Pont Neuf
16 Pont St-Louis
17 Quai d'Orléans
18 Roman Rampart Ruins
19 Square Barye
20 Square de l'Île de France
21 Square du Vert-Galant
22 Square Jean XXIII
23 Statue of Henri IV

● ACTIVITIES
24 Bains-Douches des Deux-Ponts
25 Vedettes du Pont Neuf

● SLEEPING
26 Hôtel des Deux Îles
27 Hôtel du Jeu de Paume
28 Hôtel L de Lutèce
29 Hôtel Saint-Louis en l'Isle
30 Paris Perfect

● EATING
see 30 Atelier du Geste à l'Émotion
31 Aux Petits Cakes
32 Berthillon
33 Bouillon de l'Île
34 Café Leone
35 Café Saint Régis
see 33 Hadrien
see 28 Khana
36 La Dame de Paris
37 La Sarrasine

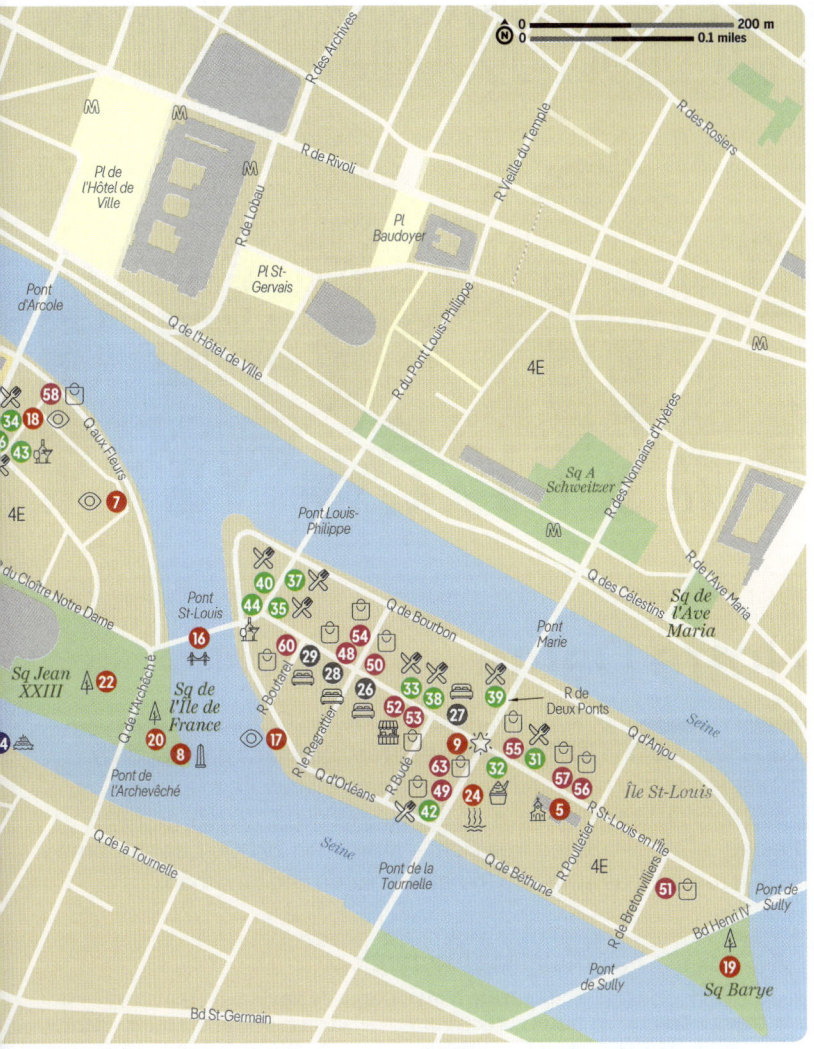

38 Le Mâche-dru
see 9 Le Sergent Recruteur
see 18 Les Deux Colombes
39 Les Fous de l'Île
40 Pierre Hermé
see 40 Poget & De Witte
41 Restaurant Paul
42 Wonderland Brunchy

● **DRINKING & NIGHTLIFE**
43 Au Bougnat
44 La Brasserie de l'Îsle Saint-Louis
45 Le Bar du Caveau
46 Les Deux Palais
see 37 L'Etiquette
see 42 Minicafé
47 Napa
see 28 Noir

● **SHOPPING**
48 78isl
49 Alexis Renard
50 Bamyan
see 48 Bhaktar
see 9 Clair de Rêve
51 Dutko

52 Fleuryan
53 Galerie Clémentine de la Féronnière
54 Galerie d'Art le 33 Mai
55 La Boucherie Gardil
see 48 La Ferme Saint-Aubin
56 L'Embrasser
see 38 L'Empire du Tapis
57 Librairie Ulysse
58 Manuelle Guibal
59 Marché aux Fleurs Reine Elizabeth II

60 Nina Kendosa
see 40 Opulence Vintage
61 Paire et Fils
62 Perspectives Studio Gallery
see 61 Raphaël Bedos Antiquités
63 Upper

● **TRANSPORT**
64 Batobus Notre Dame Stop

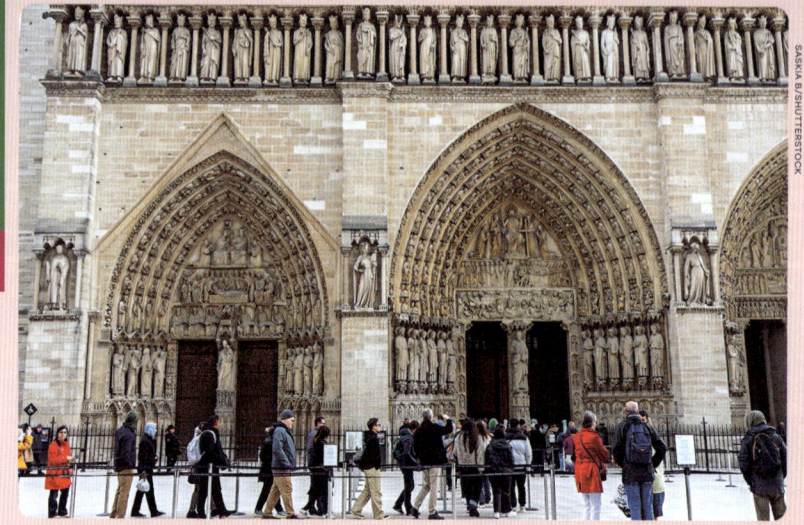

TOP EXPERIENCE
Notre Dame

Majestic and monumental, Paris' iconic French Gothic cathedral, reopened after the 2019 fire, has been restored to its original glory, its resplendent art and architecture, from bell towers to stained glass, shining like new. This is an actively working church, and also the capital's most visited free sight – more than 29,000 people come daily. It remains, as always, a Parisian beacon and landmark.

DON'T MISS
- Rose windows
- Bell towers
- Façade carvings
- Flying buttresses
- Treasury & Crown of Thorns
- The Mays paintings
- Underground ruins
- Cathedral concerts

Reigning Masterpiece

Cathédrale Notre Dame de Paris represents a generous history of building and rebuilding, long before the fire of 2019. It's constructed on the site occupied by a Gallo-Roman temple and was preceded by several earlier churches. The masterpiece we see today was begun in 1163 and largely completed by the early 14th century. It was badly damaged during the Revolution, prompting architect Eugène-Emmanuel Viollet-le-Duc to oversee extensive renovations between 1845 and 1864. That's when many of the magnificent forest of ornate

Practicalities
- notredamedeparis.fr (reserve 3 days to 2 hours ahead) ● 7.50am-7pm, to 10pm Thu, 8.15am-7.30pm Sat & Sun ● admission free, treasury adult/child €12/6, towers extra

REBUILDING NOTRE DAME

On the evening of 15 April 2019, a blaze broke out under the cathedral's roof. Firefighters were able to control the fire and ultimately save the church, but the damage was catastrophic. The restoration involved over 1000 artists and journeymen and not only repaired fire-damaged elements, but cleaned and restored everything – pipe organ, 3000 sq metres of stained glass, paintings, copper sculptures, inside and out – to the untarnished condition of the era of Viollet-le-Duc. Even the oak beams (cut from over 2000 trees) have been hand-hewn using traditional axes. It all cost about €900 million (raised via donations).

flying buttresses that encircle the cathedral chancel and support its walls and roof were added.

With the devastating 2019 fire, this French Gothic landmark, long considered the city's geographic and spiritual heart, went through a massive restoration and, amazingly, reopened its doors in December 2024. Because everything – including undamaged elements – was cleaned, the cathedral looks, literally, brand-new: stone a bright creamy-white, frescoes looking freshly painted and stained glass casting brilliant jewel tones across the walls.

Grand Plan & Fabulous Façade

Notre Dame is known for its sublime balance, though if you look closely you'll see all sorts of minor asymmetrical elements introduced to avoid monotony, in accordance with standard Gothic practice. These include the slightly different shapes of each of the three main **portals**, whose statues were once brightly coloured to make them more effective as a *Biblia pauperum* – a 'Bible of the poor' to help the illiterate faithful understand Old Testament stories, the Passion of the Christ and the lives of the saints.

Landmark Occasions

Historic events at Notre Dame abound. Henry VI of England was crowned here in 1431 as King of France. In 1558 Mary, Queen of Scots married the Dauphin Francis (later Francis II of France). At the unusual 1600 marriage of Marie de Médici to Henri of Navarre, he, as a Protestant who couldn't enter the church, stood outside. In 1804 Napoléon I was crowned by Pope Pius VII. And Joan of Arc was beatified in 1909 and canonised in 1920.

CATHEDRAL MUSIC

Music has always been a sacred part of Notre Dame's soul. Try to experience a Sunday Gregorian or polyphonic Mass or free organ recital. Or get a ticket for an evening concert (musique-sacree-notredameparis.fr).

SAVED BY THE HUNCHBACK OF NOTRE DAME

The damage inflicted on Notre Dame during the French Revolution saw it fall into ruin, and it was destined for demolition. Salvation came with the widespread popularity of Victor Hugo's 1831 novel *The Hunchback of Notre Dame*, which sparked a petition to save it. Much of the action – like when Quasimodo swings down a bell rope to save dancer Esmeralda from the gallows – takes place at the cathedral.

Towers

A constant queue marks the entrance to the **Tours de Notre Dame** *(tours-notre-dame-de-paris.fr)*, the cathedral's bell towers. Climb the 422 spiralling steps to the 69m top of the **South Tower** (the one on the right as you face the church). On your way up, you'll pass through a room with displays on the cathedral's history before you reach the **Galerie des Chimères** (Gargoyles Gallery) where gargoyles grimace and grin. These grotesque statues divert rainwater from the roof to prevent masonry damage, with the water exiting through their elongated, open mouths. They also, purportedly, ward off evil spirits. Although they appear medieval, they were installed by Viollet-le-Duc in the 19th century.

This route also brings you to Emmanuel, the cathedral's original 13-tonne bourdon **bell** (all of the cathedral's bells are named, as is the tradition). During the night of 24 August 1944, when the Île de la Cité was retaken by French, Allied and Resistance troops, the tolling of the Emmanuel announced Paris' approaching liberation. Emmanuel's peal purity apparently proceeds from the precious metals Parisian women threw into the pot when it was recast from copper and bronze in 1631.

Finish the climb at the top where there's a spectacular view over Paris. You'll also have access to a terrace running between the two towers, allowing a view of the roof and spire. There's a 1000-visitor maximum per day, so book your timed-entry ticket in advance.

Rose Windows & Organ

Inside, behold the three masterpiece rose windows colouring the cathedral's vast 127m-long, 48m-wide interior. The 13m-wide southern window is the largest and depicts the theme of the Last Judgement. The window on the northern side of the

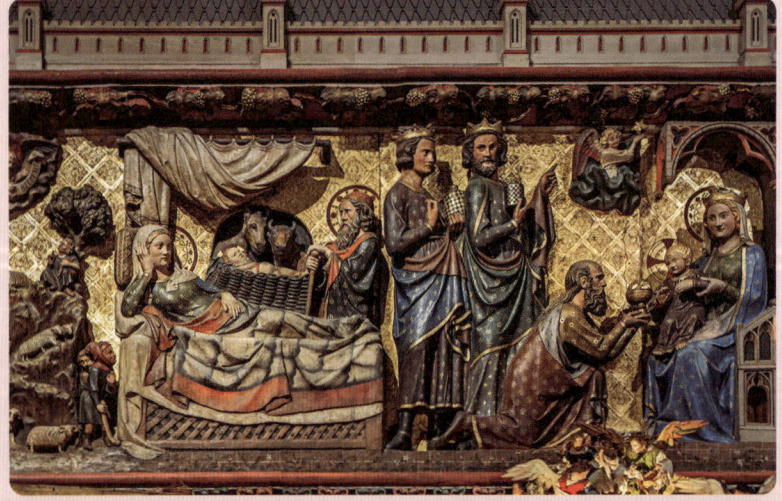

Carvings around the choir

transept remains virtually unchanged since the 13th century. Admire the 10m-wide window over the western façade, with the Virgin Mary in the centre, above the **organ**. The organ is one of the largest in the world, with 8000 pipes (900 of which have historical classification), 115 stops, five 56-key manuals and a 32-key pedalboard.

Controversially, some of the stained glass in Notre Dame's southern chapels has been commissioned to be replaced by French artist Claire Tabouret with an estimated installation of 2026. The idea is to take the originals, created by Viollet-le-Duc, and display them in a museum.

The Choir & Artwork

Don't miss the cathedral's grand wooden **choir** with its carved stalls and statues representing the Passion of the Christ. The exterior is ornately decorated with scenes from the Gospels. Admire the 13 impressive paintings, called the **Mays**, in its nave chapels. From 1630 to 1707, city goldsmiths gave 76 of these as gifts commemorating one of the acts of the Apostles. You'll also notice a collection of modern paintings and **tapestries**, including a Matisse, now hanging in place of a new collection of tapestries that's being woven.

Much of the art in the cathedral is now marked with clear signage in French, English and Spanish, making it easier to learn about each piece, sculpture or fresco.

Treasury

It is absolutely worth the fee (adult/child €12/6) to enter the *trésor* (treasury), which houses Notre Dame's dazzling sacred jewels and relics in the cathedral's southeastern transept. Check out the wonderful **Les Camées des Papes** (Papal cameos), sculpted with incredible finesse in shell and framed in silver. The 268 pieces depict every pope in miniature from St Pierre to Benoît XVI.

Crown of Thorns

The **Ste-Couronne** (Holy Crown), said to be the wreath of thorns placed on Jesus' head before he was crucified, was given to Notre Dame in 1239 by the king St Louis (he acquired it from the Emperor in Constantinople). A gigantic golden reliquary in the axial chapel was made during the post-fire restoration to house the crown, a piece of the cross and a nail from the crucifixion.

The crown is offered for viewing between 3pm and 5pm on the first Friday of the month and Fridays during Lent, plus 10am to 5pm on Good Friday.

Centre of France

Notre Dame has always been the very heart of Paris – distances from Paris to every part of metropolitan France are measured from a **bronze star** embedded in the cobbles of the cathedral's front square, called Parvis Notre Dame (p220) or place Jean-Paul II. It's also the centre of the city. The Parvis itself is undergoing a renovation that will include underground services, slated to open in 2027.

A statue of Charlemagne (742–814 CE), emperor of the Franks, prances nearby.

ANCIENT UNDERGROUND RUINS

Descend under the square in front of Notre Dame to the fascinating **Crypte Archéologique** *(crypte.paris.fr; adult/child including exhibition €11/free)*, a 117m-long and 28m-wide cavity moodily displaying 4th-century Gallo-Roman ruins and other layers of Île de la Cité history. Cool computer simulations show the area as it was in Roman times, and exhibits delve into local Roman baths and artefacts, the success of Victor Hugo's *Hunchback of Notre Dame*, and the cathedral's past.

TOP TIPS

● Huge queues get longer through the day – arrive early or go late on Thursday night.

● Fast track entrance for people with disabilities (no reservation needed).

● Collect an audioguide (€5) from the info desk inside, or download the app.

● Check online for free tours offered by volunteers.

● No public restrooms inside; paid ones on the Parvis (square) out front.

● Metro stops Cité (line 4) and St-Michel (line 4 and RER B and C) are each a five-minute walk away.

● Remember that Notre Dame is an active place of worship.

Notre Dame

Timeline

1160 Maurice de Sully becomes bishop of Paris. Mission: to grace growing Paris with a lofty new cathedral.

1182–90 The choir with double ambulatory is finished and work starts on the nave and side chapels.

1200–50 The **1 west façade**, with rose window, three portals and two soaring towers, goes up. Everyone is stunned.

1345 Some 180 years after the foundation stone was laid, the Cathédrale de Notre Dame is complete. It is dedicated to *notre dame* (our lady), the Virgin Mary.

1789 Revolutionaries smash the original Gallery of Kings, pillage the cathedral and melt all its bells except the great bell **2 Emmanuel**. The cathedral becomes a Temple of Reason and then a warehouse.

1831 Victor Hugo's novel *The Hunchback of Notre Dame* inspires new interest in the half-ruined Gothic cathedral.

1845–64 Architect Viollet-le-Duc undertakes its restoration. Twenty-eight new kings are sculpted for the west façade. The heavily decorated **3 portals and spire** are reconstructed. The neogothic treasury is built.

1860 The area in front of Notre Dame is cleared to create the **4 Parvis**, an alfresco classroom where Parisians can learn a catechism illustrated on sculpted portals.

1935 A rooster bearing part of the relics of the Crown of Thorns, St Denis and Ste Geneviève is put on top of the cathedral spire to protect those who pray inside.

1991 The architectural masterpiece of Notre Dame and its Seine-side riverbanks become a UNESCO World Heritage Site.

2013 Notre Dame celebrates 850 years since construction began with a bevy of new bells and restoration works.

2019 A fire causes devastating damage to the cathedral interior, destroys most of the roof and topples the spire.

2024 The cathedral reopens after a complete restoration returns it to Viollet-le-Duc's 19th-century original.

North Rose Window
See prophets, judges, kings and priests venerate Mary in vivid blue and violet glass, one of three beautiful rose blooms (1225–70), each almost 10m in diameter.

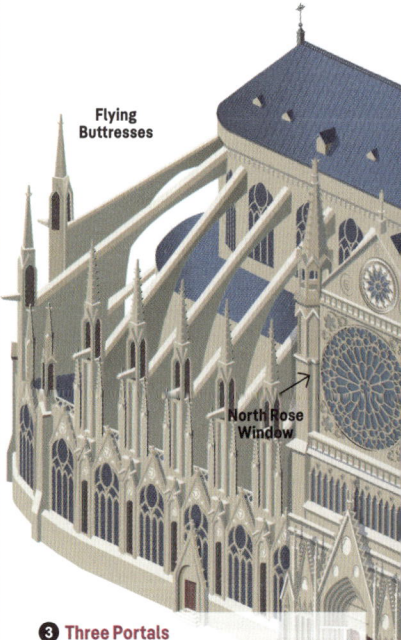

Flying Buttresses

North Rose Window

❸ Three Portals
Play 'I spy' (Greed, Cowardice et al) beneath these sculpted doorways, which illustrate the seasons, life and the 12 vices and virtues alongside the Bible.

NEIRFY/SHUTTERSTOCK

AGSAZ/SHUTTERSTOCK

Spire & Roof

Two-thirds of the roof, and the 19th-century spire, were destroyed in the April 2019 fire and have now been painstakingly replicated.

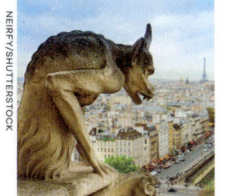

Chimera Gallery

The towers are graced with grimacing gargoyles and grotesque chimera, including celebrity chimera Stryga, which has wings, horns, a human body and sticking-out tongue. This bestial lot ward off demons.

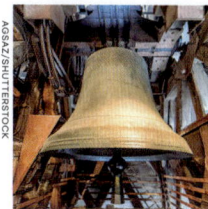

2 Great Bell

The peal of Emmanuel, the cathedral's great bell, is so pure thanks to precious gems and jewels Parisian women threw into the pot when it was recast from copper and bronze in 1631. Admire its original siblings in square Jean XXII.

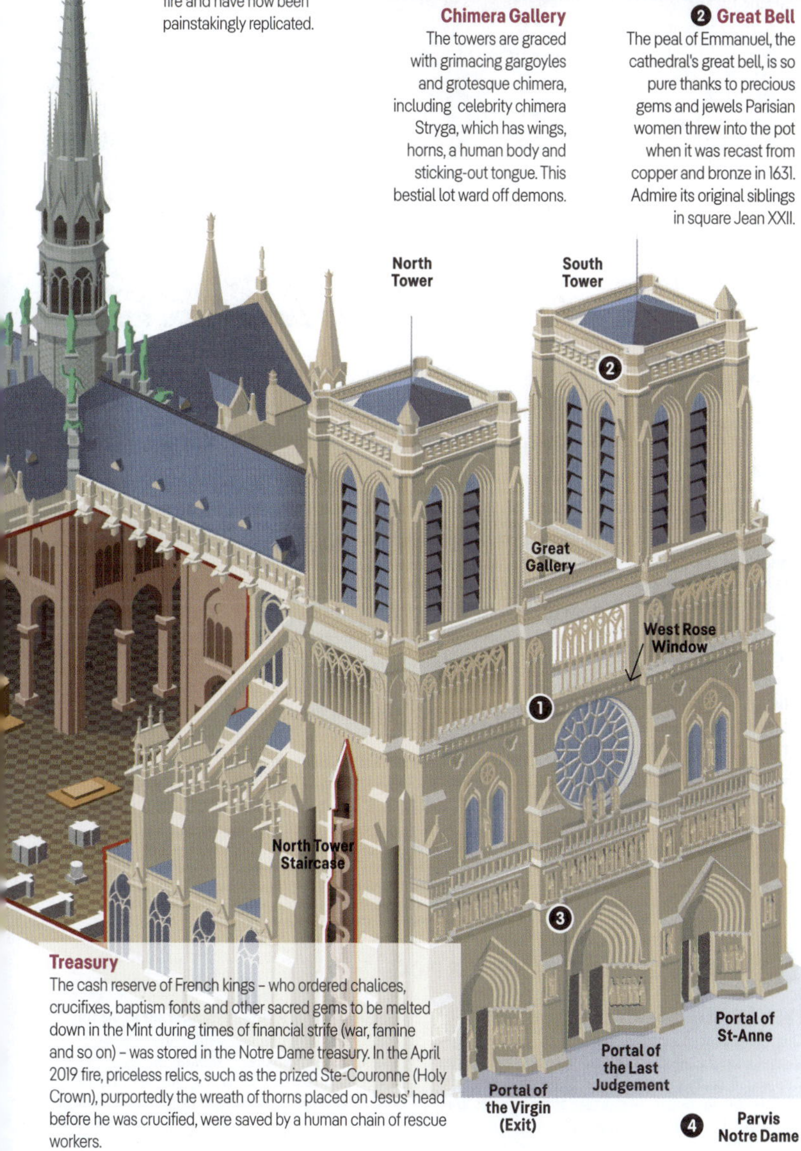
North Tower
South Tower
2
Great Gallery
West Rose Window
1
North Tower Staircase
3
Portal of St-Anne
Portal of the Last Judgement
Portal of the Virgin (Exit)
4
Parvis Notre Dame

Treasury

The cash reserve of French kings – who ordered chalices, crucifixes, baptism fonts and other sacred gems to be melted down in the Mint during times of financial strife (war, famine and so on) – was stored in the Notre Dame treasury. In the April 2019 fire, priceless relics, such as the prized Ste-Couronne (Holy Crown), purportedly the wreath of thorns placed on Jesus' head before he was crucified, were saved by a human chain of rescue workers.

Sainte-Chapelle

'READING' SAINTE-CHAPELLE'S STAINED GLASS

Statues of the Apostles, foliage-adorned capitals and beatific angels decorate this sumptuous, bijou chapel. But it is the 1113 biblical scenes, from Genesis through to the Crown of Thorns reaching Paris, depicted in its 15 soaring stained-glass windows – 15m high in the nave, 13m in the apse – and monumental, 9m-wide rose window that stun visitors. They were crafted by the artists who worked on Chartres and are generally best read from left to right and top to bottom to follow the stories. Download the Sainte Chapelle Windows app to study the windows in intricate detail. Or join a free one-hour guided tour in English (11am and 3pm; book your entrance ticket for half an hour before or other speciality tours, or rent an audioguide (€3).

Shimmering Stained Glass of Sainte-Chapelle

Glorious Gothic chapel bedazzlement

No sight in Paris is as dazzling as the radiant Holy Chapel called **Sainte-Chapelle** *(sainte-chapelle.fr; adult/child Jun-Sep €18/free, Oct-May €13, combined ticket with Conciergerie Jun-Sep/Oct-May €25/20)*, hidden away like a precious gem within the city's original, 13th-century Palais de Justice (Law Courts) and Palais de la Cité, the former royal residence. Paris' oldest, finest stained glass laces its sublime Gothic interior – best viewed on sunny days when light floods in, creating an entrancing rainbow of bold colours.

Sainte-Chapelle was built in just six years and consecrated in 1248. It was conceived by French king Louis IX to house his collection of holy relics, including the famous Ste-Couronne (Holy Crown, Jesus' wreath of thorns), which he acquired in 1239 from the Emperor of Constantinople for a sum easily exceeding the amount it cost to build the chapel. In reality, it was safeguarded at Notre Dame, as it is today.

 EATING ON ÎLE DE LA CITÉ: OUR PICKS

Les Deux Colombes: Charmingly tucked into a quiet corner of Île de la Cité with friendly service and hearty classics. *noon-3pm & 5.30-10pm Tue-Sun* €€

Café Leone: Opt for a table on the back patio looking out on quieter rue de la Colombe for tasty pizzas and pastas. *9.30am-11pm* €€

La Dame de Paris: Pick up top-notch pastries, crêpes and sandwiches from the art deco shop, or sit at its adjacent cafe. *9am-10pm* €

Restaurant Paul: The best of the charming eateries on place Dauphine, with a good lunch-time *prix fixe* menu. *noon-2.30pm & 7-10pm* €€

Enter through the lower chamber of the chapel, once used by palace staff, and mount a spiral stair signposted 'Chapelle Haute' to reach the glorious upper chapel where royals, such as Catherine de Médici, and their close friends worshipped. The relatively squat lower chamber supports the delicate masonry above, allowing for such a seemingly impossible array of windows.

Stir your soul at a classical music **evening concert** (check schedules and buy tickets at fnac.com). There are discounts on entrance on Wednesdays from April to September.

Royal Palace Turned Brig at the Conciergerie
Prisons through the ages

A royal palace in the 14th century, the **Conciergerie** *(paris -conciergerie.fr; adult/child €13/free, combined ticket with Sainte-Chapelle Jun-Sep/Oct-May €25/20)* later became a prison. During the Reign of Terror (1793–94), alleged enemies of the Revolution were incarcerated here before being brought before the Revolutionary Tribunal next door in the 13th-century **Palais de Justice**.

As you walk through the halls and cells, recall that of the almost 2800 prisoners held in the Conciergerie's dungeons (in various 'classes' of cells, no less) before being sent to the guillotine, the star prisoner was Queen Marie Antoinette. Make sure you seek out the display of some of her delicate personal items, like her camisole and cross. As the Revolution began to turn on its own, radicals Danton and Robespierre were locked up at the Conciergerie and, finally, the judges of the tribunal themselves.

Rent a HistoPad (tablet-device guide; €5) to explore in augmented reality and take part in an interactive, 3D treasure hunt. And check when you arrive, as there are often free guided tours at 11am and 3pm.

Rotating exhibitions (like displays on Paris' culinary history or travel writing and advertising) fill the beautiful Rayonnant Gothic **Salle des Gens d'Armes**, Europe's largest surviving medieval hall.

Picnic on the Banks of the Seine
The sweet island life

You can't miss the happy Parisians dotting the **quays** and parks of the islands, relaxing, reading, romancing and, of course, picnicking. Join them! Outfit yourself at the islands'

FEELING THE SEAT OF POWER

Palais de Justice stands on ground once occupied by the Romans' administrative buildings. Over time, they were replaced by other seats of power (Merovingian and Capetian kings ruled here). That ended when Charles V (1338–80) moved over to the Louvre and other palaces after he was forced to watch his trusted counsellors killed here. During the Revolution, new courts were installed on the site. Its current façade dates from the latter half of the 19th and turn of the 20th century. You can walk its near-empty halls (most tourists only snap selfies in the central **Cour du Mai**), though court proceedings are private. Enter by its dedicated security line (don't get sucked into the queue at Sainte-Chapelle, which lies in its central courtyard).

DRINKING ON ÎLE DE LA CITÉ: WINE BARS, PUBS & CAFES

Le Bar du Caveau: The wine bar of the neighbouring restaurant is an enchanting spot for a glass of wine from France's flagship regions. *noon-10pm*

Napa: Crammed-to-bursting wine shop with a few tables on place Dauphine for a sip and a charcuterie platter. Great wine advice from the owner. *10am-8pm*

Au Bougnat: Rub shoulders with area residents and workers who pop in to share a pint and catch up on all the goss. *9am-11pm Mon-Sat*

Les Deux Palais: Perfect people-watching cafe right in the middle of the action, with reasonably priced drinks for the neighbourhood. *6.30am-10.30pm*

La Brasserie de l'Île Saint-Louis

HOW TO JUMP THE LINE

Most people don't know that you can reserve your entrance (free) for Notre Dame starting three days before your desired date. Tickets keep getting released, so check back if they're not available, like it's a rock concert, and you could score a time slot and QR code that will let you use the reserved-entrance line – only a couple of minutes' wait.

Queues to swoon over Sainte-Chapelle's spectacular stained glass are also usually staggering. Book online, or visit the Conciergerie (shorter lines) for a *billet jumelé* (joint ticket) covering the old prison and the chapel. The 'priority access' line is also open to Paris Museum and Passion Monument pass holders (book online) and those under 26. Or book for an evening concert for a leisurely hour and a half inside.

lovely purveyors – from luxe sandwiches and tarts at Atelier du Geste à l'Émotion (p219) or Le Mâche-dru and excellent breads at **Aux Petits Cakes** *(aux-petits-cakes.eatbu.com)*. Buy *fromage* (cheese) from **La Ferme Saint-Aubin**, salami at **La Boucherie Gardil** or a little of everything at the small grocery store on rue St-Louis en l'Île or lovely **Fleuryan**. Pick up a bottle of wine, too, at L'Etiquette (p220). Dessert? Chocolate from Hadrien (p219) or ice cream from Berthillon (p219), *bien sur!*

Cafe Life

Lounge the day away in style

When Parisians relax, they relax. A morning coffee, lingering lunch or pre-dinner drink can stretch on, and Paris' islands offer top chances to while the day away. For excellent people-watching, head to the point where Pont St-Louis meets the island of the same name. There, you'll find one of the islands' best dining experiences: **Café Saint Régis** *(lesaintregis-paris.com)*. Waiters in long white aprons, a ceramic-tiled interior and retro vintage decor make this buzzy spot a deliciously Parisian hangout any time of the day, from breakfast

 EATING ON ÎLE ST-LOUIS: CASUAL FARE

Bouillon de l'Île: Smoothies, breakfasts and cheap-and-cheerful vegetarian lunches feature at this busy small cafe with excellent prices. *9am-3pm* €

Le Mâche-dru: Little more than a hole in the wall with two friendly guys dishing out fresh sandwiches made from top ingredients. *11.45am-5pm Tue-Sun* €

La Sarrasine: Get your crêpe fix, from buckwheat *galettes* to sugary delights, or opt for its *prix fixe menus* of classic French dishes. *11am-11pm* €

Wonderland Brunchy: All things brunch: waffles, croissants and more. Easy to spot its flower-bedecked door. *10am-5pm Mon-Thu, to 1.30pm Fri, 9am-5pm Sat & Sun* €

pastries, organic omelettes and mid-morning croques monsieurs (cheese and ham toasties) to Parisian classics – garlicky snails, onion soup, tartare – and late-night cocktails.

Or pop across the street to **La Brasserie de l'Île Saint-Louis** *(labrasserie-isl.fr)* for its broad patio with ace views. From coffees to crisp glasses of Chablis you can graduate up to hearty *choucroute* (a decadent pile of sauerkraut topped with sausage and ham), perfect to set you up for a night out.

Play on the Pont Neuf & Island Bridges
Stroll gorgeous history, modern musicians

Flâneur or *flâneuse*…a term coined in Paris: the urban saunterer. The islands' bridges call to you…to come stroll, look and see what the world of Paris is doing. Start with the city's oldest bridge, confusingly named **Pont Neuf**, or 'New Bridge'. It has linked the western end of Île de la Cité with both riverbanks since 1607, when the king, Henri IV, inaugurated it by crossing the bridge on a white stallion. The bridge's epic arches (seven on the northern stretch and five on the southern span) are decorated with 381 *mascarons* (grotesque figures) depicting barbers, dentists, pickpockets, loiterers and so on. If you can, come by at night, when they are illuminated.

As you amble onto the island, notice an equestrian **statue of Henri IV**, known to his subjects as the Vert Galant ('jolly rogue' or 'dirty old man', perspective depending) – it commemorates that inaugural crossing. From here, you can wander into the peaceful and tree-adorned **place Dauphine**.

You wouldn't imagine that place Dauphine and Pont Neuf were used for public executions in the 18th century. In the last century, the bridge became an objet d'art in 1963, when School of Paris artist Nonda built, exhibited and lived in a huge Trojan horse of steel and wood on the bridge; in 1985, when Bulgarian-born 'environmental sculptor' Christo famously wrapped the bridge in beige fabric; and in 1994 when Japanese designer Kenzo covered it with flowers.

The islands' bridges are also top spots for buskers. Stroll down the quay and through the Parvis of Notre Dame to take in the street entertainment at **Pont au Double** (linking Notre Dame with the Left Bank) and **Pont St-Louis** (linking both islands), which buzz with performers, even in winter.

In fact, the current postcard-perfect Pont St-Louis dates from 1969. It is the seventh bridge built on this spot to link the two islands. The first – made from wood – was completed in the 1630s.

ART GALLERIES

Perspectives Studio Gallery *(perspectives-studio.com)* Art photography from around the world on place Dauphine on Île de la Cité.

Raphaël Bedos Antiquités *(raphaelbedos.com)* If old-school objets d'art are your bag, this is your cabinet of curiosities.

L'Embrasser *(@lembrasser_paris)* Stylish gallery dedicated to Japanese art: think prints, paintings and pottery.

Alexis Renard *(alexisrenard.com)* Exquisite Islamic and Indian art from grand antique statues to miniature paintings.

Dutko *(dutko.com)* Fantastic contemporary art, sculpture and design with another Left Bank gallery.

Galerie Clémentine de la Féronnière *(galerieclementine delaferonniere.fr)* Focuses on fine modern photography; also a publishing house.

Galerie d'Art le 33 Mai *(le33mai.com)* Stylised contemporary painting and sculpture, from abstract to representational.

EATING ON ÎLE ST-LOUIS: LIVING IT UP

Poget & De Witte: Oysters! Paired with a crisp Chablis or a frothy Champagne. *11.45am-5pm Tue-Sun* €€

Le Sergent Recruteur: The islands' Michelin-starred treat, where plates look like art, and service is impeccable. *12.30-2.30pm Wed-Sat, 7.30-10.30pm Tue-Sat* €€€

Les Fous de l'Île: Local favourite brasserie featuring the French national symbol (cockerel) and a buzzy atmosphere. *noon-midnight* €€

Khana: Excite your palate with Afghan cuisine on the main street of Île St-Louis. *noon-3pm Wed-Mon, 5.30-11pm daily* €€

HIDDEN ISLANDS

Slip away from the hubbub of the big sights and see the unexpected side of the islands

START	END	LENGTH
Pont Neuf	Église St-Louis en l'Île	2km; two hours

Step into island life Paris-style as the ❶ **Pont Neuf** (p217) hits the tip of Île de la Cité. The emerald ❷ **square du Vert-Galant** (p220), just down the stairs, offers a bracing breath of fresh air, with stellar views, on the point where Hemingway and his pals used to fish. Amble over to hidden ❸ **place Dauphine**, built on a former marsh. If you're lucky there'll be a heated game of *pétanque* underway beneath the shade trees. Make a beeline to lovely ❹ **rue des Ursins**, which was Paris's first dock. Its pocket park comes complete with lion's-head fountain.

Meander across ❺ **Pont St-Louis** (p217) to the peaceful island named after the only sainted French king, Louis IX. Find your own quiet stretch of shade-dappled quay to picnic (p215) or embrace history and architecture on ❻ **quai de Bourbon**. Read the plaques as you go, naming venerable residents: at No 19 artist Camille Claudel had her studio; ❼ **29 quai d'Anjou** was where Ford Madox Ford founded the influential *Transatlantic Review* in 1924 with John Quinn, James Joyce and Ezra Pound.

Finish your tour of *hôtels particuliers* (private mansions) with crowning-glory ❽ **Hôtel Lambert** (1 quai d'Anjou), built by King Louis XIV's architect Louis Le Vau – also responsible for Versailles. Seek a cool and contemplative retreat in French-baroque ❾ **Église St-Louis en l'Île** (p221).

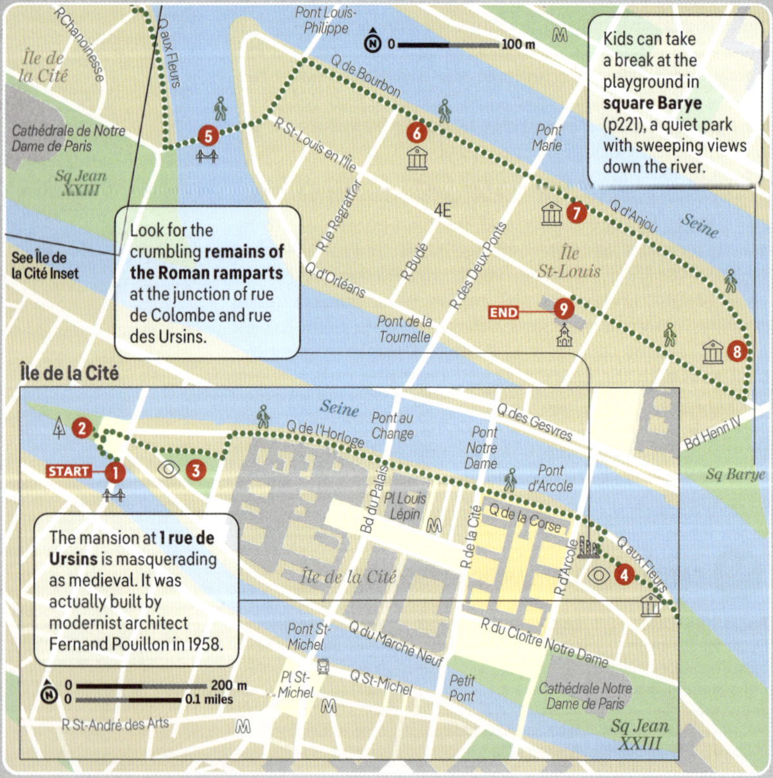

Kids can take a break at the playground in **square Barye** (p221), a quiet park with sweeping views down the river.

Look for the crumbling **remains of the Roman ramparts** at the junction of rue de Colombe and rue des Ursins.

The mansion at **1 rue de Ursins** is masquerading as medieval. It was actually built by modernist architect Fernand Pouillon in 1958.

Eclectic Keepsake Shopping
Browse Île St-Louis' surprising stores

Île St-Louis is a shopper's delight for craft-filled boutiques and tiny, enticing specialist stores and galleries (p217). A saunter down the main street, rue St-Louis en l'Île, will take you by your picnic purveyors (p215) as well as myriad locally owned emporia.

Browse antiques and jewellery at **Bhaktar** *(@gallerie bakhtar)*, handmade carpets at **L'Empire du Tapis** *(facebook.com/empire.du.tapis)* and Asian-influenced fashion at **Bamyan** *(bamyanparis.com)*. Or hit the concept store **Upper** *(upperconcept.com)*, which is part boutique, art gallery and cafe (serving coffee, tea, beer, wine). It carries men's and women's fashion and accessories as well as stationery and homewares, displayed alongside works by artists.

Or slide back in time at **Clair de Rêve** *(clairdereve.com)*, a toy store where stringed marionettes made of papier-mâché, leather and porcelain bob from the ceiling. It also sells wind-up toys and music boxes.

Towards the eastern end of the street, **Librairie Ulysse** *(ulysse.fr)* is stuffed to the rafters with antiquarian and new travel guides, *National Geographic* back editions and maps. It was the world's first travel bookshop when it was opened in 1971 by the intrepid Catherine Domaine. Hours vary, but ring the bell and Catherine will open up if she's around.

If, on the other hand, you're after mainstream souvenirs and tourist kitsch, head to Île de la Cité.

Abundance at a Historic Flower Market
Stop and smell the roses

As you stroll the Île de la Cité, look out for the sweet **Marché aux Fleurs Reine Elizabeth II**. Bang in the middle of the island, blooms have been sold at this quaint covered flower market since 1808, making it the oldest market of any kind in Paris. Browse blooming orchids, garden statuary and lavender sachets. A renovation is underway, in stages, through to 2028.

Quiet Parks & River Vistas
Slip into verdant views

In all the beauty of central Paris it's easy to forget that the Seine is a living river with a rich ecology. Get a glimpse of

---

FASHION BOUTIQUES ON THE ISLANDS

Opulence Vintage *(opulencevintage.com)* Vintage couture in a tiny storefront featuring everything from Chanel to Valentino and Versace.

Nina Kendosa *(ninakendosa.com)* On rue St-Louis en l'Île with soft, casual styles often made from natural fibres.

78isl *(78isl.com)* Think sporty, contemporary, bright and cheerful clothing and accessories.

Paire et Fils *(pairetfils.com)* Understated luxe leather loafers and boots for everyone, plus strappy sandals and ballerinas.

Manuelle Guibal *(manuelleguibal.fr)* Boho streetwear for men and women with a loose fit and insouciant vibe.

Flavours are seasonal and sorbets sensational

EATING ON THE ISLANDS: SWEET TREATS

Atelier du Geste à l'Émotion: The best bakery on Île de la Cité with superb croissants and pastries. *9am-4pm Mon, to 12.30pm Tue-Thu, to 3pm Fri* €

Hadrien: Delicate handmade chocolates, high-quality bars, hazelnut spreads and luxe hot chocolate in winter. What's not to love? *11am-7pm Wed-Mon* €

Pierre Hermé: Drop into this island outpost of the famed macaron-maker, perfect for a pick-me-up. *11am-7pm Mon-Thu, 10am-8pm Fri-Sun* €

Berthillon: Founded here in 1954, the flagship of the esteemed *glacier* (ice-cream maker) is still run by the same family. *10am-8pm Wed-Sun* €

WHY I LOVE PARIS' ISLANDS

Alexis Averbuck, Lonely Planet writer

Every time I come to Paris I make a pilgrimage to the islands. By day, by night, the views offer the soaring romance and twinkling lights we all dream about when we think of the City of Light. There's great people-watching too, as locals and tourists alike cut through on their way elsewhere or seek a picnic spot on the quay. I also love thinking about how these islands are the very root of the original city, built layer upon layer of history, from pre-Roman to Notre Dame and Sainte-Chapelle (with its heart-thrilling stained glass) and the bustling brasseries of today. I almost feel like you haven't fully experienced Paris until you've come to its islands.

Square du Vert-Galant

both wildlife and manicured gardens at the island's parks. At the westernmost tip of the Île de la Cité, migratory birds and chestnut, yew, black walnut and weeping willow trees grace the picturesque park **square du Vert-Galant**. Sitting at the islands' original level, 7m below their current height, the waterside park is reached by stairs leading down from the Pont Neuf. Especially romantic for drinks or a picnic at sunset, it can get crowded in the evenings at the beginning of summer or *la rentrée* (back to school).

Behind Notre Dame, **square Jean XXIII** is part of a massive redevelopment of Notre Dame's public spaces and is becoming a component of a linear park that will connect the **Parvis Notre Dame** with the **square de l'Île de France** across the quai de l'Archevêché. Square de l'Île de France gives superb river views and is rarely busy. It's also home to **Mémorial des Martyrs de la Déportation** (*Memorial to the Victims of the Deportation; cheminsdememoire.gouv.fr; admission free*), erected in 1962. This monument commemorates the 200,000 French (including 76,000 Jews, of whom 11,000 were children) who were deported to and murdered in Nazi concentration

Great choucroute (sauerkraut and meats) too, if you're peckish

🍸 DRINKING ON ÎLE ST-LOUIS: BARS & CAFES

L'Etiquette: Coolcat *caviste* (wine merchant) and wine bar with a couple of tables on the pavement. *11am-8pm Tue-Sun, from 2pm Mon*

Minicafé: Itsy-bitsy storefront with rich coffees, teas and matchas – both hot and cold – paired with gooey grand cookies. *10am-7pm Wed-Sun*

Noir: High-end coffee shop with delectable small baked goods on rue St-Louis en l'Île. *8am-6pm Mon-Fri, from 9am Sat & Sun*

La Brasserie de l'Île Saint-Louis (p217): Best busker- and people-watching at quai de Bourbon, with a Notre Dame backdrop. *noon-10.30pm Thu-Tue*

camps during WWII. A single barred 'window' separates the bleak, rough-concrete courtyard from the waters of the Seine. Inside lies the Tomb of the Unknown Deportee.

If you've got kids, continue along to the eastern tip of Île St-Louis where the park at **square Barye**, just across bd Henri IV, sports a jaunty **children's playground**. It's usually pretty quiet, and also has spectacular views along the river towards the Jardin des Plantes, and access to the quays below.

Virtual Reality Tour of Notre Dame
Zoom into the rafters and over the spire

VR, baby! The hunchback of Notre Dame will be spinning in his grave as you roam the rafters and roll over the rooftops of Notre Dame at this virtual reality experience called **Éternelle Notre-Dame** *(eternellenotredame.com; adult/child €35/25)*. You'll find it underground, in front of Notre Dame, and you'll save €4 and some time by booking ahead online. There's also one at La Défense.

Cool Charms of Église St-Louis en l'Île
Pretty church on Île St-Louis

For all the brouhaha around Notre Dame, you'd be forgiven for not realising there's a whole other church on the islands. When I was last there, with a line coiling in front of Notre Dame, I had the small French baroque **Église St-Louis en l'Île** *(saint louisenlile.catholique.fr)* completely to myself. Spend a calm, cool, quiet half-hour here admiring its rich decorations. It was built between 1664 and 1726 and is named after St Louis aka King Louis IX, the leader who was responsible for building Sainte-Chapelle (and so much more). Check the website for occasional classical music and organ concerts and guided tours.

Get a Free Shower
Experience a Parisian perk at Bains-Douches des Deux-Ponts

Did you know you can have a free shower in Paris? And on the Île St-Louis no less? Part of the group of municipal bathhouses, **Bains-Douches des Deux-Ponts** *(paris.fr; free)* is nothing fancy…except for the cool mosaics…but it's an uber-local experience. There's a 20-minute limit and you need to bring your own towel and soap. Also, don't believe the online times – it can vary, but you'll leave squeaky clean. It's part of Paris' commitment to clean hot water for all.

Learn About, Taste & Buy Cheese
A visit to the Musée Vivant du Fromage

Take a quick half-hour at **Musée Vivant du Fromage** to learn a little bit more about the cheese-making process and get a chance to taste several varieties. Then you can buy some at the shop, or down the street at La Ferme Saint-Aubin (p216).

BOATING AROUND THE ISLANDS

Metros, buses, bikes and *pieds* (your feet) aren't the only way to reach the islands. Travel in supreme style by getting onto a boat on the Seine. **Batobus** *(batobus.com)* runs glassed-in trimarans that dock every 20 to 25 minutes at nine small piers along the Seine, including one just across the river from Notre Dame, on the Left Bank. **Vedettes du Pont Neuf** *(vedettesdupontneuf.com)* runs one-hour cruises that depart year-round from its centrally located dock at the western tip of Île de la Cité. It delivers commentary in French and English along the way. Tickets are cheaper if you buy in advance online, and it also offers 90-minute lunch cruises, evening Champagne cruises and two-hour dinner cruises. All great chances to take in the city.

Researched by Rooksana Hossenally

LATIN QUARTER
MEDIEVAL MARVELS AND LITERARY LUMINARIES

One of the oldest neighbourhoods in Paris, explore its spectacular medieval architecture and soak up the unique atmosphere, stemming from its heyday as the heart of literary Paris.

The Latin Quarter, one of Paris' oldest and most storied neighbourhoods, grew around the Sorbonne University in the Middle Ages, becoming a hub of scholarship, debate and revolutionary ideas. Its name comes from the Latin once spoken in its medieval schools, echoes of which still shape the area's intellectual spirit. Spanning the 5th and 6th *arrondissements,* between the Jardin du Luxembourg and the Jardin des Plantes, it's crowned by the neoclassical Panthéon, resting place of France's great minds. Roman ruins, student bars and bohemian haunts coexist with arthouse cinemas, the Natural History Museum, the Césure arts hub, and cultural landmarks like the Institut du Monde Arabe and the Grande Mosquée de Paris.

TOP TIP

As the Latin Quarter is one of the biggest neighbourhoods, save at least a day to visit, to really get to know it and see its museums and parks. It spans the whole Left Bank across the River Seine from Notre Dame Cathedral. Flanking St-Germain des Prés, it goes from St-Michel (west) to the Jardin des Plantes (east), down to Censier Daubenton (south), and closes at the Luxembourg Garden.

Église St-Étienne du Mont (p227)

See p311 for places to stay in the Latin Quarter.

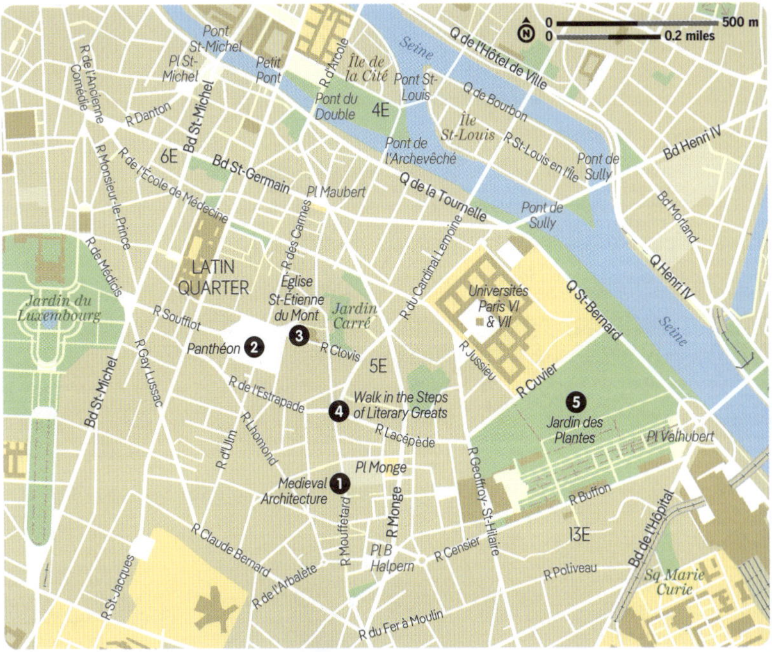

Highlights

❶ Medieval Architecture
Get lost in the maze of stone streets and soak up the singular atmosphere of Paris' oldest neighbourhood. **p229**

❷ The Panthéon
Explore the rich narratives of luminaries interred here, including Victor Hugo, Marie Curie and Simone Veil. **p226**

❸ Église St-Étienne du Mont
See the intricate carvings adorning the façade of the most beautiful building in the area. **p227**

❹ Walk in the Steps of Literary Greats
Wander streets where Hemingway and Joyce once lived, wrote and dreamed. **p232**

 ❺ Jardin des Plantes
Delve into its botanical beauty, historic greenhouses, exotic plants, zoo and museums. **p236**

Getting Around

Metro
The Latin Quarter has good transport links including metro lines 10 (Cluny–La Sorbonne) and 4 (St-Michel), and RER B (Luxembourg), which offer quick access in and out.

Bus
Hopping on a bus, like bus 38 or 47, is a more scenic and less hurried way to see the city rather than below ground. You can really see how different parts of the city fit together.

Cycling
Cycling has become more pleasant as the number of cycling lanes grows. For short hops or spontaneous detours, grab a Vélib' city rental bike.

LATIN QUARTER

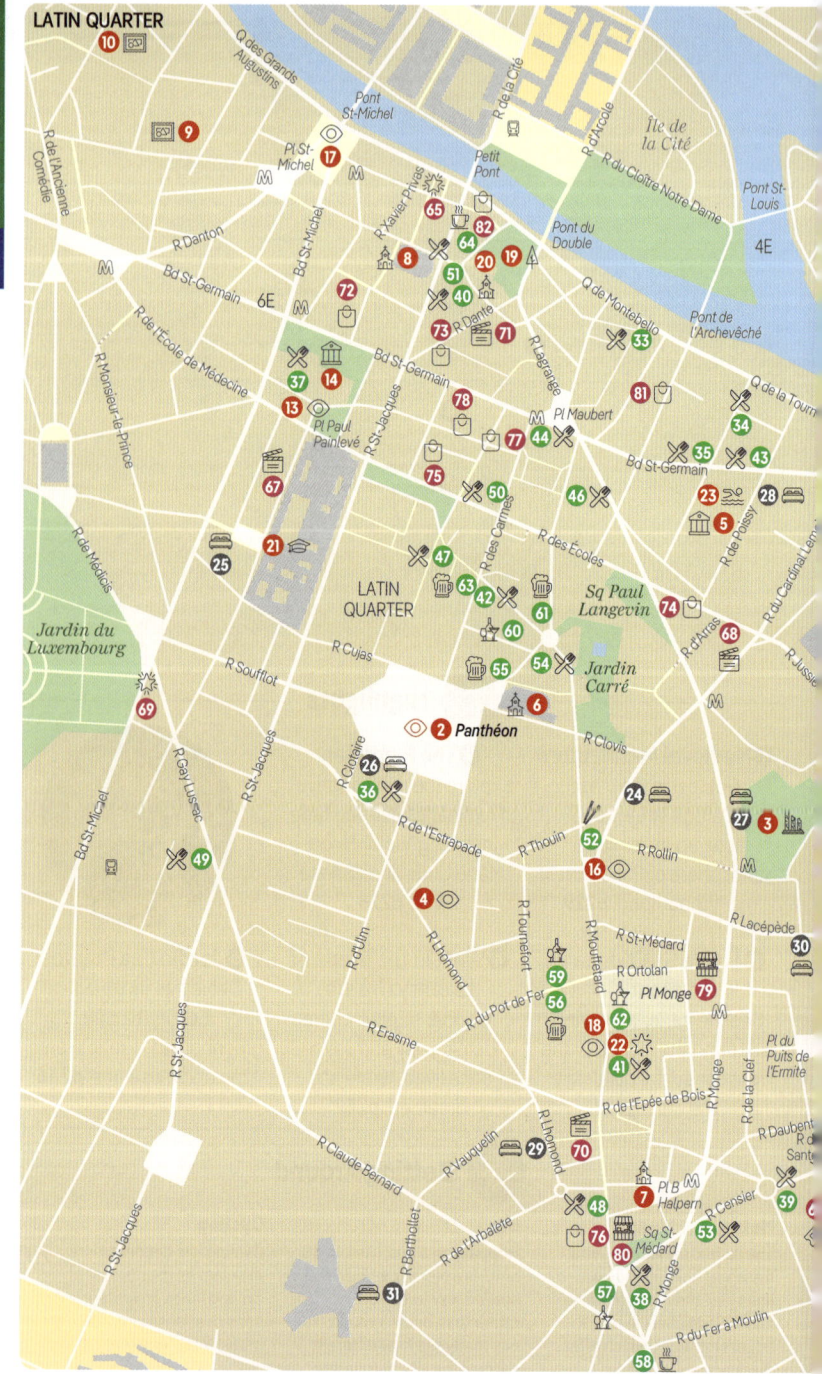

★ HIGHLIGHTS
1. Jardin des Plantes
2. Panthéon

● SIGHTS
3. Arènes de Lutèce
4. Centre Culturel Irlandais
5. Collège des Bernardins
6. Église St-Étienne du Mont
7. Église St-Médard
8. Église St-Séverin
9. Galerie Amélie du Chalard
10. Galerie Kreo
11. Grande Mosquée de Paris
12. Institut du Monde Arabe
13. Institut Finlandais
14. Musée de Cluny – Musée National du Moyen Âge
15. Musée de la Sculpture en Plein Air
16. Place de la Contrescarpe
17. Place St-Michel
18. Rue Mouffetard
19. Square René Viviani
20. St-Julien-le-Pauvre
21. Université Panthéon-Sorbonne

● ACTIVITIES
22. Bowling Mouffetard
23. Piscine Pontoise

● SLEEPING
24. Hôtel des Grandes Écoles
25. Hôtel Grand Cœur Latin
26. Hotel Les Dames du Panthéon
27. Hôtel Monge
28. Hôtel Pilgrim
29. Le 66
30. Le Jardin de Verre by Locke
31. Seven Hotel

● EATING
32. Alliance
see 32 AT
33. Atelier Maître Albert
34. Baieta
35. Bar à Iode
36. Café de la Nouvelle Mairie
37. Café Maa
38. Calice
39. Cantine de Césure
40. Chanceux
41. Dose
see 41 Flocon
42. Jozi Brunch
43. Kitchen Ter(re)
44. La Maison d'Isabelle
45. La Tour d'Argent
46. LAVA
47. Le Coupe-Chou
48. Le Verre à Pied
49. Les Papilles
50. Nuage
51. Odette
52. OTTO by Eric Trochon
53. Pot O'Lait
54. TRAM

● DRINKING & NIGHTLIFE
55. Bombardier
56. Brewberry
57. Cave La Bourgogne
58. La Brûlerie des Gobelins
59. Le Chouff'Bar
60. Le Piano Vache
61. Le Violon Dingue
62. Margen's
63. Pub St-Hilaire
64. Tea Caddy

● ENTERTAINMENT
65. Caveau de la Huchette
66. Césure
67. Le Champo
68. Le Grand Action
69. Le Petit Journal St-Michel
70. L'Epée de Bois
71. Studio Galande

● SHOPPING
72. Abbey Bookshop
73. Album BD
74. Au Bonbon du Palais
75. CrocoDisc
76. Fromagerie Androuet
see 54 La Dame Blanche
77. Le Club K7
78. Librairie Eyrolles
see 44 Marché Maubert
79. Marché Monge
80. Marché Mouffetard
81. Messy Nessy's Cabinet
82. Shakespeare & Company

THE GUIDE

LATIN QUARTER

TOP EXPERIENCE

Panthéon

The Panthéon, a neoclassical marvel, once held the title of Paris' tallest building. Today, it remains a prominent feature of the skyline, offering stunning city views from its dome, accessible by 203 steps. Inside, it honours France's greatest thinkers, with a pediment depicting key figures of the nation and Liberty, making it a symbol of intellectual and national pride.

TOP TIPS

- Demand is high, particularly in summer (July and August), so book online as far in advance as possible.

- There are no cloakrooms or luggage storage on-site, and bags or luggage exceeding the size of 20x40x40cm are not permitted inside.

- For group tickets: reservations.pantheon@monuments-nationaux.fr

PRACTICALITIES

- paris-pantheon.fr/en
- 10am-6.30pm (Apr-Sep) & 10am-6pm (Oct-Mar)
- adult/child €13/free

Know the Backstory

The building was commissioned by King Louis XV around 1750 as an abbey dedicated to Ste Geneviève, Paris' patron saint, in gratitude for his recovery from illness. It wasn't until 1790, a year after the French Revolution, that it opened, when it played a secular role as the temple of the nation and mausoleum for the remains of key figures. It did, however, revert back to religious purposes several times.

Where France's Greatest Thinkers Rest

Two-time Nobel Prize–winner Marie Curie was the first woman to be interred based on achievement. In 2018 Auschwitz survivor, feminist icon and human-rights activist Simone Veil became the fifth woman to be interred. Other notable figures include Victor Hugo and Voltaire.

Foucault's Pendulum

Taking pride of place at the very heart of the Panthéon, Foucault's Pendulum is named after French physicist Léon Foucault. In 1851 he demonstrated the rotation of the Earth using laboratory apparatus rather than astronomical observations for the first time, by suspending the revolutionary device from the Panthéon's ceiling. The original pendulum is now housed at the Musée des Arts et Métiers, while a working copy has been displayed at the Panthéon since 1995.

Architecture Worship
Medieval vestiges and Paris' oldest wall

The Latin Quarter's impressive Roman and medieval roots can be seen throughout the neighbourhood built on and around the gently sloping hill of Ste Geneviève, so if you have time for one thing while here, it has to be strolling around the area to catch glimpses of its incredible architectural heritage. The star attraction on top of the hill is the Panthéon, a regal Roman-inspired resting place for some of the country's greatest minds. Adjacent to the Panthéon, don't miss the magnificent **Église St-Étienne du Mont**, built between 1492 and 1655, whose highly ornate façade will make you gasp in amazement. The **tomb of Ste Geneviève** lies in a chapel in the nave's southeastern corner. The patron saint of Paris, she was born at Nanterre in 422 CE and is said to have turned away Attila the Hun from Paris in 451. A highly decorated reliquary near her tomb contains all that is left of her earthly remains: a finger bone. Fans of the Woody Allen film *Midnight in Paris* will recognise the stone steps on the northwestern corner as the place where Owen Wilson's character is collected by a vintage car and transported back to the 1920s.

Top picks also include the **Arènes de Lutèce**, a 2nd-century Roman amphitheatre that seated 10,000 people for gladiator fights. Found by accident in 1869 when rue Monge was under construction, it's now used by locals for playing football and boules.

You'll also notice the remains of the Philippe II Augustus wall, the **oldest city wall in Paris**. Today, visible parts pass through buildings and car parks, including on rue Clovis, where the rubble and brick core are exposed.

Other standouts include the **Musée de Cluny – Musée National du Moyen Âge** *(musee-moyenage.fr; adult/child €13/free)*, which showcases sublime treasures, from medieval statuary, stained glass and objets d'art to its celebrated series of tapestries, such as the famed *Lady and the Unicorn* (1500). It also incorporates the 15th-century **mansion Hotel de Cluny** and the frigidarium (cold room) of a Roman-era bathhouse. Designed by architect Bernard Desmoulin, the contemporary entrance building houses the ticket office, bookshop, souvenir boutique and cloakroom. Following renovations, the museum now has enhanced explanatory panels and interactive displays. It is also possible to access the 1st-floor late-Gothic chapel, La Chapelle de l'Hôtel de Cluny, with rich carvings of Christ on the cross, 13 angels and floral and foliage ornaments. Make time to visit the recently restored gardens too.

FRANCE'S ACADEMIC CENTRE

The Latin Quarter has been the heart of French academia since the Middle Ages. Its honey-hued university buildings, including the Sorbonne and the jaw-droppingly beautiful Faculty of Medicine, echo centuries of intellectual life. American authors like Ernest Hemingway once roamed its lively bars, adding to its bohemian legacy. The Sorbonne, restructured after the 1968 student protests, now comprises 10 autonomous universities with around 55,000 students. While most buildings are only open during the European Heritage Days each September, the Sorbonne Chapel welcomes visitors year-round. This historic neighbourhood blends scholarly prestige with a vibrant, lived-in atmosphere that continues to inspire students, writers and thinkers today.

EATING IN THE LATIN QUARTER: OUR PICKS

TRAM: Open from breakfast to teatime, this restaurant serves homemade fare, from chia bowls to fresh ceviche, salads and cake. *9am-7pm Tue-Sat, 10am-5.30pm Sun* €

Calice: At the southern end of the area is this retro bistro and wine bar that serves reliable staples like meaty *pâté en croûte* as well as lighter fish dishes and fancy desserts. *noon-2pm & 7-10pm Tue-Sun* €€

Café de la Nouvelle Mairie: Serving traditional bistro food, around the corner from the Panthéon on a fountained square with a breezy terrace in the warmer months. *8am-midnight Mon-Fri* €€

Les Papilles: A pocket-size old-school bistro, wine bar and *épicerie* (specialist grocer), with excellent market-driven fare and natural wines. *noon-2pm & 6.30-10pm Tue-Sat* €€

LOCAL LATIN QUARTER

Audrey Demarre (@audreydemarre) is a local embroidery artist who works from her studio at Césure (p239). These are her neighbourhood go-tos.

Messy Nessy's Cabinet
Run by Anglo-American Vanessa Grall, founder of the digital magazine *Messy Nessy Chic*, I love her boutique, which offers a charming, curious and witty selection of Parisian treasures.

Piscine Pontoise
To me, this is the most beautiful swimming pool in Paris; an art deco gem. Countless films have been shot in this stunning setting, where swimming feels like pure pleasure.

Tea Caddy
A perfect spot for English-style tea time in a timeless Parisian cafe. Just steps from the River Seine, it feels almost like cosying up by a fireplace, and it hasn't changed in decades.

Stained-glass windows, Église St-Séverin

Not many visitors or locals know about them, making them feel like a secret. They have a particular calm about them and are a good reward after a visit to the excellent museum that shines a light on the area's history. There's also a small cafe on-site that's a perfect pit stop in between sightseeing.

Another architectural marvel in the area to put on your list is the **Collège des Bernardins** (*collegedesbernardins.fr; free*). Dating back to 1248, this former Cistercian college originally served as the living quarters and place of study for novice monks. It's now an art gallery and Christian culture centre, with events ranging from lectures to film screenings and music performances. There's a stunning stone vaulted ceiling in the main hall. Closer to St-Michel is **Église St-Séverin**, a Gothic church containing one of the oldest bells in Paris, cast in 1412. Also of note are the seven stained-glass windows depicting the seven sacraments, designed by Jean René Bazaine in 1970.

One of the oldest churches in Paris is **St-Julien-le-Pauvre** (*sjlp-paris.org; free*), where piano recitals (of Chopin, Liszt and others) are staged at least two evenings a week. You'll need a ticket to attend. The bas-relief above the door, depicting the saint in a rowing boat, is a medieval sculpture from the 14th century, cited as being the oldest in Paris.

 WHERE TO DRINK IN THE AREA: OUR PICKS

Cave La Bourgogne: On pretty square St-Médard, it's perfect for soaking up the local vibes while sipping on a coffee or a glass of red. *7am-1am* €

Le Violon Dingue: 'The crazy violin' is a studenty bar with sports showing on big screens upstairs and pub quizzes downstairs. *6pm-5am Tue-Sat* €

Le Piano Vache: A 1970s rock den with live music on the weekends; it's a favourite on the student circuit. *5pm-2am Mon-Sat* €

Bombardier: An old English pub with the best view of the Panthéon, located right across from the blockbuster monument, which also serves food. *hours vary* €€

THE LATIN QUARTER'S ARCHITECTURE WALK

A compact tour that will give you a glimpse of the area's incredible history and essential stops.

START	END	LENGTH
St-Michel metro station	Grande Mosquée	One day

Start at ❶ **St-Michel**, braving the crowds for a glimpse of Notre Dame Cathedral across the River Seine. Peek at the medieval-style street ❷ **rue Galande** around the corner, and move on to the château-like ❸ **Cluny National Museum of the Middle Ages**, with its Roman thermal bath remains. As you edge closer to the grandiose Faculty of Medicine, you'll pass the art deco ❹ **Le Champo**, one of a handful of arthouse cinemas in the area. Stop for a pastry at the near-century-old ❺ **Pâtisserie Viennoise**. Continue to the ❻ **Collège des Bernardins**, a former 13th-century Cistercian college, and then to the Jean Nouvel–designed ❼ **Institut du Monde Arabe**, a centre for learning about the Arab world. Take a stroll around the 2nd-century ❽ **Arènes de Lutèce**, a Roman-era amphitheatre, then head west on rue Clovis to see a section of the ❾ **wall of Philippe II Augustus**, the oldest city wall in Paris. Continue up the slight hill to see the ❿ **Église St-Étienne du Mont** and its marvellous façade, adjacent to the ⓫ **Panthéon**, the star of the Latin Quarter, where the great thinkers of France rest. Across the square is the ⓬ **Panthéon-Sorbonne University**; this is one of the most famous buildings of the Sorbonne network. Walk southwards, past place de la Contrescarpe, and continue along ⓭ **rue Mouffetard** to see some of its medieval overhangs. Finish close to the Jardin des Plantes at the ⓮ **Grande Mosquée de Paris** for a steam bath and a bite to eat.

AN INSIDER'S LATIN QUARTER SPOTS

Neil Kreeger (neil.kreeger@gmail.com), food guide, takes visitors into the heart of the area.

Jinji
I love this store's curation of lesser-known international brands, and that here, trends and seasons don't matter – just quality and style.

Square René Viviani
This beautiful green space, boasting views of Notre Dame, is home to Paris' oldest tree, planted at the turn of the 17th century. It's one of my favourite places to sit and contemplate

Fromagerie Androuet
Androuet is one of the stars of the Parisian cheese scene. It is my go-to *fromagerie* for discovering cheeses from across the country.

La Maison d'Isabelle
Isabelle's *viennoiseries* are the best. That buttery aroma gets me every time!

Rue Mouffetard

Rue Mouffetard
Medieval streets and student bars

Another remnant from the Middle Ages, **rue Mouffetard** slopes down from the Panthéon and narrows to just 7m in places. Once named after the foul-smelling *mouffette* (skunk) due to the polluted River Bièvre (p239), this cobbled street has seen centuries of change. Though now lined with market stalls (except Mondays), casual eateries and tourist-friendly restaurants, it still retains echoes of its past. The 16th-century **Église St-Médard**, with its beautiful stained-glass windows, stands as one of the few historical landmarks that survived the Revolution and Haussmann's redesign of Paris.

At the foot of rue Mouffetard lies **place de la Contrescarpe**, once called a 'cesspool' by Hemingway for its raucous goings-on but long favoured by literary icons. From Descartes to Simone de Beauvoir, and later Joyce and Hemingway himself, the area was a magnet for philosophers and writers drawn to its boisterous bars and dance halls. While the wild nights of Parisian bohemia have faded, the square is still lively with people-watching and cafe terrace culture. Today, visitors come for croque monsieurs and a dose of Left Bank nostalgia.

EATING IN THE LATIN QUARTER: MORE OF OUR PICKS

Flocon: Flocon reimagines bistro cuisine with a lighter, plant-forward twist, guided by seasonal ingredients. *7-11pm Wed & Thu, noon-3pm & 7-11pm Fri-Sun* €€

Le Verre à Pied: A traditional bistro with bags of soul, which does a good *blanquette de veau* washed down with wine. *9am-9pm Wed-Sat, 9.30am-4.30pm Sun* €

OTTO by Eric Trochon: This tiny canteen does excellent Japanese-style bites cooked over binchotan coal, backed by a Michelin-starred chef. *hours vary* €

Bar à Iode: Locals come for the platters of well-priced oysters, prawns and whelks, as well as hearty fish-focused mains. *noon-3.30pm & 7pm-midnight Tue-Sat* €

Mouffetard: Old Soul, New Beat
Markets, student bars and timeless charm in Paris' Latin Quarter

Rue Mouffetard is now a mix of lively street life and local flavor. Tucked in the Latin Quarter's winding streets, it's one of Paris' oldest market roads, still echoing with village-like charm. On weekend mornings, the **markets** on rues Mouffetard, Maubert and Monge bustle with activity. Locals stock up on organic produce, cheeses and cured meats, perfect for a picnic or as edible souvenirs. Alongside this, the area keeps its youthful energy with a host of student bars, plus quirky spots like **Bowling Mouffetard** with its neon lights and themed nights. It's a slice of Paris where old meets new, history, hedonism and the hum of everyday life, just as in Hemingway's and de Beauvoir's days. Grab a stool at a crêperie or sip wine on a terrace as locals pass by. Whether morning markets or late-night laughs, rue Mouffetard never really sleeps.

Offbeat Shopping
Hidden gems & classic finds

The Latin Quarter offers a refined selection of shops, each with its own character. **Album BD** caters to comic-book fans with an impressive selection of artwork and rare editions. Vinyl collectors frequent **CrocoDisc** and **La Dame Blanche**, both offering a broad range of records. Coffee lovers will appreciate **Brûlerie des Gobelins**, while Shakespeare & Company remains a classic stop for book lovers. Nearby, don't miss newcomer **Messy Nessy's Cabinet** with heaps of quality and made-in-France Paris mementos to take home. Artist Marin Montagut's boutique on the other side of the area, close to the Jardin du Luxembourg, is also worth popping into for his artisan scents, crockery, decorative items and other rare finds.

Beautiful bookshops
English-language spots with Parisian soul

French literary giants and expatriate authors found creative refuge in the city's cafes but also its bookshops, like the whimsical **Shakespeare & Company** (shakespeareandcompany.com), a hub for expats since 1919. Originally it stood at 12 rue de l'Odéon as a bookshop and library, and regulars included Ernest Hemingway and F Scott Fitzgerald. When WWII broke out, it was forced to close. In 1951 new owner George

PARIS & ERNEST HEMINGWAY

In the 1920s, a young Ernest Hemingway arrived in Paris, broke but brimming with ambition. He settled in the Latin Quarter with his first wife, Hadley, writing in cafes and forging friendships with Gertrude Stein, F Scott Fitzgerald and Ezra Pound. Paris, for Hemingway, was both a muse and a proving ground, a city where he honed his spare, muscular prose. His memoir, *A Moveable Feast,* remains a love letter to those formative years. Nearly a century later, traces of his world linger: the narrow alleys, smoky bars and early-morning markets still echo with the spirit of a writer who believed Paris was 'always worth it'.

 MORE PLACES TO DRINK IN THE LATIN QUARTER: OUR PICKS

| **Margen's:** A small, dark, neon-lit pub right on rue Mouffetard that serves cocktails and pints and jumps into action to the early hours. *5pm-5am Tue-Sun* € | **Pub St-Hilaire:** A buzzy bar, usually packed out with students who come for a game of pool and the hearty food. *5pm-2am Tue-Thu, 4pm-3am Fri, 1pm-3am Sat* € | **Le Chouff'Bar:** A relaxed tavern serving Belgian beers, including extra-strong La Chouffe, and shots of all kinds. *4pm-2am Mon-Sun* € | **Brewberry:** A more modern bar, with over 20 craft beers from Paris and beyond on tap. *5pm-2am Tue-Sun* €€ |

THE LATIN QUARTER'S LITERARY WALKING TOUR

Discover the Latin Quarter's sights and delve into its literary history with this city-centre walking tour.

START	END	LENGTH
Place St-Michel	Rue Mouffetard	1.5km; two hours

Start at ❶ **place St-Michel** and the ❷ **Fontaine St-Michel**. Walk along the River Seine for views of Notre Dame Cathedral, stopping at the ❸ **bouquinistes** along the way. Take ❹ **rue de la Huchette**, passing the storied jazz club ❺ **Caveau de la Huchette**, and stop at the bookshop ❻ **Shakespeare & Company**. Head westward on ❼ **rue St-Julien-le-Pauvre**, a charming street with medieval buildings, to the ❽ **Abbey Bookshop**, before heading in the direction of the Jardin du Luxembourg to browse at the bookshop ❾ **Red Wheelbarrow**. Walk east to the ❿ **Université Panthéon-Sorbonne**, attended by numerous literary luminaries. Continue to the neoclassical ⓫ **Panthéon**.

This mausoleum is a symbol of intellectual achievement, where the remains of some of France's greatest thinkers have been laid to rest, including those of Curie, Veil and Zola. Stop for lunch at ⓬ **TRAM** before walking to ⓭ **71 rue du Cardinal Lemoine**, where James Joyce once lived, then on to Ernest Hemingway's former apartment at ⓮ **74 rue du Cardinal Lemoine**. Continue to ⓯ **place de la Contrescarpe**, a square where parties took place at clubs and cafes like the former Café des Amateurs at numbers 2–4. Pass via ⓰ **6 rue du Pot au Fer**, where George Orwell once took up bed and board. Then finish on ⓱ **rue Mouffetard**, an atmospheric medieval street.

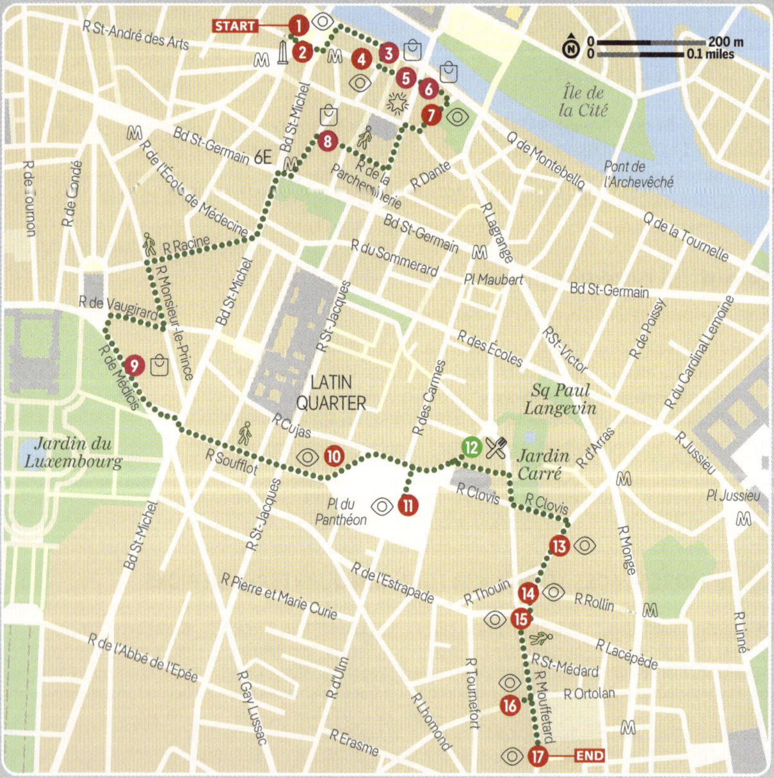

Whitman reopened the English-language bookshop in its current location at 37 rue de la Bûcherie, in a building that served as a monastery. More than 70 years later, it's still a must-visit spot for its bewitching atmosphere and selection of works.

There's also the cosy, Canadian-run **Abbey Bookshop** (*abbeybookshop.org*), where towering stacks of books and regular readings invite lingering. Also worth making a note of, **Librairie Eyrolles** is a beloved Left Bank institution, known for its vast selection of art, design and photography books. And along the Seine, the *bouquinistes* (p238) continue to sell vintage books, posters and magazines from green wooden stalls.

Literary Events
A book festival in a Roman arena

Rub shoulders with ghosts of the Parisian literary set by delving into the area on a guided tour. You can also meet contemporary writers at events like book signings, talks and readings that take place in the area's various bookshops. Check their websites for up-to-date information on future events. Also, every summer the **Festival Quartier du Livre** takes over the whole area with talks and book sales. It's held in the first week of June at venues across the Latin Quarter, including the Arènes de Lutèce (p227) and Collège des Bernardins (p228).

Calm at the Paris Mosque
A North African oasis for food and relaxation

One of the biggest mosques in France and Paris' central mosque, the **Grande Mosquée de Paris** (*grandemosquee deparis.fr*) has a striking Moorish-style minaret, which peeks out from behind smooth white walls as you approach along the street. Visit the interior to see the intricate tile work and calligraphy. There is also a **North African hammam** (steam bathhouse) with timings for women and men, a pretty courtyard **restaurant** (*la-mosquee.com*) that serves delicious couscous, tagines and meat skewers, as well as a **tearoom** where staff serve sweet, fragrant mint tea and traditional cakes. There is also the possibility of smoking **shisha** in the front garden.

LITERARY LUMINARIES

Expatriate writers from all over the world have long sought solace and inspiration in Paris, including James Joyce, Ernest Hemingway and George Orwell, who all lived here. James Joyce's flat, at 71 rue du Cardinal Lemoine, is where he finished his novel *Ulysses*. Hemingway lived close by, at number 74. Conveniently for the party-loving novelist, his apartment was right above one of the hottest dance halls in town, the Bal au Printemps. Nearby at 6 rue du Pot de Fer, George Orwell lived in a boarding house, noted as 'Hotel X' in his memoir *Down and Out in Paris and London*, before he moved to London, while French writers and philosophers like Simone de Beauvoir and Jean-Paul Sartre were often spotted at sidewalk cafes on place de la Contrescarpe, debating ideas before dancing into the night.

 LATIN QUARTER CAFES: OUR PICKS

Nuage: Lures digital nomads with its cosy, homey spaces in an old church (where Cyrano de Bergerac apparently studied). *9am-7pm Mon-Fri (Wed until 1pm), 11am-8pm Sat & Sun* €

Odette: An upstairs tearoom dishing out cream-filled choux (puff pastries) inside a charming 17th-century abode. *9am-8pm* €€

Chanceux: Replacing the popular Circus Bakery is the duo behind Café Compagnon's second location where it serves top-notch coffee, cakes and sandwiches to sit in or go. *hours vary* €€

Café Maa: Nordic design, local art and Finnish flavours meet at the Finnish Institute. Try the rye tartines, cinnamon buns, pine chai latte. €

AMERICAN JAZZ LEGENDS & PARIS

Ever since the end of WWI, France has offered American jazz musicians both a stage and a measure of respect they were often denied at home – along with basic civil rights. The Latin Quarter, in particular, emerged after WWII as a sanctuary for jazz. In the 1940s and '50s, its smoky clubs welcomed talents like Bud Powell and Sidney Bechet, who found freedom and reverence in Paris' bohemian circles. Jean-Pierre Leloir's evocative book *Jazz Images* captures this deep French affection for the music and its makers. Paris wasn't paradise, but for many, it was a vital refuge and an inspiring one.

Théâtre de l'Odéon

Savouring the Jazz Bars
The Latin Quarter's musical heritage

In the years following the war, the area pulsed with music in *bals* (evenings spent dancing) and bars, especially jazz, as crowds packed into the smoky cellars of **Caveau de la Huchette** *(caveaudelahuchette.fr)* to hear Miles Davis and Sidney Bechet play into the night. It spilled out to St-Germain des Prés at candlelit spots like **Chez Papa Jazz Club**, which you'll find just around the corner from the Café de Flore. Another key spot not to miss is **Le Petit Journal St-Michel** *(parisjazzclub.net)* on bd St-Michel. It's here, in this old cafe with a capacity of over 100, that some of the jazz world's greats have performed for more than 50 years. Today, it's at the risk of closing its doors due to lack of funds. The passionate locals, some of whom play here regularly, are calling on the Ministry of Culture to help save it.

Eat for less at lunchtime at Michelin-starred spots

FINE DINING: OUR PICKS

La Tour d'Argent: Overlooking Notre Dame, La Tour d'Argent has served pressed duck and panoramic views since 1582. *noon-2.15pm & 7-10.30pm Tue-Sat* €€€

Le Coupe-Chou: A centuries-old institution with an open fireplace, serving duck *magret* and other French classics. *7-10.30pm* €€

Baieta: Where one-star culinary sensation Julia Sedefdjian whisks up Niçoise creations like her take on bouillabaisse. *noon-2.15pm & 7-10.15pm Tue-Sat* €€

AT: Switch things up from French food with Michelin-starred chef Atsushi Tanaka's contemporary-inspired dishes. *12.30-1.30pm & 7.30-8.30pm Tue-Sat* €€€

Arty Odéon
French film, history and Paris' oldest bas-relief

Named after the neoclassical Roman-inspired **Théâtre de l'Odéon** (inaugurated in 1782), one of the most famous in the city for its classic and contemporary plays, the Odéon area is at the crossroads of St-Germain des Prés and St-Michel. The metro is marked by an Odéon cinema and there is a clutch of arthouse cinemas scattered across the Latin Quarter that are popular with figures in the film industry. The art deco **Le Champo** *(cinema-lechampo.com)* opened in 1928 and is where director François Truffaut liked to go to see other directors' film retrospectives. Other notable independent cinemas include **Christine21** *(pariscinemaclub.com)*, owned by Oscar-winning actress Isabelle Huppert and her son, and **Cinéma St-André des Arts**, on the street of the same name. **Studio Galande** *(studiogalande.fr)* is another one to have on your list, especially if you want to see *The Rocky Horror Picture Show*, which has been shown every Friday and Saturday evening for the last four decades. Back towards rue Mouffetard, built in the 1970s, the pocket-sized arthouse cinema **L'Epée de Bois** *('the wooden sword'; cine-epeedebois.fr)* has two screens and shows recent (non-dubbed) French and other European flicks, and stands on the spot of a centuries-old theatre of the same name. The cinema **Le Grand Action**, 10 minutes away, shows cult international films too.

University Territory: Jussieu
Sorbonne strolls and a sculpture park

Jussieu metro station is the closest station to the main **Université Panthéon-Sorbonne** campus, which has a mineral collection open to visitors on weekday afternoons (plus Saturdays in winter). Wander along rue Cuvier between the campus and the Jardin des Plantes and you'll reach the **Musée de la Sculpture en Plein Air**. This outdoor sculpture museum in the **Tino Rossi garden**, named after a well-liked Corsican singer, is scattered with whimsical works by artists such as César and Constantin Brâncuși. Locals also gather here in the evenings to swing and tango to their hearts' content.

ARTISAN GEMS

Vanessa Grall (@messynessychic) of the beloved blog *Messy Nessy Chic* and Messy Nessy's Cabinet shares her favourite shops.

Bourgine
An independent women's fashion label inspired by overlooked historical figures and niche subcultures. Known for blending craftsmanship with a playful edge, the brand has quietly built a cult following.

Le Club K7
This is one of the most improbable shops in Paris, dedicated to the lost world of the cassette tape. Step inside and enter the 1980s to browse iconic cassette albums and collectible Walkmans.

Au Bonbon du Palais
A sweet shop that looks like a 1950s French classroom, it stocks rare French candy, including candied fruits and *guimauve* (old-fashioned marshmallows); they're so rare they have their own patents.

 WHERE TO EAT IN THE AREA: OUR PICKS

Alliance: This one-star restaurant pairs seasonal French cuisine with Japanese touches in a serene, minimalist setting. *noon-3pm & 7.30-10.30pm Mon-Fri* €€€

LAVA: This fiery restaurant fuses a chef's love of open-flame cooking with a sommelier's flair in a celebration of travel, terroir and technique. *noon-2pm & 6.30-10pm Tue-Sat* €€

Kitchen Ter(re): Blending artisan noodles made from ancient grains with tasty Asian-inspired broths, all served in a stylish, art-infused setting. *12.15-2pm & 7-10pm Tue-Sat* €€

Atelier Maître Albert: A contemporary rotisserie offering refined traditional cuisine in a historic 14th-century setting. *noon-2.30pm & 6.30-10pm* €€

Above: Grande Galerie de l'Évolution; right: Gallery of Paleontology & Compared Anatomy

TOP EXPERIENCE

Jardin des Plantes

A garden oasis with a wealth of museums – and even a dinosaur or two – the 24-hectare botanical garden lined by a double alley of plane trees, was originally created as a medicinal herb garden in 1626. There's plenty to see here, like the wealth of exotic plants inside four elegant greenhouses (the Grandes Serres), each growing like mini-worlds of their own.

Gardens & Four Greenhouses

Wander through the Jardin des Plantes and you'll find more than just a botanical garden – it's a living museum. Paths wind past centuries-old trees, seasonal blooms and themed gardens, from medicinal plants to the tranquil Alpine Garden. Step into the soaring art deco greenhouses for a sensory journey through tropical rainforests and arid deserts. Inside, mist clings to lush leaves, orchids hang like jewels and the air is thick with green. Open year-round, the gardens are free to enter, while the greenhouses require a ticket. Arrive early for a quiet stroll, or linger at golden hour when the light feels cinematic.

DON'T MISS

The four greenhouses

Paleontology and Compared Anatomy Gallery

Gallery of Evolution

Geology and Mineralogy Gallery

Small zoo

PRACTICALITIES

● jardindesplantesdeparis.fr/en ● it's free to enter the garden and greenhouse, but you need tickets for the museums and zoo ● open every day from morning to evening (hours vary, check the website)

Gallery of Paleontology & Compared Anatomy

The spectacle is striking: a majestic herd of large terrestrial and aquatic vertebrates stretches out before you in one of Paris' most transportive museums. The Gallery of Paleontology and Comparative Anatomy invites you to journey through 460 million years of evolution, with more than 2000 fossils – including 316 complete skeletons – on display. Marvel at the 25m-long diplodocus, a cast of a tyrannosaurus rex skull, cynthiacetus the whale ancestor, and even Sacabambaspis janvieri, one of the oldest known vertebrates. Upstairs on the balcony, more than 5000 fossils trace the delicate imprints of ancient life – from insect wings to the petals of the first flowers. It's worth taking your time here as there is so much to see.

Gallery of Evolution

They don't speak, but they tell the story of life itself. In the Grande Galerie de l'Évolution, over 7000 preserved specimens trace the astonishing diversity of the natural world. Opened in 1994 within a soaring 19th-century hall designed by Jules André, the space marries history and science under a luminous 1000-sq-metre glass roof. On the ground floor, skeletons of marine giants – the southern right whale, blue whale and sperm whale – greet visitors. Upper levels showcase land mammals and birds, with sweeping galleries offering views of the great 'procession of life' below. It's a theatrical, immersive celebration of Earth's biodiversity and evolution.

Geology & Mineralogy Gallery

The Galerie de Géologie et de Minéralogie dazzles with one of the world's oldest and most prestigious collections. Inside its elegant neoclassical hall, stretching 187m and framed by columned porticoes, visitors enter the spectacular 'Earth Treasures' room. Here, Martian meteorites, colossal crystals, rare rocks and luminous minerals reveal the extraordinary story of our planet and solar system. Named after mineralogy pioneer René Just Haüy, the gallery is both a scientific and visual marvel. As you explore, learn to distinguish sulphur from quartz and cooking salt; though they have different chemical formulas, the same composition can create two distinct minerals, depending on their crystal structure. Carbon, for example, appears both as a pencil lead and as a diamond!

JARDIN DES PLANTES' ZOO

For a peaceful escape, visit the Ménagerie at the Jardin des Plantes, home to 500 animals across 150 species, many of which are endangered. One of the world's oldest zoos, it focuses on small and medium-sized species that thrive in its intimate enclosures. Wander through different habitats, from red pandas who stay in the trees to snow leopards perfectly adapted to snowy mountain environments, and witness the zoo's dedication to conservation and animal diversity. Designed for four- to six-year-olds and seven- to 12-year-olds, the Ménagerie's web app lets children discover 15 species, including red pandas and Przewalski's horses, through fun challenges and quizzes.

TOP TIPS

● Go early in the morning or late in the afternoon to enjoy the gardens at their most peaceful, especially in spring (end of March to mid-April), when the cherry blossoms or peonies are in bloom.

● Don't miss the tucked-away Alpine Garden, often overlooked by tourists

● If you're with kids, the zoo, a conservation centre in a wide open space, is a delight.

St-Michel: Gateway to the Latin Quarter
Roman history and picnicking with Notre Dame views

A historic entry point to the Left Bank, **St-Michel** is where Roman Lutetia once bridged the Seine to the **Île de la Cité**. Named after a 13th-century chapel, the area flourished in the Middle Ages as a hub for Sorbonne scholars. Today, its grand boulevard leads from the 19th-century **Fontaine St-Michel** to the Jardin du Luxembourg. The fountain, a local landmark, was built in the 19th century and depicts the archangel Michael defeating a dragon. To the east, the quai de Montebello is an offbeat picnic spot with unbeatable Notre Dame views.

Iconic Museums
Arts hubs and contemporary go-tos

At the southern end of the bd St-Germain, you'll find the **Institut du Monde Arabe** (*Arab World Institute or IMA; imarabe.org*), an unsung museum with a jaw-dropping design by the French architect Jean Nouvel. It features a metallic screen of moving geometric motifs designed to look like a *mashrabiya,* a window of ornate latticework often found in Islamic architecture, where the motifs are actually 240 light-sensitive shutters that automatically open and close to control the amount of light and heat in the building. The IMA was founded by France and 18 Arab countries with the aim of creating a research hub about the Arab world. It was established due to the perceived lack of representation for the Arab world in France, and it seeks to provide a secular location for the promotion of Arab civilisation, art, knowledge and aesthetics. The IMA consists of a museum, library, auditorium, meeting rooms and a rooftop restaurant, Dar Mima, which whisks up food with influences from North African countries, such as fish tagine and couscous. The real selling point here is the view across the Paris rooftops.

Despite the area being one of the oldest of Paris, the Latin Quarter brims with arty findings old and new. For travellers looking to put a contemporary spin on their visit to the neighbourhood, drop in at charismatic **Kamel Mennour**'s gallery spaces, three of which are in the area, with an offshoot in the 8th *arrondissement*. Mennour founded his first gallery in 1999, his hard graft propelling him onto the international art circuit. Starting out by selling artworks door-to-door,

BOUQUINISTES, THEN & NOW

Lining the top of the river banks at quai de la Tournelle, Pont Marie and quai du Louvre, you'll spot faded boxes that open to reveal secondhand book stalls (*bouquinistes*) selling out-of-print books, rare magazines, postcards and old posters, all waiting to be rediscovered.

In the 16th century, itinerant peddlers sold their wares on Parisian bridges. Sometimes their subversive (for example, Protestant) materials would get them into trouble with the authorities. By 1859 the city had wised up: official licences were issued and eventually the permanent boxes were installed.

 LATIN QUARTER QUICK BITES: OUR PICKS

Pot O'Lait: Try the tasty *galettes,* generously filled with ingredients like goat's cheese and smoked salmon. *11.15am-2.30pm & 6.30-10pm Mon-Sat* €

Dose: Get your caffeine hit with artisan-roasted craft coffee and follow with a lunch of homemade quiche on rue Mouffetard. *8am-6pm Tue-Fri, 9am-6pm Sat & Sun* €

Cantine de Césure: Art hub Césure's canteen is a good-value, zero-waste spot with easy options like burgers and salads. *10am-11pm Tue-Sat* €

Jozi Brunch: Easy plates of avocado toast and fruit pancakes served most of the day. *8am-4pm Mon-Fri, 9am-5.30pm Sat & Sun* €

Fontaine St-Michel

today he represents 40 of the art world's biggest names, from Anish Kapoor to Alberto Giacometti.

With so many students around, it's only natural that there should be more of a grassroots art scene too. Hybrid arts hub **Césure** *(cesure.paris)* has recently opened its doors inside an old Sorbonne campus building, where dorms and common rooms have been turned into exhibition spaces, artist studios and residencies. Led by several associations and collectives, the take-over will initially last two years, during which time various events will be held, from plays to parties (check the website to see what's on).

Add the **Institut Finlandais** *(institut-finlandais.fr)* to your list too: it's an independent and multidisciplinary cultural space with a pared-back cafe and various events taking place year-round. The **Centre Culturel Irlandais** *(centreculturelirlandais.com)* is also worth checking out for its well-curated exhibitions of Irish visual artists based all over the world. There are also artist residencies and a physical and digital library. For cutting-edge design, the Parisian pioneer is **Galerie Kreo** *(galeriekreo.com)*. It's the go-to for clued-up designers and collectors, located on the cusp of the Latin Quarter and St-Germain des Prés, where most galleries are clustered. For artworks from emerging and more established artists, add **Galerie Amélie du Chalard** *(amelieduchalard.com)*, where the pieces are hung in a beautiful *hôtel particulier* (private mansion) you'll wish you lived in.

PARIS' SECRET UNDERGROUND RIVER

Beneath the Latin Quarter's cobbled streets flows a hidden river: the Bièvre. Once a lively tributary of the Seine, the Bièvre shaped this historic neighbourhood, powering tanneries, dye workshops and mills from Roman times through the Middle Ages. Its waters dyed fabrics for the Gobelins Manufactory and helped establish the area's artisanal identity. By the late 19th century, pollution and urban growth led to the river being covered and diverted underground. Today, traces remain in street names and museum exhibits, and occasional plans propose uncovering sections. Invisible yet integral, the Bièvre whispers the Latin Quarter's layered, working-class past beneath the surface. Today, the local authorities are looking at how they can uncover it once again, or at least in parts.

Researched by Nicola Leigh Stewart

ST-GERMAIN & LES INVALIDES

IN THE FOOTSTEPS OF CREATIVE GIANTS

The ever-chic neighbourhoods of St-Germain and Les Invalides, in the Left Bank's 6th and 7th *arrondissements,* have long been the storied stomping grounds of modern history's greatest thinkers.

In the Middle Ages, the Left Bank was considered the countryside of Paris, dominated by open fields, known in French as *près* – hence the name St-Germain des Prés. But the development of the Abbey de St-Germain in the 6th century (where the Église St-Germain des Prés stands today) quickly turned the place into a spiritual and intellectual hot spot. The area really came into its own at the turn of the 20th century when its lively cafe scene attracted creatives from across the globe with promises of rich intellectual banter over endless carafes of cheap table wine. Today St-Germain des Prés is home to some of the city's priciest real estate, and a few film stars, but reverberations of its colourful past still echo through its immaculately preserved cobblestone streets.

TOP TIP

As you wander about, be sure to keep an eye out for plaques signposting the former abodes of creative titans. You'll quickly realise that many great thinkers of the past 200 years once called this area home.

Viewpoint from behind the original station clock, Musée d'Orsay (p250)

See p312 for places to stay in St-Germain and Les Invalides.

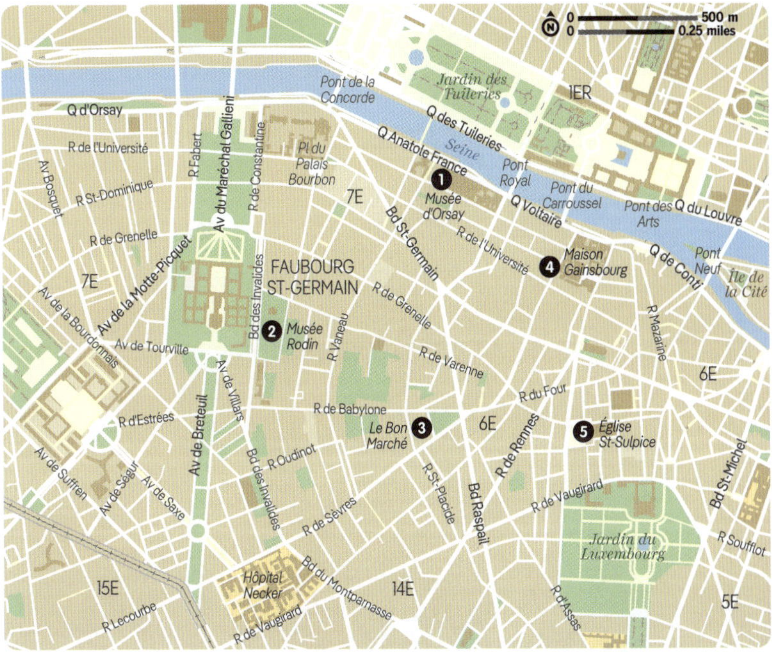

 Highlights

❶ Musée d'Orsay
Enjoy Paris' second-mostvisited museum, home to one of the world's finest collections of Impressionist and postimpressionist works. **p250**

❷ Musée Rodin
Capture a peaceful moment at this museum and sculpture garden dedicated to the sculptor Auguste Rodin. **p264**

❸ Le Bon Marché
Visit the world's first department store, today a temple of French luxury. **p252**

❹ Maison Gainsbourg
Guide yourself through French musician Serge Gainsbourg's personal abode. **p259**

❺ Église St-Sulpice
Admire the second-largest church in Paris and home to spectacular works by Delacroix and Jean-Baptiste Pigalle. **p262**

 Getting Around

Walking

Paris is a pretty compact city and easy to walk around, and St-Germain des Prés is one of the prettiest neighbourhoods for strolling.

Metro

The metro is quick, easy and cheap. The main St-Germain des Prés will put you in the heart of the 6th *arrondissement*.

Bicycle

If you're comfortable cycling you can pick up Vélib' bikes across the city. Sign up online for a one- or three-day ticket.

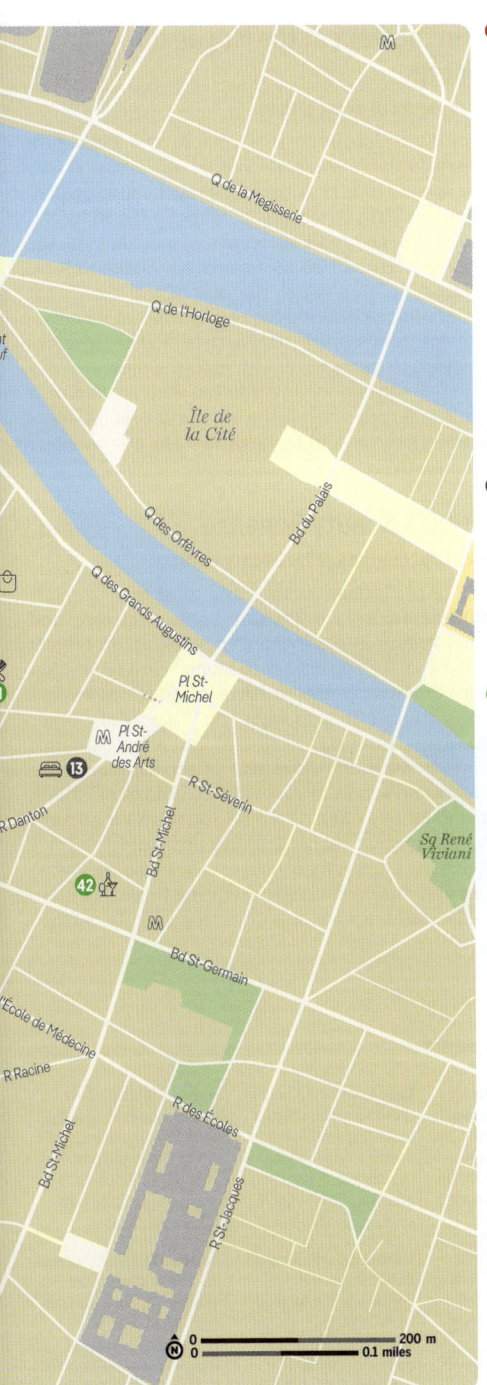

● SIGHTS
1 Bibliothèque Mazarine
2 École des Beaux-Arts
3 Église St-Germain-des-Prés
4 Église St-Sulpice
5 Fontaine Médicis
6 Jardin du Luxembourg
7 Le Bateau Ivre
8 Maison Gainsbourg
9 Monnaie de Paris
10 Musée du Luxembourg
11 Musée National Eugène Delacroix
12 Square Laurent-Prache

● SLEEPING
13 Hôtel Dame des Arts
14 Hôtel de l'Abbaye Saint-Germain
15 Hôtel St-André des Arts
16 L'Hôtel
17 Pavillon Faubourg Saint Germain

● EATING
18 Angiolo
19 Arnaud Larher
20 Aux Merveilleux de Fred
21 Boulangerie Liberté
22 Brasserie Lipp
23 Breizh Café Odéon
24 Café de la Mairie
25 Café Pavane
26 Café Pierre Hermé
27 Huîtrerie Régis
28 La Boissonerie
29 Le Christine
30 Le Comptoir des Saints-Pères
31 Le Comptoir du Relais
32 Le Pré aux Clercs
33 Le Procope
34 Le Voltaire
35 Mademoiselle Angelina
36 Polidor

● DRINKING & NIGHTLIFE
37 Augustin Marchand d'Vins
38 Bar Etna
39 Café de Flore
40 Café du Clown
41 Cafe Nuances
42 Castor Club
43 Cravan
44 Freddy's
45 La Balle au Bond
46 La Crèmerie
47 La Grande Crèmerie
48 La Palette
see 31 L'Arbre à Café
49 L'Avant Comptoir de la Mer
see 49 L'Avant Comptoir de la Terre
50 Le Bar
see 13 Le Rooftop at Hôtel Dame des Arts
51 Le Rouquet
52 Les Deux Magots
53 Maison Fleuret

● ENTERTAINMENT
54 Théâtre de l'Odéon

● SHOPPING
55 Alléno & Rivoire
56 Assouline
57 Astier de Villatte
58 Biologique Recherche
59 Caudalie
60 Chartreuse Paris-Vauvert
61 Cire Trudon
62 Citypharma
63 Compagnie Française des Poivres et des Épices
64 Debauve & Gallais
65 Dilettantes Cave à Champagne
66 Galerie Stéphane Olivier
67 La Dernière Goutte
68 La Maison du Whisky Odéon
69 La Soufflerie
70 L'Atelier 55
71 Librairie François Chanut
see 43 Librairie Rizzoli
72 L'Officine Universelle Buly 1803
73 Marché Saint-Germain
74 Marin Montagut
75 Red Wheelbarrow
76 San Francisco Book Company
77 Taschen
78 The 7L Bookshop
see 11 Yvelines Antiques

RIMBAUD'S THE DRUNKEN BOAT

Wander down quaint rue Férou (where Hemingway once lived) in the 6th *arrondissement* and you'll notice a wordy mural that's unlike any of the other graffiti scrawled across the city's façades. Take a step back from the wall and you can parse together the lengths of French poet Arthur Rimbaud's masterpiece **Le Bateau Ivre** (The Drunken Boat). Written when he was just a teenager, the symbolist ballad recounts a journey aboard a sinking ship at sea. The rue Férou mural was commissioned in 2012 by the French government, with support from a Dutch poetry society, as an homage to the poet. Local folklore has it that Rimbaud first recited it at a location nearby – hence the mural's peculiar setting.

Find Art in the Park at the Musée du Luxembourg

MAP P242

The former museum of living artists

Nestled within the Jardin du Luxembourg, the **Musée du Luxembourg** (*museeduluxembourg.fr; adult/concession €14/10*) was opened in 1818 as the first French museum dedicated to living artists. After foreign works pillaged by Napoléon I were returned to their rightful owners in 1815, the museum was conceptualised as a space to stimulate local artistic production, proving to the rest of the world that France was capable of refilling the empty walls of its museums with talent from within. After artists died, their works were transferred to the Louvre. Although the museum only plays host to two exhibitions a year (often with an emphasis on 20th-century female artists), the high calibre of its shows and its stunning location within the garden's former orangery make it well worth a visit.

Citypharma's Beauty Bonanza

MAP P242

A pharmaceutical pilgrimage for beauty addicts

In the heart of St-Germain is the city's most famous pharmacy, **Citypharma**: a place of pilgrimage for both local and international beauty lovers looking to stock up on French beauty must-haves. The pharmacy has long held a reputation for offering the lowest prices in Paris, although nowadays a lot of items are in line with what you'll pay at any other French pharmacy. However, you'll still find some bargains, and with hundreds, if not thousands, of products sprawled over two floors and across two separate buildings, one thing Citypharma definitely offers is a one-stop shop for all your beauty and pharmaceutical needs. Stock up on the usual cult favourites (Crème Embryolisse moisturiser, La Roche Posay) and don't hesitate to ask for help navigating the labyrinth of products – the staff are incredibly knowledgeable. Be warned

BEST COFFEE SHOPS: OUR PICKS

MAPS P242, P248

Ten Belles: The Left Bank outpost of beloved British Franco bakery Ten Belles, famed for its delicious sourdough loaves. *8.30am-4.30pm Mon-Fri, 9am-5pm Sat & Sun*	**Café du Clown:** Great coffee, and a good spot for people-watching from the terrace outside the Marché St-Germain. Note that the toilet is inside the market. *8am-6pm*	**Cafe Nuances:** A hole-in-the-wall coffee shop for picking up freshly baked pastries. Beans packed in reusable cloth bags make great gifts. *8am-7pm Mon-Fri, 9am-7pm Sat & Sun*	**Maison Fleuret:** A cute coffee shop inside a former bookshop. There are plant-based dishes and pastries from Maison Fleuret's own baking school. *9am-6.30pm Wed-Sun*
Wani: Cute and stylish coffee shop serving breakfast, lunch, pastries and Japanese teas. *11am-5.30pm Mon-Sun*	**Coutume:** One of the original speciality coffee shops, situated on the street where Yves Saint Laurent once lived. *8.30am-5.30pm Mon-Fri, 9am-6pm Sat & Sun*	**L'Arbre à Café:** Serious coffee lovers will appreciate the detailed menu of organic speciality beans from this artisan coffee roaster and producer. *9am-7pm*	**Terres de Café:** A pioneer in Paris' artisan coffee movement, Terres de Café has the largest range of speciality coffees in France. *8am-7pm Mon-Fri, 9.30am-7pm Sat & Sun*

Marché St-Germain

though, that photos are not allowed – and staff will tell you so – although you will find a specially designated spot on the 2nd floor, surely with Instagrammers in mind, for those who want to take a selfie.

Browse the Stalls of Marché St-Germain

MAP P242

A modern-day covered market

The **Marché St-Germain** was originally built in 1511 under the order of Abbot Guillaume and housed 300 merchants selling their wares, although it was destroyed by a fire in 1762. The market that stands today opened its doors in 2017 and although it houses some of the most modern 'merchants' you could think of, Apple for instance, it still has an attractive old-fashioned style thanks to its 112 stone arches. Inside the covered market, you'll find fruit and veg stalls, cheesemongers, and a couple of restaurants and delis, some of which, such as Poissonerie Viot, open their doors onto the outside to serve drinks and small dishes under the arcades. It's open six days a week, Tuesday to Saturday 8am to 8pm and on Sunday 8am to 1.30pm.

BEST BEAUTY SHOPS

Biologique Recherche (Map p242) This is the second Paris location from French beauty brand Biologique Recherche, whose cult products include the celebrity-approved exfoliating Lotion P50.

Caudalie (Map p242) You can easily pick up Caudalie products in the pharmacies, but fans might also want to book into the newly opened Left Bank spa.

L'Officine Universelle Buly 1803 (Map p242) Originally founded by French perfumier Jean-Vincent Bully in 1803, the brand's beautifully packaged body lotions and soaps make great gifts.

Oh My Cream! (Map p248) This fashionable beauty shop can now be found across Paris thanks to its well-curated selection of high-end and hard-to-find organic, natural and cult beauty products.

Mademoiselle Bio If you only buy organic, then this is the beauty shop for you – *'bio'* means organic in French – stocking everything from deodorant to nail polish.

ÉGLISE ST-IGNACE

Sitting on rue de Sèvres is a sign outside a modern apartment block saying *'église'* with an arrow. There is nothing too odd about that, except that the arrow is pointing to inside the apartments. Follow it and you'll be surprised to find a 19th-century Jesuit church, **Église St-Ignace** (Map p248), hidden away inside. After the Jesuits were forced to leave France in the late 18th and early 19th centuries, some returned to Paris and in 1821 moved into 33 and 35 rue de Sèvres. They later bought up numbers 37, 39, 41 and 43, giving them enough space to build the church, plus new buildings around it. These surrounding buildings were knocked down in 1971 and replaced with the apartment building that still hides the church today, creating a surprising contrast with the historic, neogothic church secreted away inside.

Bibliothèque Mazarine

An Intimate Look at Delacroix's Life

MAP P242

The painter's works and apartment

Tucked away in the charming place Furstemburg is a small museum dedicated to Delacroix, **Musée National Eugène Delacroix** *(musee-delacroix.fr; adult/under 18 years €9/free)*, housed in the painter's former apartment. Delacroix chose the location to be close to the nearby St-Sulpice church whilst he was working there on three large-scale murals, which you can still see today. It's also where Delacroix ended up spending the last few years of his life with his loyal housekeeper, whose former room is now where the museum's lift is. The rest of the rooms have been transformed into the museum, including Delacroix's atelier in the garden, although none of his possessions remain as they were all sold after his death. For Delacroix fans, seeing the smaller paintings here is a nice complement to viewing his more famous and much larger works in Le Louvre, and as you can imagine, a much quieter place to enjoy the artist's work. Note that although the museum is wheelchair accessible, Delacroix's atelier in the garden at the

 BEST SPECIALITY FOOD SHOPS ——— MAPS P242, P248

Compagnie Française des Poivres et des Épices: Stop by for high-quality peppercorns, spices, French Guérande salt, herbs de Provence, vanilla and sugars. *11am-1pm & 2.15-7pm*

Lafitte: Specialists in foie gras, rillettes, duck confits and pâtés since 1920. It also sells bottles of wine if you want to ask about a pairing. *2-7pm Tue, 10am-1pm & 2-7pm Wed-Sat*

La Belle-Iloise: Founded in 1932, this *conserverie* sells multipacks of canned fish from Quiberon, Brittany, in charmingly old-fashioned packaging. *10am-7.30pm Mon-Sat, 10am-1.30pm & 2.30-7.30pm Sun*

L'Agrumiste: Harder to find organic citrus fruits as well as fresh and zingy citrus-based products, think marmalades, yuzu granola, lemon-infused gin and delicious citrusy cakes. *11am-7pm Tue-Sat*

back isn't. If you'd like a guided tour in English, email the museum, which can organise a visit with an external guide.

Quiet Reading at Bibliothèque Mazarine

MAP P242

The oldest public library in France

Located within the Institute of France (the national body conceived to protect French culture) is the oldest public library in the country: **Bibliothèque Mazarine**. Once the private reading room of Cardinal Mazarin, today it is both a public workspace and national archive, containing a stunning collection of rare and ancient manuscripts. The resplendent reading room is open to the public from 10am to 6pm, Monday through Friday, but you must register on-site for an access card (free for five days or €15 for an annual pass).

All visitors are then required to wash their hands before entering the room in absolute silence. As you are not allowed to simply thumb through the treasured volumes, the library organises free (and wonderfully informative) daily guided tours in both French and English.

Go Organic at Marché Biologique Raspail

MAP P248

Paris' largest organic food market

Every Sunday between 7.30am and 2.30pm on bd Raspail (between rue de Sèvres and rue de Rennes) is **Marché Biologique Raspail**, Paris' top organic food market. All the 50 or so stalls here must adhere to the national guidelines on organic produce. This, in turn, means that the prices are higher than at your usual neighbourhood market, but it's a great place for otherwise hard-to-find goods such as freshly baked gluten-free bread, vegan curries and superfood powders like spirulina and maca.

THÉÂTRE DE L'ODÉON

Just a stone's throw from the Jardin du Luxembourg is the **Théâtre de l'Odéon** (Map p242). Opened in 1872, it was the first theatre in the country to have benched seating for its ground-floor audience. Many a famed French playwright debuted works here and today the program remains rather classical. But you don't have to sit through a two-hour play in French to get a taste of the theatre's history: from the outside you can admire the building's imposing neoclassical façade, in the style of Ancient Greek theatres, and then peek inside at its gilded foyer.

Don't miss Jean-Paul Hévin's hot chocolate in winter

MAP P242

 WHERE TO EAT IN ST-GERMAIN DES PRÉS

La Boissonnerie: A contemporary bistro serving seasonal dishes alongside a great wine list in a friendly, lively setting. *12.30-2.30pm & 7-10.30pm* €€	**Breizh Café Odéon:** This Paris-wide crêperie serves the best *galettes* and crêpes in Paris. A great spot for lunch or dinner and dining in groups or with kids. *10am-11pm* €	**Le Christine:** Young chef Rodolphe Despagne serves up surprising, gastronomic creations (and plant-based options) in an unpretentious setting. *noon-2pm & 7-10pm* €€€	**Café Pavane:** Run by the daughter of chocolatier Jean-Paul Hévin, the menu features Russian-inspired dishes such as borscht. *11am-7.30pm Wed-Sun* €
Huîtrerie Régis: Not the cheapest oysters in Paris, but they are the best. Make sure to reserve, as the place is tiny and can quickly get booked out. *hours vary* €€€	**Le Comptoir des Saints-Pères:** A bustling classic St-Germain des Prés bistro that pulls in a very local crowd. Hemingway and Picasso also used to pop by. *7am-11pm* €€	**Polidor:** A historic address, and affordable bistro, frequented by the likes of James Joyce and Ernest Hemingway. The *prix fixe menus* are good value. *noon-3pm and 7pm-midnight* €€	**Le Comptoir du Relais:** Classic French dishes served non-stop, which is hard to find in Paris, with a selection of natural wines. *noon-11pm* €€

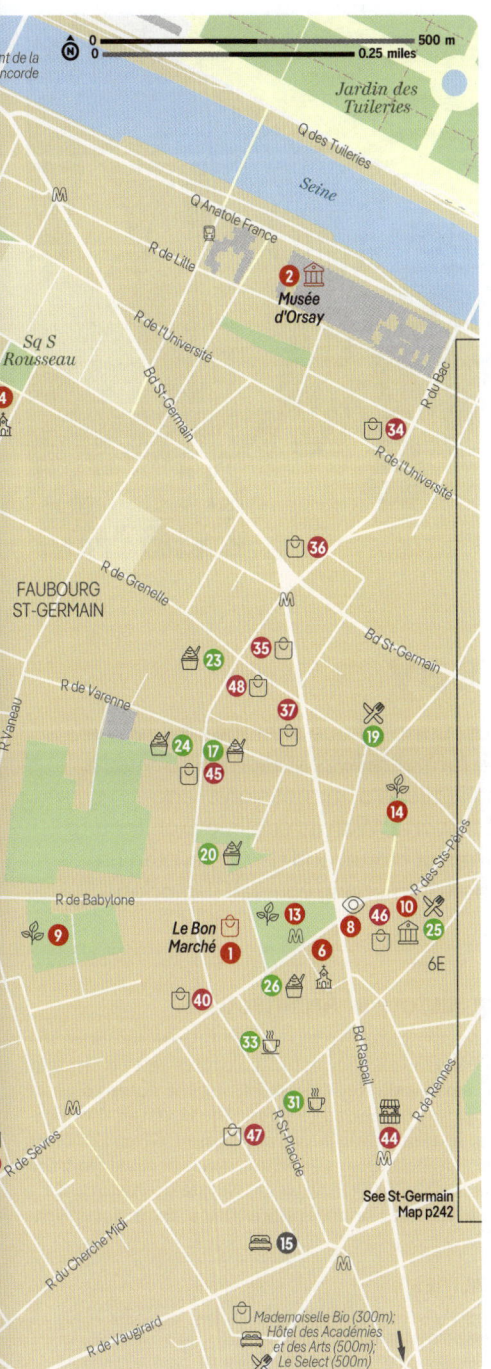

★ HIGHLIGHTS
1. Le Bon Marché
2. Musée d'Orsay
3. Musée Rodin

● SIGHTS
4. Basilique Ste-Clotilde
5. Dôme des Invalides
6. Église St-Ignace
7. Hôtel des Invalides
8. Hôtel Lutetia
9. Jardin Catherine-Labouré
10. La Maison des Histoires
11. Musée de l'Armée
12. Musée des Égouts de Paris
13. Square Boucicaut
14. Square Roger-Stéphane

● SLEEPING
15. Hôtel des Grands Voyageurs
16. Hôtel Thoumieux

● EATING
17. Des Gâteaux et du Pain
18. La Pâtisserie Cyril Lignac
19. La Petite Chaise
20. Le Bac à Glaces
21. Maison Bergeron
22. Mori Yoshida
23. Noglu
24. Philipe Conticini
25. Poilâne
26. Ritz Paris Le Comptoir
27. Tapisserie

● DRINKING & NIGHTLIFE
see 8. Bar Joséphine
28. Coutume
29. Le Flow
30. Rosa Bonheur sur Seine
31. Ten Belles
32. Terres de Café
33. Wani

● SHOPPING
34. Androuet
see 10. Chantelivre
35. Chapon
36. Deyrolle
37. Fromagerie Barthélémy
38. Fromagerie Quatrehomme
see 17. Jacques Genin
39. La Belle-Iloise
40. La Grande Épicerie de Paris
41. Lafitte
42. L'Agrumiste
43. Le Chocolat Alain Ducasse
44. Marché Biologique Raspail
45. Oh My Cream!
46. Patrick Roger
47. Plaq
48. Ryst Dupeyron

ST-GERMAIN & LES INVALIDES

TOP EXPERIENCE

Musée d'Orsay

The second-most-visited museum in France after the Louvre, the Musée d'Orsay is housed in a former railway station and contains one of the most important collections of Impressionist and postimpressionist works in the world. With its sublime architecture and masterpieces from the likes of Monet and Cézanne, plan on spending at least half a day here immersing yourself in modern French art history.

DON'T MISS

Éduoard Manet's *Le Déjeuner sur l'herbe*

Vincent Van Gogh's *Starry Night Over the Rhône*

Edgar Degas' *La Petite Danseuse de Quatorze Ans*

Claude Monet's *Londres, le Parlement*

A Living History of Architecture

As you enter the Musée d'Orsay, take a pause to notice the layout of the ground floor, with sculptures in two straight rows, and small galleries annexed along the outer edges of the space. It was organised to mimic the layout of the original railway station within which it is housed. Given the sheer significance of the encasing building, it was decided from the outset that the Musée d'Orsay would elevate the history of architecture to the same revered rung as that of the history of art.

PRACTICALITIES
- Map p248 ● musee-orsay.fr ● adult/concession €16/13 ● 9.30am-6pm Tue-Sun, until 9.45pm Thu

Accordingly, galleries dedicated to the museum's impressive collection of architectural drawings by the likes of Gustave Eiffel and Viollet-le-Duc interject those allocated to fine art.

At the end of the ground floor is a space dedicated to the history of Paris' urban development. Look below you and you'll notice an intricate scaled model of the city as it stood in 1914 when the museum first opened.

The Impressionists

Most people visit the Musée d'Orsay for its collection of Impressionist works and rightly so: the 5th floor of the museum is largely dedicated to the movement. By tracing the galleries in a clockwise direction you'll get a fairly comprehensive overview of the development of the movement from Impressionism to postimpressionism to neo-impressionism. Here is where the movement's masterpieces, such as Monet's *Londres, le Parlement,* Van Gogh's *Starry Night Over the Rhône* and Edgar Degas' sculpture *La Petite Danseuse de Quatorze Ans* are exhibited alongside other fabled modern works like Cézanne's *Nature morte* series.

Cinema as Art

Few people know that from its beginnings the Musée d'Orsay has devoted one of its sections to the history of cinema and cinematography, innovating an approach that considers film as art, and not simply as technique or entertainment. On the 5th floor, tucked away alongside the Impressionist collection, is a gallery tracing the medium's history and technical developments, with projections of short clips from pivotal films. To complement this venture, the Musée d'Orsay often holds screenings in its auditorium of some of the most important works of cinema from the early 20th century. Check the official website for a schedule.

History Through a Contemporary Lens

Although the focus of the Musée d'Orsay is art from the period between 1848 and 1914, several times a year the museum invites the biggest names in today's contemporary art scene, such as Jean-Philippe Delhomme, Marlene Dumas and Peter Doig, to curate exhibitions featuring their own works interwoven with selections from the permanent collection. By placing contemporary art in direct dialogue with historical masterpieces, it urges us to consider the works with a fresh perspective while emphasising their enduring importance. On one Thursday evening per month, the museum also hosts 'Curious Thursdays', when young artists from other creative worlds (like dance and music) are invited to perform among the art. Check the website for schedule details.

THEMED TOURS

It's impossible to view the entire collection in one day – instead it's advisable to pick one or two of the themes mentioned as entry points to discover the collection. Alternatively, take one of the museum's themed guided tours. Held daily in English, French and Italian, the 1½-hour tours are centred around fun themes such as masterpieces, animals and parties. Check the museum's website for departure times.

TOP TIPS

● Book your ticket online in advance so that you can skip the snaking queues to enter.

● The best time to visit is when it opens at 9.30am or on Thursday evenings when the museum is open until 9.45pm.

● Rent an audioguide, which provides commentary from the museum's curators on over 300 works.

● Entry to the museum is free on the first Sunday of every month, but you'll have to reserve a time slot in advance via the museum's website.

● Break up your visit with a pause in the museum's gilded tearoom, which was formerly the railway station's dining room.

THE LADIES' PARADISE

Le Bon Marché was the inspiration for the novel *Au Bonheur des Dames* (The Ladies' Paradise) by French author Émile Zola. Published in 1883, the book detailed the innovations of the department store but also its role in destroying local boutiques, as all goods were now gathered under one roof. But more pertinently for Zola, Le Bon Marché represented a step towards women's emancipation. Over half of the store's workforce were women – unheard of at the time – and unmarried women were provided accommodation in dormitories located in the store, and even classes in singing, art and so on, giving them a sense of independence and the opportunity to work in public-facing roles outside the home or factories.

La Grande Épicerie de Paris

A One-Stop Shop for French Luxury MAP P248
The world's first department store

At the intersection of the ever-chic rue du Bac and rue de Sèvres stands **Le Bon Marché**, an opulent shopping temple whose elegant architecture matches the luxurious mix of both local and international fashion brands housed within. Founded in 1838 by brothers Paul and Justin Videau, it is where shopping was transformed into an *art de vivre*.

In 1852 Le Bon Marché was taken over by marketing maverick Aristide Boucicaut and his wife Marguerite who drastically improved the customer experience with their department store vision. Before rich Parisians would shop in the *passages couverts* (covered passages) to protect them from the city's weather, noise and pollution, while everyone else would go to shops specialised in selling just one thing, and they might not even be allowed to enter to browse around. The Boucicauts introduced a fixed-price system for goods (haggling was still the way of the market at the time) and installed amenities such as a reading room where husbands could wait while their wives shopped. The pair also improved the working conditions of the employees.

Although the eye-watering price tags of the goods for sale are no longer exactly 'a good deal' (the store's name translated into English), to wander Le Bon Marché is to experience the world of historic French luxury – without having to spend a euro. Take the central escalators, which were designed by Andrée Putman with now iconic square panels to mirror the original ceiling above. In fact don't forget to always look up while you're browsing around the designer clothes and beauty brands – Gustave Eiffel designed many of the building's wrought-iron ceilings along with architect Louis-Charles Boileau. The Eiffel-designed ceiling in La Librarie, the store's bookshop, is said to hold more weight in the iron than the capital's most famous metal monolith, the Eiffel Tower. And don't forget to stop in at the bathrooms (complete with an old-school powder room) – the Boucicauts were the first to innovate in-store separate sex bathrooms. Now the store continues to innovate with a regular events program for when the store is both open and closed, with out-of-hours events including dance and acrobatic performances in the beauty area.

If all the browsing at Le Bon Marché has made you peckish, pop next door (or across one of the connecting bridges) to **La Grande Épicerie de Paris**, Le Bon Marché's gourmet food store. You can spend quite a while here just browsing the huge selection of high-quality French produce, luxury food brands, and breads and pastries, which are made fresh on-site each morning. Its basement floor has one of the largest (and most expensive) wine selections in Paris (and top tip, there's also a toilet here, usually without a queue), while the upper levels are home to a restaurant and a selection of homewares. And if you've decided on an impromptu picnic, you can even find things like paper plates and napkins on the ground floor. There are tours of the store if you're interested in learning more about the history and art deco architecture, and with a few tastings along the way.

Literary Libations

MAP P242

Raising a glass to Hemingway

According to the Parisian adage, *'La Rive Gauche, on va pour penser; la Rive Droite, on va pour depenser'*, the Left Bank is where one goes to think, while the Right Bank is for spending money. And think (and drink) on the Left Bank they did – St-Germain is home to some of the most famous dining establishments beloved by the 20th century's greatest writers, artists and philosophers.

Les Deux Magots, located on place St-Germain des Prés, is considered by many to be the birthplace of surrealism, as during the 1930s the likes of André Breton, Man Ray and Max Ernst gathered here to plan out the movement's defining manifesto. Writers James Baldwin and Ernest Hemingway were also regular customers – it is believed that the latter penned his great novel *The Sun Also Rises* at one of the back tables.

SECRET GARDENS

If you need a leafy respite from the buzz of the city then seek out one of St Germain des Prés' gardens.

Jardin Catherine-Labouré (Map p248) This little-known garden is located just a stone's throw from Le Bon Marché on the grounds of a former 17th-century convent.

Square Roger-Stéphane (Map p248) Another green oasis is square Roger-Stéphane, which you can find at the end of the pedestrian street rue Juliette Récamier, off rue de Sèvres.

Square Laurent-Prache (Map p242) It's easy to miss this little square even though it's hidden in plain sight right next to the Benedictine abbey of St-Germain des Prés.

Square Boucicaut (Map p248) This large square behind St-Sulpice metro station is great for kids, or for enjoying an ice cream from the nearby Le Bac à Glaces.

 ERNEST HEMINGWAY'S LOCAL EATING & DRINKING SPOTS —— MAP P242

Café de la Mairie:	La Closerie des Lilas:	Le Select:	Le Pré aux Clercs:
An old-school cafe located on place St-Sulpice, where it's rumoured he began plotting *A Moveable Feast*. 8am-2am Mon-Sat, 9am-midnight Sun	This is where the writer would stop for a drink on his way home. It's also where F Scott Fitzgerald showed him the original *Gatsby* manuscript. noon-2.15pm & 7-10.15pm	The original 1920s interiors make it feel like Hemingway could still be drinking here today. 7am-2am Sun-Thu, 7am-3am Fri & Sat	One of Hemingway's favourite restaurants and mentioned in a few of his works. He was a fan of the Bloody Mary, still on the menu today, 'Hemingway style'. 7am-1am

ÉGLISE ST-GERMAIN DES PRÉS

Before Notre Dame de Paris was completed, the **Église St-Germain des Prés**, (Map p242), located at place St-Germain, was the central church of worship for Parisians. The church in its current form was built in the 11th century, yet it had been the site of a Benedictine abbey since 558. In the 8th century, it was renamed in honour of St Germain, a former bishop of the city. The church has since undergone many transformations, including the addition of the flying buttresses, but the bell tower on the western façade remains practically unchanged since 990. Don't forget to visit the adjoining **Chapelle de St-Symphorien**, left over from the original abbey, under which St-Germanus is believed to be buried.

Across the road, on the corner of bd St-Germain and rue St-Benoit, is rival literary haunt **Café de Flore**. Although creative people were known to flit between each cafe, Flore had one great advantage: a fireplace-heated upper floor where writers came to work during the frosty winter months. It was here that great existentialist philosophers like Simone de Beauvoir, Jean-Paul Sartre and Albert Camus would write their defining oeuvres.

Today, it comes down to personal preference as to whether you take a seat at Les Deux Magots or Café de Flore, but be warned that you might be queuing for a while for one. Ask for a terrace table if you want to people-watch over a coffee or thick *chocolat chaud*, or go in the early evening for an apéritif.

Down the road on rue de Seine is **La Palette**, a lesser-known but equally storied bar that was frequented by artists such as Picasso and Cézanne. Today, its creative vibe lives on as it's the local hang-out spot for students from the nearby fine-arts school L'École des Beaux-Arts (p267).

Although literary folklore would make it seem like artists subsisted entirely on coffee and dry sherry à la Ernest Hemingway, even the most starved of them had to eat at some point – which is why they'd head to **Brasserie Lipp**, conveniently located directly opposite Café de Flore. Lipp was the favourite of French poets Paul Verlaine and Guillaume Apollinaire and while it's still popular with writers today, it also pulls in France's most high-profile politicians. Be sure to reserve as the restaurant is regularly full. It's a beloved spot with locals, who understandably often prefer to be in the restaurant's oldest main room, the one that looks onto the street and which still sports its original 1880 decor. It's also here where you'll find what was Jacques Chirac's favourite table, on the left of the entrance if you are looking into the restaurant, while Hemingway preferred to take his regular order of beer and *pommes à l'huile* (potato salad) at the round table under the staircase.

BEST PATISSERIES

MAPS P242, P248

Des Gâteaux et du Pain: Sublime desserts, buttery croissants, freshly baked breads, Claire Damon has it all at her second fabulous address. *10am-7.30pm Mon & Wed-Sat, 10am-6pm Sun* €€	**Mori Yoshida:** Some of the prettiest (and most delicious) desserts can be found at Mori Yoshida. Try Le Beige, his signature creation, or contemporary twists on French classics. *11am-7pm Wed-Sun* €€	**Arnaud Larher:** Fantastic desserts from Meilleur Ouvrier de France (Best Craftsman of France) Arnaud Larher, as well as chocolates, macarons and more. *11am-7pm Tue-Sat* €€	**Philipe Conticini:** The Gran Cru Vanille is the signature but it's hard to go wrong here. There's also giant (Instagrammable) croissants if that's your thing. *10am-7pm Tue-Sat, 10am-2pm Sun* €€
La Pâtisserie Cyril Lignac: French celebrity chef Cyril Lignac is now also well known for his delicious patisserie. *7am-7pm Mon, 7am-8pm Tue-Sun* €	**Ritz Paris Le Comptoir:** A taste of the Ritz Paris is through François Perret's wonderful desserts and his signature madeleines, now also available at the hotel's new Left Bank pastry shop. *9am-8pm* €€	**Noglu:** A gluten-free patisserie which also serves gluten-free breakfast and lunch. There are two locations in this area to choose from. *hours vary* €	**Café Pierre Hermé:** Pastry chef king Pierre Hermé has four spots in the neighbourhood. Look out for the cafe if you want to sit in. *hours vary* €

Café de Flore

A LEFT BANK PALACE

The **Hôtel Lutetia** (Map p248) is proudly the only palace hotel on the Left Bank, 'palace' being the prestigious status awarded to certain French hotels that deserve even more than five stars. When it opened in 1910 during Paris' Belle Époque it was to offer Le Bon Marché's well-heeled clients a suitably elegant place to stay after they arrived in town for a shopping spree. It later became a hot spot for the city's creatives; Ernest Hemingway and James Joyce drank in the bar, and it was Joséphine Baker's preferred hotel when she was in Paris. Charles de Gaulle even spent his wedding night here in 1921. Today you might spot French actors such as Marion Cotillard and Isabelle Huppert, as the hotel is a popular hangout for the neighbourhood's celebrities, and Bar Joséphine (p266; named after Baker) and Brasserie Lutetia are great spots for people-watching.

Finish off your literary tour with an after-dinner drink at **L'Hôtel**, the hotel on rue des Beaux-Arts where Oscar Wilde died in 1900 of meningitis. Wilde had made what was then known as L'Hotel d'Alsace his home and famously declared in his final days, 'My wallpaper and I are fighting a duel to the death. One of us has got to go.' Although the building – and its wallpaper – have since been given a luxurious renovation, the bar of the now five-star hotel remains open for guests wishing to pay homage to the illustrious writer.

The Oldest Restaurant in Paris?

MAP P248

Who lays claim to the title?

There are a handful of restaurants in Paris that lay claim to being the oldest in the city, and it's still undecided which one actually wins. Most people you ask would say La Tour d'Argent (p234), understandable given that it's one of the most high-profile restaurants in Paris, thanks to a Michelin star and one of the city's best views. But also on the Left Bank is another contender, **La Petite Chaise**, which actually makes the claim on its website (whereas La Tour d'Argent does not). The restaurant was founded in 1680 by wine merchant Georges Rameau, who had the novel idea of serving food to accompany his wines for sale. La Tour d'Argent is actually much older, but when it opened in 1582 it was as an inn, not a restaurant,

LA FONTAINE MÉDICIS

In the Luxembourg Garden's eastern wing is the spectacular **Fontaine Médicis** (Map p242), named after Marie de' Medici, who commissioned the grotto in homage to her home country, Italy. Today, it barely resembles its original design, yet reads as a pastiche of the different political movements that have governed Paris.

After Napoléon I added a marble statue of Venus, Baron Haussmann attempted to dismantle the fountain altogether in 1858. It was saved by architect Alphonse de Gisors, who moved the fountain 30m from its original location and added sculptures he'd salvaged during the city's replanning. Behind the grotto, he placed the Fountain of Léda, saved from rue de Vaugirard, and replaced Napoléon's Venus with three sculptures by Auguste Ottin.

Jardin du Luxembourg

which might be how À la Petite Chaise gets away with proudly proclaiming itself the winner. Similarly, **Le Procope**, founded in 1686, lays claim to the title of the oldest cafe in Paris, not restaurant, although it hasn't been in continuous operation. By the 18th century, it had become the hot spot of the intellectual elite, with the likes of Voltaire, Benjamin Franklin and Thomas Jefferson all dining here. Local legend also has it that Denis Diderot and Jean le Rond d'Alembert began writing the French encyclopaedia *(Encyclopédie)* at Le Procope over endless cups of black coffee.

St-Germain's Green Lung   MAP P242
Family fun in regal gardens

Surrounding the majestic Palais du Luxembourg, the **Jardin du Luxembourg** was the former residence of Marie de' Medici, and is beloved by children and adults alike. Construction of the garden began in 1612, with its terrain expanding across the centuries until it reached its current size in 1865. Today, the palace houses the French Senate, and the gardens are its official property.

The focal point of the garden is the *grand bassin* (central pond) around which iconic Fermob garden chairs are scattered – the perfect place to enjoy a picnic, read a book or simply rest weary legs. In the spring and summer months, the pond springs to life as toy sailing boats are raced across its waters.

Although some people bring their own boats, Les Voilieurs, the pond's official toy-boat club, has a selection available for rent.

If toy boating is not your thing – or it's simply not the right day or season for it – the garden has plenty of other activities for visitors of all ages, from *pétanque* courts to chess tables (although you'll have to bring your own balls or chess set). There's also an orchard, a greenhouse and an apiary to explore – with honey from the garden's bees sold at the end of September during the annual Fête du Miel. During spring and summer, the grassy lawns are open for visitors to picnic on, before being closed for rejuvenation during the winter months.

The garden is especially a verdant wonderland for young children, complete with a playground, sand pit and pony rides. It's also home to Paris' oldest merry-go-round, designed by Charles Garnier (the architect of the Palais Garnier), and is topped with an ancient ring-tilting game: children are equipped with a wooden stick and attempt to snatch rings off the operator as they go around the merry-go-round. To play the game is a rite of passage for many a Parisian kid.

As the opening hours of the garden vary depending on the time of year, be sure to check the official website.

An Artistic Oasis

MAP P242

Sculptor Zadkine's home and atelier

Tucked away on rue d'Assas is the little-known **Musée Zadkine** *(zadkine.paris.fr; admission free, except during temporary exhibition periods),* housed in the former home and atelier of Russian-born sculptor Ossip Zadkine. The museum contains some 300 works by the artist, from his monolithic sculptures carved in stone, wood and bronze to more delicate lithographs and photographs. Although you probably won't need more than 45 minutes to visit the entire collection, set aside extra time to rest weary museum legs in the bucolic garden.

BASILIQUE STE-CLOTILDE

Located on rue Las Cases in the 7th *arrondissement,* the **Basilique Ste-Clotilde** (Map p242), constructed between 1846 and 1856, was the first Parisian church built in the neogothic style. While the western façade is arresting in its grandeur – the twin spires each reach a soaring height of 70m – don't forget to visit the apse: its supporting iron structure was designed by Paris' favourite engineer Gustave Eiffel.

 **BEST SPOTS FOR AN APÉRO** ──────── MAP P242

Le Rouquet: Pop by for a coffee or drink (skip the food) to take in the original retro 1950s decor, which is often used in fashion campaigns for the likes of YSL. *8am-9pm Mon-Sat*	**Freddy's:** Fantastic wine list and sharing plates. Enjoy a drink and a nibble or make a whole dinner out of it. Arrive early to get a table. *12.30pm-midnight*	**L'Avant Comptoir de la Terre/L'Avant Comptoir de la Mer:** These tiny side-by-side addresses (la Terre focuses on meat, la Mer on fish) serve small sharing dishes. *noon-11pm*	**Augustin Marchand d'Vins:** Speciality wine store with a large selection of organic and natural wines. The low-lit setting makes it a good spot for more intimate evenings. *5-10pm Wed-Sun*
Bar Etna: A buzzy and cosy *bar à vin* serving natural wines and small plates. *5pm-2am Tue-Sat*	**Le Rooftop:** The seasonal rooftop bar on top of the design-led Hôtel Dame des Arts makes a great spot for a summer drink with an Eiffel Tower view. *summer only, from 4pm*	**La Crèmerie:** Very cute wine bar (you can't miss the original façade) that fills with locals. Great cheese and charcuterie boards. *6.30-10.30pm*	**La Grande Crèmerie:** Lively and friendly wine bar and restaurant where you can hang by the bar for just a drink or book a table for dinner. *5.30pm-midnight*

EAT YOUR WAY THROUGH RUE CLER

The pedestrian-only rue Cler is perhaps the most famous market street in Paris. It's open all day Tuesday through Saturday, as well as Sunday mornings – plan on spending half a day discovering the street's gastronomical goodies.

START	END	LENGTH
Petitbon	Le Chocolat Alain Ducasse	650m; one hour

As it's never a good idea to shop on an empty stomach, begin at ① **Petitbon** for sandwiches and the best coffee in the neighbourhood. Before continuing down rue Cler, take a slight detour west along rue du Champ de Mars to stock up on cheese from local legend ② **Fromager Marie-Anne Cantin** (p263).

Trace your steps back to rue Cler and continue north along the street. As no French meal can begin without an apéritif, stop at ③ **Davoli** for nibbles. Yes, it is an Italian *épicerie* but it sells the finest charcuterie on the street. Alternatively, order a glass of wine at ④ **Café du Marché** or ⑤ **Café Central**, which have the biggest terraces for people-watching. If oysters are in season stop by ⑥ **La Sablaise**, located just two doors down the street from Davoli, where the staff will happily prepare a platter to go. Pop across the road to ⑦ **Le Repaire de Bacchus** and pick up a bottle of Petit Chablis to wash the oysters down with.

For foodie souvenirs head to ⑧ **Kaviari** for caviar, and ⑨ **Mariage Frères** for some of Paris' best teas, packaged up in its signature beautiful black canisters. Saving the best until last, finish up at ⑩ **Le Chocolat Alain Ducasse**, the chocolate shop from the giant of French gastronomy, Alain Ducasse.

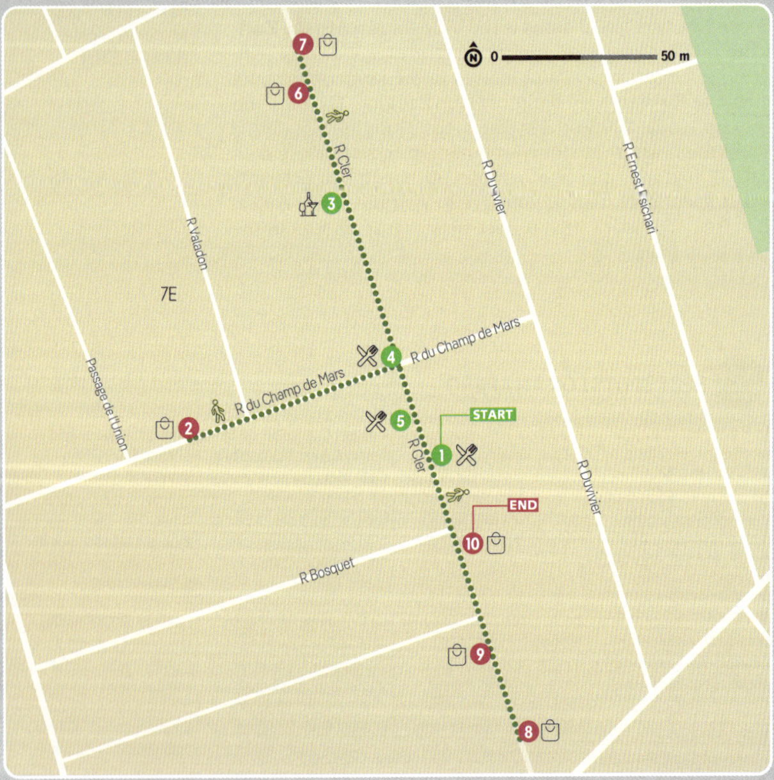

Learn the History of Money at the Monnaie de Paris

MAP P242

Paris' oldest institution

The **Monnaie de Paris** *(monnaiedeparis.fr; adult/concession €12/8)*, or Paris Mint, was the first factory in Paris when it was inaugurated in 1775, and more than 250 years later, it's now the last. Although the majority of France's coins have been minted in a new factory in Pessac, Bordeaux, since 1972, celebration and collectors' coins are still made here, as were the Olympic medals. However, the building's main purpose now is to house a permanent museum showcasing coins and minting through the ages. Even if you think a minting museum isn't for you, there's quite a lot to see here, including the oldest coin in the world, gold coins and bullion recovered from shipwrecks, and on Fridays, dramatic demonstrations of someone pouring liquid molten metal into a cast. It's also a good museum to visit if you're travelling with kids, as there's a program of children's activities (and ones for adults too, such as engraving and enamelling) and in the largest room you'll find interactive screens and hands-on activities to keep them engaged. For travellers with accessibility needs, the museum has lifts, Braille on the staircases, and even smells and noises from the minting workshop to help enhance the experience. If you're really interested in the exhibition, then allow two hours to get around it all. Like a lot of museums in Paris, the evenings with late openings (which is Wednesday here) are a good time to visit. Also look out for an open-air cinema and concerts in the courtyard in summer, and temporary exhibitions on contemporary artists, which are held in the building's beautiful gilded historic rooms overlooking the Seine.

Serge Gainsbourg's Legacy Lives On

MAP P242

Paris' most personal 'museum'

Until recently, the heavily graffitied former abode of French singer Serge Gainsbourg, located at 5bis rue de Verneil, had never been open to the public – despite being a site of pilgrimage for the singer's massive fan base.

Now, **Maison Gainsbourg** *(maisongainsbourg.fr; adult/concession €12/6, house and museum from €16)* has been opened to the public by his daughter Charlotte Gainsbourg, who has personally narrated the 30-minute audioguide to give visitors an intimate and rather poignant glimpse into his private life and her childhood. After you've finished your tour of the house, you head across the street to the museum, which showcases 450 personal objects across eight chapters of Gainsbourg's life and musical career. It's all in French, so make sure to pick up the English-language booklet that accompanies it at the entrance. There's also a cafe and cocktail bar (named Le Gainsbarre) as an homage to the late-night venues the singer was so fond of, and it's free to pop by for a drink even if you're not visiting the house or museum. Bear

FRANCE'S OLDEST BUSINESS

The Monnaie de Paris is impressively the oldest enterprise in France after being created in 864 by King Charles II. It's been in continuous operation ever since, although not always in the same majestic building that you see now. When King Louis XV realised that the 14th-century workshop on rue de la Monnaie was no longer up to scratch for minting royal coins, he decided to commission a bigger and better building on the other side of the Seine. Designed in the fashionable neoclassical style, the mint was finished in 1775, unfortunately for Louis XV, the year after he died. At this time, minting coins was serious business and forgers were boiled alive until the French Revolution came along. When it did, the building was surprisingly left untouched: even the revolutionists understood and respected how important coins were for daily life.

A TEMPLE OF TAXIDERMY

Founded in 1888 by the eponymous family, the **Deyrolle** (Map p248) taxidermy store located on rue du Bac is more than just stuffed dead animals – to step inside is to travel back in time to the heyday of old-school explorers, adventurers and curiosity cabinets. If the idea of hunting and taxidermy makes you queasy, note that the store has been curated with education in mind – informing visitors about the wonders of our natural world, the scientific systems that make sense of it all, and what we can do now to save it.

in mind that as the house is small, and to keep the personal feel of the visit, only a few people are allowed in at a time, meaning that tickets sell out well in advance. If you don't manage to get any, you can still book for just the museum so you don't miss out completely.

Parisian Waterworks

MAP P248

The Paris below our feet

As Victor Hugo put it, 'Paris has beneath it another Paris; a Paris of sewers; which has its streets, its crossroads, its squares, its blind alleys, its arteries, and its circulation, which is of mire and minus the human form'. This is kind of what you can see at the **Musée des Égouts de Paris** *(Paris Sewer Museum; musee-egouts.paris.fr; adult/concession €9/7)*, or at least a tiny section of it, and without the mire. It was after a cholera epidemic in 1832 that the city got serious about creating a modern sewer network to provide inhabitants with clean water, and when the sewers were opened up for visits during the 1867 Paris Exposition, the curious public headed down in their droves to see a part of Paris that had previously been closed off. The museum takes you through this chapter of the city's history, as well as how water is cleaned today, and has set out the street signs and galleries to mimic what's above; as Hugo said, the sewers really do have their own streets and avenues in the same layout as the ones above. I admittedly didn't find the museum quite as fascinating as Paris' other underground world, the catacombs, but if you've visited nearly every other Paris museum, or if you like more offbeat ones, or if you're travelling with kids, then it might be more for you. All signs are in French, so make sure to get the audioguide and look for any additional information online. If you're worried about being claustrophobic, you can see daylight at a couple of spots on the tour, and there's wi-fi to keep you connected to the world above.

BEST CHOCOLATE SHOPS

MAPS P242, P248

Jacques Genin: Jacques Genin makes some of the silkiest, smoothest chocolates in Paris. His caramels and *pâtes de fruits* might also be the best in the city. *10.30am-7pm Tue-Sat €€*

Chapon: There are a few Chapon addresses across Paris but try to find the ones with a Bar à Mousse aux Chocolats to take away a cone of absolutely delicious, thick chocolate mousse. *hours vary €*

Jean-Paul Hévin: Fabulous chocolate desserts as well as chocolate boxes. Pick up a box of the excellent macarons too. *10am-7.30pm Tue-Sat €*

Patrick Roger: Minimalist interiors show off the minimalist chocolates, which highlight the purity of the high-quality ingredients. There are three locations in the 6e. *hours vary €€*

Debauve & Gallais: The oldest chocolate shop in Paris, which has made chocolates for the likes of Marie Antoinette (Les Pistoles), Napoléon and Marcel Proust. *9.30am-7pm Mon-Fri, 10.30am-7.30pm Sat €€*

Le Chocolat Alain Ducasse: Famed French chef Alain Ducasse, whose restaurants have numerous Michelin stars, has many chocolate shops across Paris specialising in rich and delicious praline. *hours vary €*

Alléno & Rivoire: Young chocolatier Aurélien Rivoire has teamed up with chef Yannick Alléno to create a range of chocolates with low glycaemic birch sugar to enhance the fruit flavours. *hours vary €*

Plaq: A contemporary chocolate shop loved by some of Paris' top chefs and restaurants. *11am-7.30pm Mon-Fri, 10am-7.30pm Sat, 10am-6.30pm Sun €*

La Balle au Bond

Péniche Party

MAP P248

Apéritifs to float your boat

Where the 6th and 7th *arrondissements* meet the Seine are several *péniches* – houseboats docked permanently along the riverbanks. Some are still private homes, while others have been converted into restaurants, bars and clubs – they're a great way to experience the city's most famous waterway.

Rosa Bonheur sur Seine is the most popular *péniche*, known for its club nights and live music (with everything from salsa to jazz). Be sure to check out its official Facebook page for a complete schedule. Tickets are required for certain events and often sell out in advance. Drinks and food can be purchased on board and enjoyed on the nearby riverside benches.

If you want a more ambient apéritif, then **La Balle au Bond** (Map p242) will be your pick of the *péniches*. The plant-lined rooftop terrace makes the perfect place to relax, drink in hand, while watching the sunset over the Seine. It's open daily for apéritifs and dinner, and on Saturdays and Sundays for brunch.

If you're ready to dance the night away, head to **Le Flow**, a *péniche* with views of the glorious Pont Alexandre III. It regularly hosts live DJ sets on its rooftop and stays open until the early hours on Saturdays and Sundays.

THE ROYAL HISTORY OF CHOCOLATE

St-Germain des Prés is one of the best neighbourhoods for picking up boxes of delicious French chocolates but we've partly got Marie Antoinette, or rather her pharmacist, to thank for it. In 1779 when Sulpice Debauve was appointed Louis XVI and Marie Antoinette's pharmacist, the Versailles court had already adopted a chocolate habit. At the time chocolate was always drunk, not eaten, but when Marie Antoinette began to complain about the bitterness of her migraine medicine, Debauve had the idea to sweeten the remedy with cacao and almond milk and presented the Queen with the first solid chocolate. These round chocolate medallions, which were shaped like ancient coins, instantly won royal approval and Marie Antoinette's *pistoles*, as she called them, can still be found in the at Debauve & Gallais today.

THE REAL ROSE LINE

A note inside the Église St-Sulpice asserts that, contrary to Dan Brown's claims in *The Da Vinci Code*, the line running through the church 'was never called the Rose Line'.

The real Rose Line is known as the Paris Meridian, which, from 1678 to 1884, was the prime meridian on all international maps – until the International Meridian Convention, when it was universally agreed upon that the Royal Observatory in Greenwich, England, would be the reference for zero-degree longitude. France refused, however, to adhere to Greenwich Mean Time, implementing its own system called Paris Time. But during WWI the country found it hard to coordinate internationally on war strategies so in 1911 it officially adopted GMT.

Napoleon's tomb (p264), Musée de L'Armée

Majestic Masterpieces in St-Sulpice   MAP P242
Divine Delacroix and pious Pigalle

Despite being just 1 sq metre smaller than Notre Dame de Paris, the **Église St-Sulpice** has long lived in its shadow – until Dan Brown's *The Da Vinci Code* drew crowds to the monumental Roman Catholic church in search of the hidden treasures detailed in his epic novel.

Construction of the current church began in 1042, but it passed through the hands of several different architects – which accounts for its unique mishmash of baroque and neo-classical references – until work was halted entirely by the French Revolution. In fact, the right tower on the church's western façade (designed by Italian architect Servandoni, who drew inspiration from London's St Paul's Cathedral) remains unfinished to this day.

But what's so special about Église St-Sulpice is the artworks contained within. Immediately to your right after entering, in the Chapel of the Holy Angels, are three well-preserved wax murals painted by French artist Eugène Delacroix between 1855 and 1861. Also look out for the peculiar pair of

BEST BAKERIES

There's indoor seating here — MAPS P242, P248

Maison Bergeron: Consistently voted as having one of the top 10 croissants by the Greater Paris Bakers' Union. *7am-8.15pm Mon-Sun* €

Poilâne: Perhaps France's most famous *boulangerie*, it's known for its sourdough *miches* (round country loaf), *punitions* (cookies) and apple tarts. *7.15am-8pm Mon-Sat* €

Boulangerie Liberté: Chic, new-wave *boulangerie* with buttery croissants made on-site. Locations around Paris. *7.30am-8pm Mon-Sat, 8.30am-5pm Sun* €

Tapisserie: Delicious seasonal creations from the team behind seafood restaurant Clamato and Septime. *8.30am-7pm Wed-Fri, 9.30am-9pm Sat, 9.30am-5pm Sun* €

holy water fonts, located on either side of the nave, and the giant clam shells, which were gifted to King Francis I by the Venetian Republic, that sit atop stone bases hand-carved with sea motifs by Jean-Baptiste Pigalle. The white marble statue of Mary, located at the far end of the church, was also sculpted by the prolific artist.

Throughout the year, classical-music recitals are held at the church, with tickets available online from L'Officiel des Spectacles or directly on-site before each performance.

A Cabinet of Military Curiosities

MAP P248

Les Invalides and Musée de L'Armée

At the end of the sprawling Esplanade des Invalides stands the **Hôtel des Invalides**, the hospital commissioned by Louis XIV for wounded soldiers (partially in operation today) and from which some 32,000 weapons were pillaged by revolutionaries before the storming of the Bastille prison on 14 July 1789.

Today, the *hôtel* also houses various museums, the main one being **Musée de L'Armée** *(musee-armee.fr; adult/concession/under 26 years €17/12/free)*, France's national military museum. With over 500,000 artefacts, it boasts the third-largest collection of weapons and armour in the world. Don't be deterred from visiting if warfare and military paraphernalia are not your thing – the 8000-sq-metre complex is more of a gigantesque cabinet of curiosities with something to pique everyone's interest.

The museum is divided into various sections including French Classical Cannons, Ancient Armour and Arms (13th–17th centuries), From Louis XIV to Napoléon III (1643–1870), the Two World Wars (1871–1990), Charles de Gaulle Historical Centre, the Cathedral of St-Louis des Invalides, and special exhibition rooms (the museum hosts several temporary exhibitions, often centred around contemporary art, several times a year). It's impossible to cover the entire museum in one day – you're better off concentrating on a single section or simply wandering aimlessly, pausing at whatever grabs your attention.

Among the curiosities to be stumbled across within the museum are a taxidermy of Napoléon's last horse, Vizir (check out the Napoléonic branding on the horse's haunches), Jean Auguste Dominique Ingres' famous painting *Emperor Napoléon on his Throne*, a model of Mont-St-Michel made from playing cards by a monk in the 17th century, and ancient keys to the city of Milan from the late 1700s.

UNDER THE GOLDEN DOME

Although Napoléon I died in exile on the island of St-Helena in 1821, King Louis Philippe I ordered the repatriation of his remains to Paris in 1840, as per the emperor's wishes. His lavish tomb took more than 20 years to complete, during which Napoléon's remains were laid at the nearby Chapelle de St-Jerome, due to the difficulties in importing the speciality stone used. The actual sarcophagus, located in Musée de l'Armée is made from Russian purple quartzite, the green granite base was sourced from Vosges, and the black marble bottom is from Sainte-Luce, Martinique. Surrounding the 6m-deep open crypt are 12 statues representing Victory; on the mosaic floor are tiled the names of the battles Napoléon fought in, with his insignia also laid into the marble floors.

 **BEST CHEESEMONGERS** ——————————————————— MAP P248

Fromagerie Quatrehomme: You'll spot cheeses from this family-run *fromagerie* on some of Paris' most prestigious menus. *9am-7.45pm Tue-Sat*

Marie-Anne Cantin: The best *fromagerie* in the 7e, and where French rocker Johnny Halliday used to buy his cheese. Desserts to take away. *8.30am-7.30pm Tue-Sat, 10am-1pm Sun*

Androuet: One of Paris' best-known cheesemongers, which has been family-owned since 1909. *4-7.30pm Mon, 9.30am-1pm & 4-7.30pm Tue-Sat*

Fromagerie Barthélémy: The Left Bank's most famous cheese shop, with a huge selection of both popular and rare cheeses. *8.30am-7.30pm Tue-Sat*

THE HUMBLEST OF FRENCH DISHES

L'oeuf-mayonnaise, which is simply a hard-boiled egg halved and topped with mayonnaise, has long been the emblematic dish of the French bistro – popular dining institutions that were historically the canteen of the working-class population.

For one of the best in town, head to **Le Voltaire** (Map p242) a former bistro turned upscale eatery on the quai Voltaire (many a French politician is known to lunch here). Miraculously, the price of the *oeuf-mayo* hasn't changed since 1956: it's still only €0.90. Head here early in the evening, before service swings into full action, and the staff might let you get away with ordering just an *oeuf-mayo* and a glass of wine.

Under the arresting golden **Dôme des Invalides** lie the remains of France's Emperor Napoléon I. Entrance to the tomb is included in the ticket to the Musée de L'Armée, as is entrance to the smaller Museum of the Order of the Liberation and Museum of Relief Maps. The Cathedral of St-Louis des Invalides is open to the public and always free.

A Sculpture Garden for Thinking MAP P248
A day at the Musée Rodin

In the heart of the 7th *arrondissement* is one of Paris' most serene museums, the **Musée Rodin** (*musee-rodin.fr; €15*), dedicated to the prolific oeuvre of French sculptor Auguste Rodin. The museum is housed within the 19th-century Hôtel Biron, a former aristocratic mansion where Rodin had two showrooms and which was chosen by the sculptor himself to become a museum after his death. It now contains some 6000 sculptures and 8000 drawings by Rodin (though not all are

BEST SWEET TREATS   MAPS P242, P248

| **Angiolo:** Ultra creamy gelato made fresh in the boutique's own laboratory. *10am-10pm Mon-Fri, 10am-11pm Sat & Sun* € | **Mademoiselle Angelina:** Skip the desserts (there are better patisseries) and go straight for Angelina's famed hot chocolate. *10am-6.30pm* € | **Aux Merveilleux de Fred:** This Lille-born patisserie specialises in *merveilleux*, a meringue-based dessert usually topped with cream and chocolate shavings. *7.30am-8pm* € | **Le Bac à Glaces:** Family-owned ice cream since 1955; you can eat in or take away to enjoy in the nearby square Boucicaut. *10.30am-7.30pm Mon-Sat, from 11.30am Sun* € |

Musée Rodin

on display!), including 30 of Rodin's most iconic artworks, plus a room dedicated to sculptor Camille Claudel, who was at various points also Rodin's collaborator, muse and lover.

Rodin is considered by many an art historian to be the founder of modern sculpture, known for his unparalleled talent to translate the complexities of human emotion into meticulously sculpted clay, bronze and plaster works. Among his most famous sculptures are *The Thinker, The Kiss* and *The Gates of Hell* – all of which are on show at the museum. But what makes this museum so special is its tranquil sculpture garden, which is used to present some of Rodin's works. Although it's a beautiful space all year-round, and it's interesting to see how the sculptures catch the light in different seasons, the months of April and May are particularly lovely when the garden's Rodin roses – of course named after the sculptor – are in full bloom. There's also a cafe with an outdoor terrace, which is a particularly lovely spot to stop for a coffee and enjoy the gardens. Also look out for two temporary exhibitions a year, one of which, Atelier Rodin, is designed for children aged six months to 10 years in mind to learn about sculpture in a fun, hands-on way.

The Musée Rodin is open from Tuesday, a particularly busy day after being closed on Monday, through to Sunday. An entry ticket provides you with access to both the museum and the garden and guided tours are also available, but only in French.

BEST HOMEWARE SHOPS

Cire Trudon
(Map p242) Once the official candlemaker for the royal courts; the rue de Seine shopfront was founded in 1643.

Marin Montagut
(Map p242) Beautiful hand-painted porcelain and other decorative objects created by the French illustrator Marin Montagut.

La Soufflerie
(Map p242) Hand-blown artisanal glassware: 100% of proceeds benefit the glassmakers to help keep the dying art alive.

Astier de Villatte
(Map p242) Artisanal ceramics crafted in the store's own Paris workshop, as well as a small selection of stationery, perfumes, candles and homeware.

L'Atelier 55
(Map p242) Vintage shop specialising in mid-century and designer furniture (Gio Ponti, Charles Eames, and so on) as well as easier to pack lamps, ceramics and posters.

BEST SPECIALITY ALCOHOL SHOPS

La Maison du Whisky Odéon

(Map p242) Whiskies from around the world, as well as a 1st floor dedicated to rum and a corner showcasing around 50 different sakés.

Ryst Dupeyron

(Map p248) In the family for five generations, Ryst Dupeyron specialises in Armagnac, the oldest French brandy. The vintage bottles make great gifts.

Dilettantes Cave à Champagne

(Map p242) A female-run wine store specialising in small-producer Champagnes. Contact them to book masterclasses and tastings in English.

Chartreuse Paris-Vauvert

(Map p242) The Paris store of the famous Chartreuse drink offers tours, tastings and cocktail-making sessions.

La Dernière Goutte

(Map p242) A neighbourhood favourite that has been going for more than 20 years, this wine shop specialises in estate-bottled wines and offers tastings and classes in English.

Ryst Dupeyron

A Bibliophile's Paradise

MAP P242

Nooks and nooks of books

Given the famous literary names that once made St-Germain their font of inspiration, it's of little surprise that today the neighbourhood is the publishing heartland of French literature and home to some of the capital's most interesting bookshops.

Paris' most storied English-speaking bookstore, Shakespeare & Company (p231), originally set up shop at 12 rue de l'Odeon, where owner Sylvia Beach famously edited and published James Joyce's chef-d'oeuvre *Ulysses* in 1922. The store relocated to the 5th *arrondissement* following its closing

BEST COCKTAIL BARS

MAPS P242, P248

Cravan: The big sister to the original Cravan in the 16th. Expect cool design and excellent cocktails and as a bonus, you can even book. *5pm-1am Tue-Fri, noon-1am Sat*

Castor Club: Look out for an unnamed wood-panelled door to find this hunting lodge–inspired bar, where drinks are served to a soundtrack of country music. *7pm-2am Tue & Wed, 7pm-4am Thu-Sat*

Bar Joséphine: Once frequented by the likes of Picasso and Joséphine Baker, this palace hotel bar serves up excellent cocktails and draws a local (sometimes celebrity) crowd. *5pm-1am*

Le Bar: Chef Cyril Lignac is better known for his restaurants but his intimate and sexy cocktail bar (not to be confused with restaurant Bar des Prés) is a great spot for starting the evening. *7pm-1am Wed-Sat*

during the WWII occupation (Beach refused to sell a copy of Joyce's *Finnegans Wake* to a Nazi officer) but the neighbourhood is still home to many of Paris' notable bookshops. The **Red Wheelbarrow** sits just by the Jardin de Luxembourg and hosts regular author talks and signings. It also has a children's bookshop next door, The Red Balloon. Another bookshop for kids is **Chantelivre**, which has a children's section at the back with a small collection of books in English. It's also home to **La Maison des Histoires**, an interactive book museum for kids to play and attend story times. On rue Monsieur Le Prince, **San Francisco Book Company** is a labyrinth of secondhand books, complete with ladders so you can sail the shelves in hunt of beloved titles.

If you're looking for cool coffee-table books try the French brand **Assouline**, which has two Left Bank addresses, including one in Le Bon Marché, or head to the Philippe Starck–designed **Taschen** boutique, which has hosted events and book signings for some of the biggest names in photography, fashion, art and more. **Librairie Rizzoli** bookstore, or rather as the name implies library, can be found on the 2nd floor of the cocktail bar Cravan. You can browse books on design, fashion, film, music and more over a drink or purchase them to take home. And lastly there's the **7L Bookshop**, founded by Karl Lagerfeld, which is dedicated to all creative arts ranging from photography to gardening.

Paris' Most Prestigious Art School MAP P242
See an exhibition at the École des Beaux-Arts

Located on rue Bonaparte is Paris' **École des Beaux-Arts** (School of Fine Arts), the most competitive fine-arts school in the country. Since its inception in 1648, many of the greatest names in art history have passed through its doors: Degas, Delacroix, Renoir, Moreau and John Singer Sargent, just to name a few.

Although the school is closed to the public (you're not free to simply wander inside), it does host public exhibitions and artists' talks from both local and international talent. Check the school's website for a full schedule of events – it's an opportunity to peer inside one of the bastions of French culture.

ANTIQUE HUNTING

Marin Montagut (@marinmontagut), illustrator, designer and author, describes his favourite spots in St-Germain des Prés.

Galerie Stéphane Olivier

(Map p242) In his showroom in the heart of St-Germain des Prés, Olivier exhibits a mix of Scandinavian furniture from the 1950s to the '70s and works by contemporary designers. I love immersing myself in his timeless selection, which echoes nature and inspires harmony and poetry.

Yvelines Antiques

(Map p242) Located on the most charming square in Paris, this antiques boutique is run by Agathe Derieux, who took over from her grandmother in 2013 and continues Yveline's passion for articulated workshop mannequins. A fairy-tale setting.

Librairie François Chanut

(Map p242) This antiquarian bookshop is the most charming in Paris. Behind the converted butcher's shop, the shelves are overflowing with old volumes, precious manuscripts and rare editions reserved for the lucky few.

Researched by Jean-Bernard Carillet

MONTPARNASSE & SOUTHERN PARIS

UNDERRATED, ECLECTIC AND FULL OF SURPRISES

Unpretentious yet seductive, gritty yet full of good vibes, southern Paris is a happy mix of typical village-like areas, edgy street art, vast parks and striking architecture.

If you're in search of a Paris that few visitors take time to explore, southern Paris will appeal to you. You can start with fabled Montparnasse and its iconic brasseries before delving into the huge 15th *arrondissement*. This is a very tranquil part of Paris, with lots of greenified areas, wonderful local parks and atmospheric squares. In the 14th *arrondissement,* you'll find yet-to-be-discovered micro-neighbourhoods and great picnic-friendly parks. And then, to the east, there's the fast-evolving 13th, with Paris' largest Chinatown, pocket-sized districts that scream village life, some striking street art and even more stunning contemporary architecture, including the fabulous Duo Towers – a recent landmark in the city. Who said southern Paris was boring?

TOP TIP

The three *arrondissements* – 13e, 14e and 15e – are huge and the distance between Bibliothèque Nationale de France and Parc André Citroën is significant – about 9km. Allow sufficient time by public transport if you want to make the most of the area. Use the metro (line 6) to get from one *arrondissement* to the next.

La Butte aux Cailles (p273)

See p313 for places to stay in Montparnasse and southern Paris.

Highlights

❶ La Butte aux Cailles
Explore this yet-to-be-discovered neighbourhood with a rural feel off place d'Italie. **p273**

❷ Paris Rive Gauche
Share the buzz, energy and zeal for innovation in this fast-evolving district in the 13th. **p279**

❸ Manufacture des Gobelins
Visit this cultural institution, which has specialised in tapestries since the 18th century. **p279**

❹ Chinatown
Certainly not the largest Chinatown in Europe, but possibly the most atmospheric. **p276**

❺ Tour Montparnasse
For sweeping views of Paris (and the Eiffel Tower), climb to the top of this iconic building. **p282**

Getting Around

Metro
Use line 6 to get from one *arrondissement* to the next. Montparnasse Bienvenüe is the metro hub for Montparnasse and the 15e. Bibliothèque François-Mitterrand and Place d'Italie are convenient 13e stops.

Bus
Buses fill the gap in areas lacking metro coverage. Bus 62 travels from Bibliothèque François-Mitterrand to Javel via the southern *quartiers*. Bus 39 links Balard with Gare du Nord via Gare Montparnasse.

Bicycle
Handy Vélib' Métropole stations include 5–7 rue d'Odessa, 14e; 13 bd Edgar Quinet, 14e; 2 av René Coty, 14e; and two facing place d'Italie, 13e.

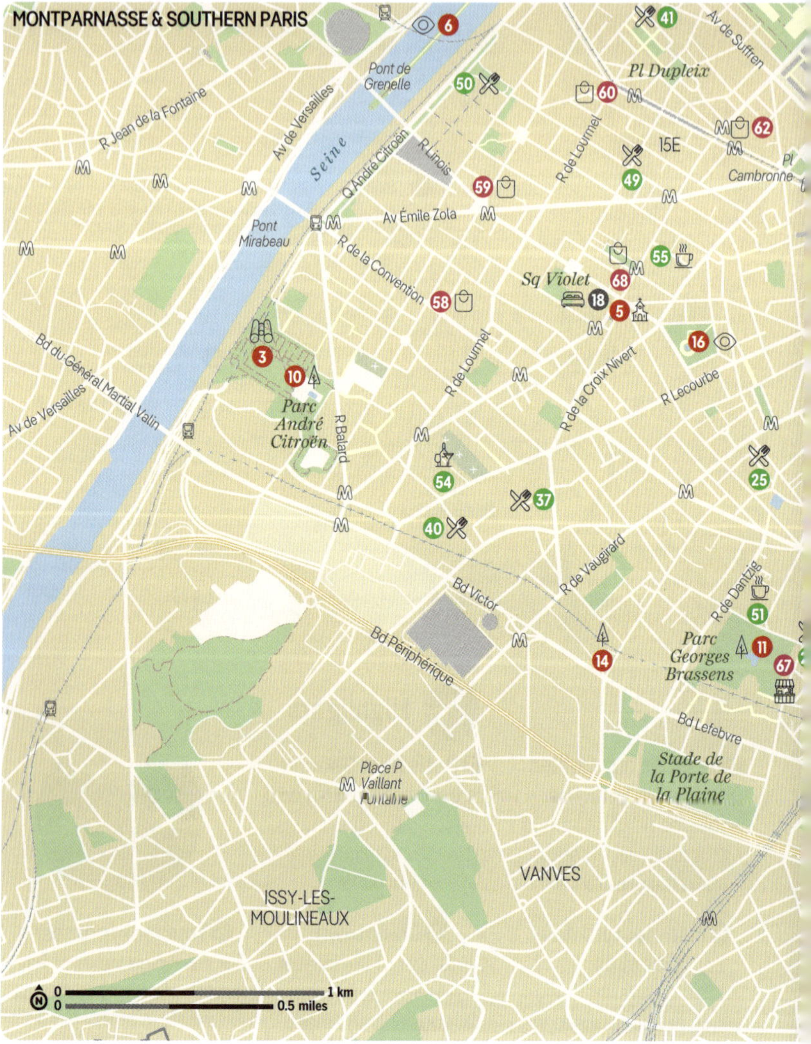

MONTPARNASSE & SOUTHERN PARIS

★ HIGHLIGHTS
1. Cimetière du Montparnasse
2. Les Catacombes

● SIGHTS
3. Ballon de Paris
4. Cité Universitaire
5. Église St-Jean Baptiste de Grenelle
6. Île aux Cygnes
7. Institut Giacometti
8. Jardin de l'Atlantique
9. Musée Bourdelle
10. Parc André Citroën
11. Parc Georges Brassens
12. Parc Montsouris
13. Petite Ceinture du 14e
14. Petite Ceinture du 15e
15. Rue Daguerre
16. Square St-Lambert
17. Tour Montparnasse

● SLEEPING
18. 3 Ducks Hostel
19. Hôtel Léopold
20. Hôtel Max
21. Hôtel Vic Eiffel
22. La Maison Lavaud
23. Villa M

● EATING
24. A Mi-Chemin
25. Bélisaire
26. Chez Walczak
27. Des Gâteaux et du Pain
28. Glazed
29. Habesha
30. Icosium
31. La Cantine du Troquet Pernety
32. La Closerie des Lilas
33. La Coupole
34. La Petite Alsacienne
35. La Rotonde
36. La Verrière
37. L'Accolade

38	Land & Monkeys Pernety	48	MoSuke	56	Poinçon	62	Le Village Suisse
39	L'Assiette	49	Panade	see 23	Villa M	63	Marché aux Puces de la Porte de Vanves
40	Le Beurre Noisette	50	Polichinelle	●	**SHOPPING**	64	Marché Biologique Brancusi
41	Le Cassenoix	see 9	Rhodia	57	Atomes		
42	Le Dôme	●	**DRINKING & NIGHTLIFE**	58	Au Cochon Rose	65	Marché de la Création
43	Les Fauves			59	Aux Vins Vivants	66	Marché Edgar Quinet
44	Les Pépites	51	Arthur & Juliette	60	Fromagerie Laurent Dubois	67	Marché Georges Brassens
45	Lokita	52	Food Society				
46	L'Opportun	53	Hexagone Café	see 34	Hazar & Co	68	Scoop Me a Cookie
47	Maison Binder	54	Les Jajas de Juju	61	Il Etait Une Fois Dix Doigts		
		55	Onoul Coffee Shop				

TOP EXPERIENCE

Les Catacombes

Paris' most spine-prickling sight are these skull- and bone-lined underground tunnels in old limestone quarries. Les Catacombes is one of the largest ossuaries in the world. Sure, it is gruesome, ghoulish and downright spooky, but it remains one of Paris' most visited sights. All in all, it's an incredible experience.

TOP TIPS

● Note that the Catacombes are not wheelchair accessible.

● Bring sturdy shoes and a light jacket; don't carry large bags or backpacks.

● Book your ticket online to save time and hassle – it guarantees a timeslot.

PRACTICALITIES
● Map p270
● catacombes.paris.fr
● adult/child €31/12
● 9.45am-7.15pm Tue-Sun

History

In 1785 subterranean tunnels of an abandoned quarry were upcycled as storage rooms for the exhumed bones of corpses that could no longer fit in the city's overcrowded cemeteries. By 1810 the skull- and bone-lined catacombs – resting place of millions of anonymous Parisians – had been officially born.

A Timeless Journey

The route through Les Catacombes begins at its spacious entrance on av du Colonel Henri Rol-Tanguy. Walk down 131 spiral steps to reach the ossuary itself, with a mind-boggling number of bones and skulls of millions of Parisians neatly packed along the walls. *'Arrête, c'est ici l'empire de la mort'* ('Stop, Here is the Empire of Death') – this inscription at the entrance to the ossuary inspires fear and respect. But there's much more than skulls and bones. The site is also of great interest from a geological, philosophical, architectural and archaeological perspective. Visits cover about 1.5km of tunnels in all, at a cool 14°C. The exit is up 112 steps via a minimalist all-white 'transition space' with gift shop at 21bis av René Coty, 14e.

People with claustrophobia may experience some anxiety in the confined environment.

Feel the Pulse of La Butte Aux Cailles

MAP P274

A mix of village life and urban vibes

Much less touristy and congested than other Parisian villages such as Montmartre or Mouffetard, **La Butte aux Cailles** extends on a gently sloping hill immediately west of place d'Italie. Wandering its cobblestoned streets bordered by low-rise buildings, you'll feel teleported to another era in rural France. Its main thoroughfare is rue de la Butte aux Cailles, lined with numerous laid-back bars, shops and restaurants, but all the adjacent streets are well worth a gander, as is the super-relaxing Parc Brassaï. A few jewel streets to stroll include passage Boiton, rue des Cinq Diamants, rue Samson, rue Alphand, passage Sigaud, passage Barrault and rue Michal, as well as the adorable rue Daviel with the Petite Alsace (Little Alsace) enclave, complete with brick and timbered houses, and Villa Daviel, which is lined with superb houses and gardens. Plan half a day to explore the area.

And there's the superb **Piscine de la Butte aux Cailles** (paris.fr/lieux/piscine-de-la-butte-aux-cailles-2927; €3.50). Built in 1924, this art deco swimming complex – a historical monument – has a spectacular vaulted indoor pool and, since 2017, Paris' only Nordic pool. In the depths of winter, we Parisians of the 13th head here to swim 25m laps in a five-lane outdoor pool, heated to a toasty 27°C.

Stroll Around the Cité Florale

MAP P274

A bucolic atmosphere deep in the 13e

A 10-minute walk south of place d'Italie lies the **Cité Florale**. This micro-neighbourhood is a gem to wander. Built in the 1920s, the Floral City included five streets that were all named after flowers (Iris, Wisteria, Bindweed, Orchid, Volubilis). They are paved and flanked by small houses whose façades are covered with ivy, vines and flowers, which adds to the serene atmosphere. A superb place to explore early in the morning when everything seems to stand still. From here, you can walk east to the leafy place de l'Abbé Georges Hénocque and its adjacent streets, including rue des Peupliers and rue Dieulafoy, lined with lovely traditional houses, some of which are made of *pierre meulières* (gritstones).

WHY I LOVE SOUTHERN PARIS

Jean-Bernard Carillet, Lonely Planet writer

Originally from Metz (Lorraine), I came to Paris as a student to complete a master's degree at La Sorbonne. I was happy to live at the Cité Universitaire de Paris in the 14e and, since then, I've called southern Paris home. I love the serenity, discretion and peacefulness of southern Paris and its numerous little gems, especially La Butte aux Cailles and its village-y atmosphere, but I also like the modern vibes and bold architecture in Paris Rive Gauche, near Bibliothèque Nationale de France – see you in TOO Tac Tac Sky Bar, one of my favourite drinking spots. In the 14e, I love hanging around Pernety, which feels so Parisian (and is totally untouristy).

 BISTRO FARE IN THE 13E: OUR PICKS ———— MAP P274

La Butte aux Piafs: Hearty bistro fare and a congenial atmosphere. Near La Butte aux Cailles. *noon-2pm & 7-10pm* €	Simone Le Resto: Terrace tables at a vibrant neobistro where inventive menus are created from high-quality products. *noon-2pm & 7-10pm Mon-Fri, 7-10pm Sat* €€	Comme Promis: Seasonal ingredients are used to prepare dishes both classic and contemporary at this gem of a bistro. *hours vary* €€	Marso & Co: This modern bistro has gorgeous fish and meat dishes, and the banana cake is a dessert delight. *noon-2pm & 7.15-10pm Mon-Fri* €€

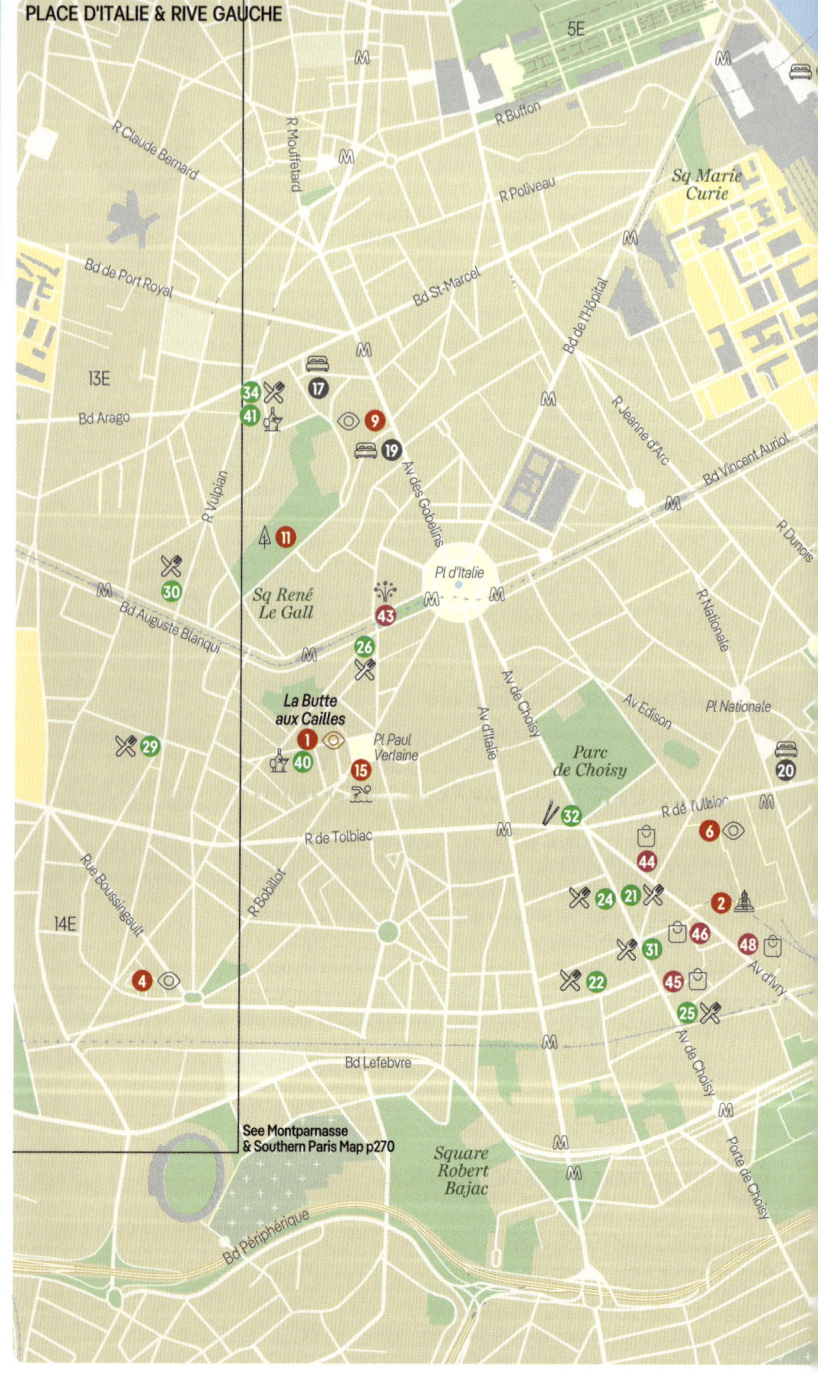

★ HIGHLIGHTS
1. La Butte aux Cailles

● SIGHTS
2. Autel du Culte de Bouddha
3. Bibliothèque Nationale de France
4. Cité Florale
5. Institut Français de la Mode
6. La Dalle des Olympiades
7. La Danse de la Fontaine Émergente
8. La Fab
9. Manufacture des Gobelins
10. Passerelle Simone de Beauvoir
11. Square René Le Gall
12. Station F
13. Tours Duo
14. Wood Up

● ACTIVITIES
15. Piscine de la Butte aux Cailles
16. Piscine Joséphine Baker

● SLEEPING
17. Hôtel Henriette
18. Off Paris Seine
19. Oops
see 13 TOO Hotel
20. Urban Bivouac Hotel

● EATING
21. Basilic & Spice
22. Bep Viet
23. Comme Promis
24. Fu Pâtisserie
25. Impérial Choisy
26. La Butte aux Piafs
27. La Felicità
28. Lao Viet
29. Laurent Duchêne
30. Marso & Co
31. Pâtisserie de Choisy
32. Pho Bành Cúon 14
33. Season Square
34. Simone Le Resto
see 13 TOO Restaurant

● DRINKING & NIGHTLIFE
35. Bateau El Alamein
36. Café Cayo
37. Café Oz Rooftop
38. Djoon Club
39. La Dame de Canton
40. Le Merle Moqueur
41. Simone La Cave
see 13 TOO Tac Tac Sky Bar

● ENTERTAINMENT
42. MK2 Bibliothèque
43. RICE – Le Marché Treiz'Asiatique

● SHOPPING
44. Aux Merveilles d'Asie
45. Exo Store
46. Kim Than
47. Little Jeanne
48. Tang Frères

THE GUIDE

MONTPARNASSE & SOUTHERN PARIS

CHINESE NEW YEAR IN THE 13E

If you happen to be here in late January or February, don't miss Chinese New Year (also known as Spring Festival). With about 2000 participants and more than 200,000 spectators, it's one of the most spectacular events in the city. Celebrations typically last about two weeks and feature colourful parades as well as lion and dragon dances. Expect brightly lit red lanterns, firecrackers and performances by ribbon dancers, drummers, cymbal players and acrobats wearing traditional costumes. There are also cultural events, including theatre, concerts, conferences and chess contests, as well as sporting events. It kicks off in front of Tang Frères supermarket (p278) on av d'Ivry. For exact dates, check mairie13.paris.fr/culture.

Autel du Culte de Bouddha

Asian Accents

MAP P274

Immerse yourself in Chinatown

Southeast of place d'Italie and near rue de Tolbiac is Paris' largest Chinatown. Don't let the massive tower blocks dating from the 1960s deter you from exploring this district. It's a fascinating piece of Southeast Asia, with plenty of surprises, including culinary delights, colourful festivals and art. It's easy to spend an afternoon in this neighbourhood.

If you're a fan of underground cultures, head to **La Dalle des Olympiades**, off rue de Tolbiac. This vast concrete esplanade with platformed pedestrian zones surrounded by towers has become the focal point for local K-Pop dancers and skateboarders. Near the Seine, on rue Paul Klee, **La Danse de la Fontaine Émergente** ('Dance of the Emerging Fountain') is a large fountain built of stainless steel, plastic and glass, designed by French Chinese sculptor Chen Zhen. Completed in 2008, it looks like a giant stylised dragon winding its way across the square, emerging and submerging from the concrete pavement. High-pressure water flows inside the sculpture. The most unusual sacred site in Paris must be the **Autel du Culte de Bouddha** (37 rue du Disque) – this small

BISTRO FARE IN THE 14E

MAP P270

L'Assiette: Chef David Rathgeber, from Auvergne, focuses on age-old traditional French dishes. Superb decor, too. *noon-2pm & 7-10pm Wed-Sun* €€

L'Opportun: This *'bistrot de copains'* (friends' bistro) near Montparnasse serves excellent French classics in cosy surrounds. *noon-2.30pm & 7-10pm Mon-Sat* €€

La Cantine du Troquet Pernety: At this jovial bistro, expect dishes made with regional products sourced from small-time producers. *noon-2.30pm & 7-10.30pm Tue-Sat* €€

A Mi-Chemin: Be it a Tunisian couscous or lamb from Auvergne, this 'fusion bistro' serves it to astonishing effect. *noon-3pm & 7-11pm Wed-Sat* €€

EXPLORE A GIANT ART SCENE

Over 30 monumental murals enliven the streets in an area between av de France, rue de Tolbiac and bd Vincent Auriol, with more added every year.

START	END	LENGTH
Chevaleret metro station	13 rue Lahire	1.6km; one hour

Start from the 1 **Chevaleret metro station**. Nearby you can enjoy the poignant 2 **Embrace and Fight** (85 bd Vincent Auriol), by Conor Harrington, *La Madone* (81 bd Vincent Auriol), a masterpiece created by famous artist Inti, and *Les Oiseaux* (The Birds; 91 bd Vincent Auriol), by Pantonio.

Continue west along bd Vincent Auriol and you'll see the monochromatic 3 **Le Visage** (The Face; 6 rue Jenner), also by Pantonio, on your right. Then the stunning 4 **Rise Above Level** (cnr bd Vincent Auriol and rue Jeanne d'Arc) comes into view, a massive mural by Shepard Fairey. On the opposite side of bd Vincent Auriol, don't miss the awesome 5 **Dancer** (98 bd Vincent Auriol), by the collective Faile.

Other great works to look for further west include 6 **Le Chat** (cnr bd Vincent Auriol and rue Nationale), the monumental *La Marianne* (186 rue Nationale) by Shepard Fairey, which represents the symbol of the French Republic, and the strikingly expressive *Turncoat* (190 rue Nationale), by D*Face (who is from London).

Be awed by the elaborate 7 **Sun Daze** (167 bd Vincent Auriol), created by the talented twins How and Nosm, and, on an adjacent building, a splendid portrait of a geisha-like woman (169 bd Vincent Auriol), by British artist Hush.

Further south, marvel at 8 **Bach** (57 rue Clisson) and the nearby 9 **colourful fresco** (13 rue Lahire) by Inti.

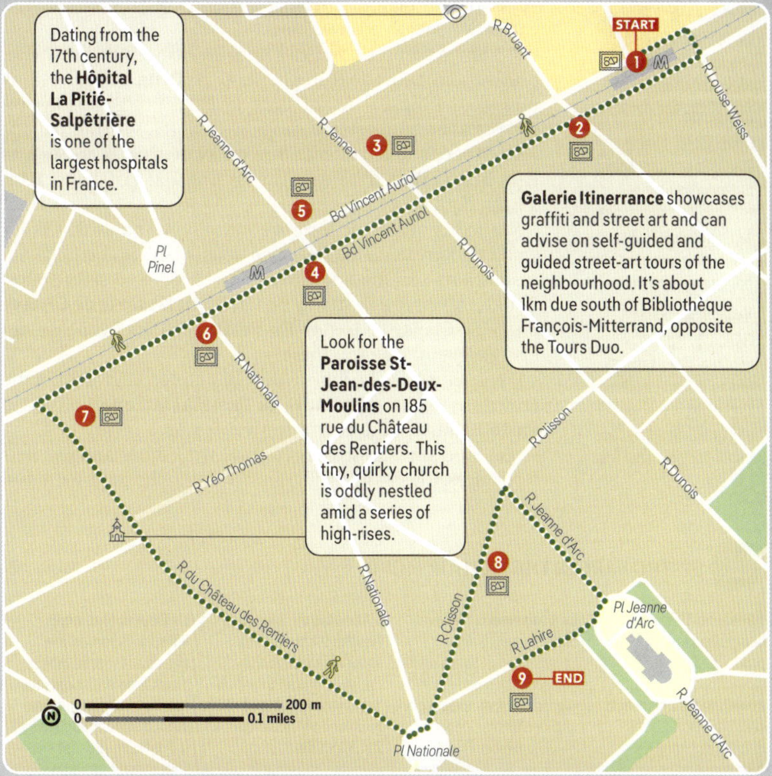
Dating from the 17th century, the **Hôpital La Pitié-Salpêtrière** is one of the largest hospitals in France.
Galerie Itinerrance showcases graffiti and street art and can advise on self-guided and guided street-art tours of the neighbourhood. It's about 1km due south of Bibliothèque François-Mitterrand, opposite the Tours Duo.
Look for the **Paroisse St-Jean-des-Deux-Moulins** on 185 rue du Château des Rentiers. This tiny, quirky church is oddly nestled amid a series of high-rises.
START
END
R Bruant
R Louise Weiss
R Jenner
R Jeanne d'Arc
Bd Vincent Auriol
Bd Vincent Auriol
R Dunois
Pl Pinel
R Nationale
R Yéo Thomas
R Clisson
R Dunois
R Jeanne d'Arc
Pl Jeanne d'Arc
R Lahire
R du Château des Rentiers
R Nationale
R Clisson
Pl Nationale
R Jeanne d'Arc
0 200 m
0 0.1 miles

Manufacture des Gobelins

BEST PANORAMAS IN SOUTHERN PARIS

TOO Tac Tac Sky Bar (Map p274) Take a lift to the bar (p287) on the 27th floor of this luxury hotel and be wowed by the sensational views of southern Paris.

Tour Montparnasse (Map p270) Enjoy one of the finest bird's-eye views of Paris from the indoor observatory of this iconic skyscraper (p282).

Café Oz Rooftop (Map p274) The rooftop bar of the Institut Français de la Mode (p281) in the 13e affords lovely views of the Seine.

Ballon de Paris (Map p270) In the 15e, this helium-filled balloon remains tethered to the ground as it lifts you 150m into the air for spectacular panoramas over Paris.

Villa M (Map p270) The rooftop bar of this elegant hotel in the 15e affords top views of Montparnasse, Les Invalides and the Tour Eiffel.

yet colourful Buddhist temple is hidden in an underground car park beneath a tower block.

For any Asian food you can imagine, as well as many decorative and household items, shop at **Tang Frères** (48 av d'Ivry), the biggest Asian store in Paris (and possibly Europe). Other atmospheric shops well worth visiting include **Exo Store**, a department store on av de Choisy, as well as **Aux Merveilles d'Asie** (great for unusual gifts) and **Kim Than**, both on av d'Ivry.

Nestled beneath the towers on av d'Ivry and av de Choisy you'll find great Vietnamese *pho* noodle bars and family-run restaurants serving homemade dumplings and spicy soups. If, like us, you're a pastry lover, fall for **Pâtisserie de Choisy** on av de Choisy or trendy **Fu Pâtisserie** (its brunches are also excellent). See you there!

If you happen to be here in September, consider joining the crowds at **RICE – Le Marché Treiz'Asiatique** on bd Auguste Blanqui. This recent festival features plenty of Asian street food stalls as well as cultural workshops and live performances. Check the Instagram @ricemarche.paris for dates.

BISTRO FARE IN THE 15E: OUR PICKS — MAP P270

Bélisaire: This elegant neobistro serves up a produce- and season-driven menu that puts a modern riff on French staples. *noon-2pm & 8-9.30pm Mon-Fri* €€

Le Cassenoix: Owner-chef Pierre Olivier Lenormand delivers dishes incorporating top-quality ingredients, including pork and beef. *noon-1.45pm & 7-9.30pm Mon-Fri* €€

L'Accolade: Neighbourhood eatery famous for its creative, modern French 'bistronomie' – bistro-style gastronomy. *noon-2pm & 7-9.30pm* €€

Le Beurre Noisette: Filled with locals, the chocolate-toned dining room here is wonderfully convivial. Great fish and meat dishes. *noon-1.45pm & 7-9.45pm Tue-Sat* €€

Travel Back in Time at the Manufacture des Gobelins

MAP P274

Meet highly skilled craftspeople

Off place d'Italie in the 13e, don't miss the **Manufacture des Gobelins** *(mobiliernational.culture.gouv.fr; 90-minute guided tour adult/child €17.50/9.90)*. It's a prestigious yet relatively unknown (even by Parisians) French institution. *Haute lice* (high warp) tapestries have been woven on specialised looms here since the 18th century, along with Beauvais-style *basse lice* (low warp) tapestries and Savonnerie rugs. Superb examples of carpets and tapestries woven here are showcased in its gallery. Note that the Manufacture des Gobelins is not a tacky museum but an actual workplace. Guided tours (in French) of the workshops are conducted on Wednesdays (book online) – it's a great opportunity to learn about an ancestral savoir-faire. There's no shop selling tapestries as all works are for official use only.

Aquatic Wonders

MAP P274

Take a dip in unique swimming pools

Floating on the Seine, the striking **Piscine Joséphine Baker** *(piscine-baker.fr; adult/child €3.50/2)* is named after the 1920s American singer. The 25m by 10m, four-lane pool and large sun deck are especially popular in summer when the roof slides back. In July and August, plus weekends from late May to September, admission is limited to two hours.

If you want to please the kids, consider the **Aquaboulevard** *(aquaboulevard.fr; adult/child €39/22)*, just outside the *Périphérique* (ring road) in the 15e. It's a huge tropical 'beach' and aquatic park with water slides, waterfalls and wave pools.

Explore Paris Rive Gauche

MAP P274

Paris' most innovative district

Paris' largest urban redevelopment since Haussmann's 19th-century reformation continues apace in the 13e *arrondissement*. Plan at least three hours to get a feel for the area.

Centred on a once-nondescript area south of the Latin Quarter spiralling out from the big busy traffic hub of place d'Italie, the renaissance of the area known as Paris Rive Gauche was heralded in the 1990s by the controversial **Bibliothèque Nationale de France** and the arrival of the high-speed metro

BEST PLACES TO PARTY IN SOUTHERN PARIS

Bateau El Alamein
(Map p274) This deep-purple boat has a Seine-side terrace for sitting amid tulips and enjoying live bands. Also has a bar.

La Dame de Canton
(Map p274) Floating *boîte* (club) aboard a Chinese junk hosting pop and indie to electro, hip-hop, reggae and rock. Skip the food.

Djoon Club
(Map p274) Glass-and-steel bar and loft club that's a stylish weekend venue for soul, funk, deep house, garage and disco.

Food Society
(Map p270) This huge food court near Montparnasse is also noted for its DJ sets and themed soirées (evenings) featuring salsa and kizomba.

 HISTORICAL BRASSERIES IN MONTPARNASSE: OUR PICKS —— MAP P270

| **La Closerie des Lilas:** Brass plaques tell you exactly where luminaries stood, sat or fell at the 'Lilac Enclosure' (opened 1847). *noon-2.15pm & 7-10.15pm* €€ | **Le Dôme:** A 1930s art deco extravaganza, monumental Le Dôme is famous for its shellfish platters. *noon-2.45pm & 7-10.30pm* €€ | **La Rotonde:** Around since 1911, elegant La Rotonde is renowned for its superior food. *7.30am-midnight* €€ | **La Coupole:** Opened in 1927, famous for its mural-covered columns, dark wood panelling and soft lighting. Great seafood. *8am-midnight Tue-Sat, to 11pm Sun & Mon* €€ |

THE HEART & SOUL OF THE 14E

South of Montparnasse, the 14e has lots of hidden corners and off-the-beaten-track areas that are well worth exploring on foot for their laid-back and bohemian atmosphere.

START	END	LENGTH
Rue Daguerre	Jardin François Héritier	3.2km; 2½ hours

Begin on lively ❶ **rue Daguerre** (p283), which is chock-a-block with restaurants, groceries and delis. Head southeast to ❷ **square Ferdinand Brunot** and the adjacent square de l'Aspirant Dunant. Both are playing grounds for kids living nearby when the sun is out. Walk east to ❸ **rue Hallé**. At No 12, there's a lovely half-moon-shaped square flanked with houses reminiscent of a French provincial town. Back on av du Général Leclerc, walk south and turn right onto passage Rimbaut, a narrow lane that leads to av du Maine. Take rue du Moulin Vert and turn onto ❹ **impasse du Moulin Vert**, flanked with houses whose façades are covered with ivy and vines – you couldn't wish for a more picturesque street.

It's a five-minute stroll westwards to ❺ **place Flora Tristan**, a bijou *placette* (small square) with pavement terraces. Continue south to ❻ **rue des Thermopyles**, arguably the most photogenic street south of the Seine. With its small houses equipped with colourful shutters, flowery gardens and serene ambience, this paved street that screams rural France is a gem to wander. You'll then emerge on busy ❼ **rue Raymond Losserand**, which has plenty of eateries, bakeries, bars and shops. Walk north and turn right onto allée du Château Ouvrier, which ushers in ❽ **jardin François Héritier**, an intimate garden where you can picnic.

line 14. With four glass towers shaped like half-open books, the National Library of France, opened in 1995, was one of President Mitterrand's most ambitious and costliest projects.

These initial developments were followed, among other additions, by the **MK2** entertainment complex on av de France, the Piscine Joséphine Baker (p279) swimming pool and Off Paris Seine (p313) hotel – both afloat the Seine – and the **Passerelle Simone de Beauvoir** (2006), providing a cycle and pedestrian link to the Right Bank.

Other institutions to have moved in include the **Institut Français de la Mode** (the French fashion institute) in the stylised former warehouse Les Docks. Framed by a lurid-lime wavelike glass façade, it mounts fashion and design exhibitions and events throughout the year. Other draws include huge riverside terraces, the odd pop-up shop and a popular rooftop bar (p278).

The area's mainline train station, **Gare d'Austerlitz**, is undergoing a massive makeover by celebrated French architect Jean Nouvel. The station itself will be overhauled, and new shops, cafes and green spaces will open up in the surrounding streets. The renovation is due to wrap up in late 2027.

Another iconic rehabilitation is **Station F** *(stationf.co)*, the world's largest start-up campus, where 1000 entrepreneurs from all over the globe dream up groundbreaking new projects and businesses. Each Wednesday or Thursday at 11.30am, guided tours in English take visitors on a 45-minute (free) waltz through the gargantuan hangar – a railway depot built in 1927–29 to house trains from Gare d'Austerlitz (book online). Spaces open to the public include the enormous Italian restaurant **La Felicità** *(lafelicita.fr),* with five different kitchens, three bars and a twinset of original, graffiti-covered train wagons.

And then there's the futuristic, iconic **Tours Duo**, which were completed in 2021. Both were designed by Jean Nouvel. Their inclined shape has changed the Parisian skyline, and they have become a landmark in southern Paris. Duo 1 and Duo 2 are 180m and 122m high respectively. Duo 1 is the third-tallest building in Paris, after the Eiffel Tower and Tour Montparnasse. Duo 2 features TOO (p313), a luxury hotel designed by Philippe Starck. Inaugurated in 2022, it ranges across 10 floors and comes with a gastronomic restaurant and a fantastic skybar. Further east, look for the 50m-high **Wood Up** tower. Inaugurated in late 2024, it's the tallest wood building in Europe.

SOUTHERN PARIS' BEST MARKETS

Marché aux Puces de la Porte de Vanves (Map p270) This flea market has over 380 stalls. Expect lots of 'curios', clothes, shoes, handbags and household items. Saturdays and Sundays, 14e.

Marché Biologique Brancusi (Map p270) This open-air market has a huge selection of *biologique* (organic) and locally sourced produce. Saturdays, 14e.

Marché de la Création (Map p270) Expect stalls overflowing with handmade arts and crafts. Sundays, 14e.

Marché Edgar Quinet (Map p270) This lively open-air street market has irresistible cheeses, as well as stalls sizzling up snacks to eat on the run. Wednesdays and Saturdays, 14e.

Marché Georges Brassens (Map p270) Our favourite is this enormous secondhand book market in the 15e, that takes place on Saturdays and Sundays. It's a great place to soak up local life.

TEMPTING PÂTISSERIES IN SOUTHERN PARIS — MAPS P270, P274

La Petite Alsacienne: In the 14e, this venture has to-die-for tartelettes, éclairs and croissants, as well as exquisite bretzels. *7am-8pm Mon-Sat* €

Land & Monkeys Pernety: In the heart of the 14e, this pastry shop has an awesome array of organic and vegan treats. *7am-7.30pm Wed-Mon* €

Laurent Duchêne: Prize-winning croissants are the speciality of this lauded bakery in the 13e. Plenty of other goodies, too, including macarons. *7.30am-8pm Mon-Sat* €€

Des Gâteaux et du Pain: This ultra-contemporary venue sells cakes, tarts and artisan breads. *9am-7.30pm Mon & Wed-Sat, to 6pm Sun* €€

WHERE TO PICNIC LIKE A PARISIAN

Marie-Louise Orlach (@marielouiseorlach), a Parisian jeweller who works in the 14e, shares her favourite places for a picnic.

Cité Universitaire (Map p270) This campus is also a large, quiet and leafy park open to the public – a great place to break for a picnic.

Île aux Cygnes (Map p270) This is a first-rate picnic destination on the banks of the Seine, with Eiffel Tower and Statue of Liberty views.

Square St-Lambert (Map p270) Another picnic heaven in the heart of the 15e. Stock up on goodies on rue du Commerce.

Square René Le Gall (Map p274) In the 13e, this is a fabulous green escape (and a secret spot) off place d'Italie. Find picnic treats on nearby rue des Gobelins.

Artistic Treasures
MAP P274

Visit an offbeat gallery

Art enthusiasts, make a beeline for **La Fab** *(la-fab.com; adult/child €7/4)*. This gallery, which occupies a striking building by SOA Architects in the 13e, was opened by French fashion designer and art collector agnès in 2020. Her 5000-plus strong collection of contemporary works is presented in themed exhibitions on the ground floor that change every three to four months. On the 1st floor, the 'galerie du jour' is styled like a home where everything, from the art to the furniture, is for sale.

Take in the Views at Tour Montparnasse
MAP P270

Iconic building and mesmerising views

Spectacular views unfold from **Tour Montparnasse** *(tour montparnasse56.com; from €18.50)*, a 210m-high, smoked-glass-and-steel office block built in 1973. A speedy elevator whisks visitors up in 38 seconds to the indoor **observatory** on the 56th floor, with multimedia displays. Finish with a hike up the stairs to the 59th-floor open-air terrace (with a sheltered walkway). Our tip: book online to avoid queues and buy a *billet jour et nuit* (night and day ticket) that allows you to visit twice – thus you can savour the views early in the morning and at sunset when the light is at its finest.

Get Away from It All at Cimetière du Montparnasse
MAP P270

Visit the final resting place of local luminaries

Opened in 1824, the 19-hectare **Cimetière du Montparnasse** is Paris' second-largest cemetery after Père Lachaise. Lesser known than Père Lachaise, it makes for a pleasant, romantic stroll along shady avenues, especially in spring and summer, when trees and flowers are in full blossom, with Tour Montparnasse looming in the background.

Famous residents include writer Guy de Maupassant, playwright Samuel Beckett, sculptor Constantin Brancusi, photographer Man Ray, legendary singer Serge Gainsbourg, and philosopher-writers Jean-Paul Sartre and Simone de Beauvoir.

Choose a calm, sunny day, ideally early in the morning, to explore its winding lanes. Allow at least one hour to soak up the atmosphere. If you want to pinpoint a few graves that

VEGETARIAN SPOTS IN SOUTHERN PARIS: OUR PICKS
MAPS P270, P274

Season Square: Homemade soups, burgers and bowls bursting with seasonal veggies are the order of the day here. *noon-2.30pm Mon-Sat* €

Bep Viet: The first 100% vegetarian Vietnamese restaurant in Paris, with excellent spring rolls. *11.30am-3pm & 6.30-10.30pm Mon-Fri, 9.30am-11pm Sat & Sun* €

Maison Binder: A creative spot, this easy-going place serves up excellent seasonal, organic fare. *noon-2pm & 7-10pm Tue-Sat, noon-2pm Sun & Mon* €

Polichinelle: Offers a tasty *cuisine légumière* (veggie cuisine). Don't miss the lavish buffet lunch. *noon-2.30pm & 7.30-10pm Mon-Sat, 11.30am-3pm Sun* €€

View from Tour Montparnasse

you'd like to visit, consult the map (and QR code) just past the entrance on bd Edgar Quinet.

Ramble Down Rue Daguerre
MAP P270
Enjoy an authentic slice of Parisian life

Paris' traditional village atmosphere thrives along **rue Daguerre**, 14e. Tucked just southwest of the Denfert Rochereau metro and RER stations, this narrow street – pedestrianised between av du Général-Leclerc and rue Boulard – is lined with florists, *fromageries* (cheese shops), *boulangeries* (bakeries), patisseries, greengrocers, delis (including Greek, Asian and Italian) and classic cafes where you can watch the local goings on. Shops set up market stalls on the pavement; Sunday mornings are especially lively. It's a great option for lunch before or after visiting Les Catacombes, or packing a picnic to take to one of the area's parks or squares.

Wander Parc Montsouris
MAP P270
A bit of fresh air

This sprawling lakeside park planted with horse-chestnut, yew, cedar, weeping beech and buttonwood trees is a delightful picnic spot and has endearing playground areas. With an

BEST PLACES TO SHOP IN SOUTHERN PARIS

Atomes
(Map p270) This concept store sells homewares, apparel, jewellery, bags and other accessories – all made by Parisian designers.

Le Village Suisse
(Map p270) Paintings, ceramics, engravings, furniture, sculptures, lights and more in a 'village' in a courtyard complex.

Hazar & Co
(Map p270) Lovely first concept store in the 14e with apparel, accessories, jewellery and homewares rarely found elsewhere.

Il Etait Une Fois Dix Doigts
(Map p270) This is a lovely creative space, where you can relax, have a drink or a snack, and shop for handmade gifts.

Little Jeanne
(Map p274) A great family store, with handmade dolls, toys, clothing, candles, lamps and decorative objects.

 ASIAN RESTAURANTS IN THE 13E: OUR PICKS — MAP P274

Pho Bành Cúon 14: This buzzy restaurant is wildly popular with in-the-know locals for its super-fresh *pho* (soup). *11.30am-10pm Wed-Mon* €

Impérial Choisy: Renowned for its Cantonese cuisine and its top-quality Peking duck. *noon-11pm* €

Lao Viet: This unpretentious eatery serves up some of the 13e's best Vietnamese and Laotian cuisine in a cosy interior. *noon-2.30pm & 6.30-10.30pm Wed-Mon* €

Basilic & Spice: This highly praised venue serves Khmer and Thai dishes such as *pad kra pao* (chicken with basil and fried egg). *noon-2.30pm & 7-10.30pm Tue-Sun* €€

GREENEST SPOTS IN SOUTHERN PARIS

Parc André Citroën
(Map p270) Its central lawn is flanked by greenhouses, dancing fountains and smaller gardens themed around movement and the (six) senses.

Parc Georges Brassens
(Map p270) Has a pond bordered by lawns and gardens featuring roses and medicinal and aromatic plants. The sloping hill is home to a wine-producing vineyard and an apiary.

Jardin de l'Atlantique
(Map p270) This hidden gem carpets the roof of the Gare Montparnasse.

Île aux Cygnes
(Map p270) For a leisurely stroll (and knockout Eiffel Tower views), nothing beats Paris' little-known third island. At the western tip is a soaring one-quarter-scale Statue of Liberty replica.

Parc Montsouris (p283)

RER station at the entrance of the park, it's an easy place to get to. In summer, you can easily spend a couple of hours here to decompress (bring a picnic).

After a visit to Parc Montsouris, I love to wander the neighbouring 1920s-built **Cité Universitaire** (student halls of residence), south of the park, which is another soothing spot, as well as rue Georges Braque, impasse Nansouty and rue du Parc de Montsouris, immediately to the west – with their paved roads and stately, ivy-clad houses, they offer a real sense of escape.

Admire the Institut Giacometti

MAP P270

Sculptures, paintings and drawings aplenty

A must for art buffs, **Institut Giacometti** (*fondation-giacometti.fr; adult/child €9/free*) is housed in the former studio of artist Paul Follot, in a gold-tiled art deco private mansion (a listed historical monument). It's dedicated to Swiss artist Alberto Giacometti (1901–66), who lived and worked in the area. The 350-sq-metre space has a reconstruction of Giacometti's

 AFRICAN RESTAURANTS IN SOUTHERN PARIS: OUR PICKS ——— MAP P270

Habesha: This Ethiopian restaurant, not far from Tour Montparnasse, has a good reputation. *7-9pm Mon, noon-2pm & 7-9pm Tue-Sat, 7-9pm Sun €*	**Lokita:** Expect West African (predominantly Senegalese) dishes with a modern twist at this great venture in the Pernety area. *noon-9pm Mon-Sat €*	**Icosium:** The best of Algerian cuisine, with tasty, rich tagine, couscous and grilled meat. In Montparnasse. *9am-2.30pm & 7-10pm Tue-Sun €€*	**MoSuke:** Michelin-starred (young) chef Mory Sacko cooks up delicious dishes that combine African and Japanese influences. *12.15-2pm & 7.30-9pm Mon-Sat €€*

A GOURMET TOUR IN THE 15E

With plenty of alluring bakeries, *fromageries* and other delis, the gourmet scene in the 15e is diverse and rich. Rent a Vélib' (Paris' bike-share scheme) and explore the area's culinary temptations.

START	END	LENGTH
Fromagerie Laurent Duchêne	Chez Walczak	6.8km; 1½ hours (by bike)

Whet your appetite at ❶ **Fromagerie Laurent Dubois**. This fabulous shop is *fromage* heaven, with tantalising cheeses carefully sourced from all four corners of France. It's a short ride to ❷ **Panade** on rue Violet, an award-winning and new-generation pastry shop that sells exquisite cakes, pastries, bread and tarts. Further west, make a beeline for ❸ **Aux Vins Vivants**, an excellent *caviste* (wine shop) famous for its 800-plus varieties of organic and natural wine. For artisanal charcuterie, there's only one address that matters: ❹ **Au Cochon Rose** on rue St-Charles. Sweet lovers will lose all self-control at ❺ **Scoop Me a Cookie** on rue du Commerce – see if you can resist the devilish pistachio cookie. Fancy a latte? Make your way to nearby ❻ **Onoul Coffee Shop**, a lovely Korean coffee shop with a couple of tables on the pavement. Now it's time for a well-deserved ice cream (or will it be a homemade scone?) at ❼ **Glazed** on bd Pasteur. Across the road, enjoy some tapas (and drink in the views) at the rooftop bar of ❽ **Villa M** (p278) before pedalling south to ❾ **Laurent Duchêne** (p281), whose croissants and other treats will tempt the devil in you. Round off the tour at ❿ **Chez Walczak**, a typical Parisian *troquet* (bistrot) with vintage decor and plenty of atmosphere.

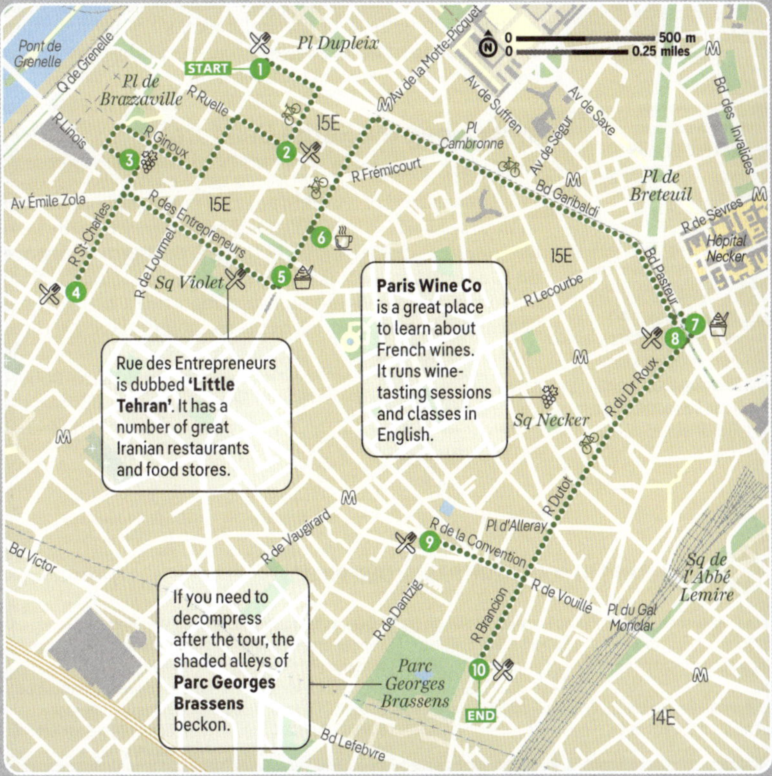

Petite Ceinture du 15e

LA SEINE MUSICALE

A landmark addition to Paris' cultural offerings, **La Seine Musicale** (laseinemusicale.com) opened on the Seine island of Île Seguin in 2017. Constructed of steel and glass, the egg-shaped auditorium has a capacity of 1150, while the larger, modular concrete hall accommodates 6000. Ballets, musicals and concerts from classical to rock are all staged here, alongside exhibitions. Outside are amphitheatres, while up above is a panoramic rooftop garden with landscaped lawns. There's also a restaurant, a brasserie, a cafe and a bar on the premises. It's the first of several arts venues, including a contemporary-art museum, planned as part of Île Seguin's transformation from a Renault factory to a cultural island.

studio, along with 70 of his sculptures, 90 of his paintings and over 2000 of his drawings. Admission is by prior online reservation only; you can't just turn up.

Walk along the Petite Ceinture MAP P270
Paris' most unusual trail

This little marvel of a walking path is not to be missed if you want to see Paris from a different perspective – it really feels like entering another world. In the 15e, the **Petite Ceinture du 15e** stretches for 1.3km, with biodiverse habitats including forest, grassland and prairies supporting 220 species of flora and fauna. In addition to the endpoints, there are three elevator-enabled access points along its route: 397ter rue de Vaugirard; opposite 82 rue Desnouettes; and place Robert Guillemard. On the eastern side of Parc Georges Brassens, a *promenade plantée* (planted walkway) travels atop a stretch of the Petite Ceinture's tracks by Porte de Vanves.

BRUNCHES IN SOUTHERN PARIS: OUR PICKS MAPS P270, P274

Les Pépites: Weekend brunch is a deliciously long and languid affair at this vibrant bistro. Most dishes are vegetarian. *10am-2pm Sat & Sun* €€

Les Fauves: Neobistro for a Sunday brunch, with a great selection of pastries, cakes and other treats. *noon-3.30pm Sun* €€

TOO Restaurant: A lavish Sunday brunch paired with some of the most spectacular views of Paris. Inside TOO Hotel. *11.30am-3.30pm Sun* €€€

La Verrière: Weekend brunch buffet with fresh breads, salads, fish and meat dishes, scrumptious pastries and vegetarian options. *noon-3pm Sat & Sun* €€€

Not enough for you? From there, get to 96bis rue Didot in the 14e, which is the access point for the 750m-long **Petite Ceinture du 14e**, which goes to Porte d'Orléans – another delightful section.

Find more information at petiteceinture.org.

Get Lost in the Heart of the 15th
MAP P270

A typical Parisian enclave that nobody knows

In the 15e, the district around **Église St-Jean Baptiste de Grenelle**, just north of the Félix Faure metro station, is well worth a gander. It feels very Parisian, supremely relaxing and is chock-a-block with interesting shops, bars and restaurants. You can also relax or have a picnic in nearby **square St-Lambert**.

See Quirky Sculptures at Musée Bourdelle
MAP P270

Off-the-radar cultural gem

You won't find many great cultural institutions in southern Paris, but there are a couple of relatively unknown yet not-to-be-missed museums, and **Musée Bourdelle** (bourdelle.paris.fr; free) in the 15e is one of them. Monumental bronzes fill the house and workshop where sculptor Antoine Bourdelle (1861–1929), a pupil of Rodin, lived and worked. The Hall des Plâtres room, with its peculiar layout and architecture, is our favourite. We also love the three oh-so-peaceful sculpture gardens, with a flavour of Belle Époque and post-WWI Montparnasse. The museum usually has a temporary exhibition (adult/child €10/8) going on alongside its free permanent collection.

Don't leave the museum without a stop at **Rhodia**. This cafe-restaurant on the 1st floor serves delectable light meals and exquisite cakes.

HISTORY OF THE PETITE CEINTURE

Long before the tramway or even the metro, the 35km Petite Ceinture (Little Belt) steam railway encircled the city of Paris. Constructed during the reign of Napoléon III between 1852 and 1869 as a way to move troops and goods around the city's fortifications, it became a thriving passenger service until the metro arrived in 1900. Most passenger services ceased in 1934 and goods services in 1993, and the line became an overgrown wilderness. Until recently, access was forbidden (although that didn't stop maverick urban explorers scrambling along its tracks and tunnels).

Of the line's original 29 stations, 17 survive (in various states of disrepair). The Petite Ceinture railway corridor is being regenerated, with the opening of several sections with walkways alongside the tracks.

Also serves top food with fresh ingredients

DRINKING IN SOUTHERN PARIS: OUR PICKS
MAPS P270, P274

Poinçon: Half trendy bar, half slick bistro, Poinçon is in a restored 1867 railway station that was part of the Petite Ceinture. In the 14e. *hours vary*	**Hexagone Café:** Award-winning Breton roaster Caffè Cataldi beans used in addictive espressos and cappuccinos. *8.30am-4.30pm Mon-Fri, 9.30am-5.30pm Sat & Sun*	**Café Cayo:** In the 13e, this is a great venue for hanging with locals over coffee, tea or cocktails. *hours vary*	**TOO Tac Tac Sky Bar:** A relaxing oasis where you can enjoy great tapas, well-crafted cocktails and, above all, panoramic views. *hours vary*
Simone La Cave: Lures a loyal wine-loving set keen to try its latest biodynamic wine selection. In the 13e. *4pm-midnight Tue-Sat*	**Arthur & Juliette:** Lap up the unpretentious Parisian vibe at this local neighbourhood bistro in the 15e. Also serves food. *9am-midnight*	**Le Merle Moqueur:** Tiny, retro Mocking Magpie carries a certain grungy appeal and serves great flavoured rums. In the 13e. *5pm-1am*	**Les Jajas de Juju:** This *cave à vin* (wine merchant) doubles as a wine bar and has a wide selection of *jaja* (French wines). In the 15e. *hours vary*

Day Trips from Paris

It may be hard to turn away from Paris, but several nearby day trips rival anything within the City of Light.

Places
Versailles p290
Chartres p296
Fontainebleau p300
Auvers-sur-Oise p304

The top day trip is Versailles: when it comes to over-the-top opulence, the colossal Château de Versailles is in a class of its own, even for France. Elsewhere, Chartres rises above fertile farmland. Its Cathédrale Notre Dame, famed for its beautiful stained glass, dominates this charming, walkable medieval town.

The lavish Château de Fontainebleau graces its elegant namesake town next to the forest that's renowned for walking and bouldering. The palace is stuffed with original furnishings and details from the time of Napoléon that bring it to life. Vincent Van Gogh spent the final days of his life in Auvers-sur-Oise, a village that's still retained the countryside charm that enticed so many artists to paint here in the 19th century.

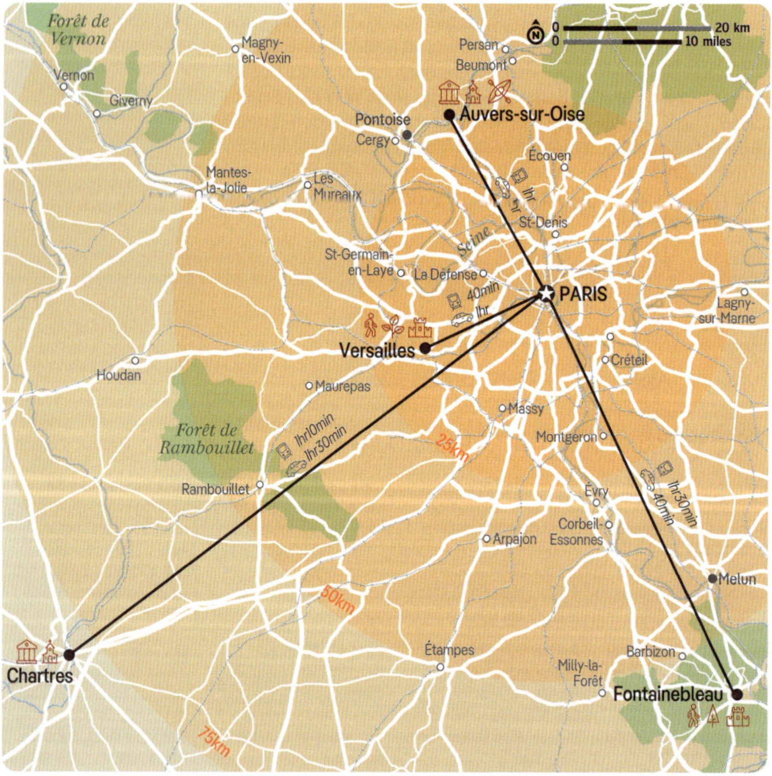

Château de Fontainebleau (p302)

Versailles Palace

TOP EXPERIENCE

Versailles

Sprawling over 900 hectares, the monumental, 400-year-old Château de Versailles is France's most famous and grand palace. It's situated in the leafy, bourgeois suburb of Versailles, 22km southwest of central Paris. The estate is divided into three main sections: the 580m-long palace; the gardens, canals and pools to the west of the palace; and the Trianon Estate to the northwest.

DON'T MISS

- The Palace
- Hall of Mirrors
- King's & Queen's State Apartments
- Formal gardens and fountains
- Lunch near the Grand Canal
- Grand Trianon

History

The estate began in 1623 as a hunting lodge for Louis XIII. Subsequently, Louis XIV transformed it into a vast, baroque château. Some 30,000 workers and soldiers toiled on the property, the bills for which all but emptied the kingdom's coffers. The Château de Versailles was the kingdom's political capital and the seat of the royal court from 1682 up until the fateful events of 1789 when revolutionaries massacred the palace guard. Louis XVI and Marie Antoinette were ultimately dragged back to Paris, where they were ingloriously guillotined. In the 19th century, Napoléon and Josephine lived on the estate, as did Charles de Gaulle in the 1940s.

PRACTICALITIES

- en.chateauversailles.fr
- adult/child from €21/ free
- 9am-5.30pm Tue-Sun

The Palace

Work on the palace began in 1661 under the guidance of architect Louis Le Vau (Jules Hardouin-Mansart took over from Le Vau in the mid-1670s); painter and interior designer Charles Le Brun; and landscape artist André Le Nôtre, whose workers flattened hills, drained marshes and relocated forests as they laid out the seemingly endless gardens, ponds and fountains.

Le Brun and his hundreds of artisans decorated every moulding, cornice, ceiling and door of the interior with the most luxurious and ostentatious of appointments: frescoes, marble, gilt and woodcarvings, many with themes and symbols drawn from Greek and Roman mythology.

Few alterations have been made to the château since its construction, apart from most of the interior furnishings disappearing during the Revolution and many of the rooms being redecorated by Louis-Philippe (r 1830–48), who opened part of the château to the public in 1837. The château is in the final stages of a lavish €400 million restoration.

Hall of Mirrors

The palace's opulence peaks in its shimmering Galerie des Glaces (Hall of Mirrors). This 75m-long ballroom shines with 17 sparkling mirrored features comprising 357 individual mirrors on one side and an equal number of windows overlooking the gardens and the setting sun on the other.

King's & Queen's State Apartments

Luxurious, ostentatious appointments adorn every feature of the palace's Grands Appartements du Roi et de la Reine (the King's and Queen's State Apartments). Rooms are dedicated to Hercules, Venus, Diana, Mars and Mercury.

Other Notable Rooms

The opulent excess is punctuated by various highlights worth seeking out. The **Galerie des Batailles** (Battle Gallery) is longer than the Hall of Mirrors and features 33 huge paintings that recall mostly forgotten French military victories. Take time to savour the thematic decor in the **Salon de la Guerre** (War Room) and the **Salon de la Paix** (Peace Room), which bookend the Hall of Mirrors.

Gardens, Estate & Equestrian Academy

A walk (p294) through the sprawling and artful formal gardens, natural areas, huge Grand Canal and the Trianon palaces is a highlight for many visitors. Or take in a horse show at the **National Equestrian Academy of Versailles**.

Getting There & Away

Versailles is best reached by the RER C line, which ends at Versailles Château Rive Gauche (some trains go elsewhere). Other stations with Versailles in their names are a much longer walk from the château and town centre. You can walk everywhere within Versailles, the palace and the estate.

HISTORIC VERSAILLES

Don't miss the historic centre of Versailles town. Build a superb picnic at the market stalls of **Les Halles de Versailles** on the place du Marché. In the old St-Louis quarter, next to the Cathédrale St-Louis, **the Potager du Roi** (King's Kitchen Garden) dates from the time of gourmand Louis XIV.

TOP TIPS

- Prepurchase tickets on the château's website for a dedicated time slot – otherwise admission is not guaranteed.

- Official group guided tours, such as the King's Private Apartments, are worthwhile.

- Consider getting tickets for a concert in the Royal Chapel or Royal Opera for a unique palace experience.

- Download the official Château de Versailles app, which is loaded with audio tours and info for the entire estate.

- The four-person rental electric carts are limited to a set route covering a fraction of the estate. Rental bikes and e-bikes allow the most freedom. Explore the Grand Canal with a rowboat. The shuttle train is very slow.

Versailles

A Day in Court

Visiting Versailles – even just the State Apartments – may seem overwhelming at first, but think of it as a house where people ate, drank, worked, slept and conspired, and you'll be on the right path.

Some two decades into his long reign, Louis XIV began turning his father's hunting lodge into a palace large enough to house his entire court (to keep closer tabs on the 6000-strong army of courtiers). Sparing no expense, the Sun King employed the greatest artists and craftspeople of the day and by 1682 he'd created the most extravagant dormitory in history.

The royal schedule was as accurate and predictable as a Swiss watch. Although it's impossible to recreate the king's day on a visit, the following itinerary does allow you to pass all of the rooms of interest. You'll start with the **1 Royal Chapel**, where morning Mass was held, followed by the **2 Hercules Drawing Room** and **3 Diana Drawing Room**, both sites of evening entertainment, while the **4 King's Library** was visited after lunch. The **5 Hall of Mirrors** was for the royal procession, and the **6 Council Chamber** for late-morning meetings with ministers. The day would have begun in the **7 King's Bedchamber** and the **8 Queen's Bedchamber**, where the royal couple was roused at about the same time.

VERSAILLES BY NUMBERS

Rooms 700 (11 hectares of roof)
Windows 2153
Staircases 67
Gardens and parks 800 hectares
Trees 200,000
Fountains 50 (with 620 nozzles)
Paintings 6300 (measuring 11km laid end to end)
Statues and sculptures 2100
Objets d'art and furnishings 5000
Visitors 8.1 million per year

8 Queen's Bedchamber
Chambre de la Reine

The queen's life was on constant public display and even the births of her children were watched by crowds of spectators in her own bedchamber.
Detour» The Guardroom, with a dozen armed men at the ready.

Gallery of Battles

LUNCH BREAK

Contemporary French cuisine at Alain Ducasse's restaurant Ore, or a picnic in the park.

2 Hercules Drawing Room
Salon d'Hercule

This salon, with its stunning ceiling fresco of the strong man, gave way to the State Apartments, which were open to courtiers three nights a week.
Detour» Apollo Drawing Room, used for formal audiences and as a throne room.

❺ Hall of Mirrors
Galerie des Glaces

The solid-silver candelabra and furnishings in this extravagant hall, devoted to Louis XIV's successes in war, were melted down in 1689 to pay for yet another conflict. **Detour»** The antithetical Peace Drawing Room, adjacent.

❼ King's Bedchamber
Chambre du Roi

The king's daily life was anything but private and even his *lever* (rising) at 8am and *coucher* (retiring) at 11.30pm would be witnessed by up to 150 sycophantic courtiers.

❻ Council Chamber
Cabinet du Conseil

This chamber, with carved medallions evoking the king's work, is where the monarch met his various ministers (state, finance, religion etc), depending on the days of the week.

❹ King's Library
Bibliothèque du Roi

The last resident, bibliophile Louis XVI, loved geography and his copy of *The Travels of James Cook* is still on the shelf here. You can only visit this room on a private tour.

❸ Diana Drawing Room
Salon de Diane

With the walls and ceiling covered in frescoes devoted to the mythical huntress, this room contained a large billiard table reserved for Louis XIV, a keen player.

❶ Royal Chapel
Chapelle Royale

This two-storey chapel (with a gallery for the royals and important courtiers, and the ground floor for the B-list) was dedicated to St Louis, patron of French monarchs. **Detour»** The sumptuous Royal Opera.

Savvy Sightseeing

Avoid Versailles on Monday (closed), Tuesday (Paris' museums close, so visitors flock here) and Sunday, the busiest day. Also, book tickets online so you don't have to queue.

WALKING TOUR

Walking the Versailles Estate

The entire Versailles estate covers over 800 hectares. The main features include the gorgeous formal gardens and groves that lead down to the Grand Canal. Then amid the hunting forests are two more palaces within the Estate of Trianon and Marie Antoinette's fanciful Queen's Hamlet. Surprises abound as the estate is filled with sculptures, water features and elegant flower gardens. On a pleasant day, you can easily spend a half-day or more exploring.

1 Gardens, Groves & Fountains

The formal gardens were laid out between 1661 and 1700 and feature geometrically aligned terraces, flowerbeds, tree-lined paths, ponds and fountains. The 400-odd statues of marble, bronze and lead were created by the most talented sculptors of the era.

Amidst soaring walls of trees and hedges are not-to-be-missed highlights such as the Bassin de Bacchus (Bacchus Fountain), the Bassin de Saturne (Saturn Fountain) and the Bosquet de l'Encelade (Enceladus Grove). The seasonal 'Musical Gardens' program pairs classical music with timed sprays of water features.

The Walk Take your time meandering through the gardens towards the Grand Canal. Pause for views at the expansive Bassin d'Apollon.

2 Grand Canal

Forming a cross that's 1km by 1.7km and orientated to catch the sunset, the Grand Canal's placid waters are the dominant

Grand Trianon

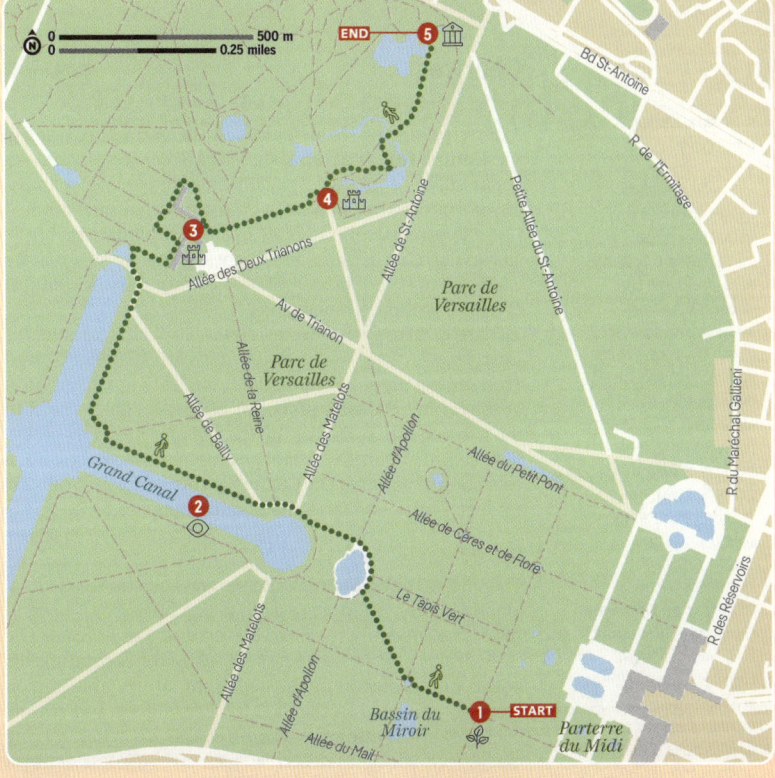

feature of the estate. At the east end is a group of good spots to eat as well as a place to rent bikes and e-bikes in case you want to save time reaching the estate's outer reaches. You can also rent a rowboat and take to the waters.

The Walk No matter how crowded the palace, you can soon feel like you have Versailles to yourself as you walk west along the north side of the water. At the crossing point, turn north.

3 Grand Trianon

In the middle of the park within the Domaine de Trianon are Versailles' two smaller palaces. The pink-colonnaded Grand Trianon was built in 1687 for Louis XIV and his family as a place of escape from the rigid etiquette of the court. Napoléon had it redone in the Empire style and a visit offers a peek at period furniture and decor. The formal gardens behind the palace are dotted with sculptures and provide a serene and shady escape.

The Walk Take the short walk through elegant flower gardens to the Petit Trianon.

4 Petit Trianon

The ochre-coloured Petit Trianon, built in the 1760s, was redecorated in 1867 by Empress Eugénie, consort of Napoléon III, who added Louis XVI–style furnishings. You can skip the interior as the allure here is all outside.

The Walk The English-style Jardins du Petit Trianon have meandering, sheltered paths and include features such as the irresistible Temple de l'Amour (Temple of Love). Stroll the paths a short distance north.

5 Hameau de la Reine

Surprisingly idiosyncratic, the Hameau de la Reine (Queen's Hamlet) is like a film set of a mock village of thatched cottages, a pond, a photogenic mill and barnyard animals. It was constructed from 1775 to 1784 for the amusement of Marie Antoinette.

Chartres

TIME FROM PARIS: 1HR

Artful museums

After viewing the stained glass in the cathedral, head to the **Centre International du Vitrail** *(centre-vitrail.org/en; adult/child €7/free)*, in a half-timbered former granary, to see reproductions up close. At the International Stained Glass Centre, you'll find blow-by-blow explanations of the stories narrated in the window panes. There are also delicate examples of Renaissance works and temporary exhibitions of contemporary stained glass.

Chartres' **Musée des Beaux-Arts** *(chartres.fr/patrimoine-historique/le-musee-des-beaux-arts; adult/child €7/ free)*, accessed via the gate next to the cathedral's north portal, is in the former **Palais Épiscopal** (Bishop's Palace), built in the 17th and 18th centuries. In this fine-arts museum, peruse 16th-century enamels of the Apostles made for François I, a collection of paintings by Chaïm Soutine and polychromatic wooden sculptures from the Middle Ages.

Mosaic marvel

There were the cathedral builders, and then there was Raymond Isidore. The story goes that as a blind boy – born in 1900 – he suddenly regained his sight at age 10 inside the cathedral. Later in life, he spent 30 years decorating his house in mosaics he fashioned from stones and broken crockery collected in the vicinity. Every nook and cranny is covered, including the furniture and his wife's sewing machine. Sometimes described as 'naive' or 'outsider art', the fantastically unique house exudes its maker's fervent religious belief. Situated 2km from the cathedral, **Maison Picassiette** *(maison-picassiette-chartres.com; adult/child €9/free)* is named as a nod to Picasso and *assiette* (plate).

ILLUMINATING HISTORY

In the 21st century, what's the best way to interest people in centuries-old cultural heritage? How can you attract a new audience? And how can you interest them in historical edifices besides the sole star attraction? These were the questions that the city of Chartres grappled with before creating a dazzling sound-and-light show in 2003. A smashing success, **Chartres en Lumières** showcases more than 20 monuments with high-tech illuminations in a nightly circuit from April to January. Images flash across old stone bridges traversing the Eure River, and medieval churches like Église St-Pierre and the Collégiale St-André glow in the darkness. With this free annual event, the city has succeeded in enticing day-trippers to stay the night and see the *ville's* charms in a new light.

Rent a pedal boat to explore the river

EATING IN CHARTRES: OUR PICKS

Le Moulin de Ponceau: Right on the water in a 17th-century mill, refined cuisine crafted from locally grown, organic ingredients that reflect the terroir. *12.15-1.30pm & 7.30-9pm Thu-Mon* €€

Les Feuillantines: The menu of traditional cuisine changes seasonally at this friendly spot in Old Chartres. *noon-1.30pm & 7-9.30pm Tue-Sat* €€

Café Serpette: The decor dates to 1900 inside a 14th-century building, with unbeatable views from the *terrasse* facing the cathedral. *8am-11pm* €

La Petite Venise: This festive, open-air hangout draws locals to the banks of the Eure. Drink an *apéro* (predinner drink), sup or listen to a concert. *noon-1.30pm & 7-9.30pm Tue-Sat* €

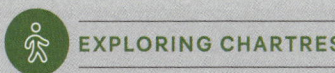

EXPLORING CHARTRES

Walking Chartres will take you up and down the steep streets and stairs between the cathedral's lofty perch and the Eure River.

START	END	LENGTH
Maison du Saumon	Musée des Beaux-Arts	2.5km; one hour

Begin on rue de la Poissonnerie at the tourist office, housed in the lavishly restored 16th-century ① **Maison du Saumon**. Loop around to ② **place Billard**, where there is usually a market. Follow rue du Soleil d'Or to the ③ **Flower Market** and the heart of the shopping district. Choose from several good, non-touristy cafes with terrace seating. Angle around to rue des Grenets, which features many half-timbered buildings. Pause at the ④ **Église St-Aignan**, then continue downhill down to the vast and shambolic ⑤ **Église St-Pierre**. Walk one street over and cross the river. Walk north and cross back west over the stone ⑥ **Pont Bouju**; the view north is sublime. Begin the trek uphill along rue du Bourg to the ⑦ **confluence of rue St-Eman and rue des Écuyers**, which has a trove of historic buildings. Turn left; after a few steps you'll reach the junction with rue aux Cois, with ⑧ **two medieval buildings**: one building is shaped like the prow of a ship, while across the way there's a beautiful turret-shaped, half-timbered staircase. Walk north on rue de la Corroierie to ⑨ **Collégiale St-André**. Follow the sinuous footpath uphill to the ⑩ **Musée des Beaux-Arts**. The former Palais Épiscopal still has flower-filled gardens and places to stop and enjoy the view.

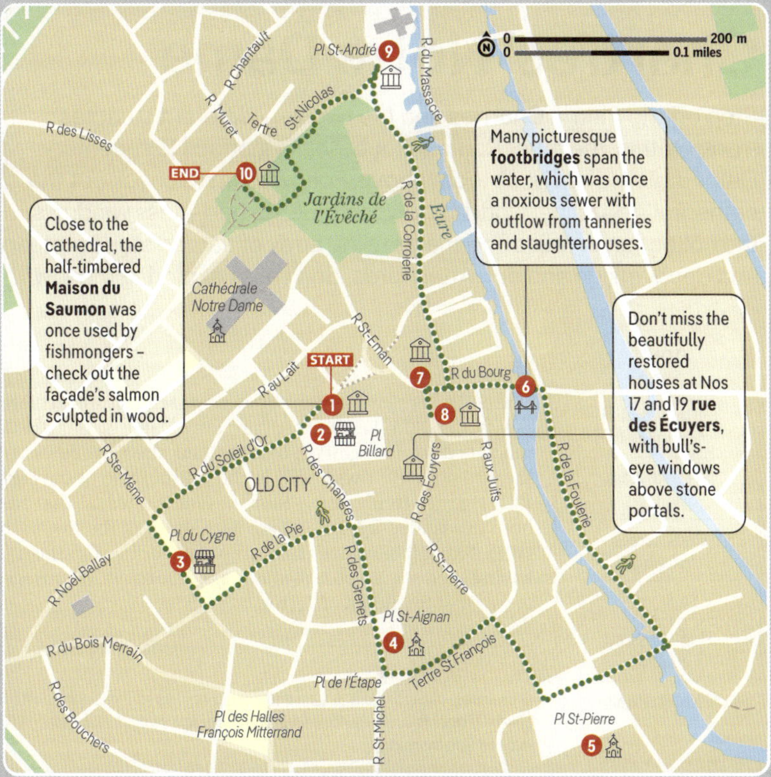

Close to the cathedral, the half-timbered **Maison du Saumon** was once used by fishmongers – check out the façade's salmon sculpted in wood.

Many picturesque **footbridges** span the water, which was once a noxious sewer with outflow from tanneries and slaughterhouses.

Don't miss the beautifully restored houses at Nos 17 and 19 **rue des Écuyers**, with bull's-eye windows above stone portals.

Notre Dame's exquisite stained-glass windows

TOP EXPERIENCE

Chartres' Notre Dame

Step off the train in Chartres and the two very different steeples – one Gothic, the other Romanesque – of its glorious 13th-century Cathédrale Notre Dame loom above. Follow them to check out the cathedral's dazzling, world-renowned blue stained-glass windows, the collection of relics and the dazzling array of carved stone statuary and decor inside and out. Afterwards, don't miss exploring the town.

DON'T MISS

- Cathedral entrances
- Stained-glass windows
- Choir screen carvings
- Saint Voile
- Half-timbered houses
- Riverside walk

History

One of Western civilisation's crowning architectural achievements, the 130m-long Cathédrale Notre Dame de Chartres is renowned for its brilliant-blue stained-glass windows and sacred holy veil. It was built in the Gothic style in the early 13th century (replacing a Romanesque cathedral that had been devastated by fire – along with much of the town – in 1194). Today, it is France's best-preserved medieval cathedral, having been spared post-medieval modifications, the ravages of war and the Reign of Terror.

PRACTICALITIES

- chartres-cathedrale.fr ● free entry (paid access to Treasury: adult/child €7/free) ● 10am-12.45pm & 2-5pm Sep-Apr, to 6pm May-Sep (closed Sun morning)

Entrancing Entrances

The cathedral's west, north and south entrances have superbly ornamented triple portals, but the west entrance, the **Portail Royal**, is the only one that predates the fire. Carved from 1145 to 1155, its splendid statues, whose features are elongated in the Romanesque style, represent Christ in the centre, and the Nativity and the Ascension to the right and left, respectively. The structure's other main Romanesque feature is the 105m-high **Clocher Vieux**, also called the Tour Sud (South Tower). Construction began in the 1140s; it's the tallest Romanesque steeple still standing.

Get up High

The climb (200 steps) up the spiral staircase to the north transept is worth the ticket price. Get top-flight views of the three-tiered flying buttresses and the 19th-century copper roof. This seasonal guided tour is only in French.

The Treasury

Closed for nearly a quarter-century, the Treasury reopened in 2024 after a massive, seven-year restoration of the Chapelle St-Piat. The remarkable collection of relics and precious objects includes shell wampums offered as diplomatic gifts in the 17th century by North American tribes. A ticket is required – book yours online or pay at the booth inside the cathedral.

Stained-Glass Windows

The cathedral's 176 extraordinary stained-glass windows, almost all of which date to the 13th century, form one of the world's most important ensembles of medieval stained glass. The three most exquisite windows, from the mid-12th century, are in the wall above the west entrance and below the rose window. Survivors of the 1194 fire, the windows are revered for the depth and intensity of their tones, famously known as 'Chartres blue'.

Mary's Holy Veil

The venerated **Saint Voile** (Holy Veil) – a yellowish bolt of silk draped over a frame, which is believed to have been worn by the Virgin Mary when she gave birth to Jesus – is displayed in a glass case in the Chapelle du St-Coeur de Marie.

The relic originally formed part of the imperial treasury of Constantinople but was offered to Charlemagne by Empress Irene when the Holy Roman Emperor proposed marriage to her in 802. Charles the Bald presented it to the town in 876; the cathedral was built because the veil survived the 1194 fire.

Deep in the Crypt

The cathedral's 110m crypt, a tombless Romanesque structure built in 1024 around a 9th-century predecessor, is the largest in France. **Tours** start at the cathedral-run shop, inside near the west entrance.

ON A PILGRIMAGE

You'll likely see hearty souls with sensible backpacks congregating in front of the cathedral. Chartres is right on the legendary pilgrimage route to Santiago de Compostela in northwest Spain. Look for the marker in the pavement that points towards their goal, some 1600km distant. The route has existed for over 1000 years; in centuries past the cathedral was also a pilgrim campsite.

TOP TIPS

- Resident expert Anne-Marie Woods leads private English tours on request (annemariechartres@gmail.com).

- The cathedral shop sells hard-to-find guides and books. Look for seminal titles by Malcolm Miller, who dedicated his life to studying the cathedral.

- Bring binoculars to appreciate the extraordinary detail of the stained glass and carvings (some Chartres shops rent them).

- Get a prime seat in one of the touristy cafes surrounding the cathedral, sit back with a favourite beverage and just gaze at the doorways. The more you look, the more you'll see.

NATURE AS SAVIOUR

The Forêt de Fontainebleau is where the world's first marked walking trails were developed in 1842. Deeply depressed, a former soldier named Claude-François Denecourt took to wandering in the forest – its beauty uplifted his spirits. He later wrote that the forest saved him. Publishing a series of guidebooks and maps, he helped to change the perception of a forest as a scary place. In fact, he pioneered hiking as a leisure activity by creating a network of more than 100km of forest paths; his *sentiers bleus* are still marked today with blue lines painted on trees and rocks – known as the Denecourt-Colinet trails. In 1861, more than 10 years before Yellowstone became the world's first national park, part of the Forêt de Fontainebleau became the world's first nature reserve.

Forêt de Fontainebleau

Fontainebleau

TIME FROM PARIS: **45MIN**

Into the woods

Fresh air fills your lungs the second you step into the **Forêt de Fontainebleau**, one of France's loveliest woods. Enveloping the town, the 200-sq-km forest is a rejuvenating expanse of pine forest and oak trees, lazy sandy clearings and curiously shaped boulders. Once a royal hunting ground, it later inspired a group of 19th-century painters, including Jean-François Millet, Camille Corot and Théodore Rousseau, who set up shop in the village of Barbizon at the forest's edge. Known as the Barbizon School, they paved the way for the impressionists who later also painted woodland scenes here.

Today the forest is as big a playground as it was in the 16th century. In fact, it's the most visited forest in France. Walking, cycling and horse-riding opportunities abound. Hikers can plot longer trips on two national walking trails, the GR1 and GR11. On weekends and holidays, the train from Paris even makes a stop in the middle of the forest, between the Bois-le-Roi and Fontainebleau Avon stations. Note that overcrowding can happen around Easter and long holiday weekends, though most picnicking urbanites don't venture far from the parking lots.

Rock-climbing enthusiasts have long come to the forest's sandstone ridges, cliffs and overhangs to hone their skills before setting off for the Alps. There are different grades marked by colours – the 'Font' bouldering scale takes its name from here. The website bleau.info is packed with info.

EATING IN FONTAINEBLEAU: OUR PICKS

Empreinte: The Hotel Napoléon's restaurant offers generous cuisine. Afternoon tea in the bar is popular with locals. *noon-2pm & 7-9.45pm Wed-Sat, to 2pm Sun* €€

Frédéric Cassel: Pair pastry with tea and peek inside the laboratory at this top chocolatier's tea room. *10am-7pm Tue-Fri, to 7.30pm Sat, to 1pm Sun* €

Le Viand'art: Dig into tasty meat-based dishes at this butcher shop that doubles as a brasserie. The weekday *plat du jour* is great value. *hours vary Tue-Sun* €

Luwei Brunch Café: A mix of classic breakfast favourites, Asian treats, and healthy staples including quinoa salad. *9am-5pm Wed-Sun* €

EXPLORING THE FONTAINEBLEAU GARDENS

Stroll the Château de Fontainebleau's stately gardens to marvel at carp-filled ponds, English landscape gardens and Europe's biggest parterre.

START	END	LENGTH
Jardin de Diane	Grand Canal	3km; one hour

Begin your walk in the formal ❶ **Jardin de Diane**, created by the infamous Catherine de Médici. Good spots for a picnic abound in this popular public park. Now move into the château complex. As successive monarchs added their own wings to the palace, five irregularly shaped courtyards were created. Start at the austere ❷ **Cour du Cheval Blanc** (Courtyard of the White Horse), which has the château's visitor entrance. Napoléon, about to be exiled to Elba in 1814, bade farewell to his guards from the magnificent 17th-century double-horseshoe staircase. Cross through the passage to the ❸ **Cour de la Fontaine** (Fountain Courtyard) and the ❹ **Étang des Carpes** (Carp Pond). Immediately west, the informal ❺ **Jardin Anglais** (English Garden) was created in 1812 to present an idealised version of the English countryside. Head east to the oldest and most interesting courtyard, the ❻ **Cour Ovale** (Oval Courtyard). Although no longer oval but U-shaped due to Henri IV's construction work, it incorporates the keep, the sole remnant of the medieval château. Just south is the geometrically pure expanse of Le Nôtre's formal, 17th-century ❼ **Jardin Français** (French Garden), also known as the Grand Parterre. Walk east, crossing av des Cascades, and follow the north bank of the ❽ **Grand Canal**, where the dense shade trees are a treat on hot days.

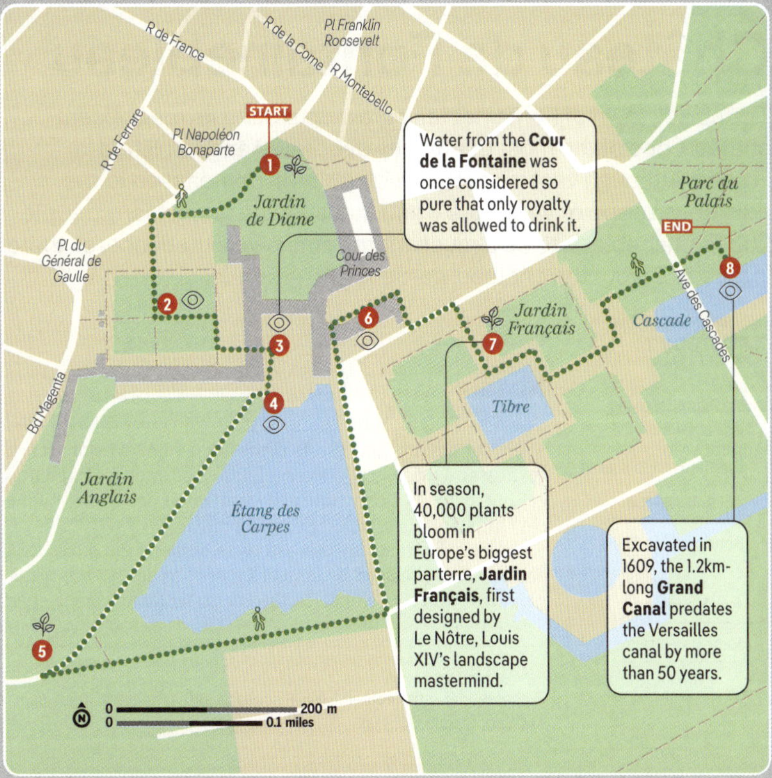

Water from the **Cour de la Fontaine** was once considered so pure that only royalty was allowed to drink it.

In season, 40,000 plants bloom in Europe's biggest parterre, **Jardin Français**, first designed by Le Nôtre, Louis XIV's landscape mastermind.

Excavated in 1609, the 1.2km-long **Grand Canal** predates the Versailles canal by more than 50 years.

Salle du Trône (Throne Room)

TOP EXPERIENCE

Château de Fontainebleau

The classy town of Fontainebleau grew up around its magnificent château, one of the most beautifully decorated and furnished in France. Although vast in scale, its size pales in comparison to the ridiculous scope of Versailles – and that's for the good. Many people find Fontainebleau to be a much more immersive experience, as there is time to savour the château, gardens and grounds.

DON'T MISS

Chapelle de la Trinité

Galerie François Ier

Salle de Bal

Boudoir de la Reine

Chambre de Napoléon

Horseshoe staircase

Cour Ovale

History

The resplendent, 1900-room Château de Fontainebleau's list of former tenants and guests reads like a who's who of French royalty and aristocracy. Every square centimetre of wall and ceiling space is richly adorned with wood panelling, gilded carvings, frescoes, tapestries and paintings.

The first château on this site was built in the early 12th century and enlarged by Louis IX a century later. Only a single medieval tower survived the energetic Renaissance-style

PRACTICALITIES
- chateaudefontainebleau.fr/en
- adult/child €14/free
- 9.30am-6pm Apr-Sep, to 5pm Oct-Mar

reconstruction undertaken by François I (r 1515–47). The *Mona Lisa* once hung here amid other fine works of art in the royal collection.

During the latter half of the 16th century, the château was further enlarged by Henri II (r 1547–59), Catherine de Médici and Henri IV (r 1589–1610). Even Louis XIV got in on the act: it was he who hired landscape artist André Le Nôtre, celebrated for his work at Versailles, to redesign the gardens.

Fontainebleau was beloved by Napoléon Bonaparte. Napoléon III was another frequent visitor. During WWII the château was turned into a German headquarters. Later, it served as the Allied and then NATO headquarters from 1945 to 1965.

Grands Appartements

The spectacular **Chapelle de la Trinité** (Trinity Chapel), the ornamentation of which dates from the first half of the 17th century, is where Napoléon III was christened in 1810. Note how the murals play with perspective.

Galerie François 1er, a jewel of Renaissance architecture, was decorated from 1533 to 1540 by Il Rosso, a Florentine follower of Michelangelo. In the seeming acres of carved-wood panelling, François I's monogram appears repeatedly along with his emblem, a dragon-like salamander.

A top sight, the **Salle de Bal**, a 30m-long ballroom dating from the mid-16th century, is renowned for its mythological frescoes, marquetry floor and Italian-inspired coffered ceiling. Its large windows afford views of the **Cour Ovale** (Oval Courtyard) and the gardens. The gilded bed in the 17th- and 18th-century **Chambre de l'Impératrice** (Empress' Bedroom) was never used by Marie Antoinette, for whom it was built in 1787. She actually favoured the **Boudoir de la Reine** (Queen's Bedroom), which attests to her under-appreciated design sensibilities. Note the lovely sunrise on the ceiling.

The gilding in the **Salle du Trône** (Throne Room), which was the royal bedroom before the Napoleonic period, is decorated in a rich tableau of golds, greens and yellows.

The **Musée Chinois de l'Impératrice Eugénie** (Chinese Museum of Empress Eugénie) offers a change from all the carved wood. It was created in 1863 for the Asian art and curios collected by Napoléon III's wife.

Echoes of Napoléon

Napoléon Bonaparte preferred Fontainebleau to Versailles because he found it more 'intimate'. The **Musée Napoléon I** presents the family history of the emperor, right down to his favourite articles of clothing. A suite of rooms recalls his time in the château: the **Chambre de Napoléon** preserves the decidedly non-minimalist decor of his bedroom. (Don't miss the great man's bathroom, complete with a very short tub.) The **Salon de l'Abdication** is where he called it quits in 1814.

HORSESHOE STAIRCASE

The couples taking wedding photos in front of the château's emblematic staircase are following in royal footsteps. Back in the day, it was where princesses like Marie Leszczyńska were greeted in pomp and circumstance before their nuptials. Commissioned by Louis XIII in the 17th century, it was widely copied across Europe. Later it was immortalised by Napoléon's farewell speech to his troops gathered in the courtyard before his exile to Elba.

TOP TIPS

● Refreshment and lunch options within the complex are limited. Outside the gates in town, you'll find good choices for picnics and meals around rue des Sablons.

● Preserve your flexibility by not buying château tickets in advance, as it draws a fraction of the crowds at Versailles.

● There are dozens of daily trains between Paris' Gare de Lyon and the Fontainebleau Avon station.

● You can easily ride the bus from the station to Fontainebleau's town centre and the château's entrance and walk all the way back as part of a tour of the gardens and grounds.

VAN GOGH'S TURMOIL

'Auvers is really beautiful, seriously beautiful', Vincent Van Gogh wrote to his brother in 1890. Here, he was under the medical supervision of Dr Gachet, a friend of the impressionists with a house in town. Far from the noise of Paris, and even further from the mental asylum where he had just been institutionalised in Provence, Van Gogh found inspiration in the picturesque countryside. Yet he also found it lonely. Paintings from this period express profound emotion: turbulent skies above the fields, a portrait of a melancholic Dr Gachet, and the local city hall on the boisterous Fête Nationale holiday, but depicted completely devoid of people. He even wrote that his wheat field landscapes were an effort to express 'sadness and extreme loneliness'.

Auvers-sur-Oise

TIME FROM PARIS: 1¼HR

Maison de Van Gogh

While the village of Giverny – a long-time place of pilgrimage for Claude Monet devotees – has become a victim of overtourism, the Paris region is home to other delightful artist villages. The country hamlet of Auvers-sur-Oise, just north of Paris, is forever linked to Vincent Van Gogh, who spent the final 70 days of his life here. He took a room at the **Auberge Ravoux** and ventured out to paint *en plein air*. It was an incredibly prolific period, resulting in masterpieces such as *Wheatfield with Crows* and *The Church of Auvers-sur-Oise*. By the time of his death by suicide, he had created 80 paintings. The small inn is now a soulful museum called the **Maison de Van Gogh** *(maisondevangogh.fr; adult/child €10/ free)*, where passionate guides lead a 30-minute visit, including a short film.

Ascend the narrow creaking staircase to room No 5 and you'll be struck by what's not there. No furnishings. Bare floors. Walls in need of a paint job. Lit by a single skylight under the eaves, the attic room has been left completely unchanged since Van Gogh's death. It's a haunting experience – you can't help but imagine the artist's brother, Théo, racing to his bedside in the nick of time before Vincent died in his arms of a self-inflicted gunshot wound. Today Van Gogh's paintings sell for astronomical prices, but in 1890 the tortured artist could only afford this cheap room.

After your visit, have lunch in the downstairs restaurant (reserve a table online in advance). The ambience is timeless: a zinc bar, bistro tables topped with vintage linen, the same style curtains hanging in the windows as in Van Gogh's day. Friendly waiters in aprons and black vests serve the *plat du jour,* such as bœuf bourguignon, or platters of Maison Verot charcuterie and cheese. Van Gogh would take his meals at the corner table in the back so he could quietly observe the room.

Church, cemetery and château

For Van Gogh fans, the **Église Notre Dame de l'Assomption** is immediately recognisable. The artist painted the 12th-century church in curving lines against a deep blue sky. Perched high above the Oise Valley, it combines Romanesque and Gothic features – keep an eye out for the fantastical creatures carved into the transept crossing. Continue walking uphill to reach the agricultural plateau, backed by endless sky, also painted by the artist. Along the road you'll come to the cemetery where Van Gogh is buried next to his brother, who died six months later. The two graves are intertwined in a blanket of ivy planted by Dr Gachet's son.

These highlights are part of a dedicated walking circuit called

FINDING VAN GOGH

You won't find original works by Van Gogh in Auvers-sur-Oise, but you can admire a number of his masterpieces in Paris at the Musée d'Orsay (p250).

Église Notre Dame de l'Assomption

the **Chemin des Peintures** (the painters' path). Along the 9km route you'll see reproductions of famous works created in situ by 19th-century artists like Paul Cézanne and Auguste Renoir. Many of these artists – household names today – came to Auvers-sur-Oise to visit their friend Charles-François Daubigny, an artist who transformed his boat *Le Botin* into a studio on the banks of the Oise. His first studio in town, its walls covered in murals, is now an excellent little museum called the **Maison Atelier Daubigny** (open weekends only). Dr Gachet's house, also a museum, is at the far end of town. Make time for the **Château d'Auvers-sur-Oise**, with its vast park and excellent exhibitions, such as 'Van Gogh: The Final Journeys'.

Get out on the water

A major tributary to the Seine, the Oise feels wild – fringed by lush trees and frequented by all kinds of birds. Canoe rentals are available through **Val d'Oise Aventures** *(val doise-aventures.paris; two hours from €14.50)*. Self-guided excursions leave from the Pont d'Auvers in the neighbouring village of Mery-sur-Oise. Or bring your family or entourage of friends aboard **Le Botin** *(lebotindauvers.fr; per person from €12)*, a replica of Daubigny's famous boat. Excursions must be booked in advance.

TRAIN TRIUMPH

Two inventions changed the art world forever. The advent of the train, and the invention of portable tubes of paint, allowed 19th-century artists to skip town and paint outside. The Auvers-sur-Oise station first opened in 1846, putting the bucolic countryside within easy reach for Parisians. Nowadays vintage postal rail cars are parked next to the charming station, and the former freight depot has been converted into a fabulous used bookstore called the **Caverne des Livres**.

In a nod to the artists who used to make the trip from Paris, SNCF offers a direct *'train des impressionnistes'* from May to late October – it departs on weekend and holiday mornings, with a return the same day in the evening. (Otherwise you switch trains at Pontoise or take a direct train to Mery-sur-Oise and walk.)

Where to Stay

Paris has a huge choice of accommodation, from hostels to palace hotels. Apartments are popular for those looking to self-cater and for more space – hotel rooms are small by international standards.

Where to Stay If You Love ...

Monuments, museums & elegant streetscapes

Eiffel Tower & Western Paris (p60) Close to Paris' iconic tower. Upmarket residential area, limited nightlife.

Parisian icons & superb shopping

Champs-Élysées & Grands Boulevards (p80) Luxury hotels, department stores, glam nights out. Some areas are pricey. Nightlife can be noisy.

Artistic treasures & epicurean treats

Louvre & Les Halles (p96) Central Paris location with excellent transport links, major museums, fashion and food shopping galore. Not cheap.

Lofty views & lively multicultural quarters

Montmartre & Northern Paris (p126) Hilly streets, village charm. Some parts very touristy. Good budget options. The red-light district around Pigalle won't appeal to everyone.

Hip boutiques & buzzing nightlife

Le Marais, Belleville & Ménilmontant (p150, p168) History-steeped streets, secret squares, copious drinking and dining choices. Can be noisy near bars.

Bustling markets, excellent eating & creative spaces

Bastille & Eastern Paris (p184) Vibrant local area with fewer tourists. Loads of restaurants, drinking and nightlife venues. Diverse accommodation options. Some areas in the east are isolated.

Heart-of-Paris setting & the Seine

The Islands (p204) Limited high-end accommodation centres on the peaceful Île St-Louis. Few self-catering shops.

History, jazz & literary connections

Latin Quarter (p222) Energetic student area with scores of eating, drinking and entertainment options. Good mix of accommodation styles.

Stylish shopping & cafe life

St-Germain & Les Invalides (p240) Quintessentially Parisian quarter close to the Seine and the Jardin du Luxembourg. High end.

Street art & expansive parks

Montparnasse & Southern Paris (p268) Villagey pockets, great outdoor bars, green space. Some areas out of the way. Good value-for-money.

€€€ Top end €€ Midrange € Budget

Eiffel Tower & Western Paris

BOUTIQUE

Hotel Beauséjour Ranelagh €€
MAP P62

A melange of museum-worthy art and designer furniture creates the feel of an elegant Parisian home at this family-run hotel that's deeply connected to the neighbourhood. Loyal regular guests love the high-quality breakfast.

Hôtel Botaniste €€
MAP P62

Accessed via a leafy garden, this tastefully decorated hotel in Auteuil offers plant-named rooms with parquet floors, organic bath products, framed flower prints and biodegradable espresso capsules – drink your morning brew from gorgeous Gien ceramics.

Hôtel Villa Nicolo €€
MAP P62

The courtyard garden adds to the charm of this friendly, 27-room hotel tucked away on a quiet street in Passy. Guestbook comments are effusive about the helpful reception staff.

CHIC B&B

Villa du Square €€
MAP P62

The Gicqueau family open the doors to their elegant townhouse next to Le Corbusier Foundation. Five guest rooms show off an eclectic mix of antiques and designer decor. Breakfast in the jasmine-infused garden is hard to beat.

WORTH THE SPLURGE

St James Paris €€€
MAP P62

The only château hotel in Paris offers a bonanza of luxuries befitting a countryside estate: wood-panelled library bar, Guerlain spa, glorious garden and a sought-after restaurant with a green ethos.

Hôtel Molitor €€€
MAP P62

More than a luxurious place to sleep, the Molitor is a landmark loaded with history. The art deco swimming pool complex was where the bikini was born, and Johnny 'Tarzan' Weissmuller was a lifeguard.

Brach Paris €€€
MAP P62

With a dazzling rooftop, locals-approved restaurant and sports club, Brach is a scene loved by stylish Parisians. Designer Philippe Starck injected playful whimsy into the stylish decor.

UNDER THE STARS

Camping de Paris €
MAP P62

On the Bois de Boulogne's western edge by the banks of the Seine, this year-round campground has 290 sites for tents or camper vans, along with kitchen-equipped wood caravans and static tents made of canvas and wood.

APARTHOTEL

Rayz Eiffel €€- €€€
MAP P62

This contemporary chic hotel has a rooftop hangout overlooking the nearby Eiffel Tower. The 25 rooms come with kitchenettes – some have furnished balconies with views.

Champs-Élysées & Grands Boulevards

ON A BUDGET

Hôtel Chopin €
MAP P82

A rare affordable hotel in Paris, and in the unique location of one of the city's historical *passages couverts* (covered shopping arcades). This historic hotel originally opened in 1846 and features classic, period-inspired rooms overlooking the Paris rooftops.

CitizenM Paris Champs-Elysées €
MAP P82

This functional but fun hotel group offers an affordable place to stay in the upmarket 8e *arrondissement*. Rooms are basic but cleverly and comfortably designed and there's an Eiffel Tower view from the rooftop bar.

BOUTIQUE

Hôtel Panache €€
MAP P82

Sitting in the heart of Grand Boulevards, this boutique address offers art deco-inspired rooms imagined by one of Paris' coolest designers, Dorothée Meilichzon.

HOW MUCH FOR A NIGHT IN

Hostel dorm bed
From €32

Boutique midrange hotel
From €160

Studio apartment
From €130

Hôtel de la Boétie €
MAP P82 ㉑

Design fans will appreciate the colourful rooms and vintage touches imagined by Swedish designer Beata Heuman at this boutique hotel, which sits amongst Paris' five-star and grande dame hotels.

Nuage €
MAP P82 ㉔

This third-generation-owned hotel is based around the concept of slow living, so expect tranquil rooms decorated in soft, soothing shades. There's also a private cinema room for a quiet night in.

CONTEMPORARY COOL

Hôtel Pulitzer €€
MAP P82 ㉓

Cosy chic rooms (which include an option for solo travellers) are dressed with warm wooden furnishings and an eclectic mix of artworks. The attractive restaurant also has an outdoor patio for summer drinks.

PLEY Hotel €€
MAP P82 ㉕

A cool lifestyle hotel with a restaurant, bar, fitness room, rooftop and even a podcast recording studio. It's also both pet- and family-friendly.

Louvre & Les Halles

CONTEMPORARY

Edgar & Achille €€
MAP P118 ⑭

An intimate hotel in the heart of Sentier, overlooking a quiet square. Each room has a distinct decoration, from a wooden cabin style to a rock 'n' roll–themed decor. The restaurant has a pleasant outdoor terrace.

Hôtel Crayon Rouge €€€
MAP P118 ⑯

Conveniently located between Palais Royal and Les Halles, this discreet hotel offers relatively large rooms for the area, with a lovely retro-chic style. Ask for the room with a Jacuzzi.

CitizenM Paris Opéra €€-€€€
MAP P118 ⑫

A bit futuristic, this modern hotel allows you to control everything with a tablet, from your check-in to the lights in your room. The rooms can be quite luminous, thanks to large bay windows.

THEMED HOTELS

123 Sebastopol €€
MAP P118 ⑪

A cinema-themed hotel where each floor is dedicated to a film director or film music composer, with an entertaining atmosphere. It is family-friendly and conveniently located between Sentier and Le Marais.

Hôtel Odyssey €€
MAP P118 ⑰

Tucked behind Palais Royal, this small hotel is designed like a wooden boat. It offers intimate rooms where you can feel like you're in a cocoon once you've drawn the curtains on your bed cubicle.

St James Paris (p307)

BOUTIQUE

Drawing Hotel €€-€€€
MAP P99 **11**

A high-standard hotel where each floor and some furniture have been designed in collaboration with an artist. Art lovers will enjoy the adjoined art gallery dedicated to contemporary drawing.

Grand Boulevards Experimental €€-€€€
MAP P118 **15**

With your room, enjoy the glass-roofed restaurant, the hotel's inner courtyard or the rooftop cocktail bar. The rooms are relatively spacious, and decorated in a late-18th-century French style.

Dandy Hotel €€-€€€
MAP P118 **13**

At the very heart of Les Halles, this hotel boasts rooms with a chic atmosphere, a restaurant with an outdoor terrace on one of the liveliest streets in Paris, and a spa to relax.

TOP END TO SPLURGE

Le Roch Hotel & Spa €€€
MAP P99 **13**

An elegant hotel where you can enjoy dinner at the restaurant below the glass roof, a coffee on the terrace tucked away from the city's noise, and even a relaxing swim in the indoor pool.

Montmartre & Northern Paris

HOSTELS

Le Village Montmartre by Hiphostels €
MAP P130 **22**

A well-priced hostel at the bottom of Montmartre and close to Pigalle's restaurants and bars; there's an outdoor patio, dorm beds and private rooms, some of which have views of the Sacré-Cœur Basilica.

Generator Hostel €
MAP P138 **10**

A buzzy, design hostel with a fun rooftop bar strung with lights, a lively social scene and industrial-chic interiors near buzzy, bohemian Canal St-Martin with its stylish boutiques and eateries.

ZEN

Hôtel HoY €€
MAP P130 **18**

One of the most restful places to stay, there's a yoga studio and in-room mats. The highlight is the ground-floor flower shop and the excellent MESA, serving up creative plant-based dishes steeped in Latin American flavours.

Hotel Élysée Montmartre €€
MAP P130 **17**

This airy, light-filled boutique stay with soothing hues is slotted between legendary music halls Elysée Montmartre and Le Trianon steps from Pigalle, blending classic wabi sabi–inspired interiors and creature comforts.

> **BOOK AHEAD**
>
> Paris has no real low season, although room rates may be less in winter (outside of the holidays) and early spring. Whether you want a hostel bed or a luxurious suite, the earlier you book the better.

Hôtel Le Ballu €€
MAP P130 **19**

An intimate hotel with sleek, sharply designed rooms just around the corner from busy Place de Clichy and Pigalle; there is a leafy outdoor courtyard restaurant and a little pool in the basement you can have to yourself.

Hôtel Eldorado €€
MAP P130 **16**

A design-forward hideaway in the village-like Batignolles, it has a fresh Mediterranean look with lots of flower-patterned wallpaper, a restaurant in a dreamy courtyard setting and an entire house you can rent.

Bloom House Hotel €€
MAP P138 **9**

A colourful, wellness-focused hotel in the 10th *arrondissement*, between Gare de l'Est and Canal St-Martin, with an attractive spa and large heated pool, perks and a sunny, resort-like feel with an outdoor patio.

COOL

Le Pigalle €€
MAP P130 **20**

There's a cool retro-vintage vibe here, from the lively ground-floor bar and restaurant with squishy vintage sofas and chairs, to the rooms that have record players, and urban photography bringing a lived-in feel.

COSY

Le Relais Montmartre €
MAP P130 **21**

A well-maintained classic abode on a quiet street, steps from the heart of Montmartre. It has lots of chintzy flower fabrics and a certain personal charm, including warm, friendly staff and rooms that are comfortable and light.

Le Marais, Belleville & Ménilmontant

CONTEMPORARY COOL

Suzie Blue €€
MAP P152 ⓰

Enjoy warm, cocooning neutral shades in this certified green key former-convent. Its eco-conscious offerings include Terre de Mars toiletries and organic refreshments. Its coffee shop is the perfect space to brunch or work before moving to the salon and relaxing to one of 1000 vinyls.

Hotel 9Confidentiel €€€
MAP P154 ⓫

Filled with delicate shades of pastel pink and yellow, this charming hotel serves signature cocktails at a glowing copper bar and has balconies perfect for a breakfast overlooking the Paris rooftops. Relax with in-room spa treatments from Codage.

Hôtel Scarlett €-€€
MAP P170 ⓳

Located at the very heart of Belleville, this charming hotel offers pretty rooms in a contemporary style. The family room opens onto a small patio.

Hotel Les Deux Girafes €€
MAP P170 ⓲

In an industrial style, this hotel between Republique and Belleville offers spacious rooms, some of which open onto a refreshing Japanese-garden patio. Art exhibitions are regularly hosted in the hall.

LUXURIOUS HISTORY

Hôtel de JoBo €€€
MAP P154 ⓬

Inspired by Empress Josephine Bonaparte, JoBo is filled with charming details drawn from her life. Pink and black wallpaper full of roses runs across walls and the cosy downstairs bar is both lavish and intimate.

Boudoir des Muses €€€
MAP P152 ⓯

Based on the building's previous uses, this stylish hotel marries convent and theatre throughout the decor and cocktails. Relax in its downstairs spa areas and enjoy monthly burlesque-inspired shows.

BOUTIQUE

Babel Belleville €-€€
MAP P170 ⓰

Conveniently located on the bd de Belleville, this hotel is welcoming and atmospheric, with a mix of natural and vintage decoration. The breakfast here is delicious and there is an open-terrace restaurant.

La Nouvelle République €-€€
MAP P170 ⓴

In the middle of bustling Oberkampf and rue St-Maur, yet in a quiet alley, this hotel offers a break from the party, with large, comfortable rooms in a vintage chic style.

HOSTELS & BUDGET

The People Belleville €
MAP P170 ㉑

Choose this international hostel for its lively atmosphere, themed parties and events – which make it easy to meet people – and its very convenient location in Belleville.

Fraternity Hostel €
MAP P170 ⓱

Located in the lively area of Oberkampf, it's a cosy hostel in a smaller alley, which makes it a little quieter. It offers dorms, but also a few double rooms for more privacy.

The People Marais €
MAP P154 ⓯

This modern hostel is built for community with well-equipped dorms, communal kitchens, and a light-filled sociable cafe and restaurant. In the evening, it transforms into an event space with a DJ and sometimes shows.

MIJE Fourcy €
MAP P154 ⓮

This winding 17th-century *hôtel particulier* has basic, clean rooms in an incredibly central location steeped in history. It only offers wi-fi on the ground floor, but rates do include a French breakfast.

Hôtel Jeanne d'Arc le Marais €€
MAP P154 ⓭

Modernised rooms retain timber beams or exposed stone walls, while others have feature walls with patterned wallpaper. The pièce de résistance: the 6th-floor attic room with a sweeping Paris rooftop view.

Bastille & Eastern Paris

HOSTELS

The People – Paris Bercy €
MAP P198 ⓳

This outlet of the Paris hostel chain is in a tranquil neighbourhood and boasts six- and eight-bed dorms as well as private rooms, a well-equipped kitchen and, most notably, a roof terrace with a panoramic view.

JO&JOE Paris – Nation €
MAP P186 ⓮

Located on the same street as a metro station, this modern, lively hostel has a busy schedule of events, comfy bunks with privacy curtains, and a 100-sq-metre rooftop that serves homemade pizzas.

ON A BUDGET

Hôtel Daval €€
MAP P186 ⓫

This renovated 23-room hotel, set in an early 1900s stone building, is in the bustling heart of Bastille. Rooms have double-glazing but ask for one facing the interior courtyard to ensure peace and quiet.

Hôtel Jeanne d'Arc le Marais

Hôtel du Printemps €€
MAP P186 ⓬

The 38-room Spring Hotel, a stone's throw from place de la Nation, offers excellent value for Paris. Set on a tree-lined boulevard in a non-touristy area, it's compact and comfortable, even if a little far from the action.

BOUTIQUE

Mama Shelter Paris East €€
MAP P186 ⓯

This hip Philippe Starck–designed, 170-room hotel, transformed from a car park, draws a younger, creative crowd to its off-grid location thanks to its bold industrial decor, rooftop bar and playful touches such as cartoon mask lampshades.

Hôtel Paris Bastille Boutet €€€
MAP P186 ⓭

This classy 80-room former joinery workshop and chocolate factory, in the heart of the 11th *arrondissement*, has a magnificent 1926 mosaic façade, timber-panelled hallways, a hammam, a sky-lit swimming pool and suites with spectacular terraces.

The Islands

BOUTIQUE

Hôtel du Jeu de Paume €€€
MAP P206 ㉗

Contemporary hotel in a former royal tennis court on Île St-Louis' main street, with rooms inspired by modern artists.

Hôtel des Deux Îles €€€
MAP P206 ㉖

Elegantly floral decor with top-floor rooms peeping out over Parisian rooftops and chimney pots.

Hôtel Saint-Louis en l'Isle €€€
MAP P206 ㉙

Swank and subtle, this stellar abode includes a 17th-century stone-cellar breakfast room.

Hôtel L de Lutèce €€€
MAP P206 ㉘

Elegant lobby-salon, with vintage fireplace and wood panelling, pairs with tastefully decorated rooms. Those overlooking the village-like street are most atmospheric.

APARTMENTS

Paris Perfect €€€
MAP P206 ㉚

High-end vacation rentals with eight luxe options right on place Dauphine, some with balconies and stupendous views.

Latin Quarter

COUNTRYSIDE VIBES

Hôtel des Grandes Écoles €€
MAP P224 ㉔

Hidden in a closed-off alleyway next door to writer James Joyce's former Latin Quarter abode, this charming three-star hotel has tables out in a leafy courtyard for breakfast in the sun.

Le 66 €€
MAP P224 ㉙

You'll find a handful of rooms inside a refitted townhouse with wooden beams, original fireplaces and a conservatory that makes it feel like you're sojourning in the French countryside.

VIEWS

Hotel Les Dames du Panthéon €€
MAP P224 ㉖

It really doesn't get better than this if you're after killer views of the Panthéon. Tucked into a building just next to it, the zany, beamed rooms here overlook the landmark.

COSY

Hôtel Monge €€
MAP P224 ㉗

A cosy boutique hotel with eclectic decor, just across the street from the Arènes de Lutèce, a 2nd-century Roman amphitheatre. Rooms have bouncy beds and colourful butterfly-print wallpapers.

URBAN

Seven Hotel €€
MAP P224 ㉛

On a quiet street in the south of the neighbourhood, the bold coloured rooms have a retro twist. There's a daily hearty breakfast buffet and also a small massage area for unwinding in.

> **CONSIDER OUTLYING DISTRICTS**
>
> Favoured neighbourhoods like St-Germain and the Marais have the highest hotel prices. If you look at less touristed areas, such as western and southern Paris, you'll find cheaper rates while still being able to enjoy the Parisian lifestyle.

Hôtel Grand Cœur Latin €€
MAP P224 ㉕

Built on the site of a 13th-century abbey, you'll find subtle nods to the past woven through the decor like stone arch wallpaper print. Rooms are simple but comfortable, and there's a bar and a pool.

Hôtel Pilgrim €€
MAP P224 ㉘

A comfortable hotel where beds have fabric headboards, there's a rooftop terrace and a pool, as well as a small gym, just a few minutes' walk to the River Seine and Notre Dame Cathedral.

APARTMENT-HOTEL

Le Jardin de Verre by Locke €€
MAP P224 ㉚

A bright and breezy apartment hotel with attractive contemporary interiors; rooms are simple but functional and the bold hues bring a cheerful twist.

St-Germain & Les Invalides

SPLASHING OUT

Pavillon Faubourg Saint Germain €€
MAP P242 ⑰

Part of a small group of charming boutique addresses, this chic hotel offers a complete set of facilities including a full spa experience with a pool big enough to swim in – a rarity in Paris.

ROMANTIC

L'Hôtel €€
MAP P242 ⑯

Oscar Wilde lived out his last days at this historic hotel. Now an intimate five-star address, its 20 rooms are romantically dressed in jewel shades and plush velvet. A small pool is hidden away underground.

Hôtel de l'Abbaye Saint-Germain €€
MAP P242 ⑭

This hotel is right in the heart of St-Germain des Prés, but quietly tucked away with its own leafy private courtyard. Rooms are just as pretty, dressed in a classic floral French style.

CONTEMPORARY COOL

Hôtel Dame des Arts €€
MAP P242 ⑬

This hip hotel is one of St-Germain des Prés' coolest addresses, with design-led rooms and a rooftop terrace with fantastic views that pulls in locals as well as guests.

Hôtel des Académies et des Arts €€
MAP P248

An effortlessly cool design hotel housed in the building where Modigliani once had his studio (book room 52 if you want to sleep in it). The hotel also has its own art atelier downstairs.

Hôtel des Grands Voyageurs €€
MAP P248 ⑮

The little sister to Hôtel Dame des Arts. Light and airy rooms take their cues from the golden age of travel with retro-inspired furnishings. The underground cocktail bar has speakeasy vibes.

BOUTIQUE

Hôtel Thoumieux €€
MAP P248 ⑯

If you like quirky design, then check into this boutique hotel decked out in a mix of floral wallpaper, bright cushions and leopard-print throws.

Hôtel St-André des Arts €€
MAP P242 ⑮

This 30-room boutique address is part of a small group of Left Bank hotels (see also Hotel Baume and La Belle Juliette) but this one feels the youngest and freshest with its bright '60s-inspired decor.

Hôtel des Académies et des Arts

Montparnasse & Southern Paris

ON A BUDGET

3 Ducks Hostel €
MAP P270 ⑱

This hostel, a 10-minute walk from the Eiffel Tower, has a good-time vibe and excellent facilities.

Oops €
MAP P274 ⑲

This colourful design hostel has four- to six-bed dorms and doubles with bathrooms as well as a wide range of facilities.

Urban Bivouac Hotel €
MAP P274 ⑳

A great base if you want to explore the Paris Rive Gauche area and the Butte aux Cailles neighbourhood.

BOUTIQUE

Hôtel Léopold €€
MAP P270 ⑲

Off Cimetière du Montparnasse, this cosy venture has only 40 rooms. They have a retro feel and feature floral-patterned wallpapers.

Hôtel Max €€
MAP P270 ⑳

All 19 rooms at this contemporary boutique hotel in the heart of the 14e have muted colours, modern art and timber floors.

Hôtel Henriette €€
MAP P274 ⑰

One of the Left Bank's most stunning boutique addresses, with designer chairs, 1950s lighting and vintage pieces. Guests can mingle in the light-flooded glass atrium and adjoining plant-filled patio with wrought-iron furniture.

Off Paris Seine €€
MAP P274 ⑱

Paris' first floating hotel is this sleek, 80m-long catamaran-design structure moored off Gare d'Austerlitz.

STYLISH

Hôtel Vic Eiffel €€
MAP P270 ㉑

A short walk from the Eiffel Tower, this pristine hotel has chic orange and oyster-grey rooms.

La Maison Lavaud €€€
MAP P270 ㉒

This super-stylish, artfully decorated gem feels like a home away from home, in a very quiet street close to Parc Montsouris. It features a giant-sized penthouse and a large apartment with a huge terrace.

Villa M €€€
MAP P270 ㉓

From its façade covered with plants to its colourful rooms with a Starck-inspired decor, the Villa M makes a perfect base in the Montparnasse area. Also has a great restaurant and a fantastic rooftop bar.

TOO Hotel €€€
MAP P274 ⑬

Opened in 2022, occupying the top floors of the Tours Duo designed by Jean Nouvel. All glassed-wall rooms have sensational city views. Its restaurant, bar and spa are also first-rate and offer unparalleled views.

TOOLKIT

The chapters in this section cover the most important topics you'll need to know about in Paris. They're full of nuts-and-bolts information and valuable insights to help you understand and navigate Paris and get the most out of your trip.

Money
p316

Family Travel
p317

Food, Drink & Nightlife
p318

LGBTIQ+ Travellers
p320

Health & Safe Travel
p321

Responsible Travel
p322

Accessible Travel
p324

Nuts & Bolts
p325

Language
p326

Breakfast with a view in Paris
FASHIONINMYSOUL/SHUTTERSTOCK

Money

CURRENCY: EURO (€)

Tipping
Taxis Round up to the nearest €1.
Restaurants Bills include a service charge; leave a few extra euros for good service.
Bars/cafes For table service, tip as you would in a restaurant.
Hotels Tip bellhops €1 to €2 per bag. Not expected for concierges, cleaners or front-desk staff.

ATMs
ATMs *(distributeur automatique de billets)* are widespread and can be cheaper than exchanging money. Check if/how much your bank charges for international withdrawals before you travel.

Digital Payments
Payments via your phone or smartwatch are common in Paris. Tap and pay is becoming ubiquitous, from shops and cafes to the metro.

Credit Cards
Visa is the most widely accepted credit card in Paris, followed by MasterCard. Amex cards are only accepted at more upmarket establishments. If paying by card, the electronic device may offer you the option to pay in your home currency. Refuse and select the euro option, as this is cheaper.

HOW MUCH FOR A...

Baguette
Around €1.20

Glass of wine
From €4

Two-course bistro menu
From €22

Louvre ticket
€22

HOW TO... Claim VAT Refunds
Non-EU residents over 16 who are visiting France for less than six months can often claim a TVA *(taxe sur la valeur ajoutée)* refund, provided the purchase amount is over €100 and made over a maximum of three days at a retailer that offers tax-free shopping (present your passport for eligibility). The retailer will provide a slip with a barcode that can be scanned at PABLO electronic terminals prior to check-in at the airport.

LOCAL TIP
Save money at restaurants by ordering tap water *(une carafe d'eau)* instead of bottled water. Take home any leftovers in a doggy bag – it's perfectly acceptable to ask your waiter.

SAVING MONEY ON MUSEUMS & SIGHTS

Most museums and monuments have discounted tickets *(tarif réduit)* for students and seniors. Children often get in for free; the cut-off age is anywhere between six and 18 years. Watch for free days.

Paris Museum Pass Gets you into 50-plus venues; a huge advantage is that pass holders usually enter larger sights at an entrance with shorter queues.

Paris Passlib' Sold by the Paris Tourist Office, this customisable city pass covers unlimited public transport, admission to dozens of museums, a Seine boat cruise, a bus tour and more.

Family Travel

Paris is a city that's made for kids. Not only is there playground equipment in virtually every square and park, but there's also a bonanza of fun things to see and do. From zoos and aquariums to theme parks, the French capital has it all. A boat ride on the Seine is always a good idea. Museums cultivate Parisians from an early age with child-friendly workshops – the Paris Tourist Office website (parisinfo.com) lists museums and activities for kids. Discounts at sights and attractions aimed at families abound.

Accommodation

Note that Paris hotel rooms can be smaller than you're used to, so keep that in mind as you think about sharing the room. Some establishments offer rooms aimed specifically at families. Rental apartments will give you – possibly – more space and let you self-cater for younger tastes and habits. Consider lift (elevator) options if you'll be dealing with prams and the like.

Theme Parks

Disneyland Resort Paris is a natural magnet for families. Located 32km east of the city, it's easily reached for day trips on the RER A. Parc Astérix, a summer-opening theme park 35km north of the city, features six 'worlds' of adrenaline-pumping attractions and shows for all ages. Jardin d'Acclimatation, situated in the Bois de Boulogne, is the only amusement park within Paris proper.

Getting Around

Children under four travel free on the metro, RER and bus network. Kids under 10 travel at half-price. Buses have low-floor entrances that are good for prams. The metro system is chaotic at rush hour; some stations have many stairs.

KID-FRIENDLY PICKS

See also Our Picks (p21) and Family Fun (p53).

Musée de la Marine (p75)

Kids find nirvana at the new-look maritime museum.

Cité de l'Architecture et du Patrimoine (p76)

Workshops let kids construct miniature skyscrapers.

Cité des Sciences et de l'Industrie (p143)

Delve into science at this sprawling venue that's way more than a museum.

Promotrain A fantastic way to explore Montmartre by avoiding the many steps.

Seine cruise (p67)

Beloved by all ages.

FABULOUS PARKS FOR KIDS

Major parks have features aimed at kids. The legendary **Jardin du Luxembourg** (p256) has playgrounds, pony rides and an old-fashioned carousel. The vintage toy sailing boats are beloved.

The elegant **Jardin des Tuileries** (p108) also has kid's activities, trampolines and its own fleet of vintage toy boats you can sail in the shadow of the Louvre.

The **Parc Floral de Paris** (p197) delights kids of all ages but particularly those eight years and older with a cornucopia of activities including climbing walls, enormous slides and a zip line.

In the **Jardin des Plantes** (p236) you can see the charming zoo that first opened in 1794 with animals from Marie Antoinette's royal menagerie at Versailles.

Food, Drink & Nightlife

When to Eat

Breakfast (7am to 9am) Typically toasted baguette and coffee, tea or hot chocolate.

Lunch (noon to 2pm) A three-course meal is the norm, though sandwiches and salads are available.

Dinner (7pm to 10.30pm) Often lighter than lunch, with two or three courses, or sharing plates at some restaurants.

Most restaurants shut for at least one full day (often Sunday, Monday and/or Tuesday). August is the peak holiday month and many places are consequently closed during this time.

Where to Eat & Drink

Bistro Small neighbourhood restaurants, often classic haunts with (good-value) chalkboard menus and zinc bars.

Bouillon What started in 1855 as a huge hall serving *bouillon*, or broth-based recipes, has evolved into a trendy, low-cost option serving traditional food.

Neobistro Trendy in Paris, where this contemporary take on the traditional bistro ranges from checked tablecloths to minimalism.

Brasserie Bustling spaces serving full meals (typical fare like *steak-frites*) and drinks from morning until night.

Restaurant Born in Paris in the 18th century, restaurants today serve lunch and dinner five or six days a week.

Cafe Basic light snacks and drinks. On seemingly every corner in Paris, often with a sidewalk terrace. They range from humble to grand, in atmosphere and pricing.

Crêperie Casual eateries specialising in sweet crêpes and savoury *galettes* (buckwheat crêpes).

MENU DECODER

Chaud Hot	**Agneau** Lamb
Froid Cold	**Escargot** Snail
Verre Glass	**Huître** Oyster
Bouteille Bottle	**Jambon** Ham
Vin Wine	**Poulet** Chicken
Bière Beer	**Veau** Veal
Lait Milk	**Champignon** Mushroom
Thé Tea	**Citron** Lemon
Beurre Butter	**Fraise** Strawberry
Fromage Cheese	**Haricots** Beans
Miel Honey	**Légume** Vegetable
Œuf Egg	**Pêche** Peach
Pain Bread	**Petit pois** Peas
Poivre Pepper	**Poireau** Leek
Sel Salt	**Pomme** Apple
Sucre Sugar	**Pomme de terre** Potato

HOW TO... Eat Like a Local

If you're travelling to Paris, keep in mind that meal times are sacred.

Petit déjeuner (breakfast) The French kick-start the day with a *tartine* (slice of baguette smeared with unsalted butter and jam) and *un café* (an espresso), a tall milky *café au lait* or – especially for kids – a hot chocolate. Croissants (eaten straight, never with butter or jam) are a weekend treat along with brioches.

Déjeuner (lunch) A meal few French would go without. The traditional main meal of the day, lunch translates as a starter and main course with wine, followed by an espresso.

Goûter (afternoon snack) The post-school treat for kids is part of the cultural tradition – you'll see the queue outside *boulangeries* around 4.30pm.

Apéritif The *apéro* (predinner drink) is sacred. Paris cafes and bars get packed from around 5pm onwards.

Dîner (dinner) Traditionally lighter than lunch, but a meal that is increasingly treated as the main meal of the day.

HOW MUCH FOR A...

Baguette
€1.20

Beer in a cafe
€6

Decent bottle of wine in a store
€10

Café in a cafe
€3

Crêpe
€5

Main in a bistro
€15–22

Two-course meal
€24–50 or more

HOW TO... Eat & Drink Like a Parisian

Eating well is of prime importance to most French people, who spend a sumptuous amount of time thinking about, discussing and enjoying food and wine. Yet dining out (learn more at p36) doesn't have to be a ceremonious occasion or one riddled with pitfalls for the uninitiated. Approach food with even half the enthusiasm *les français* do, and you will be welcomed, encouraged and exceedingly well fed.

Daily *formules* or *menus (prix fixe menus)* typically include two- to four-course meals. In some cases, particularly at market-driven neobistros, there is no *carte* (menu). Lunch *menus* are often a fantastic deal and allow you to enjoy *haute cuisine* at very affordable prices.

Order a meal and within seconds a basket of fresh bread will be brought to the table. Except in the most upmarket of places, don't expect a side plate – simply put the bread on the table.

Wine is easily the most popular beverage in Paris and house wine can cost less than bottled water. Of France's dozens of wine-producing regions, the principal ones are Burgundy, Bordeaux, the Rhône and the Loire valleys, Champagne, Languedoc, Provence and Alsace. The best wines are Appellation d'Origine Contrôlée (AOC; also labelled Appellation d'Origine Protégée, AOP).

Trying to get *l'addition* (the bill) can be maddeningly slow. The French consider it rude to bring the bill immediately – you have to be persistent when it comes to getting your server's attention. Service is included so a *pourboire* (tip) on top of the bill is not necessary, though it's appreciated.

Baguettes

Buy a baguette from a *boulangerie* (bakery), stuff it with a chunk of Camembert, pâté and *cornichons* (miniature gherkins), and, voilà, picnic perfection! A *baguette tradition/traditionnelle* will have a little more character and flavour.

THE INGREDIENTS OF A FRENCH MEAL

Knowing these terms will help you navigate a Parisian meal.

Carte Menu, as in the written list of what's on offer.

Menu Not at all what it means in English, *le menu* in French is a two- or three-course meal at a fixed price.

À la carte Order whatever you fancy from the menu (as opposed to a fixed *menu*).

Formule *Une formule* is a lunchtime option comprising a main plus starter or dessert.

Plat du jour Dish of the day, invariably good value.

Menu enfant Two- or three-course kids' meal at a fixed price.

Menu dégustation Fixed-price tasting menu served in many top-end restaurants, consisting of five to seven courses.

Amuse-bouche A complimentary savoury morsel intended to excite taste buds, served in top-end restaurants.

Entrée Starter, appetiser.

Plat Main course.

Fromage Cheese, accompanied with fresh bread; always served after the main course.

Dessert Just that, served after cheese.

LGBTIQ+ Travellers

The city known as 'gay Paree' lives up to its name. Paris is so open that there's less of a defined 'scene' here than in other cities where it's more underground. While Le Marais is the mainstay of gay and lesbian nightlife, you'll find LGBTIQ+ venues throughout the city attracting a mixed crowd.

Annual Events

By far the biggest event on the LGBTIQ+ calendar is Gay Pride Day, in late June, when the annual Marche des Fiertés through Paris via Le Marais provides a colourful spectacle, and plenty of parties take place over a two-week period.

Look for these events at other times of the year:

May Paris Ass Book Fair brings together artists, booksellers, publishers and zinesters at the Palais de Tokyo.
October to November Jerk Off is a huge series of events devoted to queer and alternative culture.
November Chéries Chéri is an annual, international LGBTIQ+ film festival supported by the French Ministry of Culture.

NIGHTLIFE

Le Marais, especially the areas around the intersection of rue Ste-Croix de la Bretonnerie and rue des Archives, and eastwards to rue Vieille du Temple, has long been Paris' main centre of LGBTIQ+ nightlife and is still its epicentre. There are also a handful of bars and clubs close by to its west, particularly around Châtelet. Bars and clubs are generally all gay- and lesbian-friendly.

Paris' Best Resource

Centre LGBTQI+ de Paris et Île-de-France *(centrelgbtparis.org)* is the single best source of information for gay and lesbian travellers in Paris, with a large library, a comprehensive website and periodicals, and a sociable bar. It also has details of hotlines, helplines, gay and gay-friendly medical services and politically oriented activist associations.

GAY TOURS

For an insider's perspective on gay life in Paris, and to learn the stories of its queer inhabitants over the centuries, take a tour with the **Gay Locals** *(thegaylocals.com)*. English-speaking residents lead tours of 'the Gaybourhood' Le Marais or Montmartre, and can provide itinerary planning based on your interests. Its website is a good source of nightlife info.

LGBTIQ+ WEBSITES

Gay Cities (paris.gaycities.com) This travel guide offers reviews of all kinds of venues, from bars and clubs to bathhouses.
Gay and lesbian cultural venues (parisjetaime.com/eng/article/gay-and-lesbian-cultural-venues-a652) The Paris Tourist Office lists 'the gayest spots in the French capital'.
Spartacus International Gay Guide (spartacus.travel) Travel site with solid recommendations for gay-friendly accommodation in particular.

Gay Paris

In 2001 Paris was the first European capital to elect an openly gay mayor. The city itself is very open – same-sex couples commonly display affection in public. In 2013 France legalised same-sex marriage (and adoption by same-sex couples).

Health & Safe Travel

INSURANCE

Citizens of the EU, Switzerland, Iceland, Norway and Liechtenstein receive free or reduced-cost, state-provided health-care cover with the European Health Insurance Card (EHIC), should medical treatment become necessary while in France. Each family member will need a separate card. Citizens of non-EU countries should check if there is a reciprocal arrangement for free medical care between their country and France.

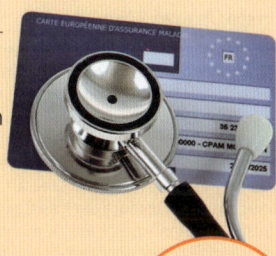

Pharmacies & Hospitals

For minor health concerns and to fill prescriptions, see a local *pharmacie* (pharmacy/chemist). For more serious problems, go to *urgences* (emergencies) wards at Paris' *hôpitaux* (hospitals).

Pharmacies are marked by a large illuminated green cross outside. At least one in each neighbourhood is open for extended hours; find a complete listing on the Paris Tourist Office website.

Luggage & Bags

Never leave baggage unattended, especially at airports or train stations. This is important not only to deter theft but because unattended bags are viewed as security threats and can cause a major law-enforcement event. Elsewhere, at museums and monuments, bags are routinely checked on entry. Avoid hassles by travelling as light as possible when you're out and about.

PICKPOCKETS

Stay alert for pickpockets, especially on the metro/RER and crowded, touristy areas. *Bornes d'alarme* (alarm boxes) are located on station platforms and some corridors.

Strikes & Protests

Sporadic train and public-transport strikes and striking taxi drivers can disrupt travel. These disruptions are usually announced in advance. Paris is the focus of public protests, some drawing huge crowds from across France. Although there's a long tradition of peacefully protesting about grievances, these events can become unsafe. Routes for demonstrations/processions are announced in advance.

DON'T WORRY

Overall, Paris (and France) is a healthy place: your main risks are likely to be sunburn, foot blisters and mild stomach problems from eating and drinking with too much gusto. Central Paris is well lit and generally safe – single travellers can play it safe by sticking to main streets at night. The important consideration is to use common sense: if an area or situation looks sketchy, leave.

Responsible Travel

Climate Change & Travel

It's impossible to ignore the impact we have when travelling; Lonely Planet urges all travellers to engage with their travel carbon footprint, which will mainly come from air travel. While there often isn't an alternative, travellers can look to minimise the number of flights they take, opt for newer aircraft and use cleaner ground transport, such as trains. One proposed solution – purchasing carbon offsets – unfortunately does not cancel out the impact of individual flights. While most destinations will depend on air travel for the foreseeable future, for now, pursuing ground-based travel where possible is the best course of action.

The **UN Carbon Offset Calculator** shows how flying impacts a household's emissions

The **ICAO's carbon emissions calculator** allows visitors to analyse the CO2 generated by point-to-point journeys

Meet the Locals

The Explore Paris website (exploreparis.com/en) offers tourism activities and guided tours that break away from the Paris classics, with an emphasis on meeting locals and artisans in the Greater Paris region.

Vegan Travellers

Vegetarian and vegan restaurants are blossoming in Paris. Franck Adandé, aka @vegantouristparis, helps you navigate the scene through guided vegan tours, a newsletter and a dedicated Vegan Tourist Map.

Refill your reusable water bottle at gorgeous green Wallace fountains all over Paris (see fontaine.eaudeparis.fr). Some contemporary fountains even offer sparkling water.

Look out over Paris from 150m up in the air aboard the helium-filled **Ballon de Paris** *(ballondeparis.com)*. Tethered in the Parc André Citroën, this sightseeing balloon monitors Paris' air quality.

SUSTAINABLE DINING

Dine farm-to-fork at Le Perchoir Porte de Versailles at Europe's largest urban rooftop farm, the 14,000-sq-metre biodiverse Nature Urbaine. The changing menu utilises all the various foods grown in this sustainable setting.

Buy fresh produce at Paris' *biologique* (organic) markets, such as Marché Raspail (Sunday), Marché Biologique des Batignolles (Saturday), Marché Biologique Brancusi (Saturday) and Marché Biologique Place du Père Chaillet (Wednesday and Saturday).

Harvest Saffron on a Rooftop
Startup **BienÉlevées** *(bienelevees.com)* cultivates saffron on Paris rooftops, including the Opéra Bastille. Various workshops are offered – you can help harvest the fragile flowers in October and November.

Learn Recycling
Take an upcycling workshop at eco-conscious cultural centre **La Recyclerie** *(larecyclerie.com)*, in a repurposed vintage train station, whose cafe utilises produce from its own urban farm on the tracks.

Electric Boats
Chart your own course and explore 40km of Paris' canals by renting an electric-powered boat (no licence required) from **Akwa Experience** *(akwa-experience.com/en)*. On the Seine, book an excursion with **Ducasse sur Seine** *(ducasse-seine.com)* or **Green River Cruises** *(greenriver-paris.fr)*.

Diverse Paris
Discover Black Paris on a guided tour with **Entrée to Black Paris** *(entreetoblackparis.com)*, take a walking or kick-scooter tour of Paris' multicultural northeastern neighbourhoods with **Ça Se Visite** *(ca-se-visite.fr)* and learn about Islamic culture on tours with the **Institut des Cultures d'Islam** *(institut-cultures-islam.org)*.

Snap up bargain-priced unsold items at merchants such as bakeries via the app **Too Good to Go** *(toogoodtogo.fr)*, which helps prevent food waste.

Browse over 1000 exquisite handcrafted items, all made in French designers' studios, at **Empreintes** *(empreintes-paris.com)*.

In Paris' pursuit of carbon neutrality by 2050, dramatic progress includes a 35% reduction in greenhouse-gas emissions between 2004 and 2021. The 'Plan Arbre', a major tree-planting scheme, has introduced 'urban forests' to the cityscape.

Sustainable Fashion
Take part in events and more through the **Paris Good Fashion** *(parisgoodfashion.fr)* initiative, which is focused on improving sourcing, traceability, eco-friendly processes and circular economies as part of Paris' aim to become the world's most sustainable fashion capital.

RESOURCES

Sustainable Paris
Embrace Paris' sustainability initiatives.

Made in Paris
Products sporting the Made in Paris label.

We Love Green
Zero-waste, renewable-energy-powered festival.

Accessible Travel

Paris is an ancient city and therefore not particularly well equipped for *visiteurs handicapés* (visitors with disabilities): kerb ramps are few and older public facilities and the metro are mostly inaccessible for those in a wheelchair *(fauteuil roulant)*. Efforts are being made to improve things, however, especially with the Grand Paris Express metro expansion project.

Helpful Paris

In general, although Paris is not always accessible, you will find that most Parisians are more than willing to help and that accommodations can be made at cultural institutions and public places like cafes.

Airport

Paris' airports are fully in line with international standards for accessibility. Note, however, that transport to and from the airports may be an issue as many metro stations in the city are not fully accessible.

Accommodation

Hotels and rental apartments are a mixed bag of accessibility. Typically, chain hotels in modern buildings meet international standards. But properties in older buildings, especially rental apartments, may lack lifts and other accessibility amenities.

TOURISM LABELS

Museums like La Monnaie de Paris have been recognised with the Tourisme & Handicap label for the quality of their amenities for those with disabilities. The Musée de la Marine pioneered special amenities for children with autism.

Taxis

Taxis G7 *(g7.fr)* has hundreds of low-base cars and over 100 cars equipped with ramps, and drivers trained in helping passengers with disabilities. Guide dogs are accepted in its entire fleet.

Accessible Culture

Many cultural attractions, including the Arc de Triomphe, offer free admission for people with disabilities and their companions, along with special discovery tours (booked in advance).

PUBLIC TRANSPORT

Much of the vintage metro system in the heart of Paris is not fully accessible; the RATP makes info available through its app and website. Paris buses, however, are all accessible, with low floors and wide doors.

RESOURCES

An excellent first stop is the website of the **Paris Tourist Office** *(parisinfo.com/accessibility)*, for a wealth of useful information organised by theme – getting there and around, attractions, accommodation and cafes/bars/restaurants – as well as practical information such as where to rent medical equipment or locate automatic public toilets. You can download the up-to-date Accessible Paris guide, which is also available in hard copy from tourist information centres in the city.

Mobile en Ville makes independent travel within Paris easier for people with mobility challenges. It organises wheelchair *randonnées* (walks) in and around Paris; those in wheelchairs are pushed by 'walkers'. Contact the association ahead of your visit to take part.

Nuts & Bolts

OPENING HOURS

The following list covers approximate standard opening hours. Many businesses close in August for summer holidays.

Banks 9am–1pm and 2–5pm Monday to Friday; some open on Saturday morning

Bars and cafes 7am–11pm or 2am

Museums 10am–6pm; closed Monday or Tuesday

Restaurants noon–2pm and 7–10.30pm

Shops 10am–7pm Monday to Saturday; hours are longer in tourist zones

Internet Access

Free wi-fi is common in many public squares, cultural institutions and cafes.

Weights & Measures

France uses the metric system. Decimal places are indicated by commas.

Smoking

Smoking is illegal in all indoor public spaces, including restaurants, cafes and bars. From July 2025, smoking in outdoor areas frequented by children is banned.

GOOD TO KNOW

Time zone
Central European Time (GMT/ UTC +1)

Country calling code
33

Emergency number
112

Population
2.1 million

Electricity

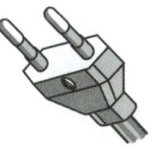

Type C
230V/50Hz

Type E
230V/50Hz

PUBLIC HOLIDAYS

New Year's Day (Jour de l'An) 1 January

Easter Sunday & Monday (Pâques & Lundi de Pâques) Late March/April

May Day (Fête du Travail) 1 May

Victory in Europe Day (Victoire 1945) 8 May

Ascension Thursday (L'Ascension) May (celebrated on the 40th day after Easter)

Whit Monday (Lundi de Pentecôte) Mid-May to mid-June (seventh Monday after Easter)

Bastille Day/ National Day (Fête Nationale) 14 July

Assumption Day (L'Assomption) 15 August

All Saints' Day (La Toussaint) 1 November

Armistice Day/ Remembrance Day (Le Onze Novembre) 11 November

Christmas (Noël) 25 December

Language

Although English is increasingly widespread in Paris, you'll have an infinitely more rewarding experience if you address locals in French, even simply *'bonjour, parlez-vous anglais?'* ('hello, do you speak English?')

Basics

Hello. Bonjour. *bon-zhoor*
Goodbye. Au revoir. *o-rer-vwa*
Yes. Oui. *wee*
No. Non. *non*
Please. S'il vous plaît. *seel voo play*
Thank you. Merci. *mair-see*
Excuse me. Excusez-moi. *ek-skew-zay-mwa*
Sorry. Pardon. *par-don*
What's your name? Comment vous appelez-vous? *ko-mon voo-za-play voo*
My name is … Je m'appelle … *zher ma-pel …*
Do you speak English? Parlez-vous anglais? *par-lay-voo ong-glay*
I don't understand. Je ne comprends pas. *zher ner kom-pron pa*

Directions

Where's …?
Où est …? *oo ay …*
What's the address?
Quelle est l'adresse? *kel ay la-dres*
Could you write the address, please? Est-ce que vous pourriez écrire l'adresse, s'il vous plaît? *es-ker voo poo-ryay ay-kreer la-dres seel voo play*
Can you show me (on the map)?
Pouvez-vous m'indiquer (sur la carte)? *poo-vay-voo mun-dee-kay (sewr la kart)*

Signs

Entrée Entrance
Fermé Closed
Ouvert Open
Sortie Exit
Toilettes/WC Toilets

Time

What time is it? Quelle heure est-il? *kel er ay til*
It's (8) o'clock. Il est (huit) heures. *il ay (weet) er*
Half past (10). Il est (dix) heures et demie. *il ay (deez) er ay day-mee*
morning matin *ma-tun*
afternoon après-midi *a-pray-mee-dee*
evening soir *swar*
yesterday hier *yair*
today aujourd'hui *o-zhoor-dwee*
tomorrow demain *der-mun*

Emergencies

Help! Au secours! *o skoor*
Leave me alone! Fichez-moi la paix! *fee-shay-mwa la pay*
I'm ill. Je suis malade. *zher swee ma-lad*
Call … Appelez… *a-play*
  a doctor un médecin *un mayd-sun*
  the police la police *la po-lees*

Eating & Drinking

What would you recommend?
Qu'est-ce que vous conseillez? *kes-ker voo kon-say-yay*
Cheers! Santé! *son-tay*
That was delicious.
C'était délicieux! *say-tay day-lee-syer*

NUMBERS

1
un *un*

2
deux *der*

3
trois *trwa*

4
quatre *ka-trer*

5
cinq *sungk*

6
six *sees*

7
sept *set*

8
huit *weet*

9
neuf *nerf*

10
dix *dees*

DISTINCTIVE SOUNDS

Throaty r, silent h, nasal vowels (pronounced as if you're trying to force the sound 'through the nose').

Street Talk

What's up? Quoi de neuf?
Drop it/nevermind! Laisse-tomber!
I can't be bothered/am feeling lazy J'ai la flemme
Enjoy your meal! Bon app!
No way! C'est pas vrai!
Let's go/do it! C'est parti!
Perfect! It's good! Nickel
Oh god! La vache! (literally 'the cow')
Good luck/break a leg Merde
There you go/there you have it Et voilà

And if you want to swear French-style (or express your joy at a gobsmackingly gorgeous view, amazement or disbelief at something...the word is used in many different ways), simply say *Putain!*

DONATIONS TO ENGLISH

Numerous – thanks to the Norman invasion of England in the 11th century, some estimate that three-fifths of everyday English vocabulary arrived via French. You may recognise *café, déjà vu, bon vivant, cliché*...

Language Family

Romance (developed from the Latin spoken by the Romans during their conquest of the 1st century BCE). Close relatives include Italian, Spanish, Portuguese and Romanian.

Must-Know Grammar

French has a formal and informal word for 'you' (*vous* and *tu* respectively); it distinguishes between masculine and feminine forms of words, eg *beau/belle* (beautiful).

False Friends

Warning: many French words look like English words but have a different meaning altogether; eg *menu* is a set lunch, not a menu (which is *carte* in French).

Why Bother to Speak French?

You may be told of a cosy bistro way off the tourist track, or discover that there's little merit in the stereotype about the French being rude.

WHO SPEAKS FRENCH?

French is an official language of 29 countries, including France, Belgium, Canada, Democratic Republic of the Congo and Vanuatu.

80 million speak French as their first language

240 million speak French as a second language

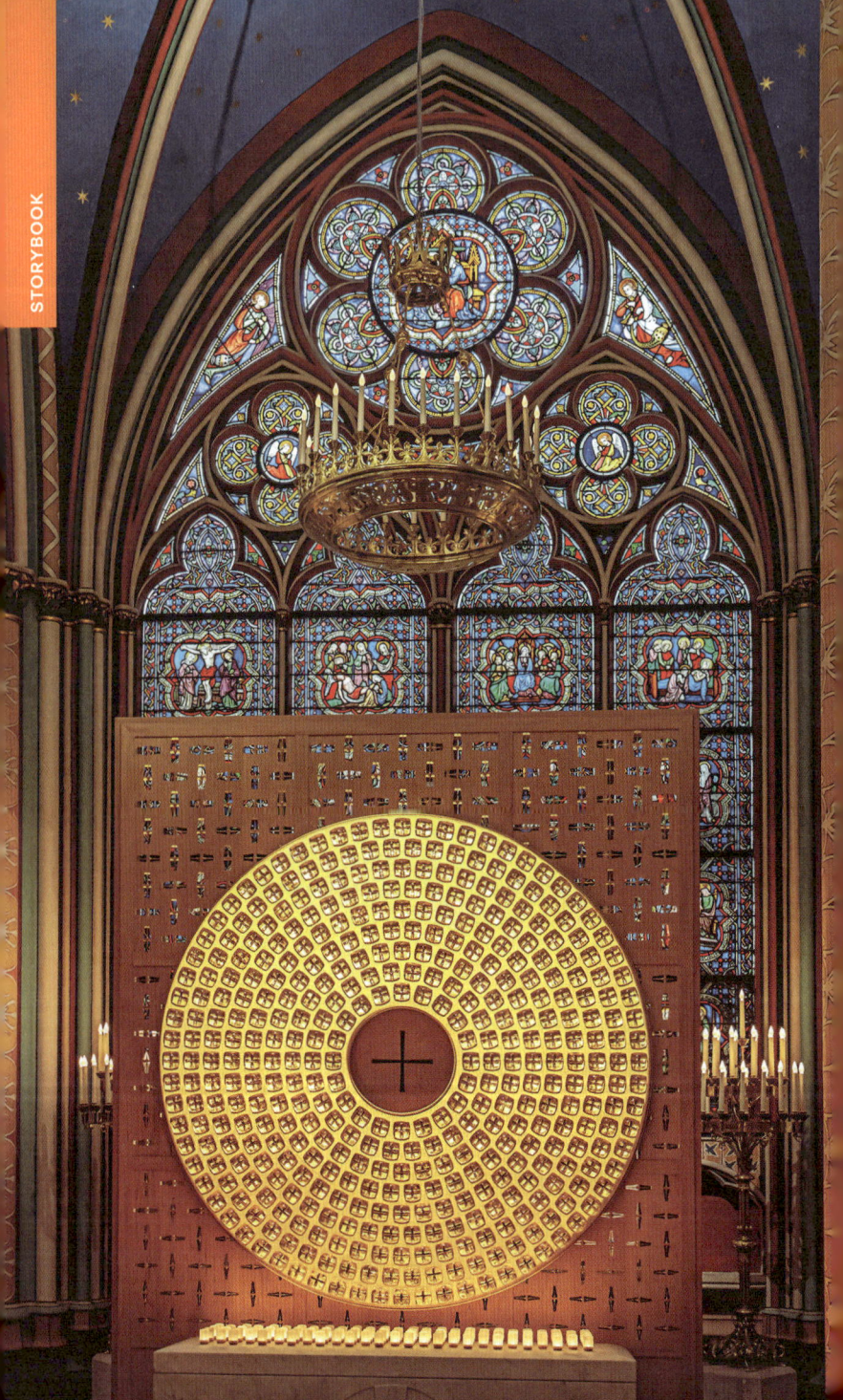

STORYBOOK

STORYBOOK

Our writers delve deep into different aspects of Parisian life.

A History of Paris in 15 Places
You can walk through centuries of history in a single day in Paris.

Mary Winston Nicklin

p330

Meet the Parisians
Paris is changing, but without losing what makes it so special and different from the rest of the country.

Jean-Bernard Carillet

p334

Paris' Marvellous Metro
Parisian life beneath the surface can be just as interesting as above ground and there's no better way to zip around the city than *le metro*.

Fabienne Fong Yan

p336

Paris on Location
Since the birth of moving pictures, France has played a major role in influencing cinema worldwide.

Alexis Averbuck

p340

Paris' Alternative Arts Scene
Derelict factories and train stations have become Paris' hottest arts venues.

Rooksana Hossenally

p344

Les Années Folles & the Cocktail Craze in Paris
The crazy years in Paris between the two world wars gave birth to the cocktail, but its history goes further back than that.

Nicola Leigh Stewart

p348

Golden reliquary, Cathédrale Notre Dame de Paris (p208)

A HISTORY OF PARIS IN
15 PLACES

In Paris, you can walk through centuries of history in a single day. Tales of battles, royal intrigue and revolution are written into the very cobblestones. Though the city by the Seine is celebrated for its enduring beauty and timelessness, make no mistake: the one thing that's constant over time is reinvention.
By Mary Winston Nicklin

DIG ANYWHERE IN PARIS – metro construction, a new hotel – and you'll turn up relics from times past. Teams of archaeologists are called to the scene to excavate the artefacts, some of which date back millennia. The most remarkable finds? Perfectly preserved dugout canoes from a Neolithic site that was the first fixed settlement in Paris, on the banks of the Seine near Bercy. (Get a glimpse at the Musée Carnavalet p157.)

It was thanks to the river that Paris developed as it did. When Julius Caesar's army conquered Gaul in the 1st century BCE, the general wrote of the Parisii, a Celtic tribe with a strategic island base from where they controlled river trade – and minted their own coins.

Paris' transformation to a major capital began in the Middle Ages, when the newly founded university attracted scholars from across Europe to the Latin Quarter. We owe the look of modern Paris to town planner Baron Haussmann (1809–91), who levelled disease-ridden medieval alleyways to make way for wide boulevards, elegant balconied buildings and vast parks.

Through centuries of upheaval and change, the Seine was the lifeblood – hence enshrined in the city's ship coat of arms and Latin motto *'fluctuat nec mergitur'* ('tossed but not sunk'). Following the 2015 terrorist attacks, this motto became emblematic of the city's resilient spirit.

These momentous events are manifest in reminders all over the city.

1. Arènes de Lutèce
THE EARLIEST SETTLERS

Colonising the Gauls, the Romans established a town in 52 BCE – Lutetia (Lutèce in French) – with the main public buildings (forum, bathhouse, theatre and amphitheatre) radiating from Île de la Cité onto the Left Bank, near today's Panthéon. Though Lutetia was not the capital of its province, it was a prosperous town, with a population of around 8000. To this day you can visit their earliest ruins at Crypte Archéologique beneath Notre Dame, the bathhouse (beneath the Cluny) and the amphitheatre at Arènes de Lutèce where you can even play boules.

For more on Arènes de Lutèce, see p227.

2. Église St-Germain des Prés
RISE OF CHRISTIANITY AND PARIS AS CAPITAL

One of the key figures in early Parisian history was patron saint Geneviève, who's said to have saved the city from Attila the Hun (451). Then there was Clovis I (c 466–511), who converted to Christianity, united the Franks into one kingdom and made Paris its capital. Under the Frankish kings, the city once again began to expand, and important edifices such as the abbey of Église St-Germain des Prés were erected. Today, the church that stands on the site of the abbey is the oldest in Paris, and it lies smack in the middle of the Left Bank's cool shopping streets.

For more on Église St-Germain des Prés, see p254.

3. Notre Dame
MEDIEVAL PARIS

In the Middle Ages, Paris became the most populous city in Europe. Merchants prospered and guilds thrived. Frenetic building marked the 12th and 13th centuries. Commissioned in 1136, the Basilique de St-Denis ushered in a new Gothic style that would later be enhanced in Notre Dame. Work on 'Our Lady of Paris' commenced in 1163 and was largely completed by the early 14th century. Schools sprang up in the vicinity, making it an important hub of learning. The geographic and spiritual centre of the city, Notre Dame has played an outsized role in its history – from royal weddings to liberation from Nazi occupation after WWII.

For more on Notre Dame, see p208.

4. Conciergerie & Palais de Justice
REIGN OF THE ROYAL COURT

The history of the Palais de Justice (Law Courts) and the Conciergerie winds through centuries of Parisian life and power. When Hugh Capet was made king in 987 (and Paris became the royal seat) he lived in the renovated palace of the Roman governor on the Île de la Cité. The buildings continued as headquarters of French kings until the 14th century (when they moved to the Louvre). In the 13th century, Sainte-Chapelle was built in six rapid years by Louis IX (St Louis, r 1226–70), and in 1391 the Conciergerie became a prison, heavily used in the French Revolution. In 2018, the Law Courts moved to an official new headquarters in the northeast of the city – the historic Palais de Justice is slated to undergo a massive restoration and transformation.

For more on the Conciergerie & Palais de Justice, see p215.

5. Pont Neuf
THE FRENCH RENAISSANCE

During the reign of François I (r 1515–47) Renaissance ideas of scientific scholarship assumed new importance, as did new architectural styles championed by disciples of Michelangelo and Raphael – on gorgeous display at the Château de Fontainebleau. Henri IV (r 1589–1610), a Catholic convert who ended the Wars of Religion, bequeathed Paris its oldest bridge. Designed with 12 arches, the Pont Neuf (New Bridge) was equipped with the world's first footpaths. It also represented a feat of civil engineering, with a pump drawing water from the Seine to supply the Louvre and Tuileries. An equestrian statue of the king overlooks the bridge today.

For more on Pont Neuf, see p217.

6. Place de la Concorde
FROM ROYALTY TO REVOLUTION

Arguably France's best-known king, Louis XIV (r 1643–1715), aka 'Le Roi Soleil' (the Sun King), built an extravagant palace in Versailles to house the entire royal court and centralise the government. But by the late 1780s his descendant, indecisive Louis XVI (r 1774–92) and his Vienna-born queen, Marie Antoinette, had alienated virtually every segment of society. On 14 July a mob stormed the prison at Bastille – a decisive moment in the French Revolution. The monarchs later lost their heads on the place de la Concorde, the city's biggest public square, constructed by Louis XV. More than a thousand people were executed there during the Reign of Terror.

For more information about place de la Concorde, see p87.

Pont Neuf (p217)

7. Arc de Triomphe
NAPOLÉON AND EMPIRE

France's post-Revolutionary government was far from stable when Napoléon Bonaparte returned to Paris in 1799. He found a chaotic republic in which few citizens had any faith. The Arc de Triomphe, built from 1806 to 1836, is a vivid reminder of his ascendancy in December 1804, when he crowned himself 'Emperor of the French' in the presence of Pope Pius VII at Notre Dame. His many reversals of fortune included an odyssey of wars and victories by which France would come to control most of Europe, but also his banishment to Elba and ultimately St Helena in the South Atlantic, where he died in 1821.

For more on the Arc de Triomphe, see p85.

8. Eiffel Tower
THE BELLE ÉPOQUE

Though a tumultuous political time, the Belle Époque (Beautiful Age) in Paris launched art nouveau architecture, a whole field of artistic 'isms' from Impressionism onwards, and advances in science and engineering, including the first metro line (1900) and train station (Gare St-Lazare). Department stores were born in Paris – *grands magasins* like La Samaritaine and Galeries Lafayette boast splendid art nouveau details. And the nightlife scene served up serious revelry, with hot spots such as Maxim's drawing a hard-partying crowd. The most famous icon of the era is the Eiffel Tower, showcased during the 1889 World's Fair. A series of such events showed off the Belle Époque's bold architectural and technical achievements, with some 50 million visitors flocking to the 1900 World's Fair to gape at purpose-built structures like the Grand Palais.

For more on the Eiffel Tower, see p64.

9. Pigalle's Cabarets
ANNÉES FOLLES – PARIS IN THE TWENTIES

In the 1920s, Paris sparkled as the centre of the avant-garde with its newfound liberalism, cutting-edge nightlife and painters pushing into new fields of art like Cubism and surrealism. African American musicians brought jazz to France beginning around WWI, and Paris' creative denizens included Joséphine Baker, Coco Chanel, Ernest Hemingway, Gertrude Stein, Pablo Picasso, Joan Miró and Salvador Dalí, to name just a few. Montparnasse and the Left Bank became hot spots, as did Pigalle and Montmartre with their speakeasies and cabarets like Moulin Rouge and Le Chat Noir.

For more on Pigalle nightlife, see p133.

10. Musée de la Libération de Paris
WWII AND THE OCCUPATION OF PARIS

During WWII, Paris was occupied by Germany, and almost half the population fled the city. The Germans divided France into two: a zone under direct German rule (including Paris); and a puppet state based in the spa town of Vichy. Collaborationists in German-occupied areas (including Paris) helped the Nazis round up 160,000 French Jews and others for deportation to concentration and extermination camps. Learn more at the Mémorial de la Shoah (p158). General Charles de Gaulle, France's undersecretary of war, fled to London and established the Forces Françaises Libres (Free French Forces). Colonel Henri Rol-Tanguy coordinated the Free French in Paris from a bunker in what is now inside the Musée de la Libération de Paris.

Sorbonne Chapel (p227)

11. Institut du Monde Arabe
COLONIALISM AND CROSS-CULTURAL INFLUENCE

France's disastrous defeat in Vietnam in 1954 ended its colonial era in Southeast Asia, and the Algerian Revolution (1954–62) ended their longstanding colony there as well. Meanwhile, almost all other French colonies and protectorates in Africa demanded and achieved independence. Some 750,000 *pieds-noirs* (black feet), as Algerian-born French people are known, came to France, and Paris remains a magnet for immigrants of all nations (making up 20% of the population in Paris and 31% in Seine-St-Denis), adding to the region's cultural wealth. A physical metaphor for modern crosscultural exchange can be seen at the Institute of the Arab World, commissioned in 1981 by 19 Arab states.

For more on the Institut du Monde Arabe, see p238.

12. Sorbonne
PIVOTAL YEAR AND FRENCH PROTESTS

The year 1968 was a watershed. In March, a large demonstration against the American war in Vietnam gave impetus to the student movement against capitalism, American imperialism and archaic institutions. In May, police broke up another demonstration, prompting angry students to occupy the venerable Sorbonne university and erect barricades in the Latin Quarter. Workers joined in, with six million people across France joining a strike that virtually paralysed the country. Slogans like *'L'Imagination au Pouvoir'* (Put Imagination in Power) took hold. Demonstrating remains a staple of Parisian life – including the Gilets Jaunes protests sparked in 2018 and 2023's unrest around the police killing of 17-year-old Nahel Merzouk.

For more on the Sorbonne, see p227.

13. Pyramide du Louvre
MODERN SOCIETY AND THE POLITICAL PENDULUM

Paris, despite appearing timeless, is always changing. As the seat of French government, it's seen political influence swing many times. De Gaulle resigning in 1969 to be replaced by Gaullist Georges Pompidou. Socialist François Mitterrand leading to Jacques Chirac. Presidential elections in 2007 ushering in dynamic, media-savvy Nicolas Sarkozy. Emmanuel Macron beating back right-wing Marine Le Pen yet again in 2022. Perhaps no one building represents change better than the Louvre. A 13th-century fortress until Charles V (1338–80) moved in, it has seen many renovations, including the IM Pei pyramid completed in 1988 – controversial and iconic at the same time, and always adapting.

For more on the Louvre, see p100.

14. Le Bataclan
TURBULENT TIMES

The year 2015 was a harrowing one for the French capital. On 7 January, the offices of *Charlie Hebdo* were attacked after the magazine published satirical images of the Prophet Mohammed; 12 people were killed and 22 injured. On 13 November 2015, coordinated terrorist attacks at a football match, a series of neighbourhood restaurants and a concert at Le Bataclan killed 130 people (89 in Le Bataclan alone), and injured 368. Paris went into lockdown. In the aftermath, Parisians took to cafe terraces and public spaces to symbolise a refusal to live in fear. The long-planned UN Climate Change Conference went ahead, yielding a historic agreement to limit global warming.

15. Paris Rive Gauche
GREEN RENAISSANCE

In 2014 socialist Anne Hidalgo became Paris' first female mayor (she was reelected in 2020). Hidalgo quickly set about greening the city and minimising car traffic and pollution while ramping up pedestrian and cycling infrastructure. Major initiatives include the 'Plan Arbre', a massive tree-planting scheme that includes 'urban forests.' In addition, the gargantuan Grand Paris (Greater Paris) redevelopment project will ultimately connect outer suburbs beyond the bd Périphérique ring road through a massive decentralised metro expansion. The transformation of Paris Rive Gauche, a formerly industrial zone of the 13e that had been left derelict, is emblematic of the city's ambitions to lower carbon footprints, create affordable housing and revitalise outlying areas.

For more on Paris Rive Gauche, see p279.

MEET THE PARISIANS

Paris is changing, but without losing what makes it so special and different from the rest of the country. JEAN-BERNARD CARILLET introduces his people.

EVERYONE IN FRANCE agrees that Parisians are different and special. When they travel around the country, it's quite common to hear the following comments: *'pfff, les Parisiens'* (oh, these Parisians), uttered with a fatalistic air. As Paris is not synonymous with France, Parisians are, firstly, Parisians, then French. In that order.

Parisians feel like they live on an island amid a sea of rough, unsophisticated provinces. That said, this perception is changing. With the pandemic and remote work, a significant number of Parisians have left Paris for other shores – especially large cities in western France, including Nantes and Bordeaux – and have been totally seduced by the quality of life they have found there. And they have realised that the rest of France is not a *désert culturel* (a cultural desert). Other French cities also have vibrancy, complexity and vitality. For Parisians, who have been living in their own bubble, this growing awareness is equivalent to a revolution. The superiority complex is fading away. French regions are taking their revenge on the capital.

Paris has never been so diverse and multicultural. It's a giant melting pot of cultures and lifestyles. Paris mixes influences like no other. Your Parisian neighbour might be from North Africa, Central Africa, Eastern Turkey, the Middle East, China or Eastern Europe. Paris is an inclusive city with a great sense of tolerance and open-mindedness.

One of the major recent changes in Paris has to do with transport. An increasing number of Parisians who had never ridden a bike have recently realised that cycling is an efficient way of getting around the city. Numerous bike lanes have been created around the city in an effort to greenify the capital. Avenues like the famous rue de Rivoli are now filled with bicycles and *trottinettes* (scooters) on lanes that previously were jammed with cars and taxis. It sometimes feels a bit chaotic – we're in Paris, not Amsterdam – but it's great fun as a visitor to observe Parisians astride their steeds!

A word about protests and strikes. Yes, it is part of our everyday life, and it can be exasperating. We are known to be rebellious and passionate, even if it's against our own interests. One way we demonstrate this is through protests and rallies, which we have developed into an art form. Whether it's to show solidarity with a cause or to voice our dissatisfaction with government policies, we take to the streets with passion and determination. That's an integral part of the city's identity, and it's not going to change anytime soon.

And when it comes to stereotypes, yes, we still buy our baguette at our favourite *boulangerie de quartier* (neighbourhood bakery). And yes, we still have to make an effort to smile.

> **How Many**
>
> There are more than two million inhabitants within Paris, and 12 million inhabitants across Grand Paris (the greater metropolitan area).

Pictured clockwise from top left: Celebrating International Workers Day; snacking on a baguette, rue Montorgueil; friends visiting the Eiffel Tower; cycling along Rue de Rivoli

I'M A PARISIAN, WITH A TWIST

I'm originally from northern Lorraine, a region that was the industrial powerhouse of France, with ironworks and coal mines dominating the landscape. Then came de-industrialisation and economic decline. I grew up amid an industrial wasteland. I realised that I needed an escape. Paris ticked all the boxes perfectly. Like many Parisians, I came to Paris as a student and stayed ever since, seduced by the energy, creative vibes and sophistication of the city. This was so reinvigorating, and a striking contrast to what I had experienced in my home region. What a change of scene and atmosphere! I was also enthralled by the many intellectual and cultural dimensions that are typical of Paris, and the sense of tolerance and diversity. This city never ages, it simply reinvents itself continuously. Over time, I've learnt to seamlessly intertwine my two identities – I'm both a Parisian and a *Lorrain*, a perfect *'bobo'* (hipster) and a provincial in his own right.

St-Michel station
BELLENA/SHUTTERSTOCK

PARIS' MARVELLOUS METRO

Parisian life beneath the surface can be just as interesting as above ground and there's no better way to zip around the city than *le Métro*. By Fabienne Fong Yan

FROM THE CRACK of dawn until the late hours, Paris' underground transport system becomes a vibrant network where workers, students, families, singles and even pets cross paths, forging connections as they traverse the city.

Unveiling the Underground

There's one landmark visitors cannot overlook while exploring Paris – it's a monumental work that has stood the test of time for over a century. Not the Louvre, nor the majestic Arc de Triomphe, or even the Eiffel Tower. In fact, it is an almost inevitable space where travellers, Parisians and people from diverse backgrounds come together: it's none other than the Parisian metro.

The metro is an intricate network that sprawls throughout the entire city, resembling a nervous system. With nearly 245km of railway, transporting 4.5 million passengers every day, and operating 365 days a year, it is a ubiquitous presence encapsulating a multitude of stories – architectural, technological and artistic. Throughout the years, it has become part of Paris' identity. Yet most Parisians possess limited knowledge about it. Beyond its characteristic faience tiles, cylindrical tunnels and crowded platforms, the metro is a testament to the modernisation of Paris, when it propelled the city into the status of an actual metropolis at the dawn of the 20th century.

The Challenging Birth of the Metro

To grasp the metro's role in urban development, we must go back to the late 19th century. The concept of an urban train was accepted, yet its implementation was uncertain. London had adopted an underground steam-powered system, which, despite running for almost four decades, proved highly polluting, drowning passengers in smoke. For years, the French government struggled to find viable technical solutions. But the urgency prompted by the 1900 World's Fair pushed the project forward: Paris could not endure trailing behind cities like London and New York.

The breakthrough of electric power at the end of the 19th century allowed Fulgence Bienvenüe, the visionary architect who eventually cracked the project, to breathe life into the underground metro.

Automated metro Line 14 train

He celebrated his own work with the words, 'By the lightning stolen from Jupiter, the lineage of Prometheus is transported into the depths.' The first line of the metro (Line 1) opened in 1900, marking the beginning of the dense urban network we know today.

Efficiency & Proximity: a Dense Underground Tapestry

Operating for more than 120 years, with 16 lines and 321 stations, the metro now connects all corners of Paris and beyond. The initial philosophy dear to Bienvenüe was to ensure that 'no place in Paris would be further than 400m away from a station and no journey would require more than two connections'. While connectivity has evolved, the imperative of proximity has led to an efficient network, with an average distance of 710m between two stations. This provides Parisians with ample choices when selecting their metro station. In this regard, the Parisian metro stands in contrast to Berlin's or London's urban railways, where several lines run on the same tracks and stations can be quite far apart. Consequently, hopping on and off the metro in the heart of Paris is like boarding and disembarking from a bus, offering passengers ease and convenience.

Navigating Paris Like a Local

This density makes the metro the ideal means to explore and discover Paris. Not only can you immerse yourself in the city like a true Parisian, but you can conveniently access all the major tourist attractions. Note that the metro has its own set of traffic rules: keep to the right on escalators and maintain your right-hand position – according to an archaic rule, blocking the flow may result in a fine, although this is rarely enforced.

To experience the city like a local, there are a few tricks. For instance, alight at Trocadéro instead of Bir-Hakeim for a breathtaking view of the Eiffel Tower, from the terraces of Palais Chaillot. Choose Abbesses over Anvers for an exit onto a charming square in Montmartre, rather than a bustling avenue. You can identify a seasoned Parisian by their mastery of navigating the metro and its most complex stations, such as Châtelet-Les Halles. Linking the underground to the above-ground map enables them to optimise their exit choices and positioning within the carriages.

Metro Stations as Cultural Landmarks

While the metro system results from architectural and technological prowess, it is widely acknowledged that passengers may not always perceive it as such, particularly during peak hours. Although certain sections may appear under constant renovation, efforts are being made to incorporate art into the subterranean world.

Here are a few stations where you can appreciate the underground artwork while discovering city landmarks: step off at Arts et Métiers to marvel at its steampunk-style station, before diving into centuries of captivating inventions at the Musée des Arts et Métiers. Get off at Concorde, where the walls are covered with 44,000 ceramic tiles displaying the text of the Declaration of the Rights of Man and Citizen of 1789, before visiting the Jardin des Tuileries and the Hôtel de la Marine. At Bastille, the platforms of Line 1 feature a striking mural commemorating the bicentenary of the French Revolution. When heading to the Latin Quarter, don't miss the mosaics of Cluny-La Sorbonne, which recreate the signatures of renowned intellectuals who once graced the area's streets and universities.

Tomorrow's Metro?

By 2031, Paris' Metro should be sprawling way beyond its historical 20 *arrondissements* and close suburbs: the Grand Paris Express project, initiated in 2010, aims to extend the current network with four new lines and facilitate connections between the surrounding cities. Its approach reflects the reality of the city's present density and shifting commuting patterns, with passengers no longer solely travelling to the city centre but also across the outskirts.

OPERATING FOR MORE THAN 120 YEARS, WITH 16 LINES AND 321 STATIONS, THE METRO NOW CONNECTS ALL CORNERS OF PARIS AND BEYOND.

Among Europe's most ambitious construction projects, this modernised underground network will eventually transcend the current star-shaped system. The 2024 Olympic and Paralympic Games prompted the first operational network extensions on Line 14. And while we're waiting for it to develop under our feet, the curious can already delve into the world of the 21st-century metro at la Fabrique du Metro, an immersive gallery where you can slip into the shoes of a future metro traveller. Alight at Mairie de St-Ouen (Line 13 or 14) and enjoy your trip!

Jean-Louis Barrault & Arletty on the set of *Les Enfants du Paradis* (1946)

PARIS
ON LOCATION

Since the birth of moving pictures, France has played a major role in influencing cinema worldwide. Are you ready for your close-up? Paris is. By Alexis Averbuck

THERE'S NO DOUBT: Paris is one of the world's most cinematic cities. It's the filming location of countless hits – for television and film – by both home-grown and foreign directors, with some 900 film shoots per year. It's also the spot where the world's first public-paying screening took place (in 1895), and Paris has since produced an absurd abundance of both independent and blockbuster filmmakers and stars.

Classic Cinema

Pretend you're a casting agent. Paris is a natural movie star. Start by looking at its past oeuvre.

Parisian filmmaker Marcel Carné (1906–96) immortalised the city in classics such as *Hôtel du Nord* (1938), set along the Canal St-Martin, and *Les Enfants du Paradis* (1946), set in 1840s Paris. Paris also spawned Jean Renoir (1894–1979), whose *La Grande Illusion* (1937) and *The Rules of the Game* (1939) are perennial entries on Best Film lists.

It's also the birthplace of the French New Wave (Nouvelle Vague). This defining cinema movement emphasised the naturalistic use of on-location shoots. Parisian film director Jean-Luc Godard (1930–2022) followed his B&W celebration of the city in *À Bout de Souffle* (*Breathless;* 1959) with *Bande à Parte* (*Band of Outsiders;* 1964), an entertaining gangster film with marvellous scenes in the Louvre.

Jean-Paul Belmondo in *À Bout de Souffle* (1959)

Entre Les Murs (2008), directed by Laurent Cantet

Similarly, François Truffaut's Paris-set, semi-autobiographical *Les 400 Coups* (*400 Blows;* 1959) is considered one of the best films in French cinematic history, a moving portrayal of the magic and disillusionment of childhood.

You can check out an anthology of short Parisian films by some of this era's directors – including Claude Chabrol and Éric Rohmer – in *Paris Vu Par...* (English title: *Six in Paris;* 1965).

The Modern Era of Parisian Film

The epicentre of France's film industry, Paris is always producing international hits, meditative studies and stars. Mathieu Kassovitz had a prescient take on social tensions in modern Paris with *La Haine* (*Hate;* 1995). Also in the 1990s, Parisian Juliette Binoche leapt to fame after diving into the turquoise water of Paris' art deco Piscine de Pontoise, in *Bleu* (*Blue;* 1993). She wooed cinema-goers with her role as a grieving mother in *Paris, Je T'Aime* (*Paris, I Love You;* 2006), 18 short films – each set in a different Parisian *arrondissement* – by directors from Gus Van Sant to Alfonso Cuarón.

Honoured with the Palme d'Or at Cannes in 2008, Laurent Cantet's *Entre Les Murs* (*The Class;* 2008) portrays a year in the school life of pupils and teachers in a Parisian suburb, an incisive reflection of contemporary multi-ethnic society.

Les Misérables (2019), directed by Ladj Ly, won the Jury Prize at Cannes. It grapples with racial and social tensions in the northeastern Paris commune of Montfermeil, the setting for parts of Victor Hugo's 1862 novel.

The terrorist attacks of 2015 are the subject of *Novembre* (2022), taking an investigative perspective, and *Revoir Paris* (2022), by Alice Winocour, taking a personal introspective one.

Parisian actress Isabelle Huppert holds the honour of having the most nominations for France's César Award. She won one for Paris-based thriller *Elle* (2016), and one of her more recent films, *The Crime Is Mine* (2023), is set in 1930s Paris.

Another Parisian superstar, Léa Seydoux, filmed well-regarded romantic-drama *One Fine Morning* (2022) in Paris, directed by Paris-born Mia Hansen-Løve. Other Paris-born directors to look for are Claire Denis (check out *35 Rhums*), Rebecca Zlotowski (try *Other People's Children*) and Mati Diop. Oscar and Palme d'Or–winner Justine Triet trained in Paris, too.

Don't forget the television hits set in Paris. They include *Lupin* (2021–present) starring Omar Sy as a master thief inspired by the fictional Arsène Lupin, a 1900s master of disguise. Thriller fans can stream *Spiral* (2005–20), a police drama, or 2023's *Thicker Than Water (Jusqu'Ici Tout Va Bien)*. *Dix Pour Cent* (*Call My Agent;* 2015–20) chronicles the hijinks of a Paris talent agency, and series creator Fanny Herrero also made *Standing Up* (*Drôle;* 2022), about Parisian stand-up comics.

Foreign Productions Set in Paris

Paris has always been a popular muse for foreign film directors, of course. Bernardo Bertolucci's *Last Tango in Paris* (1972) stars Marlon Brando, and Doug Liman's fast-paced *The Bourne Identity* (2002) features Matt Damon as an amnesiac government-agent-turned-target against a fabulous Paris backdrop. *Before Sunset* (2004) is the second part of the Richard Linklater, July Delpy and Ethan Hawke *Before* romantic trilogy.

Martin Scorsese's Oscar-winning children's film *Hugo* (2011) pays tribute to cinema and Parisian film pioneer Georges Méliès through the remarkable adventure of an orphan boy in the 1930s who tends the clocks at a Paris train station.

Many a music video has also been filmed in Paris, from Sinead O'Connor's 'Nothing Compares 2 U' to Taylor Swift's 'Begin Again' and The Carters' (Beyoncé and Jay-Z) 'Apesh*t', which was filmed in the Louvre. Foreign television shows abound, like wildly popular and polarising *Emily in Paris,* or *The Eddy,* chronicling the tribulations at a music club in Paris.

Animation

The classic animation *Ratatouille* (2007) is an American-made comedy about an ambitious rat who aims to be a chef against all odds. *Avril et de Monde Truqué* (*April and the Extraordinary World;* 2015) depicts a fictitious 1941 Paris and delightful *Dilili à Paris* (2018), by Michel Ocelot, sees its young heroine solve a series of kidnappings in Belle Époque Paris. It features famous Parisians from the era, such as artist Toulouse-Lautrec, and won the César for Best Feature.

Or check out 2025's *Marcel et Monsieur Pagnol,* by Sylvain Chomet, about iconic writer and director Marcel Pagnol (1895–1974) the first filmmaker elected to the Académie Française. Chomet also made Oscar-nominated *The Triplets of Belleville* (2003).

THE EPICENTRE OF FRANCE'S FILM INDUSTRY, PARIS IS ALWAYS PRODUCING INTERNATIONAL HITS, MEDITATIVE STUDIES AND STARS.

Frame from *Marcel et Monsieur Pagnol* (2025)
CAPITAL PICTURES/ALAMY

Documentaries

One of the earliest Parisian documentaries is *Rien que les Heures* (*Nothing but Time;* 1926) by Alberto Cavalcanti, an experimental silent film showing a day in the life of the city. Writer-director Pierre Bost's *La Libération de Paris (The Liberation of Paris;* 1944) was filmed in secret by WWII Resistance units during the battle for Paris. *La Seine a Rencontré Paris* (*The Seine Meets Paris;* 1957), directed by Joris Ivens, is told from the perspective of a boat trip through the city, showing daily life on its banks. Parisians Jean Rouch and Edgar Morin initiated the *cinéma vérité* style with *Chronique d'un Été (Chronicle of a Summer)* in 1961.

Paris' film archive, the Forum des Images *(forumdesimages.fr),* is an excellent place to discover more.

La REcyclerie (p137)

PARIS' ALTERNATIVE ARTS SCENE

Derelict factories and train stations have become Paris' hottest arts venues. By Rooksana Hossenally

IN PARIS, YOU'LL find various hybrid art hubs set up inside abandoned buildings, which have become go-tos for locals, making the Paris art scene a lot more inclusive than a decade back.

Outside the (White) Box

France ranks among the top countries in the world for injecting money into the arts, which shows the significance in which culture is held here. Paris has always had an extremely rich and vibrant art scene, as well as a plethora of theatres, cinemas, concert halls, galleries and landmark museums. However, look outside the institutions to smaller venues and grassroots collectives, and you'll find that the scene is even more diverse and multitiered than it first appears.

In the last two decades, smaller venues like La Bellevilloise, Le 104, Mains d'Oeuvres, Ground Control and Le Point Ephémère have been challenging the status quo by putting the spotlight on a broader range of artists from all over the globe, breaking the white-cube mould and opening up the arts to people who aren't necessarily part of the traditional cultural elite.

Art Squats

Before Nicolas Sarkozy became the country's president in 2007 (until 2012), much of the independent scene unfolded in art squats like La Petite Rockette (11e), Grands Voisins (12e), La Miroiterie (20e) and La Suite (13e), among others, where art collectives took over the city's empty buildings and set up their lodgings and studio spaces, and hosted events year-round. They operated like fully fledged art venues, elbowing their way onto the established arts circuit. A lot of the work was liberating and experimental. Most squats were shut down, save a handful that have been made permanent and given a right to stay. For instance, 59 Rivoli (1er) is a rare exploit where the artists took over a huge building right on Paris' main shopping street in the heart of the city. It's open to visitors, and stands as a symbol of the power of the local cultural spirit.

59 Rivoli (p120)

Reinvented Railways

In 2016 another chapter began for the local art scene when the SNCF, France's national rail giant, also the city's biggest landowner, decided to sell or lease some of its property in the city and on the outskirts. For instance, La Petite Ceinture (little belt), a disused railway that circles Paris and is scattered with empty stations, is being transformed into a bucolic promenade, its stations having been repurposed into *tiers lieux* (hybrid venues) with bars and restaurants that put on various events from concerts to exhibitions, festivals to markets, like le Hasard Ludique and La REcyclerie (both in the 18e *arrondissement*).

The SNCF even called upon the art community to suggest renewal projects for some of its abandoned buildings, such as La Gare (19e), a former train station that's now a jazz club with techno nights in the basement. There's also La Station – Gare des Mines, an experimental music venue built on the remains of an old coal station in Aubervilliers, and eco-venue La Cité Fertile in Pantin, in an old SNCF goods station that's now a place to eat and drink that hosts year-round events. Other repurposed stations include Poinçon (14e), formerly the Montrouge-Ceinture station, now a restaurant with arty events, and Brasserie d'Auteuil and Andia, two restaurants in the 16e *arrondissement* also inside former train stations.

Post-Pandemic Rejuvenation

Turning old stations into art hubs is nothing new. In the last few years, especially as the world was whirring back into action post-pandemic, Paris has seen the rise of *tiers lieux* and pop-up venues on *friches* (wasteland) as more permanent fixtures, injecting even more diversity into the city's arts offering.

Cultural associations and foundations are increasingly looking to abandoned factories on the city outskirts. In April 2022 artist incubator POUSH took over a 20,000-sq-metre derelict perfume factory in the suburb of Aubervilliers, where it now hosts 250 artists from 30 different nationalities for residencies, events and exhibitions, and takes the prize as the city's biggest arts centre. More recently, the Fiminco Foundation has opened a similar art space with residences and a beer garden in Romainville, also on the outskirts of northeastern Paris.

Cultural event organisers like Soukmachines, behind *tiers lieux* like the 6B in an abandoned Saint-Denis office block, which has been going since 2010, as well as the Halle Papin in Pantin and L'Orfèvrerie nearby, now both closed, are turning their attention to an abandoned French film laboratory, L'Eclair in Epinay-sur-Seine, where they've nabbed a six-year lease to keep organising their events and summer family barbecues. The collective has also opened a more permanent spot with the right to stay for 10 years in an old office block in Gennevilliers, a northern Paris suburb. And in Meudon, on the southwest outskirts of the city, an airship factory left empty for four decades opened as a cultural space. It has yet to build an ongoing program to attract a steady flow of returning visitors but the rehabilitation of the very lofty venue is impressive.

In the last year, Les Galeries, a new arts hub, has set up in the underbelly of the former Galeries Lafayette department store in Montparnasse, which is also a club. In fact, Paris' nightlife scene has picked up too, with Berlin-like clubs on the rise, like Essaim close to Gare d'Est and Mia Mao in La Villette, along with other smaller spots like La Fête in Place de Clichy and Fawa Wafa under the Paris flyover close to the 19th district.

Art in the Heart

While rarer, due to lack of space, disused spots in the heart of Paris are also getting the art treatment. Césure, a former Sorbonne University building in the Latin Quarter, has been turned into a creative venue for concerts, plays, exhibitions and events with a restaurant, by the Plateau Urbain cooperative, which rents cut-price space to creatives like artists as well as to students and charities.

Friches of note in Paris (open summer only) include the Jardin 21, an urban garden by the canal in the 19e *arrondissement* by the same association that runs long-standing alternative nightlife venue Glazart nearby, and 88 Ménilmontant in the location of the old Miroiterie, a squat inside an old mirror shop known for its punk-rock concerts.

Many of these old sites testify to the city's past, and dusting them off serves to retell the stories of bygone industries and disappeared railways. It gives them a new purpose and puts sleepy suburbs on the map. Restoring these vestiges of the past has also opened up the city's art scene to locals and visitors seeking something more immersive and tangible than what's on offer in Paris' more traditional museums and galleries. The new generation of cultural leaders is showing us there's a different way to interact with the arts, and that you can sip on a pint while doing it.

> **LA PETITE CEINTURE (LITTLE BELT), A DISUSED RAILWAY THAT CIRCLES PARIS AND IS SCATTERED WITH EMPTY STATIONS, IS BEING TRANSFORMED INTO A BUCOLIC PROMENADE, ITS STATIONS HAVING BEEN REPURPOSED INTO TIERS LIEUX (HYBRID VENUES) WITH BARS AND RESTAURANTS THAT PUT ON VARIOUS EVENTS FROM CONCERTS TO EXHIBITIONS, FESTIVALS TO MARKETS**

LES ANNÉES FOLLES
& THE COCKTAIL CRAZE IN PARIS

The crazy years in Paris between the two world wars gave birth to the cocktail, but its history goes further back than that.
By Nicola Leigh Stewart

PERHAPS NO DECADE has captured an image of Paris quite like *les Années folles* (the crazy years). The war was over, victory was in the air, and people were ready to celebrate life again. Paris was a young and increasingly cosmopolitan city, full of optimism and artistic innovation in every form. It's no wonder, then, that the cocktail became the drink of choice: it was new, creative and fun, and perfectly encapsulated the mood for celebrating life at every opportunity.

The Cocktail's Origins

It makes sense that a decade called Années folles would have at least some alcohol involved, but the cocktail's origins in France go even further back, as told by Franck Audoux, owner of Paris cocktail bar Cravan, in his book *French Moderne: Cocktails from the Twenties and Thirties*. In fact, it was Napoléon III who first introduced the word 'bar' to the French in the 1840s, during his exile in London, and who was a big fan of the 'coquetel', a Bordeaux drink which mixed together wine and *eau de vie* (fruit brandy). Of course, the word seems to be an early version of 'cocktail', although according to Franck, 'there are lots of stories about where the word came from and no one can agree on which one is true'.

Exposition Universelle (Paris Exposition)

It was also Napoléon III who had the idea to host the 1867 Exposition Universelle (Paris Exposition), which was a major driver behind bringing the American cocktail to France. Hundreds of international restaurants and bars opened in order to refresh the some 15 million visitors who would attend the six-month event, including an American bar where 'young women served drinks that were sipped cold through straws', a new way of drinking at the time, says Frank. At the Paris Exposition 1878, cocktails such as sherry cobblers and mint juleps were on the menu at the American bar and by the time the 1889 Exposition came around (bringing 32 million visitors) the first French cocktail book was published, aimed at helping cafe bar owners and maître d'hôtels meet the demands of Paris' new foreign visitors.

Tourists Arrive

It wasn't just international fairs that brought travellers to Paris. Tourism in general was beginning to boom. Thanks to bigger and faster cruise liners, and the founding of Air France later in 1933, it was now easier than ever to travel and explore. Curious and creative Americans came to

Paris, some of whom wanted to escape the puritanical rules of home: nationwide Prohibition began in the US in 1920 and lasted until 1933, putting a dampener on the Roaring Twenties fun (at least the legal fun). In contrast, on this side of the pond a burst of Anglo-American bars opened in Paris, serving American drinks and British and Irish dishes to appeal to an English-speaking clientele.

Horse Racing & Expats

Another American influence on the Paris bar scene was horse racing. In the early 1900s most Anglo-friendly bars would be packed out with racing fans and American jockeys, who came and outperformed the previous leaders of the sport, the English. The now world-famous Harry's Bar was one of the bars frequented by famous jockeys when it launched as the New York Bar in 1911, before being bought and renamed by Scotsman Harry MacElhone in 1923. Under Harry it became a meeting point for famed American expatriates of the time, including Ernest Hemingway and Scott and Zelda Fitzgerald, and the birthplace of cocktail classics such as the Bloody Mary, the Blue Lagoon, the White Lady and, it's also claimed, the Sidecar.

Cocktails & Creatives

But fashionable new drinks weren't limited to these expat-friendly bars. Cocktails could be found everywhere in the city, from bistros to brasseries, although the most famous at the time were huddled together in Montparnasse. Many Americans had flocked to the neighbourhood upon their arrival in Paris and it became a hub for artists, journalists, academics and publishers who ordered Martinis, Alexanders, Sidecars, Manhattans and more in neighbourhood hangouts such as La Closerie de Lilas, La Rotonde, Le Dôme and Le Select – all still open today.

Next door in St-Germain-des-Prés the Hôtel Lutetia, opened in 1910, also became a hot spot for Paris' American and international creative crowd. Hemingway and Picasso were both patrons of the bar, which is now renamed in honour of the hotel's most famous guest, American-born French dancer and singer Joséphine Baker. In the 8th *arrondissement*, the Hôtel Plaza Athénée's Jean Lupoiu, one of the key bartenders of

Les Ambassadeurs (p85)

the time, made the Relais Plaza bar another fashionable destination after the hotel's restaurant opened in 1936, particularly with the *couturiers* who had their maisons on the same street. On the menu at cocktail hour were two drinks named after the hotel: the Plaza Athénée and the Relais-Plaza. But perhaps Paris' most famous bartender at the time was Franck Meier, who oversaw the Ritz Hotel's Bar Cambon, better known simply as the Ritz Bar, where guests would sip on future classics such as the Bee's Knees.

Influence of French Spirits

Although the cocktail was an American drink, these new creations were often made with French spirits. Before the cocktail craze took off in Paris there was already a culture for *l'apéritif* and so bartenders reached for the numerous French spirits already behind the bar such as Noilly-Prat, Dolin, Suze, Cointreau and Chartreuse to shake and stir their new creations. The enthusiasm for the drinks wasn't lost on the brands either, who sponsored some of the cocktail competitions that sprang up in the late 1920s, another major driving force behind the cocktail's popularity. Some of these events welcomed amateur and even celebrity participants but the 1929 First International Championship of Professional Bartenders was, as the name suggests, for the Paris pros, and saw 40 bartenders from establishments such as Harry's New York Bar take part. The public were able to buy a ticket to enter and judge the cocktail winners, but had to try all 40 drinks to do so.

Today's Cocktail Scene

These days, the cocktail scene in Paris is thriving once again. The city's influential bartenders are leading the way with their creative concoctions, but occasionally take a look back to *les années folles* as a source of inspiration. Dirty Lemon, known for its excellent Boulevardier (invented in Paris in 1927), likes to riff on other 1920s classics such as the Negroni and the Martini while Le Syndicat has put its own spin on a French 75 by swapping out the gin for Armagnac. Back over at Cravan, Franck Audoux might have written the book, literally, on 1920s and '30s Parisian cocktail culture but he stresses that his own drinks form 'a contemporary menu dedicated to the palate of today'. This has involved reworking a couple of historic recipes in line with this concept, namely Cravan's signature Yellow Cocktail and the Tunnel. More recently, Paris' hotel bars, which were once leading the city's cocktail scene, have begun to push their creative boundaries once again to bring in a new generation of Parisians, who, unlike Londoners or New Yorkers, don't have the habit of heading to a hotel bar for their *apéritif*. Young and inventive bartenders at old influential cocktail haunts such as the Lutetia and the Ritz, as well as at the Hôtel de Crillon, the Four Seasons Hotel George V, the Hotel Lancaster and the Saint James Paris, are now playing with modern techniques such as fat washing, infusing and clarifying their ingredients, which are often local and seasonally sourced, to create cocktails that at times cause queues out the door, and which are helping to once again put the Paris cocktail scene on the map.

THESE DAYS, THE COCKTAIL SCENE IN PARIS IS THRIVING ONCE AGAIN. THE CITY'S INFLUENTIAL BARTENDERS ARE LEADING THE WAY WITH THEIR CREATIVE CONCOCTIONS

Bee's Knees cocktail
NEW AFRICA/SHUTTERSTOCK

INDEX

4Chinatown 269
59 Rivoli 20, 120

accessible travel 35, 324
accommodation 26, 306-13, 324
activities 50-2, *see also individual activities*
African culture 138
airports 31, 324
amusement parks 55, 70-1, 317
animals 55
animation 343
Appellation d'Origine Contrôlée 319
Aquarium de Paris 75
Arc de Triomphe 8, 81, 85, 92, 332
architecture 8-9, 77, 223, 227-8, 229
area codes 325
Arènes de Lutèce 227, 330
art galleries, *see* arts centres, museums & galleries
Artaud, Antonin 194
artisans workshops 191, 192
arts 20, 277, 344-7, *see also* literature, music, opera
arts centres
 Césure 239
 Ground Control 201
 La Flèche d'Or 199
 Les Galeries 347
 Maison de l'Animal 201
 Pavillon Carré de Baudoin 181
 POUSH 146, 346
 Viaduc des Arts 192
Atelier Marie La Varande 136

ATMs 30, 316
Aubervilliers, *see* St-Denis, St-Ouen, Pantin & Aubervilliers
Autel du Culte de Bouddha 276, 278
Auvers-sur-Oise 304-5
Avenue des Champs-Élysées 84, 92, 94
Avenue Montaigne 90

baguettes 36, 40-1, 319
Bains-Douches des Deux-Ponts 221
bakeries 38, 40-1, 195
Ballet de l'Opéra National de Paris 46
Ballon de Paris 278, 322
Balzac, Honoré de 72
Barbès, La Chapelle & Canal St-Martin 138-42, **139**
 accommodation 309
 entertainment 138, 140
 food 140
 highlights 127, **127**
 shopping 140, 141
Basilique du Sacré-Cœur 9, 127, 129
Bastille & eastern Paris 184-203, **186-7, 198**
 accommodation 310-11
 drinking 192, 193, 199, 201
 entertainment 192-3, 194
 food 188, 189, 193, 195, 199, 200, 202
 highlights 185, **185**
 history 188-9
 shopping 190, 192, 195
 travel within 185
 walking tours 191, **191**
Bastille Day 27

Batignolles, *see* Montmartre, Pigalle & Batignolles
Batobus 33, 67, 221
beer 44, 192
Belleville & Ménilmontant 168-83, **169, 170-1**
 accommodation 310
 drinking 177, 178
 entertainment 176-7
 food 176, 179, 183
 highlights 169, **169**
 walking tours 180-1, **181**
Belvédère de Belleville 18, 179, 181
bicycle travel 27, 34, 52
BienÉlevées 323
bistros 37-8
boat tours 17, 33, 67
 Batobus 221
 Canal St-Martin 142
 Seine 67
 Vedettes du Pont Neuf 221
 Villette to Bastille 143
Bois de Boulogne 12, 52, 70-1
Bois de Vincennes 12, 52, 185, 196-7
books 29, 122, 167, 231, 232, 233
bookshops 16, 122, 231, 233, 238, 266-7
bouillon 38
boulangeries 38, 40-1, 195
boules 52, 218
bouquinistes 16, 122, 233, 238
Bourse de Commerce 116-17
Bowling Mouffetard 231
breweries 44, 144
bridges
 Pont au Double 217

Pont Neuf 217, 331
Pont St-Louis 217
budget 316
 drinking 43
 travel 35
bus travel 31, 32-3
business hours 325

cabarets 46-7, 133, 134
 Artishow 194
 Crazy Horse 47
 Culture Rapide 176
 history 332
 Madame Arthur 47, 133
 Moulin Rouge 46, 133
Café de Flore 254
canal cruises, *see* boat tours
Canal St-Martin 13, 140-1, *see also* Barbès, La Chapelle & Canal St-Martin
canoeing 51
car travel 34
Cartier-Bresson, Henri 166
Catacombes, Les 13, 54, 272
Cathédrale Notre Dame (Chartres) 298-9
Cathédrale Notre Dame de Paris 8, 205, 208-13, 331
cathedrals, *see* churches & cathedrals
cemeteries & ossuaries
 Cimetière de Passy 68
 Cimetière du Montparnasse 282-3
 Cimetière du Père Lachaise 12, 169, 172-5
 Les Catacombes 13, 54, 272
Champ de Mars 67

351

Champs-Élysées & Grands Boulevards area 80-95, **82-3**
  accommodation 307-8
  drinking 85, 88, 94
  entertainment 95
  food 84, 86, 87, 89, 90, 91, 95
  highlights 81, **81**
  shopping 87, 93, 94-5
  travel within 81
  walking tours 92-3, **93**
Champs-Élysées, Avenue des 84, 92, 94
Champs-Élysées Film Festival 88
Chartres 296-9
Château de Fontainebleau 302-3
châteaux
  Château d'Auvers-sur-Oise 305
  Château de Bagatelle 15, 71
  Château de Fontainebleau 302-3
  Château de Vincennes 197
  Parc de Bagatelle 71
  Versailles 290-5
cheese 41, 263
chemists 321
children, travel with 21, 53-5, 122, 317
Chinatown 276
Chinese New Year 27, 276
chocolate 260, 261
churches & cathedrals
  Basilique de St-Denis 146
  Basilique du Sacré-Cœur 9, 127, 129
  Basilique Ste-Clotilde 257
  Cathédrale Notre Dame (Chartres) 298-9
  Cathédrale Notre Dame de Paris 8, 205, 208-13, 331
  Chapelle Expiatoire 94
  Église Notre Dame de l'Assomption 304
  Église St-Antoine des Quinze Vingts 192
  Église St-Étienne du Mont 223, 227
  Église St-Eustache 120
  Église St-Germain de Charonne 199
  Église St-Germain des Prés 254, 330
  Église St-Gervais-St-Protais 165
  Église St-Ignace 246
  Église St-Jean Baptiste de Grenelle 287
  Église St-Louis en l'Île 221
  Église St-Médard 230
  Église St-Paul St-Louis 165
  Église St-Séverin 228
  Église St-Sulpice 241, 262
  L'église de la Madeleine 90
  Notre Dame 8, 205, 208-13, 331
  Sacré-Cœur Basilica 9, 127, 129
  Sainte-Chapelle 205, 214-15
  St-Jean-Baptiste de Belleville 180
  St-Julien-le-Pauvre 228
Cimetière du Père Lachaise 12, 169, 172-5
cinema 47, 55, 202, 340-3
cinemas 95
  Christine21 235
  Cinéma Mac-Mahon 95
  Cinéma St-André des Arts 235
  Cinémathèque Française 185, 202
  Club de l'Étoile 95
  Elysées Lincoln 95
  Le Balzac 95
  Le Champo 235
  Le Grand Rex 124-5
  L'Epée de Bois 235
  Publicis Cinémas 95
  Studio Galande 235
Cinémathèque Française 185, 202
Cité des Arts de Montmartre 128
Cité des Fleurs 137
Cité Florale 273
Citypharma 244
climate 26-7
climate change 322, 323
cocktails 19, 44, 45, 348-50
coffee 37, 45, 166
Colette 84
Colonne Vendôme 110
Comédie Française 114
Compagnons du Devoir 165
concert venues, *see* music venues
Conciergerie 205, 215, 331
cooking courses 85-6
costs 316
Coulée Verte René-Dumont 192
Count of Monte Cristo 84
country code 325
courses 85-6, 136
credit cards 316
cruises 17, 67, 142
Crypte Archéologique 13, 211
cultural centres
  Centre Culturel Irlandais 239
  Institut Finlandais 239
  Le Carreau du Temple 160
culture 334-5
currency 316
cycling 27, 34, 52

Da Vinci Code 262
dance 46
dangers 145, 321
day trips from Paris 288-305, **288**
Delacroix, Eugène 246-7
department stores
  Galeries Lafayette Haussmann 18, 93, 95
  La Samaritaine 122, 124
  Le Bon Marché 241, 252-3
  Printemps 95
Diana, Princess of Wales 78
digital payments 316
Dior 89-90
disabilities, travellers with 35, 324
discounts 316
Disneyland Resort Paris 55, 317
documentaries 343
Dôme des Invalides 264
dragon boating 51
drinking 42-5, 318-19, 348-50, *see also individual neighbourhoods*
  beer & breweries 44, 144, 192
  cocktails 19, 44, 45, 348-50
  coffee 37, 45, 166
  wine 37, 43, 68
driving 34
Ducasse Baccarat 79

eastern Paris, *see* Bastille & eastern Paris
École des Beaux-Arts 267
Église St-Germain des Prés 254, 330
Eiffel, Gustave 64
Eiffel Tower 8, 64-7, 79, 332
Eiffel Tower & western Paris area 60-79, **62-3**
  accommodation 307
  drinking 73
  food 68, 69, 72, 74
  highlights 61, **61**
  shopping 75
  travel within 61
  walking tours 77, **77**
electricity 325
emergencies 325, 326
Emmanuel 210
Empreintes 323
entertainment 19, 46-7, *see also individual neighbourhoods*, cabarets, cinemas, theatres
  internet resources 47
  listening bars 19, 127, 140
environmental issues 16, 203
Espace Niemeyer 141-2
Éternelle Notre-Dame 221
etiquette 32
Eurostar 31
events, *see* festivals
Exposition Universelle 89

family travel 21, 53-5, 122, 317
fashion 48, 157, 323
festivals 26-7, 37
  Festival Quartier du Livre 233
  Fête de la Musique 193
  Fête des Vendanges de Montmartre 37
  LGBTIQ+ travellers 164
  Marche des Fiertés 164
  RICE - Le Marché Treiz'Asiatique 278
  We Love Green 197
Fête de la Musique 27, 193
Fête des Vendanges de Montmartre 37
film festivals
  Champs-Élysées Film Festival 88
films 47, 55, 202, 340-3
Fiminco Foundation 137
Flame of Liberty Memorial 78
Flamel, Nicolas 161, 163
Fnac 47
Fondation Cartier pour l'Art Contemporain 15, 114
Fondation Fiminco 145

Fontainebleau 300-3
food 10-11, 36-9, 318-19, *see also individual neighbourhoods*
 baguettes 36, 40-1, 319
 bakeries 38, 40-1, 195
 cheese 41, 263
 chocolate 260, 261
 cooking courses 85-6
 patisseries 38, 40-1, 86
 vegetarian & vegan travellers 37, 116, 282, 322
football 52
fountains
 Fontaine Médicis 256
 Fontaine St-Michel 238
 Fontaine Stravinsky 121
 La Danse de la Fontaine Émergente 276
free experiences 23
French Open 52, 71

Gainsbourg, Serge 259-60
Galerie des Chimères 210
Galeries Lafayette Haussmann 18, 93, 95
Gare d'Austerlitz 281
gardens, *see* parks & gardens
gay travellers 164-5, 320
Grand Palais 15, 89
Grande Arche 76
Grande Mosquée de Paris 233
Grands Boulevards, *see* Champs-Élysées & Grands Boulevards area
grands magasins 94-5, *see also* department stores
Grange aux Belles 142
Great Pyramid 106-7
guinguettes 44

Halles, Les 120
health 321
Hemingway, Ernest 231, 233, 253
highlights 8-23, 24-5
history 330-3
 Arc de Triomphe 332
 Arènes de Lutèce 330
 cabarets 332
 Chartres 296
 chocolate 261
 Conciergerie 331
 Église St-Germain des Prés 330
 Eiffel Tower 332
 Institut du Monde Arabe 333
 Le Bataclan 333
 Le Bon Marché 252
 Le Marais 160, 165
 Louvre 333
 Marianne 155
 metro 336-8
 Monnaie de Paris 259
 Musée de la Libération de Paris 332
 Notre Dame 331
 Paris Rive Gauche 333
 place de la Concorde 331
 Pont Neuf 331
 Sorbonne 333
 Versailles 290-5
holidays 325
horse racing 52
Hôtel de Ville 151, 155-6
Hôtel des Invalides 9, 263
Hôtel Lutetia 255
Hôtel Ritz Paris 110-11
hôtels particuliers 156
 Hôtel de Lamoignon 163
 Hôtel de Sens 162
 Hôtel de Sully 163
Hunchback of Notre Dame, the 210

ice skating 27
Île aux Cygnes 16, 282, 284
Île St-Louis 17, 216-17
Impressionism 251
Institut Français de la Mode 281
internet access 325
internet resources 323, 324
 entertainment 47
 food 38
Invader 21, 159
Invalides, *see* Hôtel des Invalides
Islands, the 204-21, **206-7**
 accommodation 311-12
 drinking 215, 220
 food 214, 215-17, 219
 highlights 205, **205**
 shopping 219
 travel within 205
 walking tours 218, **218**
itineraries 24-5

Jardin d'Acclimatation 55, 71
Jardin des Plantes 12, 52, 223, 236-7, 317
Jardin des Tuileries 52, 108-9, 317
Jardin du Luxembourg 21, 52, 256-7, 317
Jardin du Palais Royal 98
Jaurès to La Villette 143-5, **144**
 accommodation 309
 entertainment 143, 145
 food 144, 145
 highlights 127, **127**
jazz 46, 120, 176, 234
Jef Aerosol 177
Jewish history 158
Joyce, James 253

Kagyu-Dzong Buddhist temple 196
kayaking 51
King Philippe Auguste's Wall 163
Krasucki, Henri 181

La Butte aux Cailles 22, 269, 273
La Chapelle, *see* Barbès, La Chapelle & Canal St-Martin
La Dalle des Olympiades 276
La Défense 76
La Gare - Le Gore 137
La Géode 145
La Mouzaia 180
La Villette 127, 143-5
lakes
 Lac Daumesnil 196
 Lac des Minimes 196
 Lac Inférieur 71
language 29, 318, 326-7
Latin Quarter 222-39, **224-5**
 architecture 227-8
 drinking 228, 231
 food 227, 230, 233, 234, 235, 238
 highlights 223, **223**
 shopping 228, 231-2, 235
 travel within 223
 walking tours 229, 232, **229, 232**
Le Bataclan 333
Le Bateau Ivre (The Drunken Boat) 244
Le Bon Marché 241, 252-3
Le Corbusier 76
Le Cordon Bleu 55, 85-6
Le Marais 150-67, **152-3, 154**
 accommodation 310
 drinking 155, 157, 160, 164, 166, 167
 food 156, 159, 161, 165
 highlights 151, **151**
 history 165
 LGBTIQ+ travellers 164-5
 shopping 157, 161, 164, 167
 travel within 151
 walking tours 158, 162-3, **158, 163**
les Années folles 348-50
Les Catacombes 13, 54, 272
Les Deux Magots 253
Les Halles 120
Les Halles area, *see* Montorgueil, Les Halles & Sentier
Les Invalides, *see* St-Germain & Les Invalides
lesbian travellers 164-5, 320
LGBTIQ+ travellers 164-5, 320
libraries
 Bibliothèque Mazarine 247
 Bibliothèque Nationale de France 279-80
listening bars 19, 127, 140
literature 232, 233, *see also* books
Little India 141
live music 46, *see also* music venues
l'oeuf-mayonnaise 264
Louvre 9, 20, 97, 100-5, 333
Louvre & Palais Royal area 96-125, **99**
 accommodation 308-9
 drinking 111
 entertainment 111, 114
 food 98, 108, 109, 114-15, 115
 highlights 97, **97**
 shopping 109, 110, 115
 travel within 97
 walking tours 106-7, 112-13, **107, 113**

Madame Arthur 47, 133
Maison du Jardinage 201
Marché aux Puces de St-Ouen 23, 127, 148-9
Marche des Fiertés 164
markets 49, 323
 Le Marché des Enfants Rouges 159
 Marché aux Fleurs Reine Elizabeth II 219
 Marché aux Puces de la Porte de Vanves 281
 Marché aux Puces de St-Ouen 23, 127, 148-9

markets *(continued)*
  Marché aux Puces Porte de Montreuil 200
  Marché Biologique Brancusi 281
  Marché Biologique Raspail 247
  Marché Couvert de Passy 68
  Marché d'Aligre 185, 195
  Marché de la Création 281
  Marché Edgar Quinet 281
  Marché Georges Brassens 281
  Marché Président Wilson 74
  Marché St-Germain 245
measures 325
medical services 321
Méliès, Georges 202
Mémorial des Martyrs de la Déportation 220-1
Ménilmontant, *see* Belleville & Ménilmontant
Mesnager, Jérôme 177
metro 32, 33, 35, 159, 336-9
Mia Mao 15, 138
Miss Tic 177
Mona Lisa 103
money 30, 316
Monnaie de Paris 259
Montmartre, Pigalle & Batignolles 128-137, **130-1**
  accommodation 309
  drinking 133
  entertainment 133, 134
  food 128, 134, 136, 137
  highlights 127, **127**
  walking tours 132, 135, 136, **132**, **135**
Montorgueil, Les Halles & Sentier 96-125, **118-19**
  drinking 121, 125
  entertainment 120, 124-5
  food 116, 117, 120, 122, 124
  highlights 97, **97**
  shopping 122, 125
  travel within 97
  walking tours 123, **123**
Montparnasse & southern Paris 268-87, **270-1**, **274-5**
  accommodation 313
  drinking 287
  entertainment 279

food 273, 276, 278, 279, 281, 282, 283, 284, 286
  highlights 269, **269**
  shopping 281, 283
  travel within 269
  walking tours 277, 280, 285, **277**, **280**, **285**
Moreau, Gustave 87-8
Moulin Rouge 46, 133
multicultural Paris 323
Musée de la BNF (Bibliothèque Nationale de France) 97, 111, 114
Musée de l'Orangerie 69, 109-10
Musée d'Orsay 53, 241, 250-1
Musée du Louvre 9, 20, 97, 100-5, 333
Musée Rodin 20, 241, 264-5
museums & galleries 20, 53-4, 217
59 Rivoli 20, 120
Atelier des Lumières 21, 178
Ateliers d'Artistes de Belleville 183
Cinémathèque Française 185, 202
Cité de l'Architecture et du Patrimoine 76
Cité des Sciences et de l'Industrie 21, 53, 143, 145
Collège des Bernardins 22, 228
Dalí Museum 128
Fondation Henri Cartier Bresson 166
Fondation Louis Vuitton 20, 71
Galerie Amélie du Chalard 239
Galerie de Géologie et de Minéralogie 237
Galerie des Enfants 53
Galerie Emmanuel Perrotin 166
Galerie Kreo 239
Gallery of Paleontology & Comparative Anatomy 237
Grand Palais 15, 89
Grand Palais Immersif 189
Grande Galerie de l'Évolution 237
Hôtel de la Marine 81, 86
Hôtel d'Heidelbach 78
Institut du Monde Arabe 238, 333
Institut Giacometti 284, 286
Jeu de Paume 109-10

La Fab 282
La Galerie Dior 81, 89-90
Lafayette Anticipations 166
Louvre 9, 20, 97, 100-5, 333
M Museum du Vin 13, 68
Maison de Balzac 22, 72-3
Maison de Van Gogh 304
Maison de Victor Hugo 156
Maison Européenne de la Photographie 166
Maison Gainsbourg 241, 259-60
Manufacture des Gobelins 269, 279
Monnaie de Paris 259
Musée Art et d'Histoire du Judaïsme 158
Musée Bourdelle 287
Musée Carnavalet 151, 156, 165
Musée Cernuschi 136
Musée Clemenceau 73
Musée Cognacq-Jay 156
Musée d'Art Moderne de Paris 54, 73
Musée de Cluny - Musée National du Moyen Âge 227
Musée de la BNF (Bibliothèque Nationale de France) 97, 111, 114
Musée de la Chasse et de la Nature 156
Musée de la Libération de Paris 332
Musée de la Marine 75
Musée de la Sculpture en Plein Air 235
Musée de la Vie Romantique 134
Musée de L'Armée 263
Musée de l'Histoire de l'Immigration 195, 199
Musée de l'Homme 73
Musée de l'Orangerie 69, 109-10
Musée de Montmartre 134
Musée d'Ennery 78
Musée des Archives Nationales 156
Musée des Arts Décoratifs 109-10
Musée des Arts et Métiers 53, 151, 157, 159
Musée des Arts Forains 21, 202-3
Musée des Égouts de Paris 13, 260
Musée d'Orsay 53, 241, 250-1

Musée du Louvre 9, 20, 97, 100-5, 333
Musée du Luxembourg 244
Musée du Quai Branly - Jacques Chirac 79
Musée en Herbe 21, 53, 122
Musée Grévin 95
Musée Jacquemart-André 136
Musée Jean-Jacques Henner 136
Musée Marmottan Monet 20, 69
Musée National des Arts Asiatiques Guimet 79
Musée National Eugène Delacroix 246-7
Musée National Gustave Moreau 87-8
Musée National Picasso-Paris 156
Musée Nissim de Camondo 136
Musée Rodin 20, 241, 264-5
Musée Vivant du Fromage 221
Musée Yves Saint Laurent Paris 75
Musée Zadkine 257
Palais de la Découverte 53
Palais de Tokyo 53, 73
Palais Galliera 89
Petit Palais 81, 88, 92
Phono Museum 135
Polka Galerie 166
music 29, 209
music festivals 27, 193, 197
music venues 46
Adidas Arena 138
Elysée Montmartre 134
FGO-Barbara 138
La Boule Noire 134
La Cigale 134
La Flèche d'Or 176
La Machine du Moulin Rouge 134
La Seine Musicale 286
Le Trianon 134
Maison des Métallos 178
New Morning 138

Napoléon Bonaparte 85, 90-1, 102, 263, 332
Navigo Easy Card 33
neighbourhoods 58-9, **58-9**
Nemo 177

nightlife 318-19, 320, *see also* cabarets, drinking
Notre Dame 8, 205, 208-13, 331
Nuit Blanche 27

Olympic Cauldron 15, 108
Olympics 14, 108
online resources, *see* internet resources
opening hours 325
opera 46
  Les Rendez-Vous d'Ailleurs 194
  Opéra Bastille 189
  Opéra National de Paris 46
opera houses, *see* theatres
ossuaries, *see* cemeteries & ossuaries

palaces, *see also* châteaux
  Palais Garnier 9, 81, 90-1, 93
  Palais Royal 98
  Versailles 290-5
Palais de Justice 215
Palais de la Femme 190
Palais de la Porte Dorée 195
Palais Garnier 9, 81, 90-1, 93
Palais Royal 98
Palais Royal area, *see* Louvre & Palais Royal area
Paname Brewing Company 22, 44, 144
Panthéon 223, 226
Pantin, *see* St-Denis, St-Ouen, Pantin & Aubervilliers
Parc Astérix 55
Parc de Belleville 18, 169, 179
Parc des Buttes-Chaumont 12, 169, 180, 183
Paris 2024 Cauldron 15, 108
Paris Beer Festival 37
Paris Café Festival 37
Paris Fashion Week 157
Paris Plages 51
Paris Rive Gauche 269, 333
Parisien d'un Jour - Paris Greeters 23, 54
parks & gardens 12, 50, 74
  Bois de Boulogne 12, 52, 70-1
  Bois de Vincennes 12, 52, 185, 196-7

children, for 317
Forêt de Fontainebleau 300
Île aux Cygnes 284
Jardin Catherine-Labouré 253
Jardin d'Acclimatation 55, 71
Jardin d'Agronomie Tropicale 197
Jardin de l'Atlantique 284
Jardin de Reuilly 192
Jardin des Plantes 12, 52, 223, 236-7, 317
Jardin des Serres d'Auteuil 71
Jardin des Tuileries 52, 108-9, 317
Jardin du Luxembourg 21, 52, 256-7, 317
Jardin du Palais Royal 98
Jardin naturel Pierre-Emmanuel 173
Jardin Shakespeare 71
La Villette 143
Parc André Citroën 284
Parc Clichy-Batignolles - Martin Luther King 136
Parc de Belleville 18, 169, 179
Parc de Bercy 201
Parc de la Villette 52, 142, 143
Parc des Buttes-Chaumont 12, 169, 180, 183
Parc Floral de Paris 197, 317
Parc Georges Brassens 284
Parc Monceau 52
Parc Montsouris 283-4
Square Boucicaut 253
Square du Vert-Galant 220
Square Laurent-Prache 253
Square René Le Gall 282, 284
Square Roger-Stéphane 253
passages couverts 95, 112-13
Galerie Beaujolais 112
Galerie Colbert 112
Galerie Vivienne 113
Passage Choiseul 113
Passage des Deux Pavillons 112
Passage des Panoramas 95, 113
Passage du Bourg l'Abbé 123

Passage du Caire 123, 125
Passage du Grand Cerf 123, 125
Passage du Perron 112
Passage Jouffroy 95
Passage Molière 124
Passage Verdeau 95
passageways 181
  passage de la Main d'Or 191
  passage de l'Ancre 166
  passage des Gravilliers 166
  passage du Chantier 191
  passage Josset 191
  passage L'homme 191
patisseries 38, 40-1, 86
péniches 261
people 334-5
perfume 164
pétanque 52, 218
Petite Ceinture 22, 137, 200-1, 286, 287
pharmacies 321
Philosopher's Stone 161
Piaf, Édith 172, 183
picnics 282
Pigalle, *see* Montmartre, Pigalle & Batignolles
Piscine Joséphine Baker 17, 51, 279
pizza 38
place Colette 23, 111
place de la Bastille 188-9
place de la Concorde 9, 87, 93, 331
place de la Madeleine 90, 91, 93
place de la République 155
place des Vosges 151, 155
planning, *see also* individual neighbourhoods
  budgeting 316
  clothes 28
  etiquette 28, 32
  Paris basics 28-9
  travel seasons 26-7
podcasts 29
poetry 124
Pont Alexandre III 85
Pont Neuf 217, 331
population 325, 334-5
Promenade Plantée 23, 286
public holidays 325

Quartier du Livre 27

responsible travel 322-3
Rice du marché Treiz'Asiatique 37
river cruises, *see* boat tours
rivers
  Bièvre 239
  Seine 16-17, 44, 51, 54, 67, 203, 221
Rock en Seine 27
rooftop bars 42-3
Rose Line 262
rue Daguerre 283
rue Dénoyez 177
rue Montorgueil 11, 97, 116, 122
rue Mouffetard 230-1
rue St-Blaise 199
rugby 52

Sacré-Cœur Basilica 9, 127, 129
safe travel 145, 321
Sainte-Chapelle 205, 214-15
Salon du Chocolat 37
Salon International de l'Agriculture 37
Sentier, *see* Montorgueil, Les Halles & Sentier
Sentier de Grand Paris 51
shopping 48-9, 323, *see also individual neighbourhoods*, bookshops, department stores, markets
SIM cards 30
smoking 325
SNCF Eastern European Technical Centre 201
soccer 52
Sorbonne 227, 235, 333
souvenirs 49
sports, *see individual sports*
Square René Le Gall 282, 284
Square St-Lambert 282
stadiums
  Parc des Princes 71
  Paris La Défense Arena 71
  Stade Roland Garros 71
stand-up paddleboarding 51
Station F 281
St-Denis, St-Ouen, Pantin & Aubervilliers 146-7
  entertainment 146
  food 146, 147
steampunk 159

St-Germain & Les Invalides 240-67, **242-3**, **248-9**
accommodation 312
drinking 244, 253-4, 257, 261, 266
food 246, 247, 254, 255-6, 258, 260, 262, 263, 264
highlights 241, **241**
shopping 244-5, 252, 265, 266-7
travel within 241
walking tours 258, **258**
St-Michel 238
St-Ouen, *see* St-Denis, St-Ouen, Pantin & Aubervilliers
street art 23
 Belleville & Ménilmontant 177, 179
 Le Marais 151, 159, 166
street food 38
surrealism 253
swimming 51
 Bercy swimming area 203
swimming pools
 Aquaboulevard 279
 Piscine Joséphine Baker 17, 51, 279
 Piscine Pontoise 228
Sybille's Temple 183

taxes 316
taxidermy 260
taxis 30-1, 34
Templars 160
tennis 52, 71
theatre 46
Theatre of Cruelty 194
theatres
 Arcal 194
 Comédie Française 114
 Folies Bergère 86
 Le 100 194

Les Rendez-Vous d'Ailleurs 194
Opéra Bastille 189
Palais Garnier 9, 81, 90-1, 93
Théâtre de la Bastille 194
Théâtre de l'Odéon 235, 247
Théâtre des Abbesses 128
Théâtre des Bouffes du Nord 138
Théâtre la Boutonnière 194
Théâtre National de Chaillot 73
theft 32, 321
theme parks 55, 70-1, 317
tickets 47, 216
time 325
tipping 316
Toulouse-Lautrec 134
Tour de France 27
tours 182, *see also* boat tours, walking tours
towers
 Belvédère de Belleville 18, 179, 181
 Eiffel Tower 18, 64-7, 79, 332
 Tour Jean sans Peur 124
 Tour Montparnasse 18, 269, 278, 282
 Tours de Notre Dame 210
 Tours Duo 281
 Tour St-Jacques 18, 121
 Wood Up 281
train travel 30-1, 32
tram travel 33
travel to/from Paris 30-1
travel within Paris 32-5, 317, 324
travellers with disabilities 35, 324
Trocadéro 72

underground experiences 13
Université Panthéon-Sorbonne 227, 235, 333
universities
 Cité Universitaire 282, 284
 Université Panthéon-Sorbonne 227, 235, 333
urban agriculture 39

vacations 325
Van Gogh, Vincent 304-5
VAT refunds 316
vegetarian & vegan travellers 37, 116, 282, 322
Vélib' 52
Venus de Milo 102, 103
Versailles 290-5
Viaduc des Arts 192
viewpoints 18, 278
Village St-Paul 162-3
visas 30

walking tours
 Bastille & eastern Paris 191, **191**
 Belleville & Ménilmontant 180-1, **181**
 Champs-Élysées 92-3, **93**
 Chartres 297, **297**
 Coulée Verte René-Dumont 185, 192
 Eiffel Tower area 77, **77**
 Fontainebleau 301, **301**
 Islands, the 218, **218**
 Latin Quarter 229, 232, **229**, **232**

Le Marais 158, 162-3, **158**, **163**
Louvre & Palais Royal 106-7, 112-13, **107**, **113**
Montmartre 132, **132**
Montparnasse & southern Paris 277, 280, 285, **277**, **280**, **285**
Pigalle 135, **135**
Sentier 123, **123**
Sentier de Grand Paris 51
St-Germain & Les Invalides 258, **258**
Versailles 294-5, **295**
walks 33, 51
 Petite Ceinture du 14e 287
 Petite Ceinture du 15e 286
water 322
We Love Green 27, 197
weather 26-7
websites, *see* internet resources
weights 325
western Paris, *see* Eiffel Tower & western Paris area
wi-fi 325
Wilde, Oscar 255
wine 37, 43, 68
Winged Victory of Samothrace 103

Zola, Émile 252
zoos
 Jardin des Plantes ménagerie 237
 Parc Zoologique de Paris 197

Map Pages **000**

NOTES

NOTES

NOTES

'On a freezing winter day, I took refuge in the Auteuil greenhouses where I found I wasn't the only one soaking up the blissful tropical humidity: an artist had set up an easel among the ferns.'

MARY WINSTON NICKLIN

'The time I had Sainte-Chapelle completely to myself, jewel-toned light showering down on me through the stained glass.'

ALEXIS AVERBUCK

All rights reserved. No part of this publication may be copied, stored in a retrieval system, or transmitted in any form by any means, electronic, mechanical, recording or otherwise, except brief extracts for the purpose of review, and no part of this publication may be sold or hired, without the written permission of the publisher. Lonely Planet and the Lonely Planet logo are trademarks of Lonely Planet and are registered in the US Patent and Trademark Office and in other countries. Lonely Planet does not allow its name or logo to be appropriated by commercial establishments, such as retailers, restaurants or hotels. Please let us know of any misuses: lonelyplanet.com/legal/intellectual-property.

Mapping data sources:
© Lonely Planet
© OpenStreetMap http://openstreetmap.org/copyright

THIS BOOK

The 15th edition of Lonely Planet's *Paris* guidebook was written and researched by Mary Winston Nicklin, Alexis Averbuck, Jean-Bernard Carillet, Fabienne Fong Yan, Rooksana Hossenally, Nicola Leigh Stewart, Rowan Twine and Peter Yeung. This guidebook was produced by:

Destination Editor Annemarie McCarthy

Production Editor Katie Connolly

Image Editor Virginia Moreno

Cartographer David Connolly

Assisting Editors Janet Austin, Nigel Chin, Sally Davies

Cover Researcher Giada de Agostinis

Thanks Imogen Bannister

Paper in this book is certified against the Forest Stewardship Council™ standards. FSC™ promotes environmentally responsible, socially beneficial and economically viable management of the world's forests.

Published by Lonely Planet Global Limited
CRN 554153
15th edition – Mar 2026
ISBN 978 1 83869 862 1
© Lonely Planet 2026
10 9 8 7 6 5 4 3 2 1
Printed in China